The Syntax of Chinese

The past quarter of a century has seen a surge i
has produced a sizeable literature on the analy
in Mandarin Chinese. This guide to Chinese syntax analyzes the majority of
constructions in Chinese that have featured in theoretical linguistics in the past
twenty-five years, using the authors' own analyses as well as existing or potential
alternative treatments. A broad variety of topics are covered, including categories,
argument structure, passives, and anaphora. The discussion of each topic sums up
the key research results and provides new points of departure for further research.
This book will be invaluable both to students wanting to know more about the
grammar of Chinese, and to graduate students and theoretical linguists interested
in the universal principles that underlie human languages.

JAMES HUANG is a Professor in the Department of Linguistics at Harvard
University.

AUDREY LI is a Professor in the Department of Linguistics and Department of
East Asian Languages and Cultures at the University of Southern California.

YAFEI LI is a Professor in the Department of Linguistics at the University of
Wisconsin–Madison.

CAMBRIDGE SYNTAX GUIDES

General editors:

P. Austin, B. Comrie, J. Bresnan, D. Lightfoot, I. Roberts, N. V. Smith

Responding to the increasing interest in comparative syntax, the goal of the Cambridge Syntax Guides is to make available to all linguists major findings, both descriptive and theoretical, which have emerged from the study of particular languages. The series is not committed to working in any particular framework, but rather seeks to make language-specific research available to theoreticians and practitioners of all persuasions. Written by leading figures in the field, these guides will each include an overview of the grammatical structures of the language concerned. For the descriptivist, the books will provide an accessible introduction to the methods and results of the theoretical literature; for the theoretician, they will show how constructions that have achieved theoretical notoriety fit into the structure of the language as a whole; for everyone, they will promote cross-theoretical and cross-linguistic comparison with respect to a well-defined body of data.

Other books available in this series

O. Fischer *et al.*: *The Syntax of Early English*
K. Zagona: *The Syntax of Spanish*
K. Kiss: *The Syntax of Hungarian*
S. Mchombo: *The Syntax of Chichewa*
H. Thrainsson: *The Syntax of Icelandic*
P. Rowlett: *The Syntax of French*
R. D. Borsley *et al.*: *The Syntax of Welsh*

The Syntax of Chinese

C.-T. JAMES HUANG
Harvard University

Y.-H. AUDREY LI
University of Southern California

YAFEI LI
University of Wisconsin–Madison

CAMBRIDGE UNIVERSITY PRESS
Cambridge, New York, Melbourne, Madrid, Cape Town, Singapore, São Paulo, Delhi

Cambridge University Press
The Edinburgh Building, Cambridge CB2 8RU, UK

Published in the United States of America by Cambridge University Press, New York

www.cambridge.org
Information on this title: www.cambridge.org/9780521599580

First published 2009

Printed in the United Kingdom at the University Press, Cambridge

A catalogue record for this publication is available from the British Library

Library of Congress Cataloguing in Publication data
Huang, Cheng-Teh James.
The syntax of Chinese / C.-T. James Huang, Y.-H. Audrey Li, Yafei Li.
     p.   cm. – (Cambridge syntax guides)
Includes bibliographical references and index.
ISBN 978-0-521-59058-7 – ISBN 978-0-521-59958-0 (pbk.)
1. Chinese language – Syntax.   I. Li, Yen-hui Audrey, 1954–   II. Li, Yafei.   III. Title.
IV. Series.
PL1241.H855   2009
495.1 – dc22   2008025651

ISBN 978-0-521-59058-7 hardback
ISBN 978-0-521-59958-0 paperback

Contents

Abbreviations

A, AP	adjective, adjectival phrase
AC	Adjunct Condition
ACC	accusative case
ACD	Antecedent Contained Deletion
ADV	Adverb
AE	Anaphoric Ellipsis
ART	Article
Asp, AspP	aspect, aspectual phrase
BA	marker of the *ba* construction (see Chapter 5)
BEI	passive marker *bei* (see Chapter 4)
BPA	Binding Principle A
C, CP	complementizer, complementizer phrase
CED	Condition on Extraction Domain
CFC	complete functional complex
CL	classifier
CNPC	Complex NP Constraint
CR	Conjunction Reduction
D, DP	determiner, determiner phrase
DAT	dative case
DC	Directionality Constraint
DE	pre-nominal modification marker or postverbal resultative marker *de*
DECL	declarative
DEM	demonstrative
DrP	Duration Phrase
DRT	Discourse Representation Theory
ECP	Empty Category Principle
Fn	functional element of degree *n*
FEC	free empty category
FI	Full Interpretation
FP	Frequency Phrase

GB	Government and Binding
GC	Governing Category
GCR	Generalized Control Rule
GUO	experiential aspect marker *guo*
H	head
HMC	Head Movement Constraint
IHRC	internally headed relative clause
I, IP	inflection, inflectional phrase
L, LP	localizer, localizer phrase
LBC	Left Branch Condition
LD	long-distance
LDR	long-distance reflexive
LE	perfective marker or sentence-final particle
LF	Logical Form
LRS	lexical relational structure
LSS	lexico-semantic structure
Lv	light verb
MDP	Minimal Distance Principle
Mod	Modifier
MP	Minimalist Program
N, NP	noun, noun phrase
NOM	nominative case
NOP	null operator
Num, NumP	numeral, number phrase
OP	operator
P, PP	preposition/postposition, prep/postpositional phrase
PASS	passive morpheme
PAST	past tense
P&P	Principles and Parameters
PF	Phonetic Form
PL	plural
PLA	Principle of Lexical Association
PLI	Principle of Lexical Integrity
POV	Point-of-View Phrase
PRES	present tense
PRO/pro	empty pronominal element
PROG	progressive
QNP	quantificational NP
Q	question particle
QR	Quantifier Raising

Qu	question operator
QVE	quantificational variability effect
RNR	right-node raising
SC	Subject Condition, also for Superiority Condition
SFP	sentence-final particle
SourceP	Source Phrase
Spec	specifier
SUO	pronominal element *suo* marking object relativization or passivization
t	trace of moved element
T, TP	tense, tense phrase
TOP	topic
UG	Universal Grammar
UTAH	Uniformity of Theta Assignment Hypothesis
V, VP	verb, verb phrase
X^0	syntactic head of type X
XP	full syntactic phrase of type X
X'	intermediate syntactic phrase of type X
ZHE	durative aspect marker *zhe*

Introduction

Over the last quarter-century, there has been a surge of research on Chinese syntax. A cursory look at the programs of Chinese linguistics conferences held since 1985 shows that at least a full continuous session has been devoted to Chinese syntax throughout each day of every conference. Those who were involved in organizing such conferences can also recall the large number of syntax abstracts, routinely accounting for fifty to sixty percent of all abstracts received for review. It is also during this past quarter-century that a significant number of theoretically oriented works on Chinese syntax began to appear in major refereed academic journals published in the West. Several monographic, theoretical treatments of Chinese syntax have also appeared that distinguished themselves from earlier general descriptions or reference grammars. In the field of theoretical linguistics, more works than before make crucial reference to Chinese syntax. It is clear that research on Chinese syntax that is informed by modern linguistic theories has been productive. In turn, it is also clear that the study of Chinese syntax has played an ever-increasing role in linguists' construction of modern "mainstream" syntactic theories.

Most of these "modern syntactic theories" are in one form or another theories falling under the formal paradigm of generative grammar. Of these formal treatments, much research has been carried out in the Principles-and-Parameters (P&P) approach initiated by Chomsky and his colleagues and students around 1980, plus and minus two or three years, in its various incarnations including the so-called Government-and-Binding (GB) framework, the Barriers framework, and recent attempts at theoretical economy aimed at the ideals of the Minimalist Program (MP). The P&P approach marked the beginning of an era that distinguished itself from the first quarter-century of generative grammar (since 1957) in enabling the construction of a theory of grammar that is at once general enough to capture common properties of human language and flexible enough to account for language variations. It provided a way to make good sense of the innateness hypothesis (or "biolinguistic approach") that characterized Chomsky's approach since it was introduced twenty-five years before, a hypothesis that takes the internalized grammar of any language to be a combined product of nature and nurture.

1

It also allowed for the productive description of languages of various typological types and, most importantly, for the study of a variety of languages to directly contribute to the construction of general linguistic theory. The construction of the GB theory as we know it today, for example, was itself in part informed by some analyses of Chinese syntax.

The volume of research products that have appeared in this period, quite unlike the situation ever before, far exceeds the amount anyone can easily recall or enumerate when pondering over one particular topic or another. Various grammatical constructions have been given multiple different treatments. Some grammatical constructions that seemed irrelevant to generative grammar in its early periods are now actively analyzed, while objections to certain formal analyses have now lost ground. Yet we continue to hear objections and questions from scholars unfamiliar with the paradigm – either those who were educated in the pre-GB model with many assumptions that are no longer held by current generative researchers or those who are less informed about formal approaches. Part of this situation, we believe, arises from misunderstanding or lack of accessible information. The fact is that, for almost every topic of Chinese syntax, there now exists a sizable amount of generative literature within the P&P paradigm. The problem, for those who for one reason or another have not been able to follow the recent developments, comes in part from the fact that most research products come in single articles – from journals, edited volumes, and conference presentations – and there is no work as yet that attempts to take stock of the major results that have been produced and describe them in some depth – within one volume – that might serve the double purpose of informing the readers less familiar with (or less committed to) formal linguistics and the current status (in our view) of formal Chinese syntax, and of bringing further questions onto the research agenda for other scholars and students interested in the enterprise of providing rigorous analyses of Chinese linguistic facts and bringing them to bear on the construction of an optimal theory of human linguistic competence and its possible variations, as part of a theory of the "mirror of the mind."

The desire to take a first step toward filling this gap was a major motivation that led us to take up the project of writing this book. It is our hope that a volume consisting of the topics we have chosen will present a more comprehensive outlook of the syntactic system of the whole language to the reader, and that our discussion of the various analyses on each topic will help both to sum up some of the important results and to provide new points of departure for further research. It is also our intention to use this book to demonstrate, for each topic selected, how a formal generative analysis may help make sense of certain observed properties of the language, perhaps in ways better than other imagined approaches, and how it may be seen as a contribution to linguistic theory.

Before we go on to present the details of what this book is about, however, we must make clear what it is not. First, it is not meant to be a reference grammar for the learner of Chinese, though it might be seen as a (somewhat biased) reference on the formal linguistic analyses of Mandarin Chinese syntax. Although we have tried to include as many references as we can to the large volume of works available, we are sure to have inadvertently missed some. Even where references are included, we do not provide a detailed discussion of all alternative analyses that are worthy of consideration, other than those closely related to our own analyses. We have also excluded most references that are explicitly non-formal. Second, it is not a comprehensive treatment of Chinese syntax. As it turns out, even within formal approaches, it is impossible to touch on all the important aspects of Chinese syntax. Rather than briefly summarizing results on a comprehensive list of topics, we have chosen to provide fairly detailed analyses and argumentation of a selected number of topics, excluding some owing to space limitation and others where we have nothing new to offer. For each topic our discussion is driven by the goal of providing one or two specific analyses and explaining the rationale behind them, with the general theory of grammar in mind. It is often said that Y.-R. Chao's (1968) *Grammar of Spoken Chinese* is a comprehensive single-volume masterpiece that represents the best of the American descriptive and structuralist tradition. No single-volume formal treatment comparable to Chao's in scope has appeared in the last several decades. The rich observations and insights contained in that volume remain unsurpassed to this day. We have not attempted a comprehensive treatment of Chinese syntax in the generative tradition. Our goals are both different and limited: the book presents grammatical analyses that cover most of the constructions of (Mandarin) Chinese that have figured in the field of theoretical linguistics in the past twenty-five years, focusing on our own analyses in most cases. It is intended to show how the facts of Chinese may be profitably understood with the tools of generative linguistics, and in turn how the analyses may help settle important issues and guide further research in linguistic theory. It is intended as a contribution to Chinese syntax as a distinct subject of Chinese studies, and also to generative grammar as a hypothesis about human linguistic competence.

The rest of this book is organized into four parts comprising nine chapters. Part I (Chapters 1–3) investigates the building blocks and "canonical" structures of sentences, including the grammatically relevant properties of words and the combinatorial algorithm by which phrases are formed. Chapter 1 presents a theory of parts of speech, which we call categories. Lack of sufficient inflectional and derivational clues has made the identification of categories difficult for Chinese. Drawing on the insights gained from other languages, we rely primarily on the syntactic behaviors of a word to determine its category. It is also shown that a category is best viewed as a cluster of plus- or minus-valued features, which enables us not only to distinguish syntactically relevant categories but also to explain why some of them display identical properties. The analysis of localizers, one of the perpetually question-begging categories in Chinese, makes use of the notion of computational cost and opens up a new possibility to understand how categorial changes happen and a new category comes into existence.

Chapter 2 focuses on the nature of argument structure. Capitalizing on a long-known and puzzling fact, i.e., that the semantic relations between a verb and its subject or object are much less restricted in Chinese than in English, and drawing on recent works by others, we propose a theory of lexico-semantic decomposition of verbs that minimizes the amount of stipulated mechanisms and components and thereby maximizes the explanatory power of the theory. In particular, it is argued that a tiny set of event-typing elements interact with a lexical root to produce the more "rigid" argument structures found with English verbs, whereas the option of using bare roots as verbs in the absence of event-typers, aided with world knowledge, is responsible for the degree of semantic freedom in Chinese.

Chapter 3 covers a broad range of topics on the "canonical" structures of the sentence, with particular focus on the verb phrase and its components. It examines the systematic distinctions between adjuncts and complements, looks for the best structural representations of five different postverbal constituents (the double-object, two V-*de*'s, and the frequency and duration expressions), and discusses how such semantic notions as aspect and modality are handled in the syntax of Chinese. In the course of presentation, it is proposed that the behavioral disparity between the resultative V-*de* and its manner counterpart may be attributed to the superficially unrelated fact that Chinese has resultative compounds but not ones with a postverbal manner modifier. Attention is also given to constructions which appear to display syntax–semantics mismatches. What unifies this large collection of miscellaneous topics is a single phrase structure pattern whose restriction on possible syntactic analyses highlights an important characteristic of this model of linguistic theory: using the least amount of independently motivated tools to account for the maximal amount of data.

In Part II (Chapters 4 and 5), we take a closer look at argument structure and its relation with lexical semantics and its effects on syntactic structure, by focusing on two constructions that have been in the center of debate from the inception of Modern Chinese syntax as a field. Chapter 4 deals with the passive *bei* construction, which takes two forms depending on the presence or absence of an Agent phrase (the long and short passive respectively). After exhibiting the pros and cons of a movement-based approach and one based on complementation, it is argued that the Chinese passive involves both movement and complementation. The long passive is derived via clausal complementation where the embedded object is brought to the periphery of the complement clause (a process of "operator movement") and is predicated on the main-clause subject. The short passive, on the other hand, involves verbal complementation and the object is brought to the periphery of a verb phrase (a process of "argument movement") where it is interpreted with the subject.

Building on the findings of the passive construction, Chapter 5 compares and contrasts passives and the closely related *ba* construction. *Bei* and *ba* constructions are similar in argument structures. However, they differ in the range of (un)acceptable cases, which is attributed to the different subcategorization requirements of *ba* and *bei*, reflected in the syntactic structures with which they are associated. Nonetheless, the extant literature on the *ba* construction has not been as focused on its syntactic properties as on the special meaning of this construction and how to account for it. The *ba* construction has been noted as expressing "disposal" or "affectedness." We show that the special meaning cannot be due to any thematic-assigning capabilities of *ba*. Every *ba* sentence has a non-*ba* counterpart, which points to the irrelevance of *ba* in contributing to the argument structures. In the most typical examples, *ba* seems to be related to the notion of boundedness or requires a result expression. However, the complexities of the *ba* construction require the search for further possibilities and additional mechanisms for an "affected" interpretation.

While the passive and the *ba* construction exemplify how modifications in lexical structure affect the syntactic relations between arguments such as subject and object, other constructions exhibit syntactic properties independent of lexical semantics. Such constructions involve operations on or beyond clauses, and often concern the logical relations between clausal peripheral elements and the clauses as a whole. Part III takes up two types of logical structure: one involving (often) overt antecedent–gap relations and the other involving, as we shall argue, covert dependency relations. The first type, dealt with in Chapter 6, is best illustrated by topic and relative clause structures, in which a clause is used to modify a head noun phrase. There have been claims that a relative construction is derived from a topic structure; however, we show that the two constructions are similar but not identical. They are alike in the set of locality conditions restricting the well-formedness of these constructions, phrased in terms of constraints on movement and rules governing the distribution of empty categories. They differ in exactly which element undergoes movement and where it lands. Variations with respect to these factors are also manifested within relative constructions in a cluster of empirical generalizations that can be traced to the absence/presence of a relative operator.

In Chapter 7, we turn to the syntax of interrogative sentences with particular attention to *wh*-questions and a special type of disjunctive question called the

"A-not-A question." After clarifying the distinctness of this question type from normal *yes-no* questions, we propose and defend a modular approach to the A-not-A questions. We discuss a number of approaches to the syntax and semantics of *wh*-questions, which exhibit covert long-distance dependencies with restrictions that, we argue, follow from an appropriately formulated theory of movement, binding, and the syntax–semantics interface.

Our presentation of the syntax of Chinese would be inappropriately incomplete without some in-depth discussion of the syntax of nominal expressions and their meanings. Part IV of this book is devoted to this area. Chapter 8 takes up the syntactic structure of nominal expressions – nouns and phrases built around nouns as their heads. We note that Chinese noun phrases, on their surface, are at once more complex and more simple than their counterparts in, say, English and other languages (for example, with respect to the requirement of numeral-classifiers, the lack of true determiners, and the occurrence of "bare" singular count nouns). We argue, however, that appearance notwithstanding, Chinese noun phrases (like those in many other languages) have more structure than meets the eye. We propose a full determiner phrase that may contain other smaller phrases headed by a numeral expression, a classifier, and a noun, and show that this allows for the derivation and explanation of certain facts of (in)definiteness, specificity, and compositional semantics.

Another important aspect of the semantics of noun phrases concerns their reference and the referential dependencies they exhibit on each other. This is the subject of the final chapter. Here our discussion addresses both the syntax and semantics of coreference and of variable binding. We show that the referential properties of nominal expressions are tied to their intrinsic properties (whether they need an antecedent or not), the syntactic position of their antecedents (if they need one), and the nature of the antecedents themselves (whether they are referential or quantificational). With respect to definite noun phrase anaphora, we devote substantial space to a discussion of the Chinese reflexive pronoun *ziji*, and show that it is both an anaphor in the sense of classical Binding Theory and a logophor within contexts of "attitudes *de se*" that describe the speech, the mental state, or the perspective of an appropriate protagonist. With respect to variable binding, we show that the crucial requirement is c-command in a proper Logical Form representation. We finish Chapter 9 with a discussion of so-called "donkey anaphora," something that has a status between definite coreference and variable binding. We present two types of "donkey sentences," each with a set of distinguishing properties, and show that a proper analysis of them helps settle an important debate between two competing theories that have figured prominently in recent treatments of indefinite noun phrases and their referential properties.

There are clearly other interesting topics of Chinese syntax that deserve coverage in a book with this title, but we have had to leave them out. Several other constructions that bear on lexical structure and syntactic projection could each deserve a chapter-length full treatment. For example, the resultative construction (both the compound and the phrasal versions), touched upon briefly in Chapter 3, has further interesting properties bearing on the structure of events and their projection in syntax. The syntax of adverbials and that of aspectual markers are two other areas that have received considerable renewed interest in recent years. Other topics falling under the area of argument structure and syntactic structure include the syntax of unaccusatives, the two types of double-object constructions, and the proper syntactic treatment of various conjunctives. With respect to logical structure and the syntax–semantics interface, we have left out much work on quantification and structures bearing on focus and presupposition. And our discussion of noun phrase anaphora also does not touch upon the distribution and reference of zero pronouns, a topic of major interest to parametric theory with implications for the interface between syntax and discourse. In selecting topics for inclusion in this work, we have used three criteria. The first is our perception of relative priority in trying to strike a balance between breadth and depth within a limited space. The second is the availability of the literature: a topic is not included when it has been extensively discussed in easily accessible monographs or journals. The third one has to do with the scope of our own research: we have left out topics on which we have not ourselves carried out sufficient research and to which we do not have something new to contribute.

A word about the intended readers of this work: we prepared these chapters originally for university courses that we offer on the linguistic structure of Chinese, so the most immediate intended readers of this book are those graduate students and upper-level undergraduates who have some basic knowledge of linguistic structure. Such students, or any professional linguist of any theoretical persuasion, should find the book fully accessible, even without prior experience with the Chinese language. A student of the Chinese language may also find this work accessible with occasional reference to linguistic terminology available from syntax textbooks or linguistics glossaries. In writing the book, we have also had in mind the non-specialists who are curious about Chinese grammar and generative syntax, and have tried to briefly explain technical notions as they are first introduced. As such, we hope the book will be useful to teachers and researchers in such Chinese-related fields as language teaching, natural language processing, machine translation, language acquisition, philosophy of language, and other related areas of cognitive science.

As usual, the completion of a book of this size owes itself to the help of numerous people. It is impossible to enumerate the scholars from whom we have learned the body of knowledge represented here. We should, however, mention a few colleagues who have collaborated with us on one topic or another with results that have been included in this work. In particular, the materials on donkey anaphora and long-distance reflexives are derived from earlier work conducted with Lisa Cheng and C.-S. Luther Liu, respectively. Our discussion of argument structure and lexical relations has also benefited from our erstwhile collaboration with Lisa Cheng and C.-C. Jane Tang. Some sections on relative constructions and *wh*-questions are incorporated from work in collaboration with Joseph Aoun. The analysis of the V-*de* constructions draws on our joint work with Jen Ting. And the discussion of the interactions among different adverb classes is a direct application of the discoveries we made together with Vivian Lin and Rebecca Shields on the intervention effects of adverbs in English and Russian. We continue to appreciate the opportunities we have had to work with them. Parts of this manuscript in one of its earlier versions have been tried out in classes and read by some of the students and faculty at Harvard University, the University of Southern California, and the University of Wisconsin–Madison, as well as the National Taiwan Normal University, Stanford University, and the University of Venice. We are gratified by the interest and support shown to us by the instructors and participants and, in some cases, for their comments and suggestions – especially those of Ressy Ai, Shengli Feng, Francesca del Gobbo, Miaoling Hsieh, So-One Hwang, Soo-Yeon Jeong, Julie Jiang, Daphne Liao, Jing Rong, Peter Sells, Yang Shen, Yuan Shen, Fuzhen Si, Jen Ting, and Yaqing Wu. In our final efforts to bring this work to fruition, we owe special gratitude to Bridget Samuels for her help in making the whole manuscript more readable than it otherwise could be. Finally, but not the least, our deep-felt thanks go to Emily, Qing, and Yu-Chin for all the best of things that life can offer; something that we have taken all these years but, probably too often, for granted.

JH, AL, & YL

1

Categories

We take it as our starting point that a Chinese sentence is composed of words and that words have different behaviors in a sentence. For instance, while *dayan fei* 'wild.goose fly' is an acceptable sentence, **fei dayan* 'fly wild.goose' is not. The most obvious reason for the contrast is that *dayan* 'wild.goose' is a noun that canonically serves as the subject of the sentence and *fei* 'fly' is a verb whose canonical function is to be the predicate occurring after the subject. This means that in order to understand the syntax of Chinese, or the syntax of any language for that matter, we minimally need to understand how the words in a language are classified and how these different classes of words are put together to form sentences. In this book, word classes are referred to as *lexical categories*, or just *categories* for short, following the terminological convention of generative syntax.

While the basic distinction between nouns and verbs is universally recognized in modern literature on Chinese syntax, scholars differ, sometimes drastically, on other categories. See Chao (1968), Li and Thompson (1981), Zhu (1982), and Xing and Ma (1992) for a few examples. The differences in opinion arise partly because linguists with different theoretical backgrounds may employ different criteria for word classification, and partly because we still lack sufficient knowledge about certain words and their properties. Regardless, it is without question that the ultimate task for anyone studying lexical categories in Chinese is to identify them in such a way that they both allow an accurate description of the syntactic behaviors of the language, and provide insights into the nature of word classification.

With this goal in mind, we will introduce a theory of lexical categorization in Mandarin Chinese in this chapter. The theory consists of two intertwined parts. First, a set of categories is confirmed and examined on the basis of the syntactic behaviors of Chinese words and morphemes. Second, a decompositional theory that characterizes the intrinsic relations among these categories is defended. It is important to mention up front, however, that we do not intend to spread our discussions evenly among all issues related to lexical categorization, nor do we attempt to provide an exhaustive list of categories in the language. Rather, the chapter concerns itself primarily with where we believe new insights are available from recent research. The same approach also applies to the organization of the whole book.

1.1   Lexical categories

This section focuses on verbs (V), nouns (N), prepositions (P), and adjectives (A).

1.1.1   Verbs and nouns – basic distinctions

It is common wisdom in modern linguistics that N and V are two basic categories. In Chinese, the two categories can be clearly distinguished on the basis of their modifiability by the negative morpheme *bu*. The basic data are given in (1)–(2):

(1)   Verbs
       a. bu shui   'not sleep'
       b. bu tongzhi 'not inform'
       c. bu sai qiu   'not play ball'

(2)   Nouns
       a. *bu shu   'not tree'
       b. *bu xiaoxi 'not news'
       c. *bu qiu sai 'not ball game'

To our knowledge, all verbs can be negated by *bu*, and no noun can. It must be pointed out that *bu* can also negate adjectives such as *da* 'big' and *lei* 'tired.' As we will see in subsequent sections, this similarity between verbs and adjectives poses no problem for the N–V distinction.

Examples exist in Modern Chinese that seem to suggest that nouns can be modified by *bu*, such as *bu-ren-bu-gui* 'not-human-not-ghost.' However, there are reasons for not regarding such examples as a problem for the *bu*-test of the N–V distinction. First, they are not formed with a productive process. A change of nouns typically results in unacceptability:

(3)   a. *bu-shu-bu-bao 'not-book-not-newspaper'
       b. *bu-fan-bu-cha 'not-food-not-tea'

Second, the nouns in these examples must be monosyllabic, even when multi-syllabic counterparts exist, further confirming that *bu* cannot really modify a noun in Modern Chinese:

(4)   a. *bu-huoren-bu-sigui 'not-live.human-not-dead.ghost'
      b. *bu-renlei-bu-guilei 'not-humankind-not-ghost.kind'

Lastly, even with the nouns that *bu* can accompany, a single *bu*-N pair is not permitted, contrasting sharply with the verbs in (1):

(5)   a. *bu-ren 'not-human'
      b. *bu-gui 'not-ghost'

As a result, we regard the few exceptions not as undermining the reliability of the *bu*-test, but as idiomatic expressions not subject to the general rules we are pursuing.

   N and V also differ in many other ways reported in various grammar books (e.g., a subset of V allows aspectual suffixation, while no word used as N does). For the present chapter, the data below are of particular interest:

(6)   Verbs
      a. meiti   baodao-le na-ci   shigu.
         media report-LE that-CL accident
         'The media reported that accident.'

      b. Zhangsan fanyi-le   yi-bu   xiaoshuo.
         Zhangsan translate-LE one-CL novel
         'Zhangsan translated a novel.'

      c. laoshi piping-le   zhe ji-ge   yanjiusheng.
         teacher criticize-LE these some-CL graduate.student
         'The teacher criticized these graduate students.'

(7)   Nouns
      a. meiti   *(dui) na-ci   shigu   de baodao[1]
         media   on   that-CL accident DE report
         'the media's report of that accident'

      b. Zhangsan *(dui) yi-bu   xiaoshuo de fanyi
         Zhangsan on   one-CL novel   DE translation
         'Zhangsan's translation of a novel'

      c. laoshi *(dui) zhe ji-ge   yanjiusheng   de piping
         teacher on   these some-CL graduate.student DE criticism
         'the teacher's criticism of these graduate students'

---

[1] Parentheses are a notational convention. The expression between a pair of parentheses is optional. E.g., A(B)C indicates that both AC and ABC are acceptable facts. If an asterisk "*" immediately precedes the expression inside the parentheses, as in A(*B)C, then AC is acceptable but ABC is not. If instead the asterisk immediately precedes the left parenthesis, as in A*(B)C, then ABC is acceptable but AC is not. All the examples in (7) are of this type.

The two groups of examples, though both based on *baodao*, *fanyi*, and *piping*, exhibit three differences. Take (6a) and (7a) for example. First, the semantic object occurs to the right of *baodao* in (6a) but to the left in (7a); second, a preposition *dui* is required to introduce the object only in (7a); third, the morpheme *de* is required before *baodao* in (7a). The nature of these facts will become clearer as we proceed. For now, it is sufficient to note that nouns depend on prepositions like *dui* for the grammaticality of their object whereas verbs do not. This is a very reliable test to separate N from V, with the limitation that it only applies where the semantic subject of the N/V is present.[2]

The fundamental distinction between N and V might be a reflection of proto-categories,[3] a concept that traces its origin to psychological studies of human cognition. It is possible that our brain divides the world into two elementary kinds of entities: things that exist and situations that take place. Proto-N is the linguistic representation of the former kind, and proto-V that of the latter kind. All specific lexical categories are then the derivatives of these two proto-categories. Let us represent the proto-categories as two features, [N] and [V]. Since a word either belongs to proto-N or does not belong to proto-N, the feature for this proto-category has two values, [±N]. The same logic leads to [±V]. These two binary-valued features yield four possible combinations: [+N, −V], [+N, +V], [−N, −V], and [−N, +V]. If these feature combinations indeed correspond to lexical categories in languages, then it is obvious that nouns are [+N, −V] and verbs are [−N, +V]. That is, a noun conforms to proto-N but not to proto-V, whereas a verb conforms to proto-V but not to proto-N. The hypothesis can be summarized in a feature matrix:

(8)   Feature-based characterization of lexical categories (preliminary)

[N]	+	+	−	−
[V]	−	+	−	+
Feature / Category	N	?	?	V

To avoid confusion, we make a notational clarification: [N] and [V] are categorial features which we suggested to represent proto-categories; N and V, on the other hand, are the shorthand names of the actual lexical categories that can be decomposed into combinations of categorial features. See Chomsky (1970) for the onset of this theory. Following convention (cf. Freidin 1991), the characteristic property of a noun-like category (i.e., [+N]) is its inability to take a nominal object, at least

---

[2] This analysis is adopted from Y. Li (1997a). See Fu (1994) for a different treatment of the data.

[3] Cf. Givón (1984) and the references cited there.

in the absence of other linguistic help, whereas [+V] is defined as the ability to function as the predicate of a standalone sentence.

A natural question arises about (8): what are the lexical categories represented by [+N, +V] and [−N, −V], which are marked with "?" in the table? Answers will be given later in this section, after a unique type of noun is examined.

1.1.2   Localizers[4]

The examples below illustrate a set of words whose categorial status has always been controversial:

(9)   a. wuzi   li/limian
           room inside

       b. chuang xia/dixia
           bed   underneath

       c. da   shu pang/pangbian
           big tree side

Each expression in (9) consists of a noun followed by what Chao (1968) called a localizer. That localizers resemble nouns in syntax is widely recognized (see A. Li 1990, Y. Li 2003, and the references therein). First, to the extent that the examples in (9) are treated as phrases, which we refer to as localizer phrases (LPs) for now, they can serve as the subject or object in a sentence:

(10)   a. tamende chengshi /cheng wai   hen meili.
           their   city   /city   outside very beautiful
           'Their city/The outside of the city is beautiful.'

       b. wo qu-guo tamende chengshi /cheng wai.
           I   go-GUO their   city   /city   outside
           'I have been to their city/outside the city.'

Secondly, just as N is the last word in a noun phrase (NP), L also trails all other components in an LP, as seen in *tamende chengshi* vs. *cheng wai* in (10). In syntax, this word order is referred to as "head-final," with N and L being the "heads" of their respective NP and LP.

Another similarity between LP and NP is seen through the examples in (11):

(11)   a. ta *(zai) nage chengshi juban-guo yi-ge zhanlanhui.
           he   P   that city   hold-GUO a-CL exhibition
           'He held an exhibition *(in) that city.'

       b. ta *(zai) cheng wai/li   juban-guo yi-ge zhanlanhui.
           he   P   city   outside/inside hold-GUO a-CL exhibition
           'He held an exhibition outside/inside the city.'

---

[4] The discussion of localizers is in part based on Y. Li (1983, 2003).

For reasons to be made clear in a later chapter, NPs not functioning as the subject or the object usually need a pre/postposition (P) to occur in a sentence. As (11a) and its English translation show, this is apparently a cross-linguistic fact. In this regard, the LP in (11b) behaves exactly like NP, relying on a locative preposition to be well-formed. The same data also argue against treating L as a postposition (cf. Tai 1973, Peyraube 1980, and Ernst 1988). If L were a postposition, there would be no reason why it should not behave like one, and its presence in (11b) would be enough to introduce the nominal *cheng* 'city' just like *outside* does in English.

There is one property of L, however, that does distinguish it from N and make it resemble a postposition. It is the interaction between L and *de*, which we will turn to next. To better facilitate discussion, monosyllabic and disyllabic localizers will be examined separately.

1.1.2.1 L, *de*, and classifiers

Starting with monosyllabic L, let us first consider the interaction between the use of *de* and a group of words in Chinese called classifiers (CL). In the presence of numerals and demonstrative pronouns, a Chinese noun usually needs a classifier to specify the "unit" with which the entities denoted by the noun are measured. Crucially, different nouns require different classifiers (to maintain a minimal-pair comparison between nouns and localizers, all examples in this subsection are composed of monosyllabic morphemes at the point of relevance):

(12)   yi-zhang chuang, si-tiao tui, zhe-ke shu, na-pian pi
        one-CL   bed   four-CL leg   this-CL tree that-CL bark
        'a bed'   'four legs'   'this tree'   'that bark'

The dependency between a noun and its classifier displays interesting patterns when two nouns are concatenated with or without *de*:

(13)   a. si-tiao   chuang tui vs. *si-zhang chuang tui
           four-CL bed   leg   four-CL bed   leg

        b. zhe-pian shu pi   vs. *zhe-ke shu pi
           this-CL   tree bark   this-CL tree bark

(14)   a. (?)si-tiao   chuang de tui vs. si-zhang chuang de tui
              four-CL bed   DE leg   four-CL bed   DE leg

        b. (?)zhe-pian shu de pi   vs. zhe-ke shu de pi
              this-CL   tree DE bark   this-CL tree DE bark

In brief, *de* is independently optional between two nouns; however, a CL must match the N on the right (i.e., the head N) in the absence of *de* but can optionally associate with either N when *de* is present.

The explanation for the pattern in (13)–(14) is both simple and intuitive. Suppose that the N-N cluster without *de* is always a compound whereas the one with *de* in between is an NP in which the noun on the left modifies the one on the right. In other words, *de* necessarily and sufficiently signals a phrasal structure in the context of two consecutive nouns. Furthermore, Chinese N-N compounds are "head-final" because it is the noun on the right that determines the basic semantics of the word – a *chuang-tui* 'bed leg' is a kind of leg but not a kind of bed. As a result, only the classifier *tiao*, appropriate for legs but not for beds, is permitted in (13) where *de* is absent. When *de* is present, as in (14), the two nouns are not components of a single compound word; rather, each of them is a separate word in syntax, yielding the structure in (15) in which the pairs of brackets mark out the boundaries of noun phrases, a notational convention widely used in syntax:

(15)   [NP1 . . . [NP2 . . . bed] DE leg]

The " . . . " in each NP is where a classifier plus a numeral/demonstrative may occur. Since there are two separate nouns, each one of them may be associated with its own classifier in syntax. In other words, a classifier at the beginning of such a string may be alternatively treated as part of NP1 (i.e., associated with *leg*) or part of NP2 (associated with *bed*). Linearly, CL occurs in the same spot; the options result from different levels of word-associations that are made possible in syntax. With this explanation, we can also understand why the first example in each pair of (14) sounds somewhat strange. In these examples, the adjacent CL-N sequence is expected to match but does not because the CL is really for the second noun, thus causing difficulty in processing. Also note that no CL is required for (15) to be acceptable (e.g., *chuang de tui* 'bed DE leg'). We thus assume that an NP may be composed of a bare noun.

Turning to LPs headed by monosyllabic localizers, we note two facts: that no *de* is allowed between L and the preceding N, and that a CL before an N matches that N without a hitch:

(16)   chuang (*de) xia,   men (*de) hou,   wu (*de) li
        bed   underneath door   behind house   inside

(17)   yi-zhang chuang xia,   zhe-shan men hou,   na-jian wu   li
        one-CL   bed   underneath this-CL   door behind that-CL house inside

Example (16) distinguishes L from N and underlies the proposal that L is a post-position. (17) contrasts sharply with the *de*-less N-N compounds in (13). In both (13) and (17), only monosyllabic words are used, and in both, *de* is absent. But when the rightmost morpheme is N, a classifier matching the left-hand N is totally unacceptable; when the rightmost morpheme is L, however, the otherwise identical choice of words yields 100 percent acceptability. Given our explanation for the nominal examples in (13)–(14) above, it can be deduced that LP has the following structure:

(18)   [LP [NP . . . N] L]

Crucially, the pre-L nominal does not form a compound with L. Instead, it has its own phrase in which a classifier is permitted. Put differently, while the lack of *de* between L and the preceding N makes the cluster resemble an N-N compound in form, we have evidence now that there really is a phrasal structure.

1.1.2.2   L as a subclass of N

The structural analysis of the behavioral contrast between L and N in the previous subsection only serves to highlight an old question: What is the best categorial classification of L that explains its syntactic properties? Logically, there are three possible answers: L is a subclass of N, L is a postposition, or L is a separate category. In this book, we offer a theory in which the properties of L may be understood by pursuing the first possibility.

As we saw earlier, L exhibits three characteristic properties of N: LP is head-final, it functions as the subject or the object in a sentence, and it needs a preposition if used as a locative modifier. L also appears like a postposition because no *de* is used to associate L with the NP before it. What remains unclear is whether this NP is the object of L in the same sense that a preposition takes an NP object, since Chinese is lacking morphological cues that would help identify the NP's grammatical function. At least in theory, it is equally possible that the NP plays the role of a "possessor" in LP. Overall, if we are to choose a category for L between N and P, N seems more appropriate.

The question, then, is how to account for the lack of *de* if L is viewed as a type of N. It should be obvious that some stipulation is unavoidable in order to allow L to be N but still different from N. To this effect, we hypothesize that a language may allow a (natural) subclass of words in a given category X to "deviate" behaviorally from X.[5] Meanwhile, we propose that such deviations are not random but rather the result of a predictable nature.

_____

[5] At a more fundamental level, a categorial deviate may not be distinguishable from a new category. The more important question is whether languages may potentially allow any new category, or whether even a new one must be subject to the same principle as the core set. The second choice is obviously more restrictive and therefore is assumed here. See Y. Li (2003) for alternatively treating L as a new category "between" N and P. The basic reasoning in this section applies there too.

As the first step in our account, consider *do*-insertion in English:

(19) a. Did Sam leave?
      b. Sam did not leave.
      c. Sam left.
      d. *Sam did leave.

The semantically empty modal *do* is used in forming the interrogative in (19a) and the negative in (19b). But if *do*-insertion is a legitimate operation in English grammar, why can it not happen in the declarative (19d)? Note that (19d) would be good if *did* undertook the emphatic interpretation (plus the corresponding stress). The emphatic *did* is not the same morpheme as in (19a–b) and thus not relevant for the current discussion.

Chomsky's (1995) answer to this question is couched in the technical terms of the Minimalist Program but is, to us, intuitive in its essence. He suggests that highly language-specific operations such as *do*-insertion are more "costly" in linguistic computation because they have to be learned. In comparison, the mechanisms observed cross-linguistically, which are collectively referred to as Universal Grammar (UG), are presumably hardwired in the brain and come for free. If linguistic derivations somehow try to avoid more costly operations whenever possible, then the data in (19) are easy to explain. Example (19c) is chosen over (19d) because it results from a "cheaper" derivation by not incurring the cost of language-specific *do*-insertion. Independent reasons require the presence of a modal in interrogatives and negatives, so not having one necessarily leads to ungrammaticality. *Do*-insertion is justified in these cases only because there is no other grammatical way to form a question or negation.

Interestingly, the use of *de* is also highly language-specific. Suppose that the syntactic properties of L are decided according to (20), which in turn may be the specific manifestation of a more general principle which also produces the *do*-insertion data in (19):

(20)   In deciding the properties of a categorial deviate, anything language-specific in the original category is disfavored.

Of the cluster of properties displayed by Chinese nouns, heading an NP that functions directly as the subject or object and needs a preposition otherwise is a property that is found with nouns in every language. Being head-final inside an NP is also a typological phenomenon found in half of the world's languages (Greenberg 1963, Hawkins 1983). In comparison, the use of *de* is language-specific and therefore is a more costly operation that is subject to removal if any change is to happen to the cluster. As a result, L keeps all the syntactic properties of N except *de*.

To complete the analysis, we also make explicit an assumption underlying the previous discussion:

(21)   The choice of the syntactic properties of a categorial deviate X must guarantee that X is distinct from all existing categories.

The validity of (21) is self-evident. If X retained all the properties of the original category, there would be no X; if behavioral change resulted in X acting completely like another (existing) category, then it would be a categorial conversion, not a deviation. In sum, (21) enforces a partial change in behavior while (20) dictates the exact content of the change. In the rest of this subsection, we will continue to use the term localizer for this group of words, and noun for the standard nouns, so as to facilitate discussion. It should be noted that the theory offered here does not force a language to have a deviated L, even when N has language-specific properties. It only applies if the language opts for deviation.

1.1.2.3 Disyllabic L

The examples below illustrate disyllabic localizers.

(22)   a. chuang (de) xiamian
           bed   DE   underneath

        b. men (de) houtou
           door DE   behind

        c. wuzi   (de) libian
           house DE   inside

The analysis in the previous subsection is based on the fact that monosyllabic L differs from corresponding N in not employing *de*. In contrast, the optional use of *de* with disyllabic localizers makes them resemble disyllabic nouns:

(23)   a. men (de) bashou
           gate DE   handle

        b. wuzi   (de) houmen
           house DE   backdoor

If the presence of *de* signals "nounhood" as we have argued, then the localizers preceded by *de* in (22) are all nouns just like *bashou* 'handle' and *houmen* 'backdoor' in (23).

This may appear to suggest that the localizers without *de* are nouns as well. The classifier test, however, argues differently:

(24) a. na-shan   damen   houtou, yi-jian   wuzi   libian, ...
         that-CL   big.gate   behind   one-CL   house inside
      b. *na-shan   damen   bashou, *yi-jian   wuzi   houmen, ...
         that-CL   big.gate   handle   one-CL   house backdoor

Just as we saw with monosyllabic localizers and nouns, a classifier matching the noun immediately after it is perfect with the *de*-less localizer but results in totally unacceptable examples with typical N-N compounds. Therefore, it must be concluded that even disyllabic localizers in the absence of *de* take a preceding NP as complement (cf. the structure in (18)) but do not form an N-N compound with the preceding N. As no *de* is present between this NP and the localizer, the latter must be L, a deviate of N.

This conclusion means that, while monosyllabic localizers are exclusively L, their disyllabic cousins are ambiguous between L and N. This is actually easy to understand. After all, the morphemes *mian*, *tou*, and *bian* are nouns meaning, respectively, 'face,' 'end,' and 'side' when used alone. As a result, *libian* 'inside' can be reasonably treated as consisting of L-N. Since the nominal compounds are head-final (see discussion following (14)), it is only natural that the L-N compound inherits its category from its N head. In other words, they are simple locative nouns. It is also a fact that *mian*, *tou*, and *bian* have lost both their tones and their concrete semantic content when they occur as the second component of the disyllabic localizer. We suggest that they are on the verge of losing their categorial identity as well. If they are still treated as nouns, the disyllabic localizer is a noun, as we saw. If their categorial content is considered lost together with the tonal and semantic content, the only morpheme in the compound that can still determine the category is the monosyllabic localizer. Hence the whole compound is treated as L. See Di Sciullo and Williams (1987) for a hypothesis on computing the lexical properties of a compound from its head.

1.1.2.4   On L as a clitic

Our analysis of L is crucially built on its interaction with *de* by attributing the absence of the morpheme to L deviating from N and to *de* being more costly to use in syntactic computation. There are alternative ways to account for the distribution of *de* in such contexts. Liu (1998), for instance, treats (monosyllabic) L as a clitic carrying the [+loc] feature. As such, the NP combined with L essentially behaves as a location-denoting NP like *xuexiao* 'school,' with L being a "phrasal affix" that forms a phonological unit with the host NP (Klavans 1980,

Zwicky 1985, Anderson 1992). This account is both simple and intuitive given the well-known fact that prosody plays an active role in the syntax and morphology of Modern Chinese.[6] We see no reason against calling L a clitic since it indeed tends not to stand alone, but we do not believe that doing so can either eliminate the question regarding the categorial nature of L or provide an adequate explanation for L's behaviors.

First, it is widely accepted in the fields of generative syntax and morphology that an affix belongs in some category. Much recent research is built on assigning syntactically distinct categories to even tense and aspect affixes. Since Liu adopts Anderson's (1992) theory that a clitic differs from an affix only by attaching to a phrase rather than to a morpheme, it is expected that clitics fall into different categories as well.

Secondly, treating L as a clitic to an NP may appear to explain why *de* is absent – *de* is another clitic and incapable of serving as host for L – but actually raises various new questions. For instance, though L typically is associated with an NP, there are cases when the NP can be missing (the glossing is only suggestive):

(25)   a. X   L

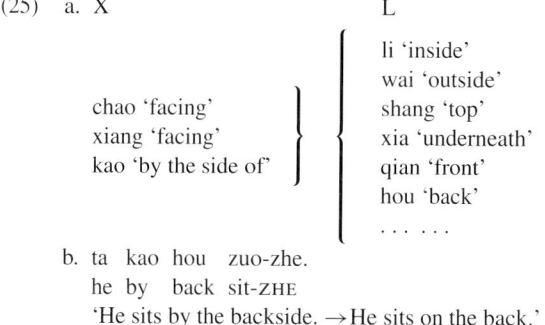

```
                                      li 'inside'
                                      wai 'outside'
           chao 'facing'             shang 'top'
           xiang 'facing'            xia 'underneath'
           kao 'by the side of'      qian 'front'
                                      hou 'back'
                                      . . . . . .
```

   b. ta kao hou   zuo-zhe.
      he by   back sit-ZHE
      'He sits by the backside. → He sits on the back.'

Whether the words in the X column are verbs or prepositions may be debatable, but they are definitely not nouns. And each one of them can be productively followed directly by any monosyllabic localizers (as well as disyllabic ones and the NP-L clusters) as exemplified by (25a–b). If L is simply a locative clitic, to what phrase does L cliticize? Note that there is no sense in which the phrase headed by, say, *kao* 'by the side of' needs L to acquire the [+loc] feature, with *kao* itself sufficiently indicating a location:

(26)   ta kao qiang zuo-zhe.
          he by   wall   sit-ZHE
          'He sits by the wall.'

---

[6] See Feng (2000) for a theory of such syntax–prosody interactions in Chinese.

On the other hand, within the theory that treats monosyllabic localizers as a deviate of N which we call L, the examples in (25) have the following structure:

(27)   by/facing [LP . . . L]

where " . . ." is a phonetically contentless pronoun which, as we will see in later chapters, Chinese employs abundantly. Technical details need to be worked out, but (27) can easily explain the intuition that when someone sits by the 'backside,' as in (25b), he sits by the backside of *something* obvious from the discourse. As we know, such reference is typical of pronouns. In contrast, claiming a clitic to take a phonetically empty pronoun as host would seem to run against the very notion of cliticization.

1.1.3   Adjectives

There are reasons for distinguishing adjectives from verbs in Chinese, in spite of the fact that a Chinese adjective functions as the predicate of a clause without the help of a copular verb. In this section, we first examine the evidence for the adjectival category (shorthanded as A), then we provide a feature characterization for it.

1.1.3.1   In comparison with verbs

Some adjectives can be used transitively, in the sense that they describe situations that involve two participants rather than one. If a clause contains such an adjective, one of the participants is expected to be represented as the subject. The other, however, needs to be introduced with *dui* (adjectives in these examples are in bold face):

(28) a. ta dui zhe-ge jieju   hen **buman**.
         he on this-CL outcome very discontent
         'He is discontent with this outcome.'

      b. ??ta hen **buman**   zhe-ge jieju.[7]
         he very discontent this-CL outcome

---

[7] Some such examples may be perceived to be acceptable by certain speakers, possibly due to dialectal differences. For these speakers, what is judged as an adjective in our book may have changed into a verb. Such a categorical shift is likely to happen more easily in Chinese than in, say, English for two reasons. First, Chinese has no morphological markers for categories found in European languages. Secondly, Chinese adjectives function as predicates without a copula, making them appear verb-like. On the second property, see Section 1.1.3.2 below.

(29) a. wo dui tade qushi   feichang **shangxin**.
         I   on his pass.away extremely sad
         'I am extremely sad about his death.'

      b. *wo feichang **shangxin** tade qushi.
          I extremely sad   his pass.away

(30) a. zhe-ge gongzuo dui ni   hen **heshi**.
         this-CL job   on you very suitable
         'This job is suitable for you.'

      b. *zhe-ge gongzuo hen **heshi**   ni.
          this-CL job   very suitable you

To the best of our knowledge, the NP after *dui* is the semantic object of the adjective. Such a relation between the two constituents not only is consistent with the semantics of the examples but also is supported by the comparison between (30) and (31):

(31)   zhe-ge gongzuo hen **shihe** ni.
        this-CL job   very suit   you
        'This job suits you well.'

Differing only in the linear sequence of the two bound morphemes *shi* and *he*, *heshi* and *shihe* are also semantically similar, especially when each one is accompanied by two NPs as in (30) and (31). Since there is no question about treating the NP *ni* 'you' as the object of *shihe*, it is only reasonable to treat the same NP in (30) as the object of *heshi*.

The different behaviors of objects in (30) and (31) are explained if the latter contains a verb while the former contains an adjective. It is established knowledge that Chinese verbs take their object directly and on the right in the unmarked context, so the linear order in (31) is expected of V. From this fact, it can be inferred that *heshi* in (30) is not a verb. In fact, as far as the use of *dui* is concerned, *heshi* patterns with nouns (cf. Section 1.1.1). Interestingly, the data here also find counterparts in English:

(32) a. She loves butterflies.
      b. her love *(of) butterflies
      c. She is fond *(of) butterflies.

In English, the object occurs consistently to the right of all categories, but the NP object must be introduced by the semantically empty preposition *of* when the word taking the object is a noun or adjective. Putting word order aside for now, this is exactly what happens in Chinese. For nouns and adjectives, the NP object must be introduced by *dui*, which not only occurs in the preverbal position typical of prepositions in the language, but also is semantically empty, as is evidenced by the fact that (30a) with *dui* does not mean any more than (31) without *dui*. In conclusion, *heshi*, *shangxin*, and *buman* in (28)–(30) are different from verbs and demonstrate typical properties of adjectives.

The use of *dui* as a test for distinguishing adjectives from verbs matches well with a long-known fact about reduplication patterns among disyllabic predicative words in Chinese (cf. Zhu 1982, Lü 1984, among many others):[8]

(33)   a. AB → ABAB
           jiancha → jianchajiancha,   jihua → jihuajihua
           examine   do a check-up of plan   do some planning

       b. AB → AABB
           ganjing → ganganjingjing, jiandan → jianjiandandan
           clean   rather clean   simple   rather simple

The words in (33a) are established verbs and can only have the ABAB pattern. Those in (33b), on the other hand, have the AABB pattern and are regarded by many grammarians as adjectives. What is interesting is that these patterns correlate with the (non-)use of *dui*. The most informative evidence comes from disyllabic transitive words such as *mingbai*, which allow both patterns of reduplication:

(34)   a. ta mingbai   zhe-ge daoli.
           he understand this-CL reason
           'He understands this reason.'

       b. ta dui zhe-ge daoli   hen   mingbai.
           he P   this-CL reason quite be.clear
           'He is quite clear about this reason.'

Applying different reduplication patterns to the word yields the sharp contrast below:

(35)   a. ta yinggai mingbaimingbai zhe-ge daoli!
           he should get.to.understand this-CL reason
           'He should get to know this reason!'

       b. *ta (yinggai) mingmingbaibai   zhe-ge daoli.
           he should   be.rather.clear.about this-CL reason

(36)   a. ta dui zhe-ge daoli   mingmingbaibai.
           he P   this-CL reason be.rather.clear
           'He is quite clear about this reason.'

       b. *ta (yinggai) dui zhe-ge daoli   mingbaimingbai.
           he should   P   this-CL reason get.to.understand

---

[8] Reduplication of this kind usually requires specific discourse contexts, which we try to take into consideration in the examples given. Various conditions apply to what disyllabic words can undergo reduplication (basically those of the "conjunctive" type), but we believe that they do not affect the validity of the analysis at hand. Also see Section 1.1.3.3 for more discussion on AABB.

In other words, the AABB pattern is correlated with using *dui* to introduce a preceding object, whereas the ABAB pattern rejects the use of *dui* and retains the object-related properties of the original verb. Later, we will provide a theoretical framework for understanding why the use of *dui* is associated with adjectives but not with verbs. For now, what is significant is the fact that the reduplication patterns corroborate with the verb–adjective distinction established on the basis of *dui*.

It is often suggested in the literature that the adverb *hen* 'very' can be used to define adjectives. While typical adjectives indeed associate well with *hen*, the following data indicate that this test does not apply exclusively to adjectives:

(37) a. ni   hen   ai   ta.
         you very love him
         'You love him very much.'

      b. ta hen ganxie   dajia   de bangzhu.
         he very be.grateful.for people DE help
         'He is very grateful of people's help.'

      c. wo hen tongqing   ni   de zaoyu.
         I   very sympathize you DE bad.experience
         'I am sympathetic with your bad experience.'

In all these examples, the object occurs without the use of *dui* or any other grammatical help. This is typical of the object of verbs. If the goal were to formulate an isolated grammatical theory of Chinese, it might be plausible to treat *ai* 'love,' *ganxie* 'be grateful for,' and *tongqing* 'sympathize' as adjectives. This is so because the test of *hen* and the test of *dui*-less object do not yield identical results, and there would be no particular reason to favor one test over the other. But we aim to capture the patterns in Chinese without losing the important fact that Chinese is also a human language. With the behaviors of adjectives in other languages taken into consideration, it is clear that the *dui* test should be favored and the words at issue in (37) are verbs, not adjectives. More generally, linguistic debates may result from lack of decisive evidence on both sides when the investigation is confined to a single language, but may be resolved, and sometimes may not even arise, if the universal aspect of language is duly considered.

1.1.3.2 As opposed to nouns

Given the fact that A patterns with N according to the *dui* test, it seems appropriate to assign [+N] to A. But it is equally clear that A and N have different syntactic behaviors. Most relevant to the current concern is the use of the copular *shi*. As the predicate of a clause, NP typically requires *shi*, with the option of omitting it in highly colloquial speech. The adjective phrase (AP) predicate, however, rejects *shi* completely. The contrast is shown below:

(38) a. ta shi yingxiong.
          he be hero
          'He is a hero.'

      b. ?ta yingxiong.
          he hero
          'He is a hero.'

(39) a. ta hen yingyong.
          he very heroic
          'He is heroic.'

      b. *ta shi hen yingyong.[9]
          he be very heroic
          Intended reading: same as (39a).

In fact, it is precisely this ability to function as the predicate without a copula that makes many researchers treat A as a subcategory of V in Chinese. In terms of categorial features, then, A is a candidate for [+V]. In sum, we see evidence that A should fill the gap of [+N, +V] in (8).[10]

1.1.3.3   More on AABB

While ABAB and AABB are shown to correlate well with the different ways in which a verb and an adjective introduce their NP objects, it would be an oversimplification to match them directly with the verb–adjective distinction because certain disyllabic verbs may also be reduplicated as AABB:[11]

(40) a. chaorang   → chaochaorangrang
          argue.yell

      b. fengbu   → fengfengbubu
          sew.mend

      c. laiwang   → lailaiwangwang
          come.go
          'mutually visit'

---

[9] One needs to distinguish the copular *shi* from the emphatic *shi*, which is permitted in this example. The most salient differences between the two morphemes are that the emphatic *shi* must be stressed in this context while the copular *shi* is typically not, and that the emphatic *shi*, as its name implies, is used only to emphasize some constituent after it, either reflecting the assertive attitude of the speaker or bringing out a contrastive interpretation. The copular *shi* in (38a) does not have this semantic property at all. The emphatic use of *shi* and its syntactic representation will be examined in detail later in the book.

[10] This conclusion fits seamlessly into Chomsky's (1970) theory of categorial features, but it also raises questions about the nature of English adjectives, which crucially cannot be used predicatively in a standalone sentence without a copula. Various possibilities arise but we will leave them aside. In essence, our analysis claims that Chinese A is the typical [+N, +V]. English A must be something else.

[11] We thank the audience of Yafei Li's Syntax of Chinese class for bringing this fact to our attention. See Lü (1984) for more examples.

For these verbs, taking the AABB form does not turn them into adjectives even though, where it is possible to tell, they do lose the ability to take a postverbal object:

(41) a. ta ba na-jian yishang fengfengbubu,   chuan-le henduo nian.
         he BA that-CL coat   sew.here.mend.there wear-LE   many   year
         'He kept sewing and patching that coat and wore it for many years.'

      b. *ta fengfengbubu   na-jian yishang, chuan-le henduo nian.
         he sew.here.mend.there that-CL coat   wear-LE   many   year
         Intended reading: same as (41a).

The use of *ba* with the preverbal NP *na-jian yishang* 'that coat' in (41a) indicates that *fengfengbubu* is still a verb (cf. Chapter 5), but the postverbal position is no longer legitimate for the NP object, shown in (41b).

Under the assumption that the AABB pattern in both (41) for verbs and in the adjectival data in Section 1.1.3.1 are produced by the same morphological process, we conclude for now that the process itself is not category-changing, although it is necessarily correlated with the lack of a postverbal object.

1.1.4   Prepositions

The class of prepositions is one of the most poorly defined categories in Chinese, due to the facts that the so-called prepositions in the language all have their historical origins as verbs, and that Chinese has no inflectional morphology to mark verbs. In this section, we examine four classes of words that are labeled as prepositions in the literature. It is not our intention to exhaust either all preposition-like words or even all the usages of any specific word in this group. Rather, we hope to provide an in-depth analysis of a subset of such words in an attempt to uncover some inner workings of the human linguistic faculty.

1.1.4.1   Behavioral clarifications

Some candidates for P are given below:[12]

(42) a. zhiyu 'as for,' guanyu 'about,' . . .
      b. cong 'from'
      c. gei 'to/for,' zai 'at,' xiang 'toward,' . . .
      d. ba, bei

The words in (42) can all introduce an NP on their right without the help of any other morpheme. This property is shared by P and V – both P and V can take a

---

[12] The English glosses are only meant as approximate translations. In fact, not every word in this list is directly translatable.

nominal object directly – but not by N or A, which are incapable of directly taking any nominal object. The reader is invited to test this claim with Chinese as well as with other languages. Given the definition of [N] above, both P and V should be [−N]. While the same logic dictates that all the words in (42) are [−N], they also differ in interesting ways, which we examine one by one. To facilitate discussion, we will temporarily call all these words prepositions until their actual categories are identified.

Though all the prepositions in (42) are typically followed by an NP, only those in (a) must occur with the NP in a pre-subject position:

(43) a. guanyu zhe-jian shi, tamen yijing   taolun-guo   le.
          about   this-CL issue they already discuss-GUO SFP
          'Regarding this issue, they already discussed (it).'

      b. ta cong nali   dai-huilai   henduo jinianpin.
          he from there bring-back many   souvenir
          'He brought back many souvenirs from there.'

      c. ta gei ban li   de ren   zuo-guo bushao shiqing.
          he for class inside DE people do-GUO not.few thing
          'He did quite a few things for the people of the class.'

      d. ta ba guizhong de shoushi cang-zai waguan li.
          he BA expensive DE jewelry hide-in   clay.pot inside
          'He hid expensive jewelry in a clay pot.'

In (b) through (d), the default position for the prepositions is between the subject and the main verb of the clause. Such a word order is not an alternative for the sentence in (43a). This fact indicates that the prepositions in (42a) occur in a syntactic position outside of or peripheral to the clausal structure. This contrasts with those in (42b–d), which clearly are inside the clause proper.

Furthermore, the pre-subject position is an option available to the prepositions in (42b, c) as long as they bring their nominal object along with them. This word order alternation, viewed as *movement* away from the default position, is not available to the words in (42d).

(44) a. cong nali, ta dai-huilai   henduo jinianpin.   (cf. (43b))
          from there he bring-back many   souvenir
          'From there, he brought back many souvenirs.'

      b. gei ban li   de ren,   ta zuo-guo bushao shiqing.   (cf. (43c))
          for class inside DE people he do-GUO not.few thing
          'For the people of the class, he did quite a few things.'

      c. *ba guizhong de shoushi, ta cang-zai waguan li.   (cf. (43d))
          BA expensive DE jewelry he hide-in   clay.pot inside
          'Expensive jewelry, he hid in a clay pot.'

The grammaticality of (44a, b) is expected if a preposition forms a phrase, PP, with the NP after it, the logic being that only words forming a constituent can move together.

If (44a, b) involve clause-initial PPs, the structure of (43a) can be analyzed analogously, with the preposition *guanyu* 'about' and the NP after it forming a PP. The difference is that the PP in (43a) does not occupy the clause-initial position through movement: where it is heard is its default position. This is why this PP cannot occur between the subject and the verb.[13] Put differently, the PP in (43a) always modifies a whole clause, while those in (43b, c) and (44a, b) typically modify only part of the clause, namely the phrasal predicate containing the verb (see Ernst (2002) for a comprehensive discussion on the locations of various adverbial modifiers). It should be noted that the PP formed with *guanyu* is also movable, as the theory expects. This can be seen in a larger syntactic environment:

(45)   guanyu zhe-jian shi,   wo tingshuo tamen yijing   taolun-guo   le.
        about   this-CL issue I   hear   they already discuss-GUO SFP
        'Regarding this issue, I heard that they already discussed (it).'

With the interpretation that I heard that they had a discussion on this issue, the PP must have originated inside the object clause. Then its actual position in the main clause results from phrasal movement.

Given this logic, the ungrammatical status of (44c) follows if *ba* and the NP after it do not form a phrase – not being a constituent, *ba* and the NP cannot move together to the clause-initial position. The same observation is true of *bei*. We will elaborate on this conclusion in Chapters 4 and 5.

A frequently mentioned factor that divides the words in (42) is whether they have the option of being used alone as verbs in Modern Chinese. Of the four classes, only (42c) has this option. In the examples below, the words at issue are in bold face:

(46) a. *women de huiyi   **guanyu** na-ci   shigu.   (cf. (42a))
          our   DE meeting about   that-CL accident
          Intended reading: 'Our meeting is about that accident.'

      b. *ta **cong** nanfang.   (cf. (42b))
          he from south
          Intended reading: 'He is from the south.'

---

[13] Logically, one could imagine that the PP in (44a) starts in the clause-initial position but moves to the post-subject position as an option. If this option were available, there would be no explanation for the pattern in (43). Later on, we will see that movement doesn't happen in all directions, and that rightward movement in Chinese is prohibited by syntactic principles that regulate all human languages; cf. Fiengo (1977), Lasnik and Saito (1993).

c. ta **gei**-le   wo yi-ba   jian.   (cf. (42c))
   he give-LE me one-CL sword
   'He gave me a sword.'

d. *ta **ba** guizhong de shoushi.   (cf. (42d))
   he BA expensive DE jewelry
   No possible interpretation.

Historically, *cong* in (46b) meant 'to follow' and *ba* in (46d) 'to hold,' both used as verbs. But these verbal usages are no longer available in Modern Chinese except inside some fossilized expressions. In contrast, it is obvious that *gei* in (46c) is used as a verb, given the aspectual markers it carries as well as the unmistakable actions it describes.

A subset of the words in class (c) of (42) may also serve productively as the second member of a complex verbal predicate, be it in a phrasal or compound form. The words of our concern are again marked in bold face:

(47) a. ta ba na-zhang zhaopian ji-**gei**-le   wo.
         he BA that-CL   picture   send-give-LE me
         'He mailed me that picture.'

      b. ta ji-le   yi-zhang zhaopian **gei** wo.
         he send-LE one-CL   picture   to me
         'He mailed a picture to me.'

(48) a. ta ba xin   fang-**zai** shu li.
         he BA letter put-at   book inside
         'He put the letter in the book.'

      b. ?ta fang-le yi-feng xin   **zai** shu li.
         he put-LE one-CL letter at   book inside
         'He put a letter in the book.'

(49)   haizi-men gaoxing de chong-**xiang** shanding.
         child-PL   happy   DE dash-toward hill.top
         'The children happily dashed toward the top of the hill.'

To our knowledge, no preposition of other classes has this property in Modern Chinese. The significance of this correlation is explored in the next subsection.

1.1.4.2 The categorially dual status

Summarizing so far, the classes (42a, b) have the typical properties of prepositions. They form a phrase with an NP object and they cannot function as verbs, as is expected of typical prepositions and postpositions in every language. Recall that the very ability to take an NP object without the help of any other morpheme indicates that these words are not noun-like, which is represented as [−N] in the theory based on categorial features (cf. Section 1.1.1). Now that classes

(40a, b) cannot be used as verbs in the typical predicative manner, it is only natural to conclude that they are not verb-like either. Namely, they are [−V]. Therefore, a preposition is [−N, −V] in terms of categorial features. This conclusion is based on the syntactic properties of prepositions, but it also fills a gap in the feature matrix in (8). To put it differently, the theory predicts the existence of a category [−N, −V], and the prediction is borne out empirically. The only structural difference between the two classes of prepositions in Chinese is that (42a) is located somewhere outside the core structure of a clause while (42b) is inside. We return to the precise locations of these phrases later.

If prepositions are [−N, −V], then the members of class (42c) cannot be treated simply as prepositions because they can also be used as verbs, which are [+V] by definition. We believe that this class has multiple statuses. As V, the words in (42c) are [−N, +V]; and as P, they are [−N, −V]. The evidence for their verbhood is already given in (46). Now consider the argument for their prepositional use, starting with the examples below. To avoid unnecessary confusions during the discussion, *gei* is glossed as a theoretically non-committal GEI in the examples:

(50)　a.　ta　gei　wo　zuo-le　henduo　shi.
　　　　　he　GEI　me　do-LE　many　thing
　　　　　'He has done many things for me.'

　　　b.　gei　wo,　ta　zuo-le　henduo　shi.
　　　　　GEI　me　he　do-LE　many　thing
　　　　　'For me, he has done many things.'

　　　c.　*ta　zuo-gei　wo　henduo　shi.
　　　　　he　do-GEI　me　many　thing
　　　　　Intended reading: same as (a) above.

　　　d.　*ta　zuo-le　henduo　shi　gei　wo.
　　　　　he　do-LE　many　thing　GEI　me
　　　　　Intended reading: same as (a) above.

Example (50b) indicates that *gei* and the NP following it form a phrase. The choice of the main verb *zuo* 'do' enforces a benefactive interpretation on this phrase. Since (50c, d) are unacceptable, it must be concluded that this interpretation is not compatible with using *gei* as part of a complex predicate, even though *gei* can be so used otherwise (cf. (47)); see A. Li (1985, 1990).

This apparently messy behavior of *gei* actually has a simple explanation. As we saw earlier, members of class (42c) can both function as standalone verbs and occur in a complex predicate. Furthermore, it is a fact that when *gei* is used as a verb, it does not have the benefactive interpretation. This is straightforward in (46c) and is corroborated by the recipient reading of *gei* in (47). Now suppose that the second part of a complex predicate must be a verb. It follows immediately that *gei* in (50c, d) cannot be understood benefactively. In contrast, the preverbal *gei* in (50a, b) is a preposition just like class (42b). Its acquisition of the benefactive meaning can be attributed to some semantic shifting and/or "bleaching."[14] In other words, the unacceptable (50c, d) with the intended readings simply result from the independent requirement in Modern Chinese that within a clause, a preposition does not ever occur after a verb. In the absence of counterexamples, we extend the same conclusion to other members of class (42c) such as *zai* and *xiang*.

It must be pointed out that this argument for treating *gei* as P in (50) does not necessarily exclude the prepositional *gei* from having the recipient interpretation. In fact, the sentence below is potentially ambiguous:

(51)   ta gei wo ji-le   yi-zhang zhaopian.
         he GEI me send-LE one-CL   picture
         a. 'He mailed a picture to me.'   or
         b. 'He mailed a picture for me.'

We see no reason to treat the recipient *gei*, reflected in (51a), as a verb when the benefactive *gei* in (51b) is a preposition. To be sure, if we ignore semantic subtleties, (51a) is synonymous with (47), where *gei* is argued to be a verb. But this is not a problem considering how the semantics of the complex predicate is computed, a topic which we return to in Chapter 2.

With this discussion of prepositions, we are also ready to be more precise about the nature of [N]. Recall that N and A are [+N] because they need a preposition, *of* in English and *dui* in Chinese, to help introduce the object NP, and that such prepositions are semantically empty. These facts only suggest one thing: that there is a pure grammatical demand for *of* and *dui* in such contexts. In the framework used in this book, the grammatical demand is to provide a Case for a nominal phrase under the following hypothesis, referred to as the Case Filter:

(52)   Every NP must have a Case.

In syntax, a Case is an NP's "certificate" to function as the object or the subject of a sentence. Languages like Russian and Korean choose to manifest Cases through morphological cases such as the nominative and accusative, but every language presumably employs the certificate system regardless of whether or not it morphologically marks arguments. In this theory, the fact that A and N are incapable of directly taking an NP object is attributed to their inability to provide a Case to the latter, and this inability is formally defined as [+N]. It follows that V and P are [−N] for being able to provide Cases to their objects. In the presence of an NP

---

[14] In Bantu and Iroquoian languages, a suffix to the verb root, called an applicative, often has the function of introducing either the goal or benefactive NP, depending on the context. Though a current analysis of applicatives treats these affixes as V (Baker 1996, Y. Li 2005), it is nonetheless worth noting that it may not be an accident that a semantically "bleached" *gei* also acquires similar semantic functions.

object for A or N, then, languages enlist a semantically empty P to provide the needed Case without altering the meaning of the expression. Hence the properties of *of* and *dui* are explained (see A. Li 1985, 1990).

1.2   Functional categories

The advantage of the feature-based theory of categories in (8) is its ability to capture shared syntactic properties of certain categories, e.g., that N and A both need a P to introduce their NP object. Such behavioral similarities would be lost if each category were treated as a non-decomposable entity in language. The disadvantage is that two categorial features maximally produce only four categories – V, N, A, P according to the previous section, a clearly insufficient outcome. As an example, the discussion of L in 1.1.2 critically relied on classifiers (CL) and *de*, neither of which can be obviously accommodated by (8). This section examines how (8) may be revised to allow more categories while remaining restrictive enough to be empirically insightful.

1.2.1   [Fn], n ≥ 0

In the tradition of Chinese linguistics, there is a widely accepted distinction between *shi-ci* 'substantive word' and *xu-ci* 'empty word.' N, V, A are classified as the former and P usually as the latter. The *shi–xu* distinction corresponds to the dichotomy of lexical categories and functional categories in the theoretical framework adopted in this book, except that P is treated as a lexical category here, not as a functional one. Regardless of where P belongs in the dichotomy, however, it is clear that languages in general, Chinese being no exception, make use of functional words in syntax.[15] In fact, one of the major theoretical claims of the past three decades is that there are more functional categories than lexical categories.

First consider classifiers (CL), introduced in 1.1.2. The nominal origin of CL is widely recognized. Below is an example to highlight the relationship between CL and N:

(53)   *gan*
     a. As N: qiang-gan
                 gun-barrel
                 'gun barrel'

---

[15] Jackendoff (2002) argues that in the course of evolution, the advent of functional words is a major marker for the critical transition from some proto-communicational system to modern language.

b. As CL: yi gan qiang
        a   CL   gun
        'a gun'

Equally obvious is the "bleached" semantic content of classifiers. In (53), for instance, the classifier use of *gan* no longer refers to any specific part of the gun, but rather to the class of objects with the general shape and texture of a thin shaft. Outside the theoretical framework of this book, the transition from N to CL is sometimes referred to as grammaticalization. Independently of terminology, however, the fact remains that a classifier does not serve as a lexical noun but rather as a "functional" one whose role in syntax is semantically less concrete.

In addition to CL, two other classes of words may also occur inside a nominal phrase:

(54)   na yi gan qiang
          that one CL gun
          Lit: 'that one gun'

The numeral (Num) *yi* 'one' typically occurs with a CL. There is also evidence that the demonstrative pronoun *na* 'that' belongs in the category of determiners (D) that is separate from N, despite the fact that the two are often placed in the same category in grammar books. Num and D will be examined in detail in Chapter 8. For now, we note that for the lexical category N, there are at least three more or less "noun-like" categories, CL, Num, and D, associated with it.

It is based on considerations of a similar kind that Grimshaw (1991, 2000) proposes to add to the existing feature set [N] and [V] another feature [Fn], where F stands for functional and n's value is equal to or larger than 0. [F0] indicates a lexical (i.e., non-functional) category; [F1] is the functional category structurally closest to [F0] in the given phrase; [F2] is farther from [F0] than [F1], etc. In this enriched theory of categorial features, the four nominal categories just discussed are described in (55):

(55)   N = [F0, +N, −V]
        CL = [F1, +N, −V]
     Num = [F2, +N, −V]
        D = [F3, +N, −V]

The precise structural relations among these categories will be discussed in detail in Chapter 8.

A similar situation exists for V. Aspectual morphemes such as *le*, *zhe*, and *guo* were historically verbs, with *guo* still capable of functioning as a standalone verb meaning 'to pass' in Modern Chinese. On the other hand, they are clearly not lexical verbs, both because they only express various kinds of aspectuality (i.e., the developmental status of an event) without changing the basic semantics of the verbs to which they affix, and because in this usage they cannot be used alone as the predicate of a clause. As a result, they seem best described as being verb-like but functional. Following the notational convention, this category is abbreviated as Asp and is defined, for now, as [F1, −N, +V], namely the closest functional word to V (= [F0, −N, +V]).

The English examples below illustrate another functional category which Grimshaw places under the verbal system:

(56)   a. Pat thinks **that** the moon is made of Wisconsin cheese.
        b. Pat asks **if** the moon is made of Wisconsin cheese.

The boldface words are complementizers (C) which have two functions: introducing an embedded clause in a bigger context and marking the type of the clause. In (56), both *that* and *if* introduce an embedded (object) clause, but the former indicates the clause to be declarative while the latter marks out the interrogative. This view, however, proves to be oversimplified when East Asian languages are taken into consideration. The Korean examples below are quoted from Y. Li (2005):

(57)   a. John-nun Mary-ka   kocen   umak-lul   cohaha-n-ta-ko   mit-nun-ta.
           John-TOP Mary-ACC classical music-ACC like-PRES-DECL-C believe-PRES-DECL
           'John believes that Mary loves classical music.'

        b. John-nun Mary-ka   tungsan-lul   cohaha-nya-ko mwul-ess-ta.
           John-TOP Mary-ACC mountain.climbing-ACC like-Q-C   ask-PAST-DEC
           'John asked if Mary liked mountain climbing.'

In each example, the verb of the embedded clause is suffixed with two morphemes, *ko* for introducing the embedded clause, and the other for "typing" it, with *ta* for the declarative (glossed as 'DEC') and *nya* for the interrogative (glossed as 'Q'). In addition, only the clause-typing morpheme *ta* occurs with the matrix verb. This makes perfect sense. After all, the matrix clause is itself the largest syntactic construction. As it is not embedded, there is no need for *ko*. In conclusion, to the extent that we accept Grimshaw's view that there are functional categories associated with V, analogous to the functional categories associated with N in (55), it is necessary to distinguish two more categories of morphemes, those that introduce embedded clauses, for which the name complementizer (C) is kept, and those that signal the types of clauses, which we call clause-typers (CT). In (57), C is immediately to the right of CT and thus is farther from V. So if CT = [Fi] for any value of i greater than 1 (Asp = [F1]), then C = [Fi+1]. As for English, *that* and *if* must be the result of merging both CT and C into a single morpheme, a phenomenon not surprising for European languages where two conceptually separate pieces of information, such as agreement and tense, are characteristically represented as a single morpheme.

Turning back to Chinese, consider the following examples:

(58)   a. ni-men zou   ba.
          you-PL leave SFP
          'You can leave (now).'

       b. ta qu-guo ma?
          he go-GUO Q
          'Was he there (before)?'

       c. shei xie   zhe yi   zhang   ne?
          who write this one chapter Q
          'Who will write this chapter?'

Each of the three morphemes, *ba*, *ma*, and *ne*, signals a particular clause type. *Ba* is for imperatives, *ma* for *yes-no* interrogatives, and *ne* for interrogatives containing question phrases such as *shei* 'who' and *shenmo shihou* 'what time.' Furthermore, these morphemes occur at a position peripheral to the clause, just like CT in Korean matrix clauses. We thus propose to treat clause-final morphemes such as *ma*, *ba*, and *ne* as CT. What remains unclear is why CT in Chinese never occurs with embedded clauses. Possibly, there are unidentified discourse functions that *ma*, *ba*, and *ne* perform that are associated only with matrix clauses (see Cinque (1999) for a list of functional categories in the typical clausal structure). For the purpose of this book, these morphemes can be roughly treated as CT composed of [Fn, $+$V, $-$N], where n is a number sufficiently large to distinguish itself from the values of those functional categories more closely associated with the lexical verb.

To summarize so far, N and V each have a set of related functional categories, which are distinguished through incremental values of [F]. This analysis also suggests a route for diachronic changes. In the literature, both the shift from V to Asp and from N to CL has sometimes been called grammaticalization or *xu-hua*, meaning that a lexical morpheme adopts a more abstract meaning and starts to perform grammatical functions. One way to grammaticalize, then, is to shift from [F0] to [Fi], $i > 0$, while all other categorial values remain intact.

1.2.2   *[F] and the modifier-introducing* de

That *de* belongs to a functional category for its lack of tangible semantic content is the conventional wisdom and will be adopted here as well. The question is where it stands in the [$\pm$N, $\pm$V] system. Descriptively, *de* occurs in the syntactic context of [X *de* Y]. If Y = N, X can be an NP, an AP, a PP, or a full clause, as shown in (59):

(59)   a. zhe-wei xuezhe de guandian
          this-CL scholar DE opinion
          'this scholar's opinion'

     b. shifen youren de tiaojian
          very enticing DE term
          'very enticing term'

     c. guanyu zhanzheng de chuanyan[16]
          about war   DE gossip
          'gossip about war'

     d. wo qu guowai de liyou
          I go abroad DE reason
          'the reason for my going abroad'

In contrast, X is largely restricted to AP when Y = V, with *de* being optional even then.

Pending a better understanding of this morpheme, two categorial characterizations seem plausible to explore. First, *de* may be [Fi, +N, +V], where $i > 0$. Under this interpretation, *de* is an adjectival functional word which turns a phrase inside a larger NP into a modifier. Functional morphemes that may alter the category of phrases are found in other languages as well. Consider the English example below:

(60)   Beth is proud of Christine's winning the prize twice.

On the one hand, *winning* functions as a verb because it can assign a Case to the object NP *the prize*. On the other hand, it also displays two nominal properties: providing the Genitive Case for the semantic subject *Christine* and needing *of* to be the legitimate object of the adjective *proud*. As we saw in 1.1.3.1, *of* is required in this context only when the object is nominal and thus needs to satisfy the Case Filter in (52). This mixture of verbal and nominal properties follows if *-ing* in (60) is [Fj, +N, −V] ($j > 0$), which nominalizes the whole VP rather than just the verb *win*. Since *win* remains V inside VP, its ability to assign Case to the object remains intact; the whole VP, however, is nominalized by *-ing* and therefore needs a Case for itself, just like any other nominal phrase. For the same reason, the semantic subject in the nominal phrase receives the Genitive Case.[17]

---

[16] Note that (59c), as well as the good examples in (7), determines that *de* cannot be a morphological marker of Case, for the simple reason that PPs (*guanyu zhanzheng* 'about war') don't need any Case (cf. (52)). The same logic applies to *no* in Japanese, which is sometimes treated as the Genitive Case marker but is actually suffixed to either an NP or a PP.

[17] Also see Huang (1994b) for a related treatment of the gerundive construction.

One may wonder why *de* is needed even for an AP in (59b). A possible answer relates this to another property of A. Unlike their English counterparts, Chinese adjectives play the role of a predicate directly, without any copula (cf. 1.1.3.2). In this use, AP behaves just like VP. It follows that an AP modifier may in fact be a relative clause, which in turn is "adjectivized" by *de*. The same analysis may even apply to PP modifiers, given the well-known fact that Chinese prepositions originated as verbs. Caution is called for, however, as there is no evidence that *guanyu* 'about' has any verbal property in Modern Chinese. Another area of concern is why *de* is not as widely used with modifiers for V.

De may also be analyzed as [F*x*, N, V], i.e., a word without any value for the categorical features [N] or [V] nor for the [F] feature. According to common assumption (cf. Di Sciullo and Williams 1987), the constituent composed of such an unspecified *de* and a pre-*de* phrase of category X (i.e., [XP *de*]) inherits X as its category; that is, X provides the values for [F], [V], and [N]. In effect, then, a noun allows modification by NP, AP, PP, and clauses, as is the case in many other languages, while *de* serves merely as a morphological linker. For practical purposes, this analysis treats *de* on a par with a subordinate conjunctive in the conventional sense, linking a modifier phrase to the modified (see Aoun and Li (2003) for a proposal in this direction). Again, complications arise which are yet to be resolved, one of which is why *de* is even needed in the first place. We suspect that the ultimate account of *de* in Modern Chinese depends partially on understanding its predecessors at various historical stages of the language.[18] Still, we have seen the potential for the [F, N, V] system to accommodate this morpheme, and equally importantly, *de* in either analysis is of a clearly language-specific nature and thus is disfavored in the case of categorial deviation (cf. 1.1.2.2).

---

[18] *De* results from two separate morphemes, *di* and *di*, distinguished through tones, in an earlier stage (Lü 1984: 130–31). Of the two *di*'s, one was used to introduce a "descriptive" phrase for N whereas the other, judging from the examples in Lü's work, was limited to introducing AP modifiers that are "qualitative" (p. 126). Lü's classification of NP-internal modifiers into descriptive and qualitative might correspond to the distinction between individual-level and stage-level predicates (Carlson 1977).

2

Argument structure

Each category affects the grammaticality of a sentence differently. For verbs, the most conspicuous property is transitivity, which we investigate in this chapter. Following the convention in theoretical syntax, the subject and object(s) of a verb are called its *arguments*, and the semantic relation between a verb and any of its arguments called a *thematic* relation. The first section introduces the basic properties of thematic relations and demonstrates how they can help explain certain linguistic phenomena. A few recent attempts to understand the nature of thematic relations are critically reviewed in Section 2.2. An alternative theory is proposed in Section 2.3.

2.1   Arguments and theta-roles

It is obvious to any linguistically minded observer that in a typical[1] active sentence built around a transitive action verb, such as *ta chang minge* 'she sing folk.song' or *ni xie shi* 'you write poem,' the subject argument is always the one initiating and performing the action while the object argument is always what is acted upon. This simple fact suggests the possibility that not every detail in the thematic relation between an argument and a verb matters in syntactic computation. For instance, *ta* 'she' and *ni* 'you' are subjects only because these NPs represent the "doers" of the actions; whether an action is done through singing or writing has no effect on qualifying an NP as the subject argument.

Based on this fact, thematic relations are classified into types. *Agent* is the relation where the argument is the doer/initiator, *Patient* labels the "do-ee" argument, *Theme* is for the argument that undergoes change, and a few others like *Beneficiary*, *Goal*, and *Source* all represent self-explanatory relations. The guiding principle

---

[1] By "typical," we hope to leave room for certain uses of transitive verbs where no Agent or Patient/Theme argument is required; cf. Sections 2.2 and 2.3.

here is that such relations are identified because of their relevance to syntax. A metaphor is typically adopted to talk about this aspect of language: Agent, Patient, etc. are called *thematic roles*[2] (theta-roles); a lexical word W, usually a verb, is said to have a certain number of theta-roles to *assign* to arguments; the set of theta-roles that W has for assignment is referred to, somewhat confusingly for historical reasons, as W's *argument structure*.

2.1.1   Basic properties of theta-roles

Recall that in a typical active sentence, Agent is always assigned to the subject and Patient to the object. One way to look at this correlation is that theta-roles are intrinsically ranked, with Agent being the highest in the hierarchy, Patient being lower, and so on. It is already well established that arguments are structurally ranked in the syntactic structure in the sense that the subject is more prominent than the object(s). The precise nature of this structural prominence will become clear later. For now, it will suffice to hypothesize a linking operation in the human language faculty that aligns the thematic hierarchy among theta-roles with the structural hierarchy among syntactic arguments.

Another property of theta-roles is shown with the examples in (1):

(1)   a. tamen gei-le   jingli   *(yi-fen baogao).
          they   give-LE manager   a-CL report
          'They gave the manager *(a report).'

      b. ta zou-le   (*women).
         he walk-LE   us
         'He walked (*us).'

Out of context, (1a) is unacceptable without the second object *yi-fen baogao* 'a report.'[3] It is intuitively clear why this is so: the verb *gei* 'give' has three theta-roles to assign, namely Agent, Goal, and Theme, but in the bad sentence, there are only two arguments to receive them – *tamen* 'they' as Agent and *jingli* 'manager' as Goal. There is no other argument available for assignment to the Theme role.

---

[2] See Gruber (1965) and Jackendoff (1972) for initial works on this concept.

[3] Unlike its English counterpart, a sentence like (1a) might be allowed if a report is mentioned earlier in the discourse. This doesn't pose a problem for our analysis because there is independent evidence that languages like Chinese but not English use a phonetically empty constituent as the "missing" object in the presence of a discourse topic. See Chapter 6 for relevant discussions. Also see Sections 2.2 and 2.3 for another property of Chinese verbs: that the thematic relations a verb holds with its arguments are not as restricted as in many other languages.

In other words, (1a), as well as its direct translation in English, justify the cross-linguistic generalization in (2a):

(2)   a. Every theta-role must be assigned to an argument.

Example (1b) proves the inverse of (2a) to be true as well. The postverbal NP *women* 'us' makes the sentence bad because semantically it cannot be integrated with the rest of the sentence. Again, the explanation is simple: with the meaning of 'walk,' *zou* has only one theta-role to assign, the Agent role, but there are two NPs in the sentence. Hence we arrive at the statement in (2b):

(2)   b. Every argument must receive a theta-role.

Together, (2a–b) constitute the *theta-criterion*.

2.1.2   *Chinese resultative compounds: a case study*

That theta-roles do more to language than classifying the semantic types of arguments is best illustrated by resultative compounds in Chinese. A couple of examples are given below, with the compounds marked out in bold face:[4]

(3)   a. tamen **za-sui**-le   yi-kuai boli.
           they   pound-broken-LE a-CL   glass
           'They smashed a piece of glass.'
       b. wo **zhui-lei**-le   ta   le.
           I   chase-tired-LE him   SFP
            i. 'I chased him, which made him tired.'
           ii. 'I chased him, which made me tired.'

The two verbal morphemes[5] in each compound are in a causal relation, with the one on the left (hereafter referred to as V1) indicating a causing event and the one on the right (V2) indicating the resulting event. The most common form of the compound is found in (3a), in which V1 is a transitive verb, V2 is an intransitive, and the object NP *yi-kuai boli* 'a piece of glass' is understood as having been pounded on and consequently broken. The semantics of this interpretation can be easily captured if certain theta-roles from V1 and V2 merge into a composite theta-role as the verbal morphemes merge into the compound. Example (4) below illustrates this thematic composition, called *theta-identification* in Higginbotham

---

[4] Much of this section is based on Y. Li (1990).
[5] For the purpose of this discussion, we will not distinguish A from V, given the fact that both categories can directly function as the predicate in a clause (cf. Chapter 1, Section 1.1.3) and a resultative compound essentially puts two [F0, +V] words into a bigger [F0, +V] word.

(1985), by giving the argument structures of V1, V2, and the compound:

(4) *za* 'pound': $\langle$Agent $\langle$Patient$\rangle\rangle^6$
     sui 'broken': $\langle$Theme$\rangle$
     za-sui 'pound-broken': $\langle$Agent $\langle$Patient-Theme$\rangle\rangle$

The theta-identification of the Patient role from V1 and the Theme role from V2 is indicated with a hyphen. Once theta-identified, the two theta-roles are assigned together to the object NP, yielding the reading in (3a).

From the point of view of linguistic computation, theta-identification is a random process. Under certain conditions, one of which may be pragmatics, a resultative compound can be ambiguous, as shown in (3b). In terms of thematic composition, therefore, the single theta-role of V2 may be optionally identified with either the Agent role or the Patient role of V1:

(5) *zhui* 'chase': $\langle$Agent $\langle$Patient$\rangle\rangle$
     lei 'tired': $\langle$Experiencer$\rangle$
     zhui-lei 'chase-tired': $\langle$Agent $\langle$Patient-Experiencer$\rangle\rangle$ or
                                 $\langle$Agent-Experiencer $\langle$Patient$\rangle\rangle$

It is this option that allows either the subject or the object of the compound in (3b) to be understood as the one becoming tired from chasing. In fact, even theta-identification itself is optional in the context of resultative compounding. Consider the examples in (6), with the corresponding argument structures in (7). Given the general nature of this analysis, we use $\theta 1$, $\theta 2$, etc. to represent theta-roles in our discussion in place of specific labels:

(6) a. ta   xiao-feng-le.
        he laugh-insane-LE
        'He laughed to the extent that he became insane.'

     b. ni   ku-zou-le   henduo keren.
        you cry-leave-LE   many   guest
        'Your crying made many guests leave.'

(7) V1: $\langle\theta 1\rangle$
     V2: $\langle\theta 2\rangle$
     V1-V2: $\langle\theta 1\text{-}\theta 2\rangle$ (for (6a))   or
             $\langle\theta 1 \langle\theta 2\rangle\rangle$ (for (6b))

We leave it to the reader to verify that the argument structures of the V1-V2 compound in (7) indeed corresponds to the semantics of the examples in (6).

---

[6] Pairs of angled brackets are used to reflect the thematic hierarchy. The fewer pairs a theta-role is surrounded with, the higher it is ranked in the argument structure. This notation is from Y. Li (1995). Grimshaw (1990) uses parentheses for the same purpose.

At this point, one naturally wonders whether the creation of the composite argument structure for the compound out of those of V1 and V2 is subject to any restrictions. It is. First, though theta-identification is an optional process in itself, its actual application is partially driven by the Case Filter (as introduced in Chapter 1). Consider (5) again. When the two verbal morphemes collectively have three theta-roles, each of them expected to be assigned under the theta-criterion in (2a–b), three NP arguments would be needed. However, the Case Filter requires that every NP receive a Case. In the context of a typical clause which contains a verb, in this case the compound, and no other Case-assigners, there are maximally two Cases, one for the subject and one for the object. This limit on the number of available Cases effectively forces two of the three theta-roles to be merged into one so as to be assigned to a single NP. Provided that this merging can satisfy the Case Filter, it is up to the speaker to decide how exactly to implement theta-identification. This is the source of the ambiguity in (3b)/(5).

Support for this analysis comes from the correct prediction it makes: that no theta-identification is needed precisely when the total number of Cases available matches that of the theta-roles from V1 and V2. The example in (6b) already illustrates one possible scenario where this may happen: when V1 and V2 together have two theta-roles, the compound may assign them separately to the subject and object, each receiving a Case in a typical clause. Note that theta-identification may still take place so that the compound has one composite theta-role, as shown in (6a). In terms of theta-role and Case assignment, the compound with such an argument structure is no different from a monomorphemic intransitive verb. Chinese also has ways to provide extra Cases in a clause, one of which is the use of the morpheme *ba*. Certain semantic and syntactic details of *ba* will be investigated in Chapter 5. It suffices for now to simply recognize the fact that *ba* can license a third NP in a clause:

(8)   ta **ba** naxie tudou qu-le   pi.
        he BA those   potato remove-LE skin
        'He peeled those potatoes.'

As is typical of transitive verbs, *qu* 'remove' provides Cases only to the subject *ta* 'he' and the postverbal object *pi* 'skin.' So *ba* must be the provider for the Case needed by *naxie tudou* 'those potatoes.' With this in mind, consider the following example:

(9)   a. (?)ta ba wo chang-wang-le yi-tian-de fannao.
          he BA me sing-forget-LE a-day-DE   worry
          'His singing made me forget the whole day's worry.'

      b. chang 'sing': ⟨Agent⟩
         wang 'forget' ⟨Experiencer ⟨Patient⟩⟩
         chang-wang 'sing-forget': ⟨Agent ⟨Experiencer ⟨Patient⟩⟩⟩

The three theta-roles from V1 and V2 are assigned individually to three NP arguments in (9), one of which receives a Case from *ba*. No theta-identification is necessary.

The second restriction on composite argument structure formation can be appreciated, again, by considering (6b), where the two theta-roles are not identified. Taking for granted that the event in question is one party's crying leading to the other party's leaving, why can't (6b) mean that many guests' crying made you leave? To obtain this reading, the same compound *ku-zou* 'cry-leave' would need the impossible argument structure in (10):

(10)   cry: $\langle \theta 1 \rangle$
         leave: $\langle \theta 2 \rangle$
         cry-leave: *$\langle \theta 2 \langle \theta 1 \rangle \rangle$

In Y. Li (1990) and (1993a), it is suggested that, of the two verbal components in the compound, V1 serves as the morphological *head*.[7] It is a well-established fact that certain key properties of the head H are always maintained in the word containing H (cf. Lieber 1983, Di Sciullo and Williams 1987). For instance, in *xiao-hai* 'little-child,' *xiao* is A in category and *hai* is N; the whole compound is N, inheriting the category from *hai*, the head of the word. Extending the list of inheritable properties to thematic information, it is proposed in Y. Li (1990) that the prominences of the theta-roles of the head, i.e., V1, must not be altered in the resultative compound. Since $\theta 1$ is, trivially, the most prominent theta-role in the argument structure of V1, it must stay as the most prominent in the composite argument structure of the compound. This explains why (10) is ungrammatical, where $\theta 1$ is placed lower than $\theta 2$ from V2, the non-head. Meanwhile, since no similar restriction applies to V2, $\theta 2$ may be either treated as a less prominent theta-role in the argument structure of the compound, or it may be merged with $\theta 1$, as seen in (6).

2.1.3   *Compounds vs. phrases*

We start with a brief introduction of the basic theory for phrase structure. There is no doubt that language employs some combinatorial algorithm so as to construct a potentially infinite number of phrases and clauses from words. A major task of syntax is to figure out what this algorithm is. The most widely adopted

---

[7] The most direct support for this claim lies in comparing resultative compounds in Chinese and in Japanese, the latter being a well-known head-final language. Y. Li (1993a) shows that the different locations of the head lead to differences in the two languages both in the semantic behavior of the compound and the transitivity options of its components. The reader is referred to the original work for details.

hypothesis at the moment is the X′-theory (read as X-bar), initially proposed in Chomsky (1970) and revised into the current form via the works of many subsequent researchers:

(11)

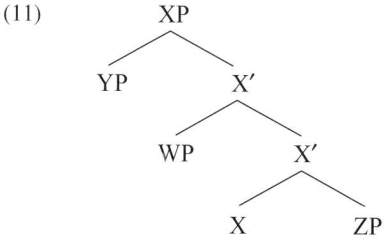

X is a word/morpheme and serves as the head of its own phrase, XP. ZP is the *complement* of X. When X is a lexical item such as a verb (cf. Chapter 1, Section 1.2), ZP would be called the object of X in traditional terminology. The head and its complement combine, as indicated by the linking branches, to form a "sub-phrase" inside XP, labeled as X′. WP is the *adjunct*, performing the typical function of a modifier. Merging WP with X′ yields another X′. X′-theory itself imposes no intrinsic limit to the number of adjuncts inside any given phrase, i.e., XP may contain any number of X′ nodes. YP is the *specifier* (*Spec*) which corresponds to, among other things, the subject if X is a verb and the possessor if X is a noun.

In (11), X, Y, W, and Z are variables ranging over all lexical and functional categories. In other words, this theory claims that the way a phrase is constructed is cross-categorial. Example (11) is also held to be cross-linguistic with respect to the hierarchical relations among the constituents in it. The most important hierarchical relation for syntax is *c-command*, defined as follows:

(12)   Let A, B, and C be any symbols in a tree, then
        A c-commands B iff
        a. neither A nor B contains the other, and
        b. every C containing A contains B.

For instance, the specifier YP in (11) c-commands the complement, ZP, because neither of them is a component of the other (i.e., (12a)) and YP is part of XP which also contains ZP (= (12b)). The same logic prevents ZP from c-commanding YP, as the reader can verify. While this asymmetric c-command relation between the specifier and the complement of the same phrase is taken to hold for all phrases in all languages, linear relations among constituents vary from language to language and sometimes perhaps from category to category. If the head precedes the complement, as in Chinese VP, the phrase structure is *head-initial*; if the head follows the complement, found in Japanese and Korean, then the phrase is *head-final*.

Now consider the examples below:

(13) a. ta   sheng-chi-guo henduo shucai.
          he   raw-eat-GUO   many   vegetable
          'He has eaten many (kinds of) vegetables raw.'

      b. ?/*ta sheng-zhe chi-guo henduo shucai.
          he   raw-ZHE   eat-GUO many   vegetable
          Intended reading: same as above.

      c. henduo shucai,   ta sheng-zhe chi-guo.
          many   vegetable he raw-ZHE   eat-GUO
          Same as (13a).

Upon first hearing it, native speakers' judgments of (13b) vary somewhat, from marginal to downright bad, but everyone we consulted agrees that it sounds worse than the other two sentences. That (13a) is good is no surprise. The two morphemes, *sheng* 'raw' and *chi* 'eat,' have the argument structures $\langle\theta1\rangle$ and $\langle\theta a \langle\theta b\rangle\rangle$, respectively. (The numbers and letters after θ are used to help distinguish the theta-roles from the two verbs.) In (13a), they form a compound with the argument structure $\langle\theta a \langle\theta b\text{-}\theta 1\rangle\rangle$. These theta-roles are assigned to the subject and object of the compound in syntax, yielding the reading that the object of the verb *chi* also refers to the material which is raw. As we would expect from the previous section, this is legitimate given that *chi* is the head of the compound.

In contrast with (13a), *sheng* and *chi* in (13b–c) are in separate phrases, as indicated by the presence of the aspectual suffix *zhe*. Omitting many irrelevant details (via triangles, as is the convention), the VP structure of (13b) is given in (14):

(14)

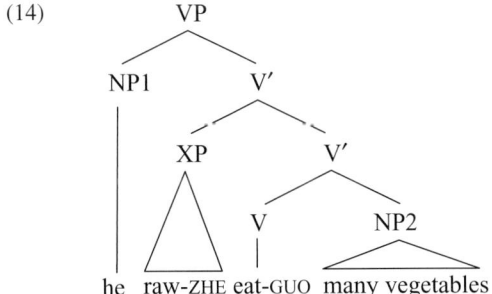

Whatever is the category of the phrase containing *sheng* 'raw' and the aspect marker *zhe*, the single theta-role of *sheng* needs to be assigned under the theta-criterion. Anticipating more substantial justification in later chapters, we assume that this theta-role is assigned to a phonetically empty pronoun, call it Pro, in the Spec of XP in (14). Cross-linguistically, a basic property of Pro is that its antecedent, if there is one, must c-command it (Chomsky 1981, Y. Li 1985, Huang 1989). In (14), NP2 doesn't c-command the Pro inside XP, so it is not a good antecedent, and the poor acceptability of (13b) is explained.

This analysis receives support from its predictive power. First, it predicts that putting NP2 at the beginning of the sentence improves its acceptability. As (14) suggests, constituents occurring earlier in the utterance generally c-command those occurring later (cf. Kayne 1994). It follows that if the object *henduo shucai* 'many vegetables' is placed at the beginning of the sentence, it will c-command every other constituent, including the Pro inside XP. As a result, it becomes a legitimate antecedent for Pro. This is corroborated by (13c). Second, we also expect a good sentence if Pro can take the subject as antecedent, for the simple reason that the subject NP c-commands Pro, among other things. The examples below confirm this prediction:

(15)   a. ta ku-su-le   qinluezhe-de baoxing.
           he cry-tell-LE invader-DE   atrocity
           'He complained about the invaders' atrocities tearfully.'

       b. ta ku-zhe   sushuo-le qinluezhe-de baoxing.
           he cry-ZHE   tell-LE   invader-DE   atrocity
           Same as (15a).

Example (15a) contains the compound *ku-su* 'cry-tell.' If *ku*'s argument structure is $\langle\theta 1\rangle$ and *su*'s is $\langle\theta a \langle\theta b\rangle\rangle$, the compound has the structure $\langle\theta 1\text{-}\theta a \langle\theta b\rangle\rangle$. In (15b), *ku* heads a separate phrase and is suffixed with the aspectual marker *zhe*. The VP structure of this example is identical to the one in (14). But the subject of the whole sentence, *ta* 'he,' is a semantically felicitous antecedent for the Pro inside XP. Since the subject also c-commands Pro, (15b) is 100 percent acceptable.

2.2   On the nature of theta-roles

Given the fact that theta-roles and thematic operations participate significantly in linguistic computation, as illustrated in the previous section, it is inevitable to wonder why theta-roles have the particular properties that they do. In this section, we review three works, Hale and Keyser (1993), T.-H. Lin (2001), and Borer (2005), which attempt to answer this question.

2.2.1   Theta-roles produced by the syntax

Hale and Keyser (1993) (hereafter referred to as H&K) are the first authors to attempt an explicit theory on the origin of theta-roles. Specifically, they hope to explain why there are so few theta-roles and why language links theta-roles to syntactic arguments in this particular manner (cf. 2.1.1).[8] In their view, both of these properties of theta-roles result from a particular form of syntax in the lexicon.

2.2.1.1 Hale and Keyser's theory

The key assumption in H&K is given in (16):

(16)   At the lexical level, a verb can be represented as a *lexical relational structure* (LRS) which is constructed only with the four lexical categories, V, N, A, P, associated with four elementary notional types: event, entity, state, and interrelation, respectively.

Given the X′-template in (11) minus the irrelevant adjunct, (16) produces four possible LRSs for verbs, in which the relation between V and its complement phrase translates to semantic "implication." The LRSs based on A and P are given below:

(17)   a.   b.

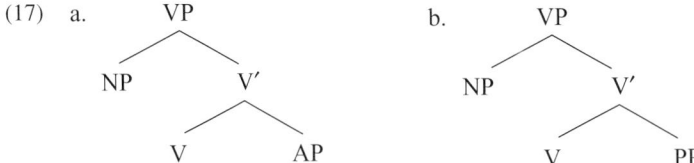

Example (17a) is the LRS for intransitive verbs like *clear* as in *The sky cleared*, with the adjectival root √*clear* heading the AP. (We use √ to mark a root, borrowing from Pesetsky's (1995) notation.) Semantically, it represents an event implicating a state. For H&K, this is interpreted as a "change resulting in a state" (p. 73). The subject of AP (= NP in the tree) is therefore understood as the Theme of the whole verb because it refers to an entity undergoing a change of state. In other words, the Theme role is nothing more than the semantic interpretation of the NP being in the Spec of VP in this particular LRS. The semantics associated with (17b) is

---

[8] Actually, H&K's second question is about the Uniformity of Theta Assignment Hypothesis (UTAH), as defined by Baker (1988):

(i)   Identical thematic relations are represented by identical syntactic relations.

The UTAH is a stronger condition on theta-role assignment than simply aligning the thematic hierarchy with the syntactic hierarchy of arguments, as we introduced in 2.1 above. Since the content of this book doesn't hinge on the UTAH, we will not bring it into the text. See Y. Li (2005) for a critical evaluation of its status in the human language faculty.

Also worth noting is that the theory in H&K differs in many ways from Hale and Keyser (2002). However, the essence of H&K remains intact in their later work, and the essence of our discussion in this section applies accordingly.

an event implicating an interrelation, or in plainer words, the situation in which an entity, referred to by the NP, "comes to be involved in an interrelation" (p. 71) expressed through the PP. This LRS again expresses the meaning of change, so the NP also carries the Theme reading.

A verb also may be formed out of a nominal or verbal category. Rather than directly substituting NP and VP for AP and PP in (17), however, H&K propose two extra conditions for LRS:

(18)   a.   The Spec position of VP in the LRS representation of a lexical verb is filled only when forced by predication (p. 76).

    b.   NP and VP are not predicates in the LRS (pp. 76, 80).

The direct consequence of (18) is the following LRSs:

(19)   a.   b.

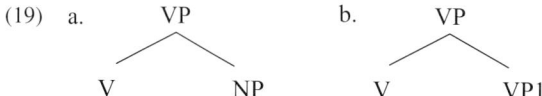

Given (18b), neither the NP in (19a) nor the VP1 in (19b) is a predicate; namely, neither supports an external subject. In the absence of an external subject, then, no constituent will fill the Spec position of the (upper) VP according to (18a). The LRSs in (19) illustrate the "Specless" LRSs. In contrast, since AP and PP are predicates, each has a subject. This forces the Spec position of the VP to be filled, as shown in (17) above.

The LRS in (19a) is for denominal verbs such as *sneeze* in *The colt sneezed*. This LRS explicitly codes the verb's relation with the corresponding noun in *the colt had a sneeze*, translated as an event implicating an entity (e.g., a sneeze). H&K paraphrase (19a) as "the implicating event is completed, or perfected, by virtue of the 'creation,' 'production,' or 'realization' of the relevant entity" (p. 74). Example (19b) describes an event implicating another event, the typical causal relation. This LRS also provides the basis for *recursion*. With VP being a possible complement of V, any basic LRS in (17) and (19) may occur as a complement, giving rise to new and more complex LRSs and hence more verb types. For instance, the LRS for the verb *put* is analyzed as substituting (17b) for VP1 in (19b), roughly paraphrased as someone "causing X to be in an interrelation with whatever is the object of P." For reasons to become clear shortly, H&K also adopts (20) (cf. pp. 78, 82), which is based on Marantz' (1984) study of syntactic idioms (also see Kratzer 1996):

(20)   The subject of the verb types in (19) are external to the LRSs and occur only in a clausal context. The relation between this subject and the VP is interpreted as Agent.

In summary, H&K propose that the two most fundamental theta-roles, Agent and Theme, are nothing more than relations between an NP and the rest of a given LRS, which is composed of some generic type of V and other lexical categories. In the literature, the generic verb type is often called a *light verb*[9] and attributed with more graspable semantic content in the given context. In this tradition, a light verb is conventionally, though not necessarily accurately, expressed with a capital lettered verb – CAUSE for (19b), DO or HAVE for (19a), and BE or BECOME for (17a–b). This tradition is adopted in this section merely to facilitate discussion.

In support of this syntactic representation of a verb's LRS, H&K offer arguments most of which are based on denominal verbs in English. Due to limited space, only two of their arguments are presented below for illustration. One of these concerns English denominal verbs, which show the following pattern:

(21)   a.   A cow calved.
        b.   *It cowed a calf.

Assuming both of them to correspond to *a cow had a calf*, the generalization is then that a denominal verb can be formed only when the nominal root is understood as the object of the light verb HAVE, but not as the subject. This follows directly from (19a), repeated below with details:

(22)

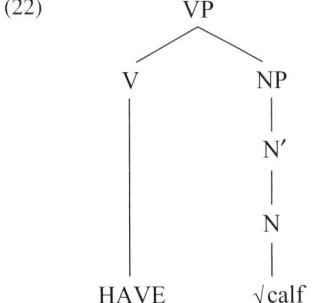

By hypothesis, the nominal root, say √*calf*, must be merged with the light verb in order to appear as a verb. In the current theory, this merger of two lexical categories is done through movement, as was systematically used first by generative semanticists in the late 1960s and early 1970s and later popularized by Baker (1988).

---

[9] The term "light verb" was originally used to refer to verbs like *take* and *give* in expressions such as *take a walk* and *give him a kick*, which are lexical verbs that are semantically "light" because the action is actually described by the nominal object. In current syntactic literature, a light verb is typically a structural or semantic component of a lexical verb and hence often has no independent phonetic form of its own. This is the sense used in the text.

Critically, √*calf* as the head of the object NP can move to HAVE because movement is known to obey the *Proper Binding Condition* (cf. Fiengo 1977, Lasnik and Saito 1993):

(23)   Movement must target a c-commanding position.

In (22), V c-commands N, so the nominal root may move to the light verb as desired. On the other hand, the subject of the whole VP (= √*cow* in (21b)) is not even part of the LRS in (22) because of (20). It follows that the head of the subject NP cannot be c-commanded by V at all. This is sufficient to block the merging of √*cow* with HAVE, and the contrast in (21) is thus explained.

The conditions in (18) and (20) are also used by H&K to account for the impossible examples in (24):

(24)   a. *The clown laughed the child.
                (cf. The clown made the child laugh.)
        b. *The alfalfa sneezed the colt.
                (cf. The alfalfa made the colt sneeze.)

As intransitive denominal verbs such as *sneeze* have the LRS in (19a), substituting this LRS for the VP complement in (19b) would generate (25), with √*sneeze* moving to V2 and V1 to produce the hypothetical causative variant of *sneeze* in (24b):

(25)

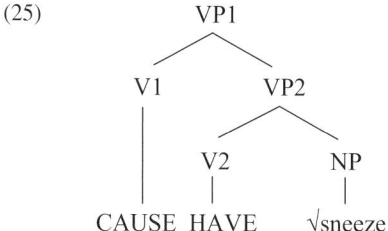

This LRS determines, however, that *the alfalfa* in (24b) is the Agent subject of CAUSE and *the colt* is the Agent subject of HAVE, and that both are necessarily outside the LRS and represented only via a clause. This variant of *sneeze* would be a "double-subject" verb. If each clause can only license one subject, there is no legitimate way in syntax to license both *the alfalfa* and *colt*, and the impossibility of (24) is expected.

Denominal locatum verbs such as *saddle* and *blindfold* provide another argument for H&K when compared with impossible verbs like *church* in the pair below:

(26)   a. She saddled the horse.
        b. *She churched her money.

Taking the verbs in these examples to have the same LRS in (27) below,[10] the question is why the noun root $\sqrt{}$*saddle* can become a verb whereas $\sqrt{}$*church* can't.

(27)

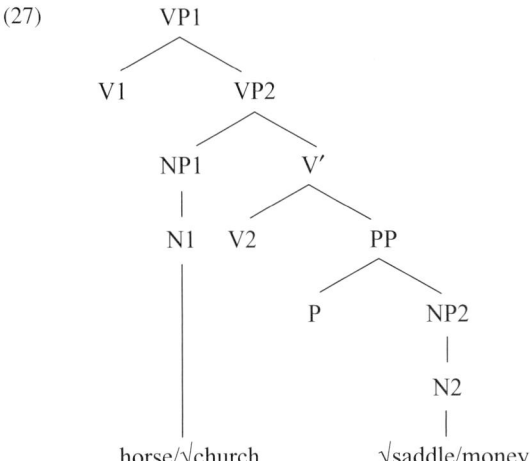

The answer lies with another UG principle that has the following effect:

(28)   No constituent can move out of a non-complement phrase.

That is, non-complements (adjuncts and subjects) are "islands" (in the sense of Ross 1967) that block extractions, but complements are not.[11] This straightfor-wardly prohibits N1 from merging with V1 (or V2), explaining the impossibility of (26b). On the other hand, N2 can move to P, V2, and finally V1, at each step moving out of a complement phrase and to the closest c-commanding position, in satisfaction of (28) and the Proper Binding Condition in (23). This explains the grammaticality of (26a).

---

[10] H&K paraphrased *church her money* in two different ways: *give a church her money* and *provide a church with her money*, but paraphrased *saddle the horse* only as *provide the horse with a saddle*. Meanwhile, the LRS they provide for both verbs seem to follow the *provide . . . with* pattern. This illustrates an intrinsic weakness in semantic decomposition: how do we know for sure that a verb's LRS takes one form but not another? We leave this question open.

[11] This falls under Huang's (1982b) Condition on Extraction Domain (CED). H&K actually used a version of the Empty Category Principle (ECP) in Chomsky (1981, 1986b) to account for the data. Also see Y. Li (1997c) for a Minimalist derivation of part of the ECP. Some principles mentioned in this book, as well as in the general literature, overlap in the range of data they deal with. For thoughts on the redundancy of the UG theory, see Y. Li (1997d).

2.2.1.2 The critique

H&K's theory of theta-roles and syntactic LRSs for lexical verbs (which they call l-syntax in order to distinguish it from the conventional sense of syntax, referred to as s-syntax) is influential among scholars working on the interactions between the lexicon and the syntax. In this subsection, we evaluate some technical claims in their theory, hoping to arrive at a better understanding of the issues involved.

To begin with, we note that the essence of H&K's proposal, that the general types of semantic roles of a lexical verb (i.e., theta-roles) are associated with the small number of lexical categories available in the lexical-relational decomposition of the verb, is independent of their particular utilization of the l-syntactic LRS. Suppose that a lexical verb may indeed be decomposed into various "atoms" (root and light verb(s)) but the relation between these atoms are not syntactic, with "syntactic" meaning conforming to the X'-structure and subject to various constraints at the sentential level (cf. (23) and (27)). Dubbed as *lexicalist*, this alternative view on word-formation was first explicitly articulated in Chomsky (1970) to counter the attempt at the time to unify both word-formation and sentence-formation with syntactic tools. In a typical lexicalist theory, the components of a word are directly concatenated and interpreted accordingly, without the help of a syntax-like structure. For a representative of this approach, see Di Sciullo and Williams (1987). In such a theory, one may still treat a theta-role as the semantic relation resulting from combining a light verb with the lexical root of a particular category, simply minus the syntactic structures shown in the previous subsection. With this in mind, one way to evaluate H&K's l-syntactic theory is to see how it compares with a lexicalist alternative in accounting for various theta-role-related facts.

Suppose that we agree with H&K and adopt (20). Then the data in (21), which provides one of the arguments for H&K's l-syntax, have an alternative explanation. In particular, H&K's decomposition of the denominal verbs *calve* and **cow* in (22) can be directly translated into the two lexicalist representations in (29), which we call lexico-semantic structures (LSS) (with linear order between components for facilitating discussions only):

(29)   a. [HAVE-$\sqrt{}$calf] → calve   (cf. (21a))
          b. [$\sqrt{}$cow-HAVE] → *cow   (cf. (21b))

That (29a) is allowed is straightforward: the light verb HAVE requires an object in its basic semantics, and the noun $\sqrt{}$*calf* fills the spot. The result is the intransitive verb *calve* meaning 'to have a calf.' Example (29b), on the other hand, is in violation of the principle of Full Interpretation (FI; cf. Chomsky 1995: 151), which is also adopted by H&K:

(30)   An element can appear in a representation only if it is properly interpreted.

According to (20), HAVE is incapable of supporting a subject until a VP is constructed from it in syntax. Because there is no VP (or any phrase) at the word-formation level under the lexicalist theory, $\sqrt{cow}$ in (29b) cannot bear the intended semantic relation with the light verb HAVE and thus has no interpretation. It follows from (30) that *cow* cannot be used as a verb this way. Note that both the lexicalist theory and H&K's allow *cow* to mean 'to have a cow.' Whether this reading is indeed available depends on factors outside the current concern. In sum, with assumptions such as (20), the contrast in (21) can be explained with the Proper Binding Condition in (23) through H&K's l-syntactic LRS, but can also be naturally accounted for in a lexicalist theory which critically employs no syntactic LRS. In other words, this argument for their theory is weak in the sense that the data *can* be handled by the theory, not that the data *must* be handled by it.

Next consider H&K's argument based on (26). Given their LRS of locatum verbs such as *saddle*, the generalization from (26) is that the head of the nominal complement may merge with a light verb to form a denominal verb, whereas the head of an NP in the Spec position may not undergo this process even when the NP is understood as an object of the whole denominal verb. For H&K, this fact follows directly from a general UG principle (i.e., our (28)). However, this theory also wrongly rules out well-formed compounds such as *horse-saddling* and *book-shelving*. The LRS of these verbs is given below, adapted from (27):

(31)

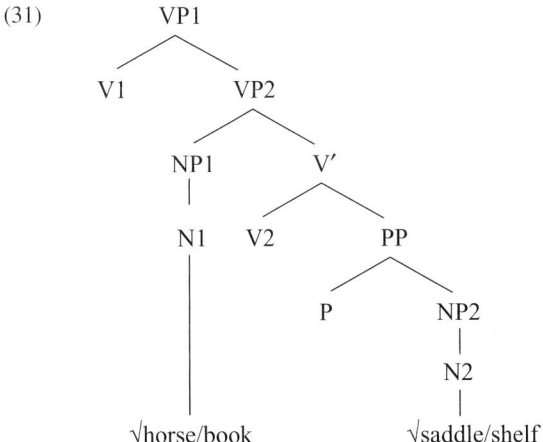

N2 moves up via P, V2, and V1 to form the verbs *saddle* and *shelve*, but N1 is prohibited from merging with any of these heads because of the CED violation it would incur, for the same reason that **church the money* is not possible (cf. (26b)). But this predicts *horse-saddling* to be bad, contrary to fact. It is also worth noting that this conclusion stays unchanged whether such compounds are formed in l-syntax or s-syntax, because for H&K, the l-syntactic LRS of a lexical verb is "inserted into an s-syntactic structure as a phrasal category, and its insertion will be grammatical if the point of insertion sanctions a verb phrase" (p. 95). Minimally, this means that both l-syntax and s-syntax refer to the same structure, (31) in our case.

In comparison, a lexicalist theory of word-formation, without utilizing X′-structures and syntactic principles such as the CED, can handle the relevant data without a hitch. Let the LSS of *saddle* be something like [CAUSE [BE [P √saddle]]]. Since there is no known reason against associating such a structure with the argument via the Theme relation, *horse-saddling* is permitted in a trivial manner. We return with a more specific account in a later section. Overall, the data H&K use to argue for an l-syntactic theory of word-internal structure and theta-roles all have a straightforward lexicalist explanation, whereas certain compounds prove to be problems for them but not for a lexicalist theory. See Y. Li (in progress) for details in this regard.

2.2.2   What's in a verb?

T.-H. Lin (2001) observes that the thematic relations between a Chinese verb and its arguments are more miscellaneous than those found in English. First consider the thematic interpretations of the subject:[12]

(32)   ta kai-guo   zhe-sou[13] motuoting.
      he drive-GUO this-CL   motorboat
      'He drove this motorboat before.'

(33)   a. zhe-sou motuoting yijing   kai-le   xuduo nian le.
         this-CL motorboat already drive-LE many year LE
         'This motorboat has already been driven for many years.'

      b. zhe-tiao he   bu neng kai   motuoting.
         this-CL   river not can   drive motorboat
         'A motorboat can't be driven on this river.'

In (32), *kai* 'drive' is used as a transitive verb, as in any other language. Unlike English, however, the subject of the verb is not limited to being an Agent. Example (33a) shows a Theme subject and (33b) a Location, and in both examples, the verb form remains intact, in contrast to the required passive form in English when the Agent subject is absent (cf. the English glosses). To this observation, we also add the following fact:

---

[12] All the examples in this section are ours, but where it matters, they confirm Lin's original observation on the freer theta-relations between the verb and the subject/object in Chinese.

[13] According to the *Ci Hai* dictionary, this classifier may also be read as *sao*.

(34) a. zhe-sou motuoting yijing   bei xiaoxinyiyi de kai-le   xuduo nian le.
          this-CL motorboat already BEI cautious   DE drive-LE many year SFP
          'This motorboat has already been cautiously driven for many years.'

      b. ??zhe-sou motuoting yijing   xiaoxinyiyi de kai-le   xuduo nian le.
          this-CL motorboat already cautious   DE drive-LE many year SFP
          Intended reading: same as (34a).

The adverb *xiaoxinyiyi de* implies an Agent. Example (34a) is perfectly acceptable, where this adverb is coupled with *bei*, a "passive" morpheme to be carefully examined in Chapter 4. This is compatible with the general understanding that passives have an implied Agent.[14] In contrast, though native speakers' judgment varies somewhat, (34b) without *bei* is generally perceived to be less acceptable. The contrast can be explained if *kai* 'drive' in (33a) and (34b) are truly Agentless for the purpose of syntax. The reason that (34b) is not totally ruled out can be attributed to a separate fact mentioned earlier: that Chinese allows a phonetically empty Pro subject. Those who find (34b) marginally acceptable perhaps try to treat an otherwise ungrammatical sentence as if it had an Agent subject in the form of Pro.

Chinese also differs from English in allowing non-Theme objects more freely:

(35) a. ta kai-guo   weixian   shuiyu.
          he drive-GUO dangerous waters
          'He drove in dangerous waters.'

      b. ta xihuan kai   shangwu.
          he like   drive morning
          'He likes to drive in the mornings.'

      c. ta neng kai   yibiao.
          he can   drive instrument
          'He can drive only by instruments.'

As reflected through the English translations, the object in (35a) is actually a Location, the one in (35b) a Time, and the one in (35c) an Instrument. Before turning to Lin's specific proposal, it should be pointed out that the situation is not as clear-cut as it appears. Even though Chinese allows *he da bei* 'drink big cup,' presumably another case of an Instrument serving as an object, it is nonetheless very odd to say *he ci shao* 'drink porcelain spoon' with the same Instrumental reading, at least when out of context. Also, there are actually various expressions in English where a verb typically taking a Theme object can take an Instrument instead. *Drive the stick* is an idiomatic expression for driving a car with a manual transmission, which sports a gear shift control in the vague shape of a stick. Less idiomatically, one can either *slash someone with a sword* or *slash a sword at*

---

[14] For proposals that implement this idea syntactically, see Baker, Johnson, and Roberts (1989), Feng (1995), Ting (1995, 1998), and Chapter 4.

someone. Still, we agree with Lin that Chinese is far less restrictive in this respect than English. The examples below make the point:

(36)   a. xie maobi
           'write calligraphy.brush = write with a calligraphy brush'
       b. za da chui
           'pound big mallet = pound with a big mallet'
       c. chang yangsangzi
           'sing Western.style.of.singing = sing in Western style'
       d. ci hongyingqiang
           'stab red.tasseled.spear = stab with a red tasseled spear'
       e. ... ...

In sum, Chinese verbs are demonstrably less rigid than their English counterparts in terms of thematic relations, a fact deserving an explanation.

Along the lines of H&K's l-syntactic decomposition of lexical verbs, T.-H. Lin (2001) proposes a theory for the data in question that consists of two assumptions:

(37)   a. A verb contains both the lexical root and the light verb(s) in English but only the lexical root and no light verb in Chinese (p. 109).[15]
       b. The combination of lexical roots and light verbs can be "quite liberal" in s-syntax (p. 106).

The l-syntactic LRS of *drive* in English is given below (Lin deviates from H&K in various technical details, one of which is to ignore (20) by placing every argument, including the subject, in the Spec of a VP headed by a light verb):

(38)

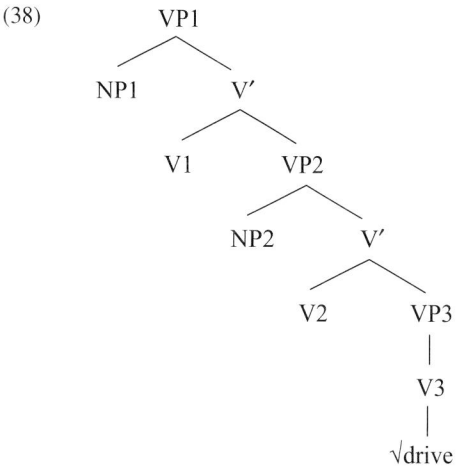

---

[15] This is only part of Lin's theory, which is actually based on a three-way contrast among Chinese, Japanese, and English. We focus on the Chinese–English contrast here due to the nature of this book. Also see Y. Li (in progress) for a critical review of Lin's three-way contrast.

Moving $\sqrt{drive}$ to the light verbs V2 and V1 derives the transitive verb *drive*, with NP1 the Agent subject and NP2 the Theme object. Crucially, the lexical entry of *drive* contains no more and no less than (38), and the thematic relations encoded in the structure are not subject to change. *Kai* 'drive' in Chinese differs from English *drive* in having only VP3 as the lexical entry (cf. (37a)). It may merge with the same light verbs as *drive* does, but only in s-syntax. The result would be non-distinguishable from *drive*, as shown in (32). But given (37b), other light verbs are also available in s-syntax that may be "quite liberally" merged with $\sqrt{kai}$. Depending on the selection of these light verbs, some licensing an Instrument relation and some a Location, all the examples in (33) and (35) are generated. Lin's theory interprets theta-roles in the same way as H&K's, i.e., that a theta-role is simply the relation between a light verb V and the argument in the Spec of the VP headed by V. However, given the difference between Chinese and English, as stated in (37b), the theta-roles of an English verb are all determined in l-syntax, whereas those of a Chinese verb come into existence only in s-syntax.

Lin's theory offers a way to account for the Chinese–English contrast in a verb's permitted argument structure(s) which we find insightful. In effect, (37b) also recognizes that the lexicon, with its mechanism for generating lexical entries, needs to be somewhat autonomous from syntax despite all the efforts, as exemplified in H&K, to assimilate it into syntax – in order to explain certain critical facts, we need lexical operations to behave differently from those in syntax. This is a point we made in the previous section while reviewing H&K's third argument for an l-syntactic LRS; it is restated via (37b). Lin's theory also raises questions. First, by adopting H&K's l-syntax to represent the compositional structure of a verb and by placing all arguments in the Spec positions, Lin inherits H&K's problem with compounds such as *horse-saddling* (cf. 2.2.1.2). Second, the assumption in (37b) inevitably makes one wonder why the combination of light verbs and roots is not as liberal in the lexicon when, by hypothesis, the same X'-structure is used as the combinatorial mechanism. The question is actually weightier than it first appears. If Chinese employs all those light verbs in s-syntax to provide arguments of Instrument, Location, and several more (cf. Lin, Chapters 3 and 4), are these light verbs part of UG? If they are, why doesn't English (or Japanese) use them in l-syntax or even s-syntax? If they are not part of UG, then something more needs to be said in order to properly constrain the utilization of light verbs in the cross-linguistic context.

2.2.3   *Squeezing a lexical foot into a functional shoe*

Whereas H&K and Lin have attributed the origin of theta-roles to relations between arguments and particular light verbs in some syntactic structure, Borer (2005) goes further by claiming that a theta-role, to the extent we can still refer to it as such, only reflects the interpretation that a phrase acquires in the Spec position of a certain functional category in syntax. Given the voluminousness of Borer's theory, only what we consider to be directly relevant to the content of this section is addressed. To avoid sophistications unnecessary for this book, not all terminology in Borer's work is adopted here.

Briefly, Borer proposes that the linguistically critical properties of the event described by a clause are largely determined not by the lexical root $\sqrt{}$ of the verb, contra intuitions and common beliefs, but by the syntactic environment that $\sqrt{}$ is placed in, with the syntactic environment being the phrases headed by the event-related functional categories. The sentence *Anna read the book*, for instance, is given the following (somewhat simplified) structure (cf. p. 85):

(39)

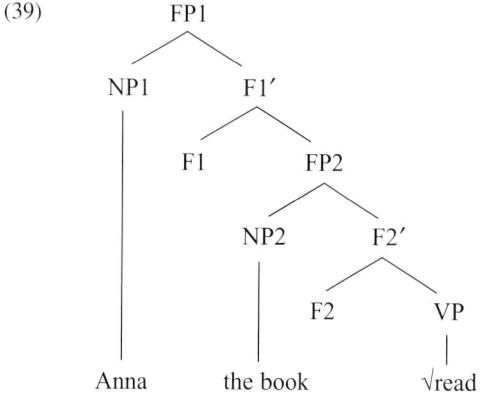

F1 and F2 are the event-related functional heads. Together with the constituents that fill the Spec positions of their phrases, these functional heads define a particular type of event labeled with the root. Roughly, (39) is interpreted as "there is an event e such that Anna is the originator of e, the book measures e,[16] and e is an event of reading." In this theory, the small number of event-related functional categories determines that there can be only a few interpretations (e.g., originator, . . .) for the phrases in their Spec positions. The $\sqrt{}$ doesn't participate in semantic role-assignment at all (e.g., see p. 227); it functions in the sentence merely as a modifier to the event type defined by FP1 and FP2 (p. 30). It doesn't change the event type thus defined but is instead affected by it.

One of the motivations for this theory is the class of "variable-behavior" verbs, the intransitive verbs whose single argument functions like either an Agent or

---

[16] That the object of a verb provides a way to measure the event is generally accepted in the field; see Dowty (1991) for an explicit proposal on this. We return to this issue in Chapter 3.

Theme, depending on the context. Borer drew data from Dutch, Italian, and Hebrew. We use Chinese to illustrate the same point. In Chinese, as in any other language, there are adverbs that specifically require the subject of the sentence to be an Agent. The examples in (34) were such, and more are given in (40):[17]

(40) a. ta (guyi)   han/chang/tiao.
         he intentionally yell/sing/jump
         'He intentionally yelled/sang/jumped.'

      b. yi-kuai boli (*guyi)   sui/diao-le.
         a-CL   glass intentionally   break/fall-LE
         'A piece of glass (*intentionally) broke/fell.'

Given this fact, the examples below show that in a resultative compound, the second verb (V2) must not be one with an Agent:

(41) a. tamen za-sui/peng-diao-le   yi-kuai boli.
         they   smash-break/knock-fall-LE a-CL   glass
         'They smashed/knocked to the ground a piece of glass.'

      b. *tamen qi-han/da-tiao/dou-chang-le   na-ge   moshengren.
         they infuriate-yell/hit-jump/cheer-sing-LE that-CL stranger

Compare the examples in (41b) with another resultative form, call it V-*de*, in (42):

(42) a. tamen qi-de   na-ge moshengren dasheng han.
         they infuriate-DE that-CL stranger   loudly yell
         'They made that stranger so angry he yelled loudly.'

      b. tamen da-de na-ge moshengren luan   tiao.
         they hit-DE that-CL stranger   aimless jump
         'They hit that stranger and made him jump around.'

      c. tamen dou-de   na-ge moshengren chang-le qilai.
         they cheer-DE that-CL stranger   sing-LE up
         'They cheered that stranger into singing.'

We return to some properties of this V-*de* construction in Chapter 3. For now, (42) indicates that there is nothing semantically or pragmatically wrong with (41b) because both groups use the same V1 and V2 sets and are meant to have the same interpretations.

    Given the contrast in (40a–b), it is interesting to note that certain Agentive verbs are nonetheless permitted as V2 in a resultative compound:

(43) a. ta guiyi   xiao/ku/pao/zou-le.
         he intentionally laugh/cry/run.away/leave-LE
         'He intentionally laughed/cried/ran away/left.'

---

[17] For using *guyi* 'intentionally' to force the Agent reading, see Cheng and Huang (1994).

b. ta ba haizi dou-xiao/ku-le.
   he BA child play.with-laugh/cry-LE
   'He treated the child playfully and made him laugh/cry.'

c. ni   ba huaidan da-pao/zou-le.
   you BA bad.guy hit-run.away/leave-LE
   'You hit the bad guy and made him run off.'

One must conclude from (40), (41), and (43), then, that certain verbs have variable behaviors. In the literature, intransitive verbs with an Agent argument are called *unergative* verbs and those with a Theme argument, *unaccusative* verbs. Variable-behavior verbs alternate between the two classes.

For Borer, the existence of such verbs suggests that the lexical root does not determine the argument structure, the decisive factor being the environment in which the root occurs. But if the lexical root is ruled out, it must be functional categories that perform the task of introducing arguments, hence the theory shown in (39). Compared with miscellaneous proposals, including Lin's, which quite freely use light verbs with lexical meanings (e.g., CAUSE, USE, AT) in syntax to introduce thematic arguments, Borer's theory is more restrictive: no matter what the lexical root is, the number and the semantic content of the arguments in a clause are already determined by the couple of event-related FPs. If such FP structures are part of UG, then it automatically follows that languages in general have only a tiny number of "theta-roles" with cross-linguistically identical behavior. What is not addressed sufficiently in her theory is the lexical root. This is where Lin's study of Chinese becomes significant.

As we saw in (33)–(35), Chinese allows more thematic relations to be associated with the subject and object of a clause. Later on, we will examine another fact in Chinese where even the basic thematic hierarchy appears to be violated. The question is how such "anomalies" are to be accounted for. Chomsky (1995) proposes that the syntax consists of a set of simple structure-building and structure-altering operations that function identically in all languages, with linguistic variations solely due to parametric differences among languages at the lexical level. From this perspective, the reason for the Chinese–English contrast can be sought only in the lexicon, and Lin's theory points at a viable solution: in comparison with English, a verb in Chinese is underspecified in thematically relevant ways, which in turn gives syntax more freedom in choosing what arguments to represent.

2.3   Sketching an alternative theory of theta-roles

The theories reviewed in Section 2.2, and indeed all the theories regarding theta-roles and arguments, have tried to answer one central question: How much information does a lexical verb contain that bears on syntactic computation? For

H&K, each lexical verb contains a fully developed syntactic structure (l-syntax) and much of what is coded in l-syntax is also available to clause-formation (their s-syntax). Borer (2005) denies any direct involvement of lexical roots in argument-related syntactic computation, exploring the possibility that what participates in syntactic computation is purely syntactic, with the lexical root contributing only as a modifier with semantic details that enrich but don't fundamentally determine the representation of arguments. Lin (2001) leans on H&K's view while arguing that languages may vary in how much syntactically coded information is in a lexical verb. In this section, we articulate a theory that combines some important ideas from these authors. To keep the task more manageable, we focus only on verbs that describe dynamic events.

2.3.1 *How a lexical entry contributes to the argument structure*

To begin with, it must be noted that the very fact that Borer can talk about the class of variable-behavior verbs entails that there are verbs that behave differently. For instance, though *xiao* 'laugh' and *ku* 'cry' may alternate between having an Agent argument or a non-Agent (cf. (43)), there are also many verbs that either intrinsically reject an Agent, as in (40b), or cannot acquire a non-Agent interpretation even in the context that converts *xiao* and *ku* (41b). At least on the surface, this rigidity suggests that a lexical entry affects argument-representation in non-trivial ways, irrespective of the structural context in which it occurs. Borer's theory attempts to address this problem by saying that lexical entries determine the functional structure only "insofar as some denote concepts which are 'odd' in certain grammatical contexts, in the sense that such grammatical contexts return an interpretation that conflicts with world knowledge" (p. 1). Logically, this is a plausible way out of the problem. Whether it is how language works, however, can only be determined empirically.

Both resultative constructions in Chinese, the compound (in 44) and the V-*de* construction in (45), exhibit a phenomenon that has been known for a long time due to its apparent thematic oddity:

(44)　a. na-ping jiu　he-zui-le　　　quan　zhuo de ren.
　　　　　that-CL　wine　drink-drunk-LE　whole　table　DE　person
　　　　　'Drinking that bottle of wine made everyone at the table drunk.'

　　　b. zhe-pi ma　qi-lei-le　　wo le.
　　　　　this-CL　horse　ride-tired-LE　me　SFP
　　　　　'Riding this horse made me tired.'

(45)　a. na-ping jiu　he　de ta zui-le　　san-tian.
　　　　　that-CL　wine　drink　DE　he　drunk-LE　three-day
　　　　　'Drinking that bottle of wine made him drunk for three days.'

b. zaochen de xinwen ting   de dajia   feichang zhenfen.
   morning DE news   listen DE everyone very   excited
   'Listening to the morning news made everyone excited.'

All these examples share the same three traits: the first verb (V1) is a typical transitive verb, the subject of the whole sentence is interpreted as the Theme argument of V1, and the NP after V1 carries the reading of V1's Agent. In other words, with respect to the argument structure of V1, the thematic hierarchy seems to be associated with the two NP arguments in the sentence in reverse order.

Various analyses have been proposed within the theoretical framework we adopt here (Cheng and Huang 1994, Y. Li 1995, 1997b, 1999, Sybesma 1992). Regardless of the technicalities used to account for this phenomenon, however, it is clear that the fundamental factor cannot be syntactic in Borer's sense. English also has a resultative construction, but no thematic inversion is allowed:

(46)   a.   Bill drank himself into a stupor.
       b.   *This bottle of whisky drank Bill into a stupor.

If the argument structure of a predicate were solely determined by the event-related functional structure of a clause and the effect of the lexical verb were merely found at the level of naturalness with respect to world knowledge, then the fact that *he* 'drink' in Chinese can be used as in (44a) should be enough to prove that this particular way of utilizing Borer's universal functional structure (cf. (39)) is not at odds with world knowledge. The ungrammaticality of (46b), then, must have an explanation outside Borer's system. An obvious possibility is to attribute the Chinese–English contrast to intrinsically lexical differences. In fact, it is quite straightforward to link the apparent thematic anomalies in (44)–(45) to the facts behind Lin's theory: that Chinese transitive verbs like *he* 'drink,' *qi* 'ride,' and *kai* 'drive' may easily drop their Agent argument (cf. 2.2.2).

2.3.2   The theory

The essence of the theory is simple: a lexical root $\sqrt{}$ conceptualizes a set of events e and contains the information on all the participants of e; a lexical verb V is composed of $\sqrt{}$ and a small number of light verbs (Lv) which indicate the event type(s) of e; only the information on those participants of e which bear directly on the nature of the event type sifts through Lv and remains accessible to syntax – this is the origin of stereotypical theta-roles; Chinese differs from English in allowing the option of not having any Lv in V, exposing all participant information encoded in $\sqrt{}$ to syntax and thereby creating the effect of thematic liberality. The theory is more explicitly defined as follows:

(47) $V \in \{(\sqrt{}), [Lv1 \; \sqrt{}], [Lv2 \; \sqrt{}], [Lv2 \; [Lv1 \; \sqrt{}]]\}$, where the option of $V = \sqrt{}$ is available only in Chinese.

(48)   Let E stand for a dynamic event, S for a state, and R for a relation, then:

a. Lv1 manifests the type of event which happens without an external cause and may be approximately described as "enter S" or "enter R." The participant that enters the state or relation is interpreted as Theme.

b. Lv2 manifests the type of event with an external cause which may be approximately described as "bring about E" or "bring about R."[18] The external cause, interpreted as Agent (or perhaps more accurately, Originator; cf. van Voorst 1988 and Borer 2005), is implicated by Lv2 but is not an argument of V because, as an external factor, it is *not* conceptualized as part of the event described by V.

c. Other intrinsic participants of E, S, and R are manifested as optional or obligatory theta-roles, as determined by $\sqrt{}$.

d. The choice of an Lv must not conflict with the type of event already coded in $\sqrt{}$.

(49)   Participant-information resulting from (48) must satisfy the theta-criterion.

Other than the language-specific option of V = $\sqrt{}$, to which we return shortly, (47) is a lexicalist adaptation of H&K's theory of l-syntactic LRSs. With these authors, we assume that there must be intrinsic reasons for why, when both Lv1 and Lv2 are in V, the former combines with $\sqrt{}$ first – somehow, the fact that Lv2 is associated with an external cause determines its peripheral position, but we will not speculate any further at this point. Another insight from H&K (also see Hale and Keyser 2002) finds its place in (48a–b), namely the theta-roles Theme and Agent/Originator are the results of Lv1 and Lv2 combined with $\sqrt{}$. Where we differ from H&K, and indeed from every other author working with light verbs, is that for us, an Lv does not add meaning to $\sqrt{}$; rather, it only spells out the event type already included, albeit "mixed" with other information, in the meaning of $\sqrt{}$. Likewise, a theta-role such as Theme is not provided by Lv1. The root already contains information about participants and other relevant factors for the event; Theme is simply the one that is "selected" by Lv1 because it is the participant in the Lv1-type of event.

Condition (48c) is best illustrated with an example. Consider V = [Lv2 $\sqrt{}$] with Lv2 marking an event of "bring about R." It is the intrinsic property of a relation to involve two parties. According to (48c), then, both participants can be manifested via the theta-roles of V; that is, this particular type of event may maximally have three theta-roles, two due to the nature of R and one implicated as Agent/Originator. Whether or not a given verb actually has the two R-related theta-roles depends on the event conceptualized in $\sqrt{}$. $\sqrt{}$*give* describes the bringing about of the transactional relation between an entity and goal of the transaction

---

[18] For lack of space, we leave aside the discussion on whether Lv2 has the interpretation of "bring about S."

(cf. Bowers 1993 and H&K), with both parties viewed as necessary participants of the event. This results in *give* with two object theta-roles, as in *give X to Y*. Aside from semantic details irrelevant at the thematic level, $\sqrt{}$*donate* conceptualizes the same type of event as $\sqrt{}$*give*, but differs from the latter in not treating the goal of transaction as a necessary participant. Hence we have *donate X (to Y)*.

That the theta-roles a given V may or must have are fundamentally determined by the type of event already coded in the root is stated in (48d), contra Borer. With this information carried in the root, an Lv, by default, is only a linguistic "spell-out" of that information, not something totally independent of the semantics of the root. It is for this reason that $\sqrt{}$*sneeze* in English and $\sqrt{}$*han* 'yell' in Chinese are compatible only with Lv2, which implicates an external Agent role, whereas the intransitive use of verbs such as *melt* and *hua* 'melt' must consist of the root plus Lv1 and thus necessitates a Theme role. Presumably, in human conceptualization, events of sneezing and yelling necessarily have an originator but the melting of snow is identified as an event that simply comes about, with snow being an intrinsic part of melting. The event of snow-melting may also be viewed as being caused by an external factor, resulting in both Lv1 and Lv2 inside the verb. In this view, variable-behavior verbs exist precisely because certain events are perceived to be ambiguous between the two types. In this respect, one language may opt to define the set somewhat differently from another. English simply treats laughing and crying on a par with sneezing, but Chinese regards such events as either ones with an originator or involuntary outbursts of emotions that just happen in the right context.[19] Below are the LSSs of these Chinese verbs:

(50) a. han 'yell': [Lv2 $\sqrt{}$*han*]
     b. hua 'melt': [Lv1 $\sqrt{}$*hua*] or [Lv2 [Lv1 $\sqrt{}$*hua*]]
     c. ku 'cry': [Lv2 $\sqrt{}$*ku*] or [Lv1 $\sqrt{}$*ku*]

Example (50a) represents the unergative; (50b) shows the alternation between the unaccusative and the causative. Verbs with these two options are also referred to as being *ergative*. Example (50c) characterizes Borer's variable-behavior verbs.

As it is, (48d) also leaves room for denominal verbs like *calve*. In itself, the nominal root $\sqrt{}$*calf* doesn't describe any event. Combining it with Lv2, then, would have no interpretation unless a calf is the intrinsic participant of some presumed event which is compatible in type with Lv2. In the case of *calve*, the presumed event is to give birth to a calf. In other words, $\sqrt{}$*calf* functions as a cue to help "fill up" the missing information about the exact nature of the event. Similarly, we find the following data in certain subdialects of northern Chinese:

---

[19] A similar idea was independently expressed in Gu (1992).

(51) a. ta   caoji-le.
      he   hen-LE
      'He chickened out.'

    b. *ta   zhengzai   caoji.
      he   PROG   hen
      'He is chickening out.'

    c. *ta   guiyi   caoji-le.
      he   on.purpose   hen-LE
      Intended reading: 'He chickened out on purpose.'

The unacceptable (51b–c) suggest that *caoji* 'grass.chicken = hen' in this use is perhaps not an action verb or does not have an Agent subject. If this is correct, then *caoji* should be decomposed into [Lv1 $\sqrt{caoji}$], with the interpretation of, roughly, 'entering a hen-like state,' i.e., being cowardly like a chicken. As in the case of *calve*, $\sqrt{caoji}$ does not describe any event in itself, only helping to furnish the missing information of the Lv1-type event.

Two points are worth making at this moment. First, it should be noted that in neither Chinese nor English are these brute-force conversions from a nominal root to a verb fully productive. It is impossible to say *ta laohu-le* 'he tiger-LE' to mean he was fierce or fearless like a tiger, nor is it considered acceptable to replace *This hen just laid an egg* with *This hen just egged*. This fact has a natural explanation in our theory. The function of Lv is to spell out the event type of a root. Once the UG mechanisms in (47)–(48) are in place, a language may choose to allow non-event-describing roots to merge with an Lv provided that the critical information can be recovered from the root on the basis of world knowledge, but doing so is a stretch of the Lv-system, not the norm. The second point, closely related to the first, is that when the root is non-event-describing, the interpretation of the relation between the root and the light verb is essentially out of the control of the deterministic mechanisms of UG and into the hands of pragmatics, idiomaticity, and language-specific choices.[20] So even though English allows a cow to calve and a mare to foal, Chinese has no denominal verbs of this kind, nor should English be expected to apply this form of denominalization to all offspring-denoting nouns.

Lin's proposal on the Chinese–English distinction is incorporated in (47). We directly adopt from Lin the notion that a Chinese verb may consist of the bare root regardless of its event type and thereby differs from its Lv-containing counterpart in English. Departing from his theory in (37), however, ours does not reallocate these Lvs to syntax. Conceptually, (47) retains the logical minimum of (37) by discarding two stipulations. First, if an Lv is not present in a lexical entry, we see no logical necessity that it must be found another home. By default, a verb with a

---

[20] This is the same idea as Borer's (cf. Section 2.2.3) but applied inside a lexical verb.

missing Lv in the lexicon remains that way in all other components of language and thus exhibits whatever behavior the lack of Lv causes during subsequent linguistic computation. As the direct consequence of this minimalist approach to Lv, (47) also avoids another and arguably more problematic stipulation in Lin's theory: that light verbs are used "liberally" in syntax. As we note in Section 2.2.2, this liberality is a powerful mechanism with unclear theoretical and empirical repercussions.

Last, to the extent that Lv1 and Lv2 give rise to what are called theta-roles, it is self-evident in the UG framework that such theta-roles obey the theta-criterion, as specified in (49). Especially worth clarification is the Agent role. According to (48b), the external cause of an event is "implicated" by Lv2 but not considered part of the event described by the lexical verb containing Lv2. What this means is best illustrated by an analogy. Consider a university in which a faculty committee is designated to provide advice to the president. The committee has its own composition (chair and a set number of members), and its existence necessarily implicates the existence of the president who is, nonetheless, not part of the committee. Comparably, when Lv2 implicates Agent, the latter must satisfy the theta-criterion even though it is not regarded as part of the event described by the lexical verb containing Lv2. Now we proceed to demonstrate how the theory formulated in (47) through (49) works toward accounting for various English and Chinese data, taking for granted that a function of syntax is to license NPs, via the Case filter, etc., so as for the NPs and the verb to satisfy the principle of Full Interpretation defined in (30).

2.3.3   Facts explained

The basic subject–object asymmetry in denominal verb formation, demonstrated in (21), follows straightforwardly from our theory. That *calve* means 'to give birth to a calf' is just accounted for. The impossible *cow*, meaning 'a cow gives birth to,' is the outcome of (48b). Since Lv2 implicates an Agent role but does not "have" it, merging $\sqrt{cow}$ with Lv2 at the lexical level leaves the root semantically unconnected from Lv2, in direct violation of Full Interpretation. This is the same analysis we gave in Section 2.2.1.2 while evaluating H&K's work. The ungrammatical *The alfalfa sneezed the colt* in (24b) also has a simple account. Adopting the essence of H&K's LRS of the transitive *sneeze* in (25) yields (52):

(52)   *sneeze*:   [Lv2 [Lv2 $\sqrt{sneeze}$]]

This LSS is not legitimate according to (47), which in turn is based on the assumption that in human conceptualization a single event may have no more than one external cause (cf. Borer 2005 for the same effect achieved via syntax).

The same logic also explains why the second verbal morpheme of a resultative compound must be non-Agentive (cf. (41)). To the extent that such a compound behaves like a regular verb (cf. Y. Li 1997b, 2005), what it encodes must be regarded as one (albeit internally complex) event, with (53) being the maximum composition it may have ($\sqrt{1}$ and $\sqrt{2}$ standing for the two lexical roots[21]):

(53)   [Lv2 [Lv1 $\sqrt{1}$–$\sqrt{2}$]]

Given the fact that $\sqrt{1}$ is the head of the root-cluster and determines the fundamental properties of the whole word (Y. Li 1990, 1993a, Cheng and Huang 1994; also see note 8 of this chapter), whether the event they together describe has an external cause hinges on $\sqrt{1}$. Put differently, if the compound verb has Lv2 in its composition, the light verb must spell out the event type of $\sqrt{1}$, the head. As there is no more than one Lv2 per verb, $\sqrt{2}$ is effectively prevented from having its own Lv2, resulting in the data in (41). In contrast, the resultative V-*de* construction in (42) consists of two separate verbs, each heading its own clause (Huang 1989, Y. Li 1999) and thus describing a separate event. It is only expected that each event may have its own external cause.

Proceeding to the locatum verbs in (26), suppose the LSS of the denominal verb *saddle* is as follows, a lexicalist conversion of H&K's (27):

(54)   *saddle*:   [Lv2 [Lv1 $\sqrt{saddle}$]]

As in the case of *calve*, the root in (54) doesn't describe any event, making it necessary to provide the missing information on the event in question, with $\sqrt{saddle}$ being the only overt cue. If H&K are correct (cf. (27)), [Lv1 $\sqrt{saddle}$] is to be interpreted as entering a relation R with a saddle. The precise nature of R is again determined by factors outside the theory of (47)–(49).[22] Next consider the impossible *church used in *church the money (cf. (26b)). Given H&K's decomposition of *church* in (27), where the nominal root $\sqrt{church}$ is interpreted as a Theme, it is straightforward that the hypothetical verb violates the principle of Full Interpretation in (30). Recall that in our theory (and in H&K but not in Lin), Lv1 does not create the Theme theta-role by itself; rather, the Theme is that participant of the event, described by the root, which enters the specific state or relation and is thus "picked out" by Lv1. Since there is no Theme from Lv1 alone, merging $\sqrt{church}$ with a bare Lv1, with the intended Theme reading, would only leave the root semantically unrelated with the light verb, making it impossible for

---

[21] See Borer (2005) for a comparable analysis of the resultative cluster, out of partially overlapping considerations.

[22] Again, Borer's world-knowledge factor may be at work, with $\sqrt{saddle}$ restricting the plausible nature of R. It has also been suggested that spatial relations are among the most basic notions in human conceptualization of the world. For recent works on this fairly old idea, see Svorou (1994) and Haspelmath (1997). In this view, it is natural for R to be understood as a spatial relation when $\sqrt{}$ fails to provide relevant information.

church to have the hypothetical use in (26b). This theory can also explain why, though *church the money* and *horse the saddle* are bad, *horse-saddling* is acceptable, a problem intrinsic to H&K's l-syntactic theory of denominal verb formation (cf. 2.2.1.2). Since *saddle* has a legitimate derivation in (54), in which Lv1 and $\sqrt{saddle}$ are properly combined, the resulting denominal verb does have a Theme role, which *horse* receives in *horse-saddling* to satisfy Full Interpretation.

It is worth noting that locative and locatum denominal verbs also require filling the missing information on events by means of world knowledge and/or language-internal choices. This explains why such verbs, though quite popular in Modern English (*can the beans, cradle the child,...*) as well as in Old Chinese (*sheng zhi yi fa* 'rope him with law,' *yi zhi* 'clothe him,'...), are hard to find in Modern Chinese.

Now we move to the differences between Chinese and English, a significant fact being that the thematic relations between a transitive verb in Chinese and its NP arguments are generally more flexible (cf. (33), (35), (36)). Two possibilities arise from (47). If the event type intrinsically coded in the root is spelled out with an Lv, the resulting verb in Chinese is thematically the same as its counterpart in English. Apparently, this is the cross-linguistic norm. Alternatively, a Chinese verb may choose to contain the lexical root only. When such a verb, call it V_{root}, appears in syntax, two factors come into play:

(55)   a. V_{root} has no theta-roles in the sense defined in (48) and therefore, according to (49), whatever semantic relations the lexical root encodes between the event and its participants are not subject to the theta-criterion.

   b. Syntax provides ways, through such mechanisms as the X'-structure (cf. (11)) and the Case Filter (cf. (52) of Chapter 1), to license NPs that are independently expected to satisfy the principle of Full Interpretation.

From (55a–b) one deduces that an NP may function legitimately as the subject or object of V_{root} provided that it bears some compatible participant-relation with V_{root}. This, we suggest, is the reason for the "liberal thematic relations" found with the Chinese NP subject and object.

As a specific example, when *kai* 'drive' takes the Lv-less option, the NPs in the subject and object positions of the clause may still satisfy Full Interpretation, as long as they are understood as, say, the location where the driving event takes place and the vehicle that is involved in the driving event. Hence the example in (56):

(56)   zhe-tiao he   bu neng kai   ni-de na-sou po   motuoting.
         this-CL river not can drive your that-CL shabby motorboat
         'That shabby motorboat of yours can't be driven on this river.'

In fact, at least given the way our theory is formulated at the moment, it imposes no restriction on how these semantic relations are represented in syntax. Therefore, unless there are other independent principles preventing it, the semantic relations, which we still call Location and Theme just for the purpose of easy discussion, may be reversely represented as well:[23]

(57)   ni-de na-sou po   motuoting bu   neng kai   zhe-tiao he.
        your that-CL shabby motorboat not can drive this-CL   river
        Intended meaning: same as (56).

The examples below illustrate other "thematic" relations represented in this flip-flopped manner:

(58) a. xiao bei he   lücha.   (subj = Instrument, obj = Theme)
         small cup drink green.tea
         'Use the small cup to drink the green tea.'

      b. lücha   he   xiao bei.   (subj = Theme, obj = Instrument)
         green.tea drink small cup

(59) a. ni-de keren shui na-zhang chuang ba. (subj = Experiencer?, obj = Location)
         your guest sleep that-CL   bed   SFP
         'Let your guest sleep on that bed.'

      b. na-zhang chuang shui ni-de keren ba. (subj = Location, obj = Experiencer?)
         that-CL   bed   sleep your guest SFP

(60) a. jieri   liwu dou gei-le   pengyou-men le.   (subj = Theme, obj = Goal)
         holiday gift all give-LE friend-PL   SFP
         'Holiday gifts were all given to the friends.'

      b. pengyou-men dou gei-le   jieri   liwu le.   (subj = Goal,[24] obj = Theme)
         friend-PL   all give-LE holiday gift SFP
         'Friends were all given gifts.'

---

[23] This may also be the reason why temporal and locative adjuncts don't display intrinsic hierarchy even in English, where other classes of adverbs are known to be hierarchically arranged:

    (i)   Sam chased the coyote noisily deliberately.
    (ii)   *Sam chased the coyote deliberately noisily. (only good if *deliberately* modifies *noisily*)
    (iii) Sam chased the coyote yesterday in the woods.
    (iv)   Sam chased the coyote in the woods yesterday.

Assuming that manner and subject-oriented adverbs are parts of corresponding functional phrases (Cinque 1999), then their linear order is determined by the intrinsic hierarchy in which their functional phrases are arranged in a clause. On the other hand, if time and location are two of the relations already coded in the lexical root as part of the event, the fact that they are not "picked up" by Lv1 and Lv2 exempts them from the θ-criterion. Then whatever reason allows the flip-flop in (57)–(58) in Chinese allows these adjuncts to do the same in English.

[24] The subject NP of this sentence may also take the Agent reading, which is irrelevant to our discussion at this point.

We hasten to note that it is not our intention to claim that such "thematic liberality" is a fully productive process in Chinese. In fact, it is easy to find action verbs in the language that do not permit such swaps. This alone, however, does not falsify the theory because there may well be other principles/factors at work. The question we hope to address with the proposed theory is why the examples above and in Section 2.2.2 are not observed in English or many other languages, though they are so easily produced in Chinese. Also, quite independently of the thematic flip-flop, Lin's original observation is still valid: the subject and object in Chinese are not limited to Agent and Theme even with an action verb in a non-passive context. At a dinner party not long ago, a university professor of Chinese linguistics passed a pair of chopsticks to one of the authors and said:

(61)   ni   chi zhe-shuang kuaizi   ba.
        you   eat this-CL   chopstick SFP
        'Use this pair of chopsticks for the dinner.'

Such sentences, perhaps deemed unacceptable in formal texts, are nonetheless produced by native speakers in everyday conversations quite freely. This is a fundamental difference between Chinese and many other languages; our theory, built on Lin's initial proposal, aims to address it.

Another issue worth bringing up is the Agent interpretation. In the presence of Lv2, a verb necessarily implicates an Agent/Originator. Given (49), this theta-role must be borne out by an argument in syntax. We side with the various authors (Marantz 1984, Hale and Keyser 1993, Kratzer 1996, Borer 2005, among others) that syntax provides a particular way to manifest this Agent argument in a clause, which will be elaborated on in Chapter 3. The question for now is what happens when Lv2 is not present. The most straightforward answer is that without Lv2, no Agent theta-role is implicated, the theta-criterion doesn't apply, and therefore a verb that would have an obligatory Agent subject in English can occur without one in Chinese. This explains the fact in (33).[25] Interestingly, though such data from Chinese argue against Borer's indiscriminate claim that the Agent/Originator and Theme (Subject-of-quantity for her) roles are purely from syntax (cf. 2.2.3), our treatment of Chinese V_{root} is conceptually very close to

---

[25] Another question is whether in the absence of Lv2, the NP bearing the interpretation of the external cause, which we conveniently call Agent, is also subject to the kind of flip-flop shown in (56) through (60). The logic of the theory suggests that it is not, because the external cause is not part of the event and therefore depends on a syntactic structure outside VP to be introduced. This seems to be consistent with the facts: typical action verbs reject an Agent reading on the object.

her theory: the verb without any Lv in it has no theta-role, the NPs structurally licensed in syntax are "thematically" interpreted based on their semantic relations with the root, and as we saw through the examples above, such miscellaneous "thematic" readings are characterized with a certain degree of context-dependent flexibility. Meanwhile, we disagree with Borer by recognizing that given the contrast between Chinese and English, if Chinese verbs are best analyzed this way, then English verbs, at least typical ones, must not be. The solution lies in keeping syntax universally identical and accounting for the thematic "anomalies" in Chinese via differences at the lexical level. In this respect, we echo with Chomsky (1995; also see Chomsky 1970) that linguistic variations should be attributed to the lexicon.

The last phenomenon to be addressed is the apparently reversed theta-role assignment in Chinese resultative constructions, shown in (44)–(45). The compound form of the data is schematically illustrated below, with a simple explanation:

(62)   wine drink-drunk me

Since Chinese has the option of not including Lvs in a verb, the whole compound as a verb may be composed of just the two roots $\sqrt{drink}$ and $\sqrt{drunk}$.[26] Specifically, in the absence of Lv2, no Agent reading is required under the theta-criterion. When this V_{root} compound is placed in syntax, the NP *wine* is interpreted in connection with $\sqrt{drink}$ as the passive participant of drinking, and the NP *me* is interpreted in connection with $\sqrt{drunk}$. Both NPs satisfy Full Interpretation semantically and are licensed syntactically by receiving the subject and object Cases, respectively. That *me* is also understood as the drinker can be attributed to "world knowledge" without any structurally established relation between *me* and $\sqrt{drink}$ (cf. Hoekstra 1988): in a normal world, if wine-drinking caused me to get drunk, then I must have done the drinking. In brief, the problematic thematic reversal is only apparent, due to the unique property of Chinese in (47).[27] The V-*de* construction receives the same account:

(63)   wine drink-DE I drunk

The only difference is that with two separate verbs, only the first verb needs to be a V_{root} to generate (63). In this analysis, English (or any other language we know

---

[26] Unlike in English, these two roots are not derivationally related in Chinese.

[27] This account, arrived at from a different perspective, resembles in spirit the analysis in Her (2007), which proposed accounting for Y. Li's (1995) data by suppressing the subject theta-role of V1. Her's theory is constructed in Lexical Functional Grammar.

of) doesn't have the comparable phenomenon precisely because the Agent subject is obligatory for such verbs, which in turn is attributed to (47).

Direct support for this analysis comes from the examples below:

(64)　a. na-shou ge   chang-ku-le wo le.
　　　　that-CL song sing-cry-LE me SFP
　　　　'Singing that song made me cry.'

　　　b. na-shou ge   chang-de wo luo-le   lei.
　　　　that-CL song sing-DE I   shed-LE tear
　　　　'Singing that song made me shed tears.'

Pertinent to the current discussion is that the singer in these sentences can be either me or some unidentified person. At least with the second reading, *chang* 'sing' must be used as an Agentless verb, necessarily excluding *wo* 'me' as the thematic subject of the first verb morpheme. Further substantiating the V_{root} analysis are the examples in (65):

(65)　a. ?na-zhi da wan he-zui-le   wo le.
　　　　that-CL big bowl drink-drunk-LE me SFP
　　　　'Drinking with that big bowl made me drunk.'

　　　b. xin   kai   de na-jia   fanguan   chi de tamen zhang-le haoji   bang.
　　　　newly open DE that-CL restaurant eat DE they   gain-LE   several pound
　　　　'Eating in that newly opened restaurant made them gain several pounds.'

In (65a), the subject of the sentence is understood as the instrument of eating; in (65b), the subject of the matrix clause is the location of eating. Similar examples may be easily constructed, indicating that the Theme reading on the subject is not required. Given the option of treating the compound or the matrix verb in the V-*de* construction as V_{root}, this thematic flexibility is expected.[28]

---

[28] Jen Ting pointed out the following contrast (personal communication):

　(i)　　*wo he-zui-le   jiu.
　　　　　I   drink-drunk-LE wine
　　　　　'Drinking wine made me drunk.'

　(ii)　　*wo he-zui-le   da wan.
　　　　　I   drink-drunk-LE big bowl
　　　　　Intended reading: 'Drinking in a big bowl made me drunk.'

To this data, we add (iii):

　(iii)　　*wo he-zui-le   xiangbin/na-ping   jiu/henduo jiu.
　　　　　I   drink-drunk-LE champagne/that-CL wine/much wine

Apparently, there are restrictions even on the Patient/Theme PN object of *he* 'drink' when the verb is used in the context of the compound, indicating factors at work independently of thematic flexibility.

Also pertinent is the next set of examples, starting with (66):

(66)   a. gangcai de bisai pao de tamen manshendahan.
            just.now DE race run DE they   sweat.all.over
            'Running the race a moment ago made them sweat profusely.'

       b. *gang lai   de jiaolian pao de tamen manshendahan.
            just arrive DE coach   run DE they   sweat.all.over
            Intended reading: 'The new coach made them run to the extent
            of sweating profusely.'

Example (66a) is a perfect sentence because the verb *pao* 'run' may independently take *bisai* 'race' as the object (cf. *pao yi chang bisai* 'run a race'). As long as the verb takes the form of V_{root}, the Agent argument is "dropped," with *tamen* 'they' understood as the runners only on the basis of world knowledge. That is, the sentence receives the same analysis as a typical "thematically anomalous" case. Example (66b) is unacceptable because, under the intended interpretation, there is no plausible semantic relation between the subject *xin lai de jiaolian* 'new coach' and the verb *pao* 'run,' whether the latter is V_{root} or has corresponding Lv(s) in it.[29]

In comparison, (67) below look like similar examples but display a milder contrast:

(67)   a. (?)na-chang dianying ku de wo xin   dou sui le.
            that-CL   movie   cry DE I heart even broken SFP
            'I cried so much during that movie that even my heart broke.'

       b. ?(?)na-ge   dianying ku de wo xin   dou sui le.
            that-CL movie   cry DE I heart even broken SFP
            'That movie made me cry so much that even my heart broke.'

---

[29] This NP, of course, may serve as the Agent of the verb, creating a totally different reading. The problem then would be lack of real world plausibility: Why would the coach's running make THEM sweat? If a different predicate is used, then the sentence becomes acceptable:

(i)   xin lai   de jiaolian pao de tamen dou buhaoyisi le.
      new arrive DE coach   run DE they   all   embarrassed SFP
      'The new coach's running made them feel not at ease.'

The scenario may be, for instance, that the coach ran so fast or practiced so hard that the athletes felt embarrassed because they should have done better.

Worth stressing is that the unacceptability of (66b) suggests that thematic interpretations, whether via theta-roles resulting from Lvs or through more liberal participant interpretations between an NP and a verb root, don't come out of the blue. Logically, it is imaginable that the coach functions solely as the "causer" for making the athletes run and sweat. But √*pao* 'run' does not encode such a causer participant (nor does √*manshendahan* 'sweat profusely'), so what's logically possible in the real world is not allowed in a linguistic construction such as (66b).

The native speakers we consulted vary in how readily they accept (67b), but there is a consensus that (67b) is not as good as (67a). Especially interesting is that the two examples differ only in the choice of the classifier inside the subject NP. The explanation, we believe, lies in the fact that the classifier *chang*, meaning a ground for a special purpose in its original nominal interpretation, allows the NP to mean either a movie or the space/time in which a movie is shown. Example (67a) is acceptable, then, because the matrix verb *ku* 'cry' can be used as V_{root} and the subject NP is interpreted as holding a space/time relationship with the event of crying. In (67b), however, the classifier *ge* limits the interpretation of the subject NP to the movie itself, which has no natural semantic relation with the verb *ku*.[30] That the example isn't as bad as (66b) is the result of a separate fact in Chinese, i.e., under marked contexts, *ku* may indeed be used as a transitive action verb:

(68)   a. Zhuge Liang ku   Zhou Yu.
          Zhuge Liang cry.for Zhou Yu
          'Zhuge Liang cried for (= mourned weepingly for) Zhou Yu.'

        b. ni   zai ku   shenme? wo zai ku   shidao de bu gongping!
          you ASP cry.about what   I   ASP cry.about world   DE not fair
          'What are you crying about? I'm crying about the lack of fairness in the world!'

This use of *ku* is not fully productive in Modern Chinese, but it helps salvage (67b). That is, *na ge dianying* in the sentence may be marginally understood as what the crying is about, making it more interpretable than (66b).

Comparing (67) with two other pairs of examples lends support to this analysis. First, substituting *ku* with *kan* 'watch' eliminates the contrast caused by the two different classifiers:

(69)   a. na-chang dianying kan   de wo feichang bushufu.
          that-CL movie   watch DE I   very   uncomfortable
          'Watching that movie made me very uncomfortable.'

---

[30] The contrast in (67) is likely to be connected with the following contrast:

(i)   ?ta ku-le   zhengzheng yi-chang dianying.
       he cry-LE   whole   a-CL   movie
       'He cried throughout the whole time of the movie.'

(ii)   *ta ku-le   zhengzheng yi-ge dianying.
       he cry-LE   whole   a-CL movie

Only the NP with *chang* as the classifier and thus meaning the time of the movie is acceptable in the postverbal position. So (i) may be the base for the example in (67a). For sure, the subject NP in (67a) doesn't just have the space/time/process reading; it is also understood as the cause for my broken heart. But there is evidence that this is the result of a separate semantic factor at work; see Y. Li (1995, 1999).

b. na-ge   dianying kan   de wo feichang bushufu.
   that-CL movie   watch DE I   very   uncomfortable
   Intended meaning: same as (69b).

This is because the normal use of *kan* allows both *na chang dianying* and *na ge dianying* as the semantic object. As a result, the subject NP in (69) is consistently associated with the V_{root} *kan* as the "Theme," unlike in (68b) where the semantic relation between the two components can be established only through a stretch. Second, compare (67) with (70):

(70) a. na-chang xiangsheng xiao de wo duzi   dou teng-le.
        that-CL   cross.talk   laugh DE I   stomach even ache-LE
        'I laughed during that talk show so much that even my stomach ached.'

     b. na-ge   xiangsheng xiao de wo duzi   dou teng-le.
        that-CL cross.talk   laugh DE I   stomach even ache-LE
        'That piece of talk show made me laugh so much that even my stomach ached.'

The two examples both use *xiao* 'laugh' as the matrix verb, differing again in choosing between the classifiers *chang* and *ge*. Remarkably, both examples are perfect, in contrast to (67). At first sight, it may seem unexpected that *ku* and *xiao* should differ in this way. But the difference correlates with another one between these otherwise similar verbs:

(71)   zui   xiao-ren   de shi   vs. *zui   ku-ren   de shi
        most laugh-person DE thing   most cry-person DE thing
        'the most amusing thing'   'the most saddening thing'

Independently, *xiao* has a causative use, shown in (71), whereas *ku* doesn't. No matter why this happens (recall from 2.2.3 that both *ku* and *xiao* may be used as Agentless verbs in certain contexts, suggesting that the contrast in (71) is language-specific in nature), (71) is sufficient to help understand (70) vs. (67). That is, if *xiao* already has a causative use, (70b) doesn't even need to involve V_{root}. *na ge xiangsheng* 'that piece of talk show' is already the thematic subject of the verb with *wo* 'I/me' being the object. Each NP has the standard thematic interpretation, fundamentally different from the stretched semantics involved in interpreting (67b).

2.4   In place of a conclusion

We finish this chapter with a question and an observation. The question is why Chinese differs from English in the manner of (47) in the first place. A possible direction in which to look is whether the existence of V_{root} is correlated with its high degree of analyticity. For example, compared to Old Chinese, where words were primarily monosyllabic, Modern Chinese has clearly shifted to a disyllabic- or multi-syllabic-word language. Logically, if a monosyllabic word is deprived of its "wordhood" and reused as a component of the new disyllabic word, then its original lexical boundary might be removed, exposing the inside. Possibly, this process involves separating the Lvs from the lexical root.[31]

The observation is with respect to the status of theta-roles and the various analyses based on them. If Chinese allows V_{root} which, by definition, has no theta-roles and provides semantic interpretations for NPs in the syntactic structure only on the basis of world knowledge more or less in the sense of Borer (2005), then are those theta-role-based accounts of Chinese compounds in 2.1 still valid? The answer is yes, for the following reasons. First, there is no evidence that Chinese verbs *always* take the V_{root} form. At least when verbs do contain Lvs, everything we have said remains valid. Second, whether a compound always consists of two bare roots or not, the fact remains that a given NP may still be interpreted as the participant of the subevents described by both morphemes in the compound. At some level of description, multiple semantic relations can still be said to converge on a single NP argument. In other words, we still need the identification, in Higginbotham's (1985) sense, of semantic relations, thematic or not. Third, regardless of the nature of these semantic relations, the number of NPs available in a given clause is still restricted by such principles as the Case Filter – Chinese may allow thematic liberality as Lin calls it, but it doesn't mean a Chinese verb could take five or eight NP arguments. Fourth, even in the cases where the compound can be shown to be a V_{root}, the first root ($\sqrt{1}$) still determines the basic properties of the compound. For instance, there is no proper use of the compound where the subject of the sentence is semantically related only with $\sqrt{2}$. In short, all the basic principles introduced in 2.1 are intact. It is for this reason that in subsequent chapters, unless necessary, we will simply use the term theta-role to describe all the semantic relations between a verb and its arguments.

---

[31] For works that explore the extensions of this possibility, see Huang (2005, 2006, to appear) and Y. Li (in progress).

3

The verb phrase

The notion of a phrase came up many times in Chapter 1. One of the main discoveries in the past thirty-plus years is that a phrase is much more than simply a group of words acting as a unit. Phrases have several important characteristic properties. One of them was introduced in Chapter 2, i.e., that words inside a phrase are combined according to a particular schema which holds across categories and, linear order aside, perhaps across all languages as well. In this chapter, we focus on the verb phrase (VP), examining the various constituents affiliated with V.

3.1 Adjuncts and complements

Consider a typical verb phrase in the example below:

(1)   ta   dasheng   chang   minge.
        he   loud   sing   folk.song
        'He sings folk songs loudly.'

In addition to the verb *chang* 'sing' which we refer to as the *head* of the VP, the phrase also contains the verb's object, *minge* 'folk song,' and a modifier, *dasheng* 'loud,' that describes the manner of singing. That non-head components inside the VP are divided into objects and modifiers is long-held wisdom with its basis in intuition. The object is an intrinsic participant of the event described by the verb whereas a modifier provides more "peripheral" information about the event such as time, location, and the manner in which the event is carried out. The X'-theory introduced in Chapter 2 captures the object–modifier distinction as follows (for now, we treat the subject as the Spec of VP; but see definition (20), Chapter 2, and Section 3.2 below):

(2)

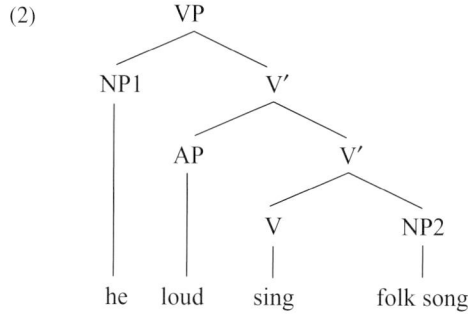

Treating the modifier as AP, we already saw in Chapter 2 that the AP in (2) is in the adjunct position and the object, NP2, in the complement position. Note first that merging V with NP2 produces V′, which is notationally different from either V or NP2; in contrast, merging AP with V′ results in another V′. This labeling system is meant to reflect two important facts about language. First, an adjunct is only peripheral to the VP because its addition does not alter the original structure – when it attaches to V′, we still have a V′, not a node of a different nature. Second, if adjunct + V′ = V′, it follows automatically that modifier-adjunction may intrinsically happen an indefinite number of times, restricted only by other factors. It is this *recursive* nature of syntactic structure, not limited to adjuncts, that accounts for the ability of language to produce a potentially infinite number of sentences. Also worth observing in (2) is that adjoining AP to V′ yields the correct word order, with AP necessarily preceding the verb and its complement. But what distinguishes complements and adjuncts is actually more subtle and interesting.

The examples in (3)–(4) illustrate questions about the complement and adjunct of the basic sentence in (1):

(3)   a. ni   chang shenme minge?
           you sing   what   folk.song
           'What folk songs do you sing?'

         b. ni   zenme chang minge?
           you how   sing   folk.song
           'How do you sing folk songs?'

(4)   a. ta shuo [ni   chang shenme minge]?
           he say   you sing   what   folk.song
           'What folk songs did he say that you sing?'

         b. ta shuo [ni   zenme chang minge]?
           he say   you how   sing   folk.song
           'How did he say that you sing folk songs?' [with *how* modifying *sing*]

Each example in (3) is a simple sentence, whereas each example in (4) consists of two clauses with the embedded one marked with brackets. Regardless, either the object or the modifier of *chang* 'sing' can be questioned. It appears then that the question expressions (e.g., *shenme minge* 'what folk song' and *zenme* 'how') can occur freely either in a simple sentence or in an embedded clause.

The generalization falls apart in several ways, however. Consider the context of indirect questions, first discovered in Huang (1982a):

(5) a. ta xiang zhidao [shei chang minge].
    he want know who sing folk.song
    'He wants to know who sings folk songs.'

   b. (?)ta xiang zhidao [shei chang shenme minge]?
     he want know who sing what folk.song
     *'What song does he want to know who sings?'[1]

   c. *ta xiang zhidao [shei zenme chang minge]?
     he want know who how sing folk.song
     *'How does he want to know who sings folk songs?' [with *how* modifying *sing*]

Note that (5b) and (5c) would be equally acceptable if the two question words in each sentence were both part of the indirect question; under this interpretation the examples are not understood as questions in themselves. Example (5b) would be translated as 'he wants to know who sings what folk songs' and (5c) 'he wants to know who sings folks songs in what manner.' The contrast appears when *shenme minge* 'what folk song' and *zenme* 'how' are meant to turn the whole example into a question, as indicated by the question mark in (5b–c). Under this condition, the subject in the indirect question may still participate in forming an interrogative whereas the adjunct appears to resist such an interpretation.

The same differentiating pattern is found when the main verb is negated:

(6) a. ta mei gaosu dajia [ni zheme chang nei-shou minge].
    he not tell people you this.way sing that-CL folk.song
    'He didn't tell people that you sang that folk song this way.'

   b. (?)ta mei gaosu dajia [ni zheme chang shenme minge]?
     he not tell people you this.way sing what folk.song
     'What folk song(s) did he not tell people that you sing this way?'

   c. *ta mei gaosu dajia [ni zenme chang zhe-shou minge]?
     he not tell people you how sing this-CL folk.song
     Intended reading: *'How did he not tell people that you sing this folk song?'
     [with *how* modifying *sing*]

---

[1] See Huang (1982a) for a discussion on why the corresponding English example is ungrammatical. The contrast between (5b–c) may not be equally clear to every native speaker of Chinese. What is important is that if there is a contrast in acceptability, (5b) is always the better one, a generalization to which we know of no counterexamples.

The contrast between (6b) and (6c) varies among native speakers of Chinese. For some, (6b) also sounds somewhat strange. But overall, (6c) is perceived to be significantly more difficult to interpret even though the sentence otherwise feels "grammatical," meaning that every word seems to occur in the right spot. The following triplet, using a different main verb, confirms that the contrast is not a coincidence:

(7) a. ta bu xiangxin [ni zheme   chang-guo nei-shou minge].
        he not believe   you this.way sing-GUO that-CL folk.song
        'He doesn't believe that you sang that folk song this way.'

     b. ta bu xiangxin [ni zheme   chang-guo shenme minge]?
        he not believe   you this.way sing-GUO what   folk.song
        'What folk song does he not think that you sang this way?'

     c. ??ta bu xiangxin [ni zenme chang-guo nei-shou minge]?
          he not think   you how   sing-GUO that-CL folk.song
          *'How does he not think that you sang that folk song?' [with *how*
          modifying *sing*]

In conclusion, the adjunct inside VP is much harder to question than the complement when the main clause is negative. And judging from the English translations, the same complement–adjunct asymmetry holds in English as well.[2]

  The same pattern is found when certain adverbs are used in the main clause:[3]

[2] This "inner island" phenomenon was first noticed in English by Ross (1983). See Rizzi (1990) for a theory of why it arises. At least in Chinese, this contrast seems to hold only of embedded clauses that would be represented as tensed clauses in other languages. If the clause is non-tensed, the asymmetry disappears:

  (i)   ta mei ting-guo ni   chang shenme minge?
         he not hear-GUO you sing   what   folk.song
         'What folk song has he not heard you sing?'

  (ii)   ta mei ting-guo ni   zenme chang minge?
         he not hear-GUO you how   sing folk.song
         *'How has he not heard you sing folk songs?'

[3] That adverbs of different types may show an interference effect when one of them is a question word has been reported by many authors; see Jackendoff (1972), Schlyter (1974), Koster (1978), Travis (1988), Alexiadou (1997), Laenzlinger (1998), Cinque (1999), Rizzi (2001), Ernst (2002), among others. The generalization that holds among all types of adverbs is reported in Li, Lin, and Shields (2005):

  (i)   Let X range over types of movement and [±X] indicate whether a given adverb
         (or adverb class) can undergo X-type movement, then adverb A1 prevents adverb
         A2 from undergoing X-type movement iff

         a. A1 c-commands A2, and
         b. A1 = [+X].

(8)   a. ?ta xiaoxinyiyi de shuo [ni   chang-guo shenme minge]?
            he cautiously   DE say you sing-GUO   what   folk.song
            'What folk song did he cautiously say that you sang?'

       b. *ta xiaoxinyiyi de shuo [ni   zenme chang-guo minge]?
            he cautiously   DE say you how   sing-GUO   folk.song
            *'How did he cautiously say that you sang folk songs?'
            [with *how* modifying *sing*]

Again, while (8a) may not be a natural question, it is much easier to understand with the intended meaning than (8b), which is essentially uninterpretable. Replacing the manner adverb *xiaoxinyiyi de* 'cautiously' with another, e.g., *dasheng (de)* 'loudly' or *xinbuzaiyan de* 'absent-mindedly,' produces the same result.

In sum, the object and the adverbial modifier, while both inside VP, consistently exhibit different behaviors in syntax. In the theoretical framework in which the current book is written, this difference is ultimately attributed to the intuition that the object holds a thematic relation with the verb that adjuncts do not. See Chapter 2 for a theory about thematic relations. For now, we focus on its significance for the structure of phrases.

It should also be noted that the data discussed so far, neat as they are, are not without apparent counterexamples. For instance, not every kind of adverb in the main clause creates the complement–adjunct asymmetry seen in (8). The examples below use *gangcai* 'a short moment ago' and *daochu* 'everywhere' to illustrate one such "counterexample."

(9)   a. ta gangcai/daochu   shuo [ni   chang-guo shenme minge]?
            he just.now/everywhere say   you sing-GUO   what   folk.song
            'What folk song(s) did he say just now/everywhere that you sang?'

       b. ta gangcai/daochu   shuo [ni   zenme chang-guo minge]?
            he just.now/everywhere say   you how   sing-GUO   folk.song
            'How did he say just now/everywhere that you sang folk songs?'
            [with *how* modifying *sing*]

But these sentences do not falsify the asymmetry established with (8). For one thing, there is no known data showing the reversed pattern. That is, there are no examples comparable to (8) and (9) except that the sentence questioning the embedded object is bad whereas the one questioning the adverbial modifier is good. This rules out the possibility that the asymmetry in (8) is random. Also, there is independent evidence from English and other languages that the difference between (8) and (9) is largely predictable once adverbs are more finely classified. See Cinque (1999)

Critically, and unlike what has been proposed in the literature, what turns A1 into a blocker in this case is not that A1 also needs to undergo X-type movement, but that A1 has the potential for X-type movement.

for various subclasses of adverbs. For theories on how different adverb classes interact with one another, see Ernst (2002) and Li, Lin, and Shields (2005), as well as note 3.

3.2   Postverbal constituents

In this section, we take a close look at three types of constituents occurring after the verb – double objects, V-*de* (cf. 2.2.3 in Chapter 2), and Frequency/Duration Phrases – and examine their implications for the syntactic structure of language.

3.2.1   *Double objects and the structure of VP*

Certain verbs allow or require two objects. Throughout the recent history of syntax, double-object constructions have always posed a problem for constituency:

(10) a. ta di-gei   gege   yi-hu jiu.
          he pass-give brother one-CL wine
          'He passed his brother a jug of wine.'

      b. ?ta di-gei   gege   yi-hu jiu,   jiejie yi-pan cai.
           he   pass-give brother one-CL wine sister one-CL dish
           'He passed his brother a jug of wine and his sister a dish.'

      c. *ta di-gei   de shi gege   yi-hu jiu.
           he pass-give DE be   brother one-CL wine
           *'What he passed was his brother a jug of wine.'

While (10b) may sound somewhat strange out of the context, it is not difficult to find a colloquial context where it is perfectly acceptable. Example (10c), however, remains bad regardless of the context. The same pattern, though sharper, is also found in English, as seen in the translations of (10). The problem with such data is the apparent contradiction that different constituency tests create. The conjunctive construction, shown in (10b), is generally believed to require each conjunct to be a constituent. Therefore, it must be concluded that the two NP objects of the compound *di-gei* 'pass-give' form a constituent of some sort. Meanwhile, the pseudo-cleft construction in (10c) is also a well-established constituency test, with whatever is after the copula *shi* 'be' being a phrase. Then why does one test say *gege yi-hu jiu* is a constituent while the other says it isn't? Different solutions have been proposed, most of which are based on Larson's (1988) work.[4] In this

---

[4] See Pesetsky (1995) for a different approach based on a double structure for any given sentence.

book, we adopt a variant of Larson's theory, articulated in Chomsky (1995), which meshes well with our analysis of Chinese in other chapters of the book.

Recall from Chapter 2 that the Agent theta-role is the direct result of syntax, not of the lexical verb per se, because it represents the cause that is external to the event the verb describes. Given the universally accepted belief that all and only the theta-roles of the verb are assigned to arguments inside VP, it follows that there is a component, separate from VP, which is responsible for introducing the Agent argument. In Chomsky (1995), the Agent-introducing job is attributed to v, a soundless verbal head which is somewhat "less lexical" than V (cf. Chapter 1). If VP is taken to be the structural complement of v, then, the X'-theory applied to v and V yields (11):

(11)

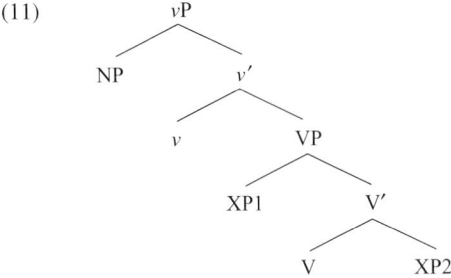

From the semantico–syntactic perspective, (11) is the minimal "complete functional complex" (CFC; cf. Chomsky 1986b) because it is the smallest structure in which all the external and internal participants of the given event are represented.

As an immediate consequence of adopting (11), we are provided with a solution to the dilemma in (10). Let NP be the subject and XP1 and XP2 be the two objects. For some cross-linguistic reason which we will gloss over for now, the lexical V clearly must move to v in order to yield the subject-verb-object1-object2 sequence in both Chinese and English. In the case of (10a), the structure after V-to-v movement is (12), with the generic XP objects replaced by NPs:

(12)

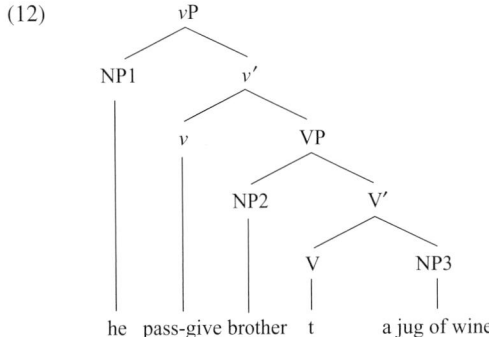

In the tree, *t* stands for the "trace" that marks the original position of a moved constituent. When the conjunctive construction in (10b) appears to take NP2 (i.e., *gege* 'brother') and NP3 (*yi-hu jiu* 'a jug of wine') as conjuncts, it really takes the whole VP. Since the V position is now a phonetically null trace, NP2 and NP3 are the only constituents that can be heard. As for (10c), recall that the CFC is not VP but *v*P. It is possible then that the pseudo-cleft construction, when targeting phrases containing thematic arguments, must always apply to a CFC and never part of it. This differs from the conjunctive construction, which is more flexible on what qualifies as a conjunct (conjuncts are in bold face; the conjunctive *he* 'and' may alternate with a pause):

(13)   ta de **qinqi**   (he) **pengyou** dou lai-le.
        he DE relative and friend   all   come-LE
        'His relatives and friends all came.'

If the conjunctive construction can link two nominal constituents smaller than a full NP in (13), it is no surprise that part of a CFC in (10b) may serve as a conjunct as well. Also note that in (11)–(12), one of the objects is in fact in the Spec position of VP. Certain consequences of this configuration will become clear shortly.

3.2.2   *V*-de

Other than objects, two phrasal constituents may also occur postverbally, both of which are characterized by a morpheme *de* suffixed to the verb. Consider first the resultative:[5]

(14)   a. ta zou-de   qichaunxuxu.
          he walk-DE breathe.heavily
          'He walked so fast that he breathed heavily.'

       b. ta qi-de   wo bu xiang xie   xin   le.
          he annoy-DE me not want   write letter SFP
          'He annoyed me so much that I didn't want to write the letter.'

Descriptively, the semantically obscure *de* introduces a clause that describes the result of the event denoted by V. (14a) is an example with V being intransitive. Given the theta-criterion, we take the subject of *qichaunxuxu* 'breathe heavily' to be Pro (cf. Chapter 2, Section 2.1.3):

(15)   he walk-DE [s Pro breathe heavily]

---

[5] The analysis in this subsection is an extension of Y. Li (1995) and Ting and Li (1997). Also see Huang (1988c) for arguments that the post-*de* constituent is structurally a clausal complement, and Cheng and Huang (1994) for related discussion.

When V is transitive as in (14b), the NP after it (i.e., *wo* 'me') is interpreted as both the object of V and the subject of the result clause. But in syntax, this NP can only serve either as the object of *qi* 'annoy' or as the subject of *bu xiang xie xin* 'not want to write the letter' but not as both – otherwise the NP would get two theta-roles from different sources and violate the theta-criterion. There is evidence that this NP is the object of *qi*.

The interjection *ya* can be inserted between a verb and its clausal object, but never between the verb and the postverbal NP object. In each example below, the object clause is between brackets. Pro is again used in the absence of an overt subject.

(16)   a. ta gaosu pengyou ya, [$_S$ Pro qu touben   qinqi].
          he tell   friend   YA   go seek.refuge.with relative
          'He told his friend, um, to go to the relatives for shelter.'

        b. *ta gaosu ya, pengyou [$_S$ Pro qu touben   qinqi].
            he tell   YA   friend   go seek.refuge.with relative
            *'He told, um, his friend to go to the relatives for shelter.'

        c. ta shuo ya, [$_S$ pengyou qu touben   qinqi   le].
           he say   YA   friend   go seek.refuge.with relative SFP
           'He said, um, that his friend went to the relatives for shelter.'

The unacceptability of (16b) is the result of inserting *ya* in front of the NP object. In contrast, the overt NP *pengyou* 'friend' after *ya* in (16c) is the subject of the embedded clause, making *ya*-insertion possible.

Applying *ya*-insertion to the resultative (14b) yields the following contrast:

(17)   a. ta qi-de   wo ya, bu xiang xie   xin   le.
          he annoy-DE me YA not want write letter SFP
          'He annoyed me so much, um, that I didn't want to write the letter.'

        b. #ta qi-de   ya, wo bu xiang xie   xin   le.
            he annoy-DE YA   me not want write letter SFP
            = '#He was so annoyed that I didn't want to write the letter.'
            ≠ (17a).

Example (17a) is directly comparable to (16a), with *ya* between the postverbal NP and what we believe to be an embedded clause expressing the result. When *ya* occurs between the verb *qi* and the NP *wo*, however, the sentence still sounds grammatical but has the pragmatically strange interpretation, marked "#," that he was so annoyed that I didn't want to write the letter. In other words, the insertion of *ya* forces *wo* to be understood as the subject of the embedded clause because, with *ya* in between, this NP cannot be the object of *qi*. Consequently, the verb *qi* is forced to take an intransitive reading. Crucially, (17a) does not have this strange interpretation, suggesting that *qi* in it is used transitively and that *wo* is indeed the object of *qi*. Since the *ya*-less (14b) has the same basic semantics as (17a) but not as (17b), we conclude that the verb *qi* is also a transitive with *wo* as its object. The structure of (14b) is thus (18):

(18)   he annoy-DE me [ₛ Pro not want write letter]

The next question is where exactly the result S is seated in the *v*P-VP configuration in (12). Recall from Chapter 2, definition (28), that a complement does not create any island effect but an adjunct does. It follows that the precise location of S may be tested: if movement out of it is good, S is in the complement position; otherwise, it must be in some kind of adjunct position. The examples below are designed for this test. Example (19a) involves the topicalization of the NP object inside the result S; in (19b), the same NP participates in relativization, a process which, in Chinese, moves the NP to the edge of the relative clause (see Chapter 6 for details), leaving a trace at the original site:

(19) a. na-feng xin,   ta   qi-de   wo [ₛ bu xiang xie   t le].
          that-CL letter he   annoy-DE me   not want write   SFP
          Lit: 'That letter, he annoyed me so much that I didn't want to write.'

      b. [ta qi-de   wo [ₛ bu xiang xie   t]] de na-feng xin.
          he annoy-DE me   not want write   DE that-CL letter
          Lit: 'The letter that he annoyed me so much that I didn't want to write.'

Other than being a little too long, these sentences show no deterioration in acceptability when compared with (14b). Thus, it is confirmed that the result S is indeed in the complement position. Putting aside certain details to which we will return later, the structure below represents the *v*P in (14b):

(20)

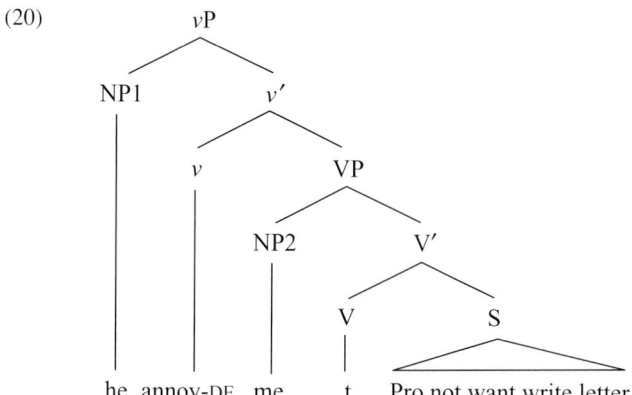

With a careful design, the same CED test may be applied to the manner V-*de* as well. The examples in (21) illustrate the construction, while those in (22) involve movement out of the postverbal manner phrase:

(21) a. ni   chang-de [$_Z$ tebie   haoting].
         you   sing-DE   especially pleasant.to.listen.to
         'You sing especially well.'

      b. ?ta pao-de [$_Z$ kuai-dao neng   zhuishang   tuzi].
         he   run-DE   fast-till   be.able.to catch.up.with rabbit
         'He ran fast enough to catch up with a rabbit.'

(22) a. ?na-zhi tuzi, ta pao-de [$_Z$ kuai-dao neng   zhuishang   t].
         that-CL rabbit he run-DE   fast-till be.able.to catch.up.with
         Lit: 'That rabbit, he ran fast enough to catch up with.'

      b. ?[ta pao-de [$_Z$ kuai-dao neng   zhuishang   t]] de na-zhi tuzi.
         he run-DE   fast-till be.able.to catch.up.with   DE that-CL rabbit
         Lit: 'the rabbit that he ran fast enough to catch up with'

The bracketed phrases in (21)–(22), marked Z, have the semantic function of a manner or degree modifier for the verb suffixed with *de*. Example (21b) sounds marginal because Z itself contains an embedded clause *neng zhuishang tuzi* 'Pro can catch up with a rabbit.' Topicalization and relativization are applied to (21b) to yield the examples in (22). Other than the fact that they are both long and clumsy, these examples exhibit no detectable deterioration from (21b) in acceptability. Hence, it is concluded that even the manner phrase is in fact located in a complement position.[6]

Though both V-*de* constructions contain a complement (S in (19) and Z in (20)), there is a difference between them: only the resultative V-*de* allows the object NP of the verb to occur postverbally. Compare (14b)/(18) with the examples below:

(23) a. ta chang-de tebie   haoting.
         he sing-DE   especially good.to.listen to
         'He sang especially well.'

      b. *ta chang-de xiaoqu tebie   haoting.[7]
         he sing-DE   ditty   especially good.to.listen to
         Intended reading: 'He sang ditties especially well.'

---

[6] One question is what types of constituents that are not thematic objects may or must occur in the complement position and why. Huang (1988c, 1992) suggests, in the spirit of Larson (1988, 1991) and McConnell-Ginet (1982), that a postverbal manner phrase is a secondary predicate (whereas a preverbal manner phrase is an adjunct). A secondary predicate is property denoting, and it may combine first with the main verb and form a complex predicate (V′) before the thematic object is merged to Spec, VP.

[7] This sentence has a fully acceptable interpretation in which *de* is not manner-denoting but signals a relative clause, i.e., (23b) can mean the folk song he sang was especially nice to listen to. This is irrelevant to our current concern.

c. xiaoqu ta chang-de tebie   haoting.
   ditty he sing-DE especially good.to.listen to
   'Ditties, he sang especially well.'

d. ta chang-de tebie   haoting   de na-shou xiaoqu
   he sing-DE especially good.to.listen to DE that-CL ditty
   'the ditty that he sang especially well'

When the verb *chang* 'sing' is used transitively, the object NP *xiaoqu* 'ditty' can either be topicalized as in (23c) or undergo relativization as in (23d). But when it stays in situ, as in (23b), the sentence becomes unacceptable. Since topicalization and relativization both leave a trace in the object position (cf. (19), (22)), the contrast between the manner V-*de* and the resultative V-*de* can be summarized as follows:

(24)   A phonetically overt NP object is permitted postverbally only in the resultative V-*de* construction.

Condition (24) may be linked to another fact in Modern Chinese, namely that there is no verbal compound in which the morpheme on the left (V1) is modified by the one on the right (V2):[8]

(25)   fei-kuai, jing-zuo, sheng-chi, zhong-shi,   nu-hou, . . .
        fly-fast quiet-sit raw-eat   heavy-view   angry-shout
        very fast sit quietly eat raw   take seriously shout angrily

In all these examples, V1 modifies V2. *Fei-kuai* 'fly-fast,' for instance, means only 'fast like flying' and never 'fast flying.' This independent fact in Chinese word formation creates a conflict of requirements. On the one hand, the manner *de* must be suffixed to a verb. On the other hand, because it ultimately introduces a manner phrase, the only possible relation it holds with the verb is one of modification, a relation that prevents it from occurring after the verb morpheme. The only way to resolve the conflict is for *de* and the verb to be separate constituents structurally but pronounced as a unit. That is, V and *de* form a phonological word based on pure linear adjacency. Since they do not form a structural unit in the sense of lexical word-formation, the compounding pattern shown in (25) becomes irrelevant.

That phonological words may be formed without structural constituency is best illustrated with the following typical Kwakw'ala example, quoted from Anderson (1992: 18):

---

[8] In order to avoid irrelevant complications, we do not distinguish A from V. See Chapter 1 for their similarities and differences.

(26)   nanagə sil-ida i?gəl'wat-i əliwinuxʷa-s-is mestuwi la-x̣a   migʷat-i.
        guides-ART   expert-DEM hunter-instru-his harpoon prep-ART seal-DEM
        'An expert hunter guides the seal with his harpoon.'

In general, the functional morphemes suffixed to each lexical stem belong structurally not to their hosts but to what follows them. For instance, the demonstrative suffix *-i* following the noun *i?gəl'wat* 'expert' actually is part of the nominal phrase headed by *əliwinuxwa* 'hunter,' which in turn is followed by the
instrumental suffix *-s* and the possessive pronoun *-is* 'his' that actually are part
of the syntactic phrase *with his harpoon*. Given (26), we claim that the manner *de* forms a syntactic constituent with the subsequent AP (e.g., *tebie haoting* 'especially good to listen to' in (23a)) but suffixes to the preceding verb as
part of a phonological word. This is directly comparable with what happens in
Kwakw'ala.

The following structure illustrates the syntactic context for (23), based on the
earlier conclusion that the manner phrase is in the complement position:

(27)

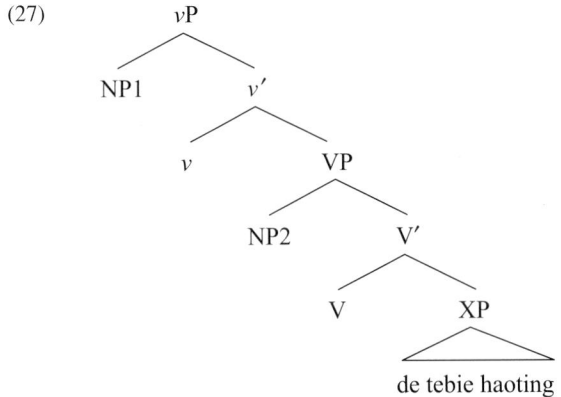

The verb *chang* 'sing' raises from V to *v*. If it is used intransitively as in (23a),
there is nothing in the position of NP2. The verb in the *v* position remains linearly
adjacent to *de*, making it possible to form the phonological word *chang-de*. If the
verb is transitive, NP2 is the object *xiaoqu* 'ditty.' Once raised to *v*, the verb is separated from *de* by NP2 and no phonological word can be formed. The "dangling"
de is unacceptable for lack of a verbal host. Of course *de* can form a phonological
word with the verb before the latter raises. But because the verb and *de* do not
form a structural constituent, they cannot raise together to *v*, which *chang* 'sing'
presumably must do. As a result, there is no good way to form the phonological
word *chang-de* while still meeting all the relevant requirements. This is why (23b)

is bad.[9] As for (23c–d), both contain a moved object, leaving the position of NP2 occupied by a trace. As traces are phonetically empty, they do not break the superficial adjacency between the verb and *de*, leaving both examples well-formed.[10]

The manner *de* forms a contrast with the resultative *de*. Along the same line of reasoning, if there is any semantic relation between V and the resultative-introducing *de*, it must be comparable to the one between the two verbal morphemes in the resultative compound such as *chang-lei* 'sing-tired' (cf. Section 2.1.2). But resultative compounds are highly productive in Chinese. It follows that V-*de* can be formed with the same lexical compounding rule that is responsible for the resultative compounds. In turn, this means that *qi-de* 'annoy-DE' in (14b), for

---

[9] The example below, illustrating post-subject contrastive topicalization (or focalization), seems relevant to the proposed theory:

(i)   ta xiaoqu chang-de hen   haoting.
       he ditty   sing-DE   very well
       'He sang folk songs well.'

On the one hand, since the object NP *xiaoqu* 'ditty' precedes the verb, (i) may be part of the pattern seen in (23c–d), which are accounted for below. On the other hand, however, the fact that this NP object follows the subject might seem to suggest that the verb does not have to raise to *v* after all. Suppose the verb stays in V and forms the phonological word with *de*. Then (i) can be generated by (27) right away, with the object between the subject and the verb. However, there is evidence that the preverbal object in (i) is in fact outside of VP rather than staying in the NP2 position in (27).

(ii)   ta xiaoqu mei-you chang-guo.
        he ditty   not-have sing-GUO
        'Folk songs, he hasn't sung.'

(iii)   *ta mei-you xiaoqu chang-guo.
         he not-have ditty   sing-GUO

Aspect words such as *you* 'have' (as well as negation) are known to be outside VP (and indeed *v*P, as we will see below). The contrast between (ii) and (iii) indicates that the post-subject topic/focus has been moved out of VP to a much higher position. In other words, (i) should pattern with the examples in (23c–d) where the object has moved away.

[10] The English data below are taken to indicate that a trace blocks phonological word formation:

(i)   I want to win.
(ii)   I wanna win.
(iii)   I want Bill to win the prize.
(iv)   *Who do you wanna win the prize?

In (iv), the trace of *who* should be between *want* and *to*. The fact that *wanna* cannot be formed, therefore, follows from the trace blocking the contraction of the two otherwise adjacent morphemes. However, there is no evidence that traces interfere with phonological word-formation cross-linguistically. So (i)–(iv) are not considered necessary counterexamples to the analysis proposed with the Chinese manner V-*de*.

instance, may enter syntax as a single word. All we need to assume is that *de* takes a clausal complement in itself, so merging the argument structure of *qi* 'annoy' with that of *de* generates a complex verb that takes a clausal complement in addition to the arguments of *qi*. See Chapter 2 for how the argument structures are treated in compounding. Since V-*de* is a single verb from the perspective of syntax, it starts in the V position and raises to *v* as a unit, crossing the object NP2 in the process:

(28)

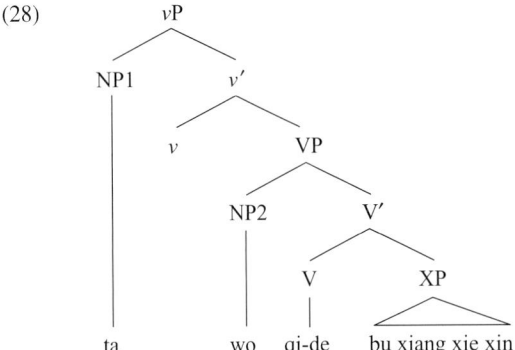

3.2.3   *Frequency/Duration Phrases (FP/DrP)*

Another type of postverbal phrase describes the frequency or duration of an event:

(29)   ta   chang-le wu   ci   / liang-ge zhongtou.
       he   sing-LE   five time / two-CL   hour
       'He sang five times/for two hours.'

In this section, we try to determine where the Frequency and Duration Phrases (FP/DrP) are located in VP and how they interact with other postverbal components.

3.2.3.1   FP/DrP as adjuncts to V′

The *v*P-VP structure in (11) conforms to a general perception about language: that verbs take at most two objects, not three or six. Inside VP, there are only two positions for arguments, the specifier and the complement. If (11) accurately describes the verbal structure available to syntactic computation, it limits the maximal number of objects any verb can take. This property of (11), when combined with the conclusion in 3.2.2 that the postverbal phrase in V-*de* occupies the complement position, makes a prediction: that V-*de* doesn't occur with two objects (Ting and Li 1997). The logic is simple: with the postverbal phrase as the complement, there is only one position left inside VP, the Spec. No more than one object can be accommodated in this one remaining position. The prediction is borne out:

(30) a. wo gei-le   ta   henduo liwu.
          I   give-LE him many gift
          'I gave him many gifts.'

      b. *wo gei-de   ta   liwu duicheng-le shan.
          I   give-DE him gift pile.into-LE hill
          Intended reading: 'I gave him so many gifts that they piled up like a hill.'

(31) a. ta gaosu-le renmen zhege xiaoxi.
          he tell-LE people this   news
          'He told people this news.'

      b. *ta gaosu-de renmen zhege xiaoxi jiayuhuxiao.
          he tell-DE   people this   news be.known.by.everyone
          Intended reading: 'He told people this news so often that it was known
          to everyone.'

There is nothing semantically wrong or pragmatically implausible about the (b) examples. Still, with two NP objects and one result clause all competing for only two syntactic positions, their unacceptability is expected.

Now consider the examples below, each with an optional and legitimate FP:

(32) a. wo shang-guo ta   (liang ci) jinyinzhubao.
          I   award-GUO him two time money.jewelry
          'I awarded him money and jewelry (twice).'

      b. ta gaosu-guo wo (haoji ci) tamen bu gai   jin   cheng.
          he tell-GUO   me several time they not should enter city
          'He told me (several times) that they shouldn't go into the city.'

In the presence of two objects in each sentence, we must conclude that the FP is an adjunct and thus does not compete with the objects, unlike the result clause in the V-*de* construction. This is illustrated in (33):

(33)

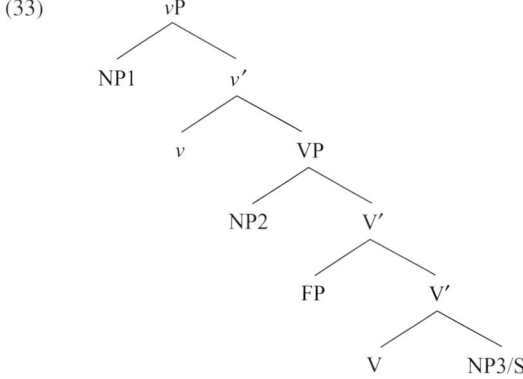

Raising V to *v* yields the word order in which there are two postverbal objects with the FP between them.

Occasionally, the FP may appear after the second object, a linear arrangement that (33) is unable to generate:

(34)   wo shang-gei ta   jinyinzhubao   yijing   liang ci   le.
        I   award-give him money.jewelry already two   time SFP
        'I already awarded him money and jewelry twice.'

But there is evidence that (34) may have a different structure from (32a). Note the adverbial *yijing* 'already' immediately before the FP. This same adverbial can never precede the FP when it comes between the two objects, regardless of the specific form of the double-object verb:

(35)   a. *wo shang-guo ta   yijing   liang ci   jinyinzhubao.
            I   award-GUO him already two   time money.jewelry
            Intended reading: 'I already awarded him money and jewelry twice.'
        b. *wo shang-gei ta   yijing   liang ci   jinyinzhubao le.
            I   award-give him already two   time money.jewelry SFP
            Intended reading: same as (34).

One possibility investigated by A. Li (1987) is that the FP in (34) is actually the predicate of a sentence whose subject is the whole clause in front of *yijing* 'already,' which modifies the predicate FP. In any case, (34) needs to be analyzed differently from (32a) and therefore offers no obvious counterargument against treating the latter example with the tree in (33).

Example (33) also makes it easy to accommodate transitive verbs with only one object. The examples below illustrate the alternative word order between the NP object and FP:[11]

(36)   a. wo da-guo   liang ci   qifu   haizi de huaidan.
            I   beat-GUO two   time bully child DE bad.guy
            'I twice beat bad guys who bullied children.'
        b. ta da-guo   neixie huaidan liang ci.
            he beat-GUO those   bad.guy two   time
            'He beat those bad guys twice.'

The first example may be directly represented as (33) minus NP2. The raising of the verb *da* 'beat' from V to *v* yields the actual word order. Example (36b) is formed with the object NP in the Spec of VP plus, again, V-to-*v* movement. It is

---

[11] Apparently, native speakers differ in whether to accept a post-FP NP with a demonstrative pronoun in it. On the variations and their theoretical consequences, see C.-C. Tang (1990), Kung (1993), Huang (1994c), Lin (1994), and Soh (1998).

not yet clear whether this NP originates as the Spec or moves into place from the complement position.[12] Either way, the account for the word order variation in (36) remains intact.[13]

The V′-adjunction analysis of FP can be directly carried over to the postverbal DrP:

(37) a. ta yilian   jiao-le   wo shi tian Henan hua.
         he in.a.row teach-LE me ten day Henan dialect
         'He taught me the dialect of Henan for ten days in a row.'

      b. wo mai-guo yi   nian yu.
         I   sell-GUO one year fish
         'I sold fish for a year.'

If these examples are compared with (32a) and (34a), respectively, it is rather straightforward to see that adjoining the DrPs *shi-tian* 'ten days' and *yi-nian* 'a year' to V′ yields the correct word order.

---

[12] Baker (1988) postulates the Uniformity of Theta Assignment Hypothesis (UTAH), which associates each theta-role with a constant structural position. In this view, if the NP *bad guys* holds the same theta-relation with *beat* in both examples, then they should originate in the same position, presumably as the complement of V (cf. Soh 1998). If they originated in the Spec, downward movement from the specifier to the complement position would be necessary to derive (36a). This is not allowed as movement always targets c-commanding positions (cf. Chapter 2). On the other hand, Y. Li (2005) discusses various problems with the UTAH and its stipulated roles in syntax. Also see Borer (2005) for arguments against the UTAH as well as our own discussion below on the interactions between FP/DrP and the definiteness of the object.

[13] It should be noted that, abstracting away from details, (36b) might also be analyzed on a par with (34), with the sentence-final FP serving as the predicate of a clausal subject. The structural ambiguity results from the absence of the second object which, necessarily in the complement position of V, would serve as the reference point for determining the nature of FP. There is still reason, however, to continue treating the FP in the specific example in (36b) as an adjunct rather than a predicate. When a bare FP occurs at the end of a double-object clause, it acquires a contrastive reading:

(i)   wo shang-gei ta   jinyinzhubao   liang ci.
       I   award-give him money.jewelry two   time
       'I awarded him money and jewelry twice (and other things once).'

But no such contrastive interpretation is required of (36b). Since the two objects in (i) force the FP to be a predicate, there must be some difference between (i) and (36b). Why the predicative use of FP in (i) is associated with the contrastive reading is still unknown, but given the contrast, treating the sentence-final FP in (36b) as the V′-adjoined adverbial at least offers a structural base for distinguishing the two sentences.

In addition to accounting for the linear locations of FP/DrP, the structure in (33) also provides a means to accommodate the following fact:

(38) a. ta ma-le   san   ci   ren.
         he scold-LE three time person
         'He scolded people three times.'

      b. zhe-ge laoshi jiao-guo   shi nian xuesheng.
         this-CL teacher teach-GUO ten year student
         'This teacher taught students for ten years.'

(39) a. *ta ma-le   ren   san   ci.
         he scold-LE people three time

      b. *zhe-ge laoshi jiao-guo   xuesheng shi nian.
         this-CL teacher teach-GUO student ten year

(40) a. ta ma-le   na-ge   ren   san   ci.
         he scold-LE that-CL people three time
         'He scolded that person three times.'

      b. zhe-ge laoshi jiao-guo   na   jige xuesheng shi nian.
         this-CL teacher teach-GUO that few student ten year
         'This teacher taught those few students for ten years.'

In general, bare NP objects must occur after the FP/DrP adjunct while definite NPs are permitted before it.

A remarkable property of the bare NPs in (38)–(39) is that, unlike their definite counterparts in (40), they do not refer to individuals.[14] Anticipating extensive discussions of the syntax and semantics of nominal phrases in Chapter 8, we consider these bare NPs non-referential and propose (41) as a hypothesis for Chinese and, perhaps, for other languages too:

(41)   A non-referential constituent which bears a theta-relation with a head H should be combined with H to form the smallest possible constituent.

In the construction of VP, the smallest possible constituent is the (smallest) V′. This explains why the non-referential bare NPs must come after the FP/DrP (cf. (38)) but not before (cf. (39)) – only the former word order reflects the smallest V′ consisting of the V and the bare NP; the latter would place the bare NP in the Spec, directly under VP, a much larger constituent than V′. Definite NPs, on the other hand, are referential and thus are not subject to (41). This explains the grammaticality of (40).

---

[14] For a brief summary of the thoughts on bare NPs, see Longobardi (2001) and the references therein.

As it is formulated, (41) also allows the examples below:

(42) a. ta gei-guo   ren   henduo ci   guizhong de liwu.
          he give-GUO person many   time expensive DE gift
          'He gave people expensive gifts many times.'

      b. zhe-ge laoshi   jiao-guo   xuesheng shi-nian wuli.
          this-CL teacher teach-GUO student   ten-year physics
          'This teacher taught students physics for ten years.'

In these sentences, the bare NPs (*ren* 'person' and *xuesheng* 'student') indeed occur before FP/DrP and, given the structure in (33), are placed in the Spec of VP rather than inside V′. However, assuming that theta-relations are intrinsically ranked so that Recipient is more prominent in the hierarchy than Theme (cf. Chapter 2 and Y. Li 2005), the VP structure conforming to the thematic hierarchy must be (43):

(43)

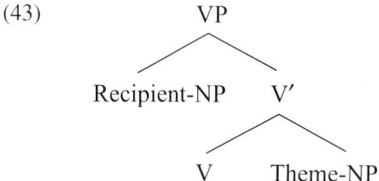

Given (43), the smallest possible constituent containing V and the Recipient bare NP *is* VP. This contrasts with the earlier cases in which V is a simple transitive verb. As both the complement and Spec positions are available, V′ becomes the only constituent satisfying (41).

3.2.3.2 A syntax–semantics mismatch

For all the similarities between FP and DrP, there is an intriguing difference: that *de* may be optionally added between only DrP and the subsequent NP object without semantic change. This section examines two possible analyses of this phenomenon, starting with the basic fact:

(44) a. ta yilian   jiao-le   wo shi-tian de Henan hua.
          he in.a.row teach-LE me ten-day DE Henan dialect
          'He taught me the dialect of Henan for ten days in a row.'

      b. wo mai-guo yi-nian   de yu.
          I   sell-GUO one-year DE fish
          'I sold fish for a year.'

Native speakers' intuitions are that with *de*, which characteristically introduces a modifier to the succeeding head (cf. Section 1.2.2), DrP and the NP form some kind of constituent, even though DrP is still interpreted as measuring the temporal length of the event described by the verb. How is this syntax–semantics mismatch explained?

One possibility, proposed in Huang (1997, 2005), is to hypothesize the existence of a phonetically empty verb DO, which in turn takes a nominalized clause (e.g., a gerundive clause). Example (44b), for instance, may in fact have the following structure (irrelevant details are put aside):

(45)

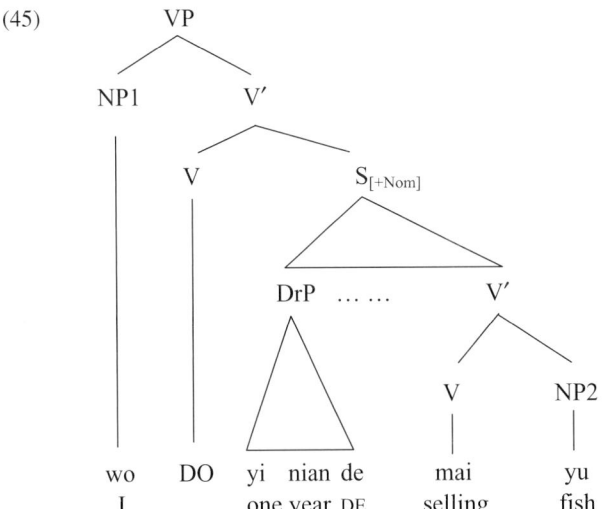

wo	DO	yi nian de	mai	yu
I		one year DE	selling	fish

Moving *mai* 'selling' to the matrix verb DO, a type of movement we have seen many times by now, will yield the actual word order in (44b) because the trace of *mai* has no phonetic content. With (45), the syntax–semantics mismatch in (44) is no longer a real problem as DrP indeed modifies the verb *mai* 'sell,' both semantically and structurally. The perception that DrP and NP are both part of the same constituent is also correct, with the gerundive clause properly containing both of them plus the trace of the raised verb.

Huang further shows that the postulation of movement out of a nominalized VP readily extends to an account of mismatches of the following sorts:

(46) a. tamen ge- tamen-de -xin, women fu- women-de -gu.
          they   DE- their   -xin we   fu- our   -gu
          'They carried out their [project of] innovation, but we went
          on with our restoration of ancient ways.'

      b. ta-de laoshi   dang-de hao.
          he-DE teacher do-DE   well
          'He serves well as a teacher.'

In (46a), the first item of the sequence *ge-xin* meaning 'to innovate' moves out of a phrase following the possessor 'their'; and the first item of the sequence *fu-gu* meaning 'to return to the old' moves out of its original position following 'our.' As indicated in the translations, the possessives are understood as relating to the action denoted by *ge-xin* and *fu-gu*, not as possessives of *-xin* 'new,' and *-gu* 'old.' In (46b), *ta-de laoshi* does not denote 'his teacher,' but is understood as 'his service as a teacher,' being a result of the verb *dang* having moved out of the domain *ta-de dang laoshi* 'his serving-as teacher.' The possessives are, in other words, "fake possessives" of the noun that immediately follows them. (For more details and arguments, see Huang 2005.)

Another possible approach toward understanding the syntax–semantics mismatch in (44) is to follow Dowty's (1991) theory of Incremental Theme. Consider these examples:

(47)   a. chi pingguo
           eat apple
           'eat apples'

       b. chi yi-ge   pingguo
           eat one-CL   apple
           'eat an apple'

       c. chi yi   kuang pingguo
           eat one basket apple
           'eat a basket of apples'

Dowty notes that in examples like (47b), the apple in fact measures the progress of the event of apple-eating – if half of the apple is gone, the event is also half accomplished; when the whole apple disappears, the event is completed. In other words, *an apple* sets boundaries for the beginning and end of the event because the apple has a physical boundary in itself; or in Tenny's (1994) terms, this object *delimits* the event. In contrast, (47a) does not have such a property because *pingguo* 'apple' is (or at least can be) generic and possibly plural in meaning and therefore provides no intrinsic beginning and end for apple-eating. In principle, apple-eating may last indefinitely as long as one has the stomach and there is an ample supply of apples. To describe this semantic property, Dowty proposes that the object NP in (47b) bears the thematic relation of Incremental Theme. The same relation also holds for *a basket of apples* in (47c) which again measures the progress of apple-eating through the fullness of the basket. The gist of Incremental Theme is that *the boundaries of the object delimit the event described by the verb.*

It is clear that Incremental Theme, unlike the theta-roles such as Agent and Theme, is not solely determined by the verb. Examples (47a–c) all contain the same verb, differing only in the definiteness of the NP object. In other words, calling Incremental Theme a theta-role is a misnomer; it in fact describes a semantic phenomenon which is brought into existence by the collective work of certain syntactic components.

With this caveat in mind, let us return to (44). Note first that *mai yu* 'sell fish' in itself lacks intrinsic boundaries for the event just as (47a) does. Modifying the verb with the DrP *yi-nian* 'a year' (cf. (37b)) is a straightforward way to delimit the event of fish-selling. This is accomplished structurally by adjoining DrP to V′ and semantically by restricting the event to the temporal boundaries set by DrP. The object NP *yu* 'fish' contains no constituent to delimit any boundary and no Incremental Theme is created. Now suppose that DrP is coerced into the object NP via the use of *de*. This creates no structural problem because *yi-nian de yu* 'a year's fish' is syntactically identical to the well-formed NP *yi-nian de diaocha guocheng* 'a year's investigative process.' At the semantic level, *yi-nian de yu* is odd and most likely uninterpretable by itself. But the DrP inside the object NP may trigger the mechanism of Incremental Theme into action, transferring the boundaries defined by the DrP to the whole event of fish-selling as Dowty has observed. This analysis explains why (44b), for instance, is semantically identical to (37b) regardless of *de*. In both constructions, DrP delimits the whole event. Without *de*, this is done directly through modification to V; with *de*, the delimitation happens indirectly via Incremental Theme. It also follows that NPs such as *yi-nian de yu* 'a year's fish' cannot be used as anything other than the object: for independent reasons, only the Theme argument may display the "incremental," event-delimiting quality (Tenny 1994).

This alternative account of (44) does not automatically require that the examples in (46) be reanalyzed differently from a structure like (45). After all, while English has nothing like (44), it does exhibit a productive (46)-style syntax–semantics mismatch in, say, *You teach your economics and I'll hunt my coyotes. Let's see who'll get rich faster.* The default interpretation of such a sentence is that you do your economics teaching and I do my coyote hunting, not that economics is yours and the coyotes to be hunted are mine. The fact that the two types of mismatches do not necessarily co-occur makes it logically possible to treat them differently.

There are unresolved issues with both the gerundive-based account and the one utilizing the Incremental Theme, the most conspicuous being why the phenomenon in (44) isn't found in, say, English. At this moment, we can only point at a possible direction of investigation: the Chinese–English contrast at issue may be correlated to another one, namely that Chinese nouns depend on classifiers for quantitative specification whereas English nouns don't. If the use of classifiers means a noun contains no information about the unit of quantity measurement, it may become more tolerant for combining with quantitative constituents (of which DrP is one), provided that each constituent eventually receives full interpretation (cf. Chapter 2) through legitimate linguistic mechanisms such as Incremental Theme. Similarly, on the account assuming verb-movement out of nominalized domains, the high degree of analyticity in Chinese provides for a route for *syntactic* V movement that results in apparent syntax–semantics mismatches. In particular, as Hale and Keyser (1993) have argued, many unergative, action verbs in English are derived via denominalization in the lexicon. It is not unnatural that the same process can occur in Chinese, but in more analytic fashion in the domain of syntax.

3.3   Preverbal constituents

Given the proposal that FP/DrP, when used as adverbials, adjoin to the left of V′, it is plausible that other types of adverbial phrases may adjoin to the left of v'. This immediately accounts for preverbal PP and ADV modifiers:

(48) a. ta cong Xi'an hui-lai-le.
        he from Xi'an come-back-LE
        'He came back from Xi'an.'

      b. wo xiaoxinyiyi de xie-le   yi-feng xin.
        I   cautious   DE write-LE one-CL letter
        'I cautiously wrote a letter.'

Adjoined to v', the adverbial is to the left of v, to which the lexical verb raises to generate the verb-object word order. The only detail to be added is that multiple adverbials are allowed preverbally while postverbal FP and DrP exclude each other:

(49) a. ta cong Xi'an xiaoxinyiyi de hui-lai-le.
        he from Xi'an cautious   DE come-back-LE
        'He cautiously came back from Xi'an.'

      b. *wo mai-guo liang ci   yi nian yu.
        I   sell-GUO two   time one year fish
        Intended reading: 'I sold fish for a year twice.'

An explanation for (49) may exist somewhere between two possibilities. First, if (49b) is taken to mean that each XP may have no more than one adjunction to X′, either in the nature of the syntactic structure (see Kayne 1994 for a theory in this direction) or due to semantic reasons, then multiple preverbal adjuncts should be equated to multiple functional phrases (cf. Chapter 1), as is indeed proposed in Cinque (1999). In such a theory, (49a) is the result of having the PP and AP adjuncts each adjoin to a different functional X′ at least as "high" as v' while V only raises up to v. The word order follows automatically, as the reader can verify. Alternatively, it may be the case that lexical categories allow only one adjunction in each phrase but functional categories, including v, allow an indefinite number of adjunctions.[15]

[15] A version of this idea is already proposed to handle multiple subjects in East Asian languages like Japanese, first in Fukui and Speas (1986) in Government-Binding Theory and later in Ura (1996) in the framework of Chomsky's (1995) Minimalist Program.

A few more types of constituents occur before the verb and after the subject, including the aspectual auxiliaries *you* (perfective as in *mei-you*) and *zai* (progressive) and modals such as *neng* 'can' and *yinggai* 'should.' The traditional wisdom is that these are all part of the predicate. More recent research confirms this insight, but distinguishes the traditional sense of predicate from the structurally defined VP. In fact, there are reasons to believe that some of these constituents are outside VP. Nonetheless, we will examine certain syntactic details of these elements in the rest of this chapter because, after all, they are intrinsically associated with the verb.

3.3.1   Aspectual phrase

From the cross-linguistic perspective, it is obvious that human languages distinguish *tense* (T) from *aspect* (Asp). Briefly, tense marks the relation between the time of a described event and the time at which the description is given, whereas aspect signals the speaker's viewpoint on the progress of the event (cf. Smith 1991): the perfective aspect focuses (typically) on the final state of the event and the progressive aspect on an interval somewhere between the event's beginning and end. This section examines the aspectual morphemes in Chinese. Given the fact that most languages have morphemes for tense, we also assume that tense exists in Chinese, though no part of this book hinges on this assumption. For some possible motivations for syntactically represented tense in Chinese, see A. Li (1985, 1990) and Simpson and Wu (2002). For alternative views see Lin (2003, 2006) and references cited.

Chinese has two systems for aspect, preverbal and suffixal, illustrated respectively in (50) and (51) with the aspectual morphemes in bold face:[16]

(50)   a. ta **zai** chang ge.
          he at   sing   song
          'He was singing.'

       b. wo mei-**you** hui   jia.
          I   not-have return home
          'I didn't go home.'

(51)   a. ta chang-**zhe** ge.
          ta sing-ZHE   song
          'He was singing.'

---

[16] The semantic properties of some of these aspectual morphemes are discussed below. The English translations of the examples are only approximate because the aspectual information in each Chinese sentence is often difficult to show precisely with a single English word. See Smith (1991) for detailed discussions and comparisons of aspectual morphemes in several languages, including Chinese and English.

b. wo hui-**le**   jia.
   I   return-LE home
   'I went home.'

c. zhe-ge ren   sha-**guo** laohu.
   this-CL person kill-GUO tiger
   'This person once killed a tiger.'

Anticipating a unified analysis of both systems to be introduced shortly, we adopt the following structure for aspect:

(52)

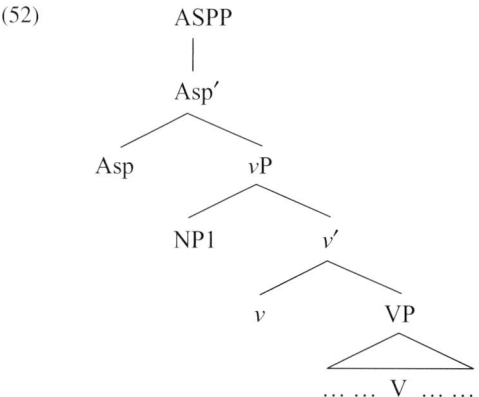

The preverbal *you* and *zai* directly fit into the Asp position, provided that NP1 eventually moves to whatever clause-initial position for the subject. The location of the suffixal *-zhe*, *-le*, and *-guo*, however, is not as straightforward.

Conceptually, it is clearly desirable that they are affiliated with Asp. If they are also generated under Asp, the fact that they are affixed to the verb could only be because the morphemes undergo a merging process which, in syntax, means moving one of them to the other. Recall from Chapter 2 that movement must be out of a complement and target a c-commanding position. The configuration in (52) meets both requirements if V raises, via *v*, to Asp. There is evidence, however, that V doesn't go out of *v*P:[17]

(53) a. ta zai dasheng chang ge.
         he at   loud   sing   song
         'He was singing loudly.'

      b. *ta dasheng zai chang ge.
          he loud   at   sing   song
          Intended reading: same as (53a).

---

[17] The argument below is based on Cheng and Li (1991), which in turn takes advantage of the insight in Pollock's (1989) comparative study of French and English.

(54) a. wo mei-you qiaoqiao de hui   jia.
         I   not-have quiet   DE return home
         'I didn't go home stealthily.'

      b. *I qiaoqiao de mei-you hui   jia.[18]
         I quiet   DE not-have return home
         Intended reading: same as (54a).

Since the modifiers *dasheng* 'loud' and *qiaoqiao de* 'quietly' occur before the verb but after Asp, they must be adjoined to v' (cf. (52)).

Now consider the linear relation between such modifiers and the aspectual suffixes:

(55) a. ta dasheng chang-zhe ge.
         he loud   sing-ZHE   song
         'He was singing loudly.'

      b. *ta chang-zhe dasheng ge.
         he sing-ZHE loud   song
         Intended reading: same as (55a).

(56) a. wo qiaoqiao de hui-le   jia.
         I   quiet   DE return-LE home
         'I went home stealthily.'

      b. *wo hui-le   qiaoqiao de jia.
         I   return-LE quiet   DE home
         Intended reading: same as (56a).

(57) a. na-ge   jiahuo chishoukongquan sha-guo laohu.
         that-CL guy   bare-handed   kill-GUO tiger
         'That guy once killed a tiger bare-handedly.'

      b. *na-ge   jiahuo sha-guo chishoukongquan laohu.
         that-CL guy   kill-GUO bare-handed   tiger
         Intended reading: same as (57a).

Descriptively, the verb-suffix cluster must occur after the v'-adjoined modifiers (cf. (a) examples) and not before ((b) examples). This is not expected if *-le*, for instance, occupies the Asp position with the verb raising out of vP to merge with it.

The solution lies in one of the oldest ideas in linguistics combined with one of the major discoveries in modern syntax. It has long been tradition to regard a verb plus its inflectional affix as a form of the verb. Take the English verb *play-s* for example. While the correct use of this inflected verb is clearly dependent on the syntactic context, *play-s* itself can be formed with a word-formation rule

---

[18] This sentence is good with the reading that I was cautious (about the trip) and therefore didn't go home, which is irrelevant to the issue here.

independently of syntax. By the same logic, the concatenation of *hui* 'return' with the perfective suffix *-le* should not rely on syntactic movement either, as long as the syntactic context that *hui-le* occurs in guarantees a match between the aspectual information of the clause and the suffix *-le*. In particular, if Asp is the syntactic node representing aspect but *hui-le* 'return-Perf' as a verb form is initially placed under V, syntax must provide a way to match the perfective suffix on the verb with whatever aspectual information is coded under Asp. This is easily accomplished given the progress of our syntactic knowledge in recent years.

A prominent assumption in recent and current syntactic theory is that there exists an abstract level of syntactic derivation, called *Logical Form* (LF), which will be the central concern of some later chapters of this book. For now, it may be described as follows. While various constituents undergo movement in syntax, some of these movements happen "prior to" the point at which the sentence is uttered. All these pre-utterance movements are overtly reflected because the moved constituents are already in their landing sites at the point of utterance. But certain constituents move after that point, at the abstract level of LF. In these cases, the movement is not heard for the simple reason that by the time of utterance, the movement has not taken place yet. Anticipating independent evidence for LF later, we suggest that *hui-le* 'return-LE' in (56a), for instance, moves from V to *v* overtly but continues to move to Asp covertly at the level of LF. Since the second step of movement is covert, *hui-le* is heard in the *v* position after the adjunct phrase *qiaoqiao-de* 'stealthily.' But because *hui-le* eventually lands in Asp, albeit covertly, the perfective *-le* does end up in Asp, thereby matching itself with the syntactic node that carries the aspectual information. It should be pointed out that the covert movement at LF is also expected to be subject to all restrictions on movement. Given (52), the landing site, Asp, c-commands the *v* position from which *hui-le* moves, and the movement is out of *v*P, the complement of ASP.[19]

---

[19] Historically, there has been a fundamentally different approach to the one presented in the text, which, in the case of the Chinese data, takes V-Asp as a result of Affix Hopping in *Phonetic Form* (PF), the component of grammar that is pronounced but does not have direct consequences on the meanings of sentences. That is, we may assume that *-le* is an affix heading the aspectual phrase. Rather than the verb raising to Asp, the affix *-le* lowers to the verb. This gives the correct word order as desired, and because this "lowering" is not syntactic but phonological, it is not subject to the constraints for syntactic movement. This is in line with a number of recent treatments of English main verb morphology, and the English–French differences (Emonds 1978, Pollock 1989, Lasnik 1999) with respect to the position of the main verb. Chinese, in this respect, behaves on a par with English, in contrast to French. But unlike English (which does raise its *be* and auxiliary *have* to T), no auxiliary raising across adverbials or negation occurs in Chinese (see Huang 1994b). A variant of this idea is for both a functional morpheme such as *-le* and the lexical verb to stay in their respective positions and to merge into a morphological complex at PF

This syntactic representation of aspect also helps us understand the contrast below:

(58) a. *ta mei-you hui-le   jia.
          he not-have return-LE home
          Intended reading: 'He didn't go home.'

      b. ta mei-you hui-guo   jia.
          he not-have return-GUO home
          'He hadn't been home.'

In (58a), the perfective preverbal *you* and the perfective suffixal *-le* cannot co-exist. This follows if both morphemes reflect the same aspectual information under Asp. Then it is natural that the same information under the same syntactic node does not get manifested twice. For the same reason, the co-existence of *you* and the experiential suffix *-guo* is possible because the two morphemes do not carry identical information (cf. Smith 1991). Needless to say, each aspectual marker has its own ASPP. When *you* and *-guo* are both present, the relevant structure prior to LF movement is (59):

(59)

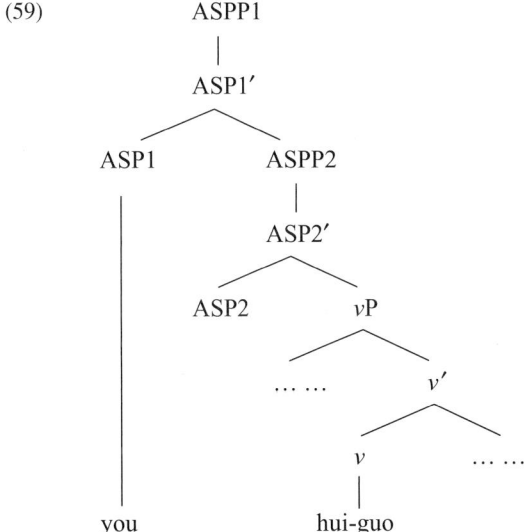

By convention, a clause contains as many ASPPs as there are identifiable aspectual markers. In the absence of any such marker, no ASPP is present in the structure.

---

via linear adjacency. Certain typological facts may be accounted for this way (Baker 2002, Y. Li 2005), with implications regarding more fundamental distinctions between adjuncts and other constituents in the X′-structure.

What remains to be answered is why the negative form of perfective aspect must choose *you* and not -*le*.[20]

3.3.2   Modals

Examples of Chinese modals are given in (60), drawn from D. Zhu (1982):

(60)   a.   keneng 'be possible,' hui 'be likely to,' keyi 'be permitted to,' yinggai 'ought to,' gai 'ought to,' . . .

       b.   gan 'dare,' ken 'be willing to,' yuanyi 'be willing to,' yao 'want to,' neng 'be able to,' nenggou 'be able to,' keyi 'be able to,' hui 'be able to,' . . .

It will become clear why we divide them into two groups and why some occur in both groups. The discussion in this section is primarily based on Lin and Tang (1995).[21]

In languages like English, modals have been traditionally placed under inflection (I), a functional head position. Though recent work (e.g., Cinque 1999) has explicitly argued that this treatment may be overly simplistic, there is still consensus that English modals belong to a functional category. Example (61) represents the (simplified) structure of the phrase headed by an English modal, using I merely as a convenient label (no ASPP is shown):

(61)

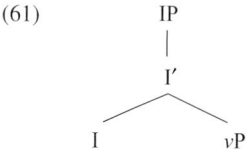

---

[20]   There are many possible reasons for this. It may be the result of a historical accident that the Mandarin dialect of Chinese acquired two separate perfective markers along different routes of linguistic change, and opted to make use of them for separating positive and negative clauses. Or there may be a deeper reason for the distinction, considering the similarity, at least on the surface, between the Chinese perfective aspect and the English tense, both represented with functional categories:

   (i)   ta de-le jiang.   → ta mei you de jiang.
   (ii)   He received an award. → He did not receive an award.

In both cases, a suffix is used on the lexical verb in the positive form while a totally different morpheme accompanies negation in a preverbal position. Still another possibility may be that negation (Neg) is a bound form whose morphological host must have certain as yet unclear properties. In the case of perfective aspect, the host must be the Asp (because *mei you kanjian ta* denotes the negation of the perfectiveness). This can be done with *you*, easily. But -*le* is too far for *bu* to attach to, with V-*le* raised to Asp only in LF, too late to support Neg.

[21]   Lin and Tang's work is in turn a further development of Huang (1988a). For earlier discussion, see T. Tang (1979).

Such an analysis of modals cannot be directly adopted for Chinese, however. At least those in (60a) have distinctive behaviors of lexical verbs.[22] Below, we examine arguments for this claim.

To begin with, while all modals in (60) may occur between the subject and the predicative VP as expected, many of those in (60a) may also occur after a full clause, especially in colloquial Chinese:

(62) a. ni   cizhi   keyi,   ta jieban   bu   xing!
          you resign be.permitted he take.over.one's.position not all.right
          'You may resign, but he can't be hired for your position!'

      b. tamen zheyang xiang bu yinggai.
          they   this.way   think   not ought.to
          'They shouldn't think this way.'

      c. zhe-ge ren   shou   fa   gai-bu-gai?
          this-CL person receive punishment should-not-should
          'Should this person receive the punishment?'

      d. rang   wo gen ni   zuodui keneng   ma?
          make me with you oppose be.possible Q
          'Is it possible to let me be against you?'

The sentence-final location of the modals in (62) is not expected if they are under I because vP comes after I, not before it. On the other hand, if these modals are in fact lexical verbs that can take a clause as a subject, the word order in (62) is exactly what is predicted. Take the first half of (62a) as an example (with V raised to v):

(63)

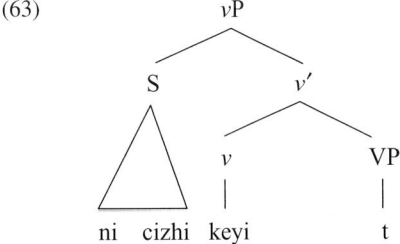

This structure is further confirmed by the parallelism between the two halves of (62a), a pattern used widely in Chinese under the condition that the two aligned constituents have the same syntactic structure. Since *xing* 'be all right' in the second half of (62a) is clearly used as the matrix verb taking a clausal subject (*ta jieban* 'that he took your job'), the modal *keyi* in the first half must be comparably constructed. The same conclusion is also corroborated by the fact that these modals can take the pronoun *zhe* 'this' as the subject that refers to the previous sentence,

---

[22] D. Zhu (1982) also lists modals under the large category of verbs.

illustrated schematically with (64) below:

(64)   a. ni   dasuan cizhi? zhe zenme keyi?
          you plan   resign this how   be.permitted
          'You plan to resign? That's not allowed!'

       b. ni   touxiang-le? zhe bu   keneng.
          you surrender-LE this not be.possible
          'You surrendered? That's impossible.'

Also common is for a modal of this group to occur sentence-initially:

(65)   a. keyi   ni qu, ye keyi   ta qu.
          be.permitted you go or be.permitted he go
          'You may go or he may go.'

       b. (ying)gai zanmen zhexie ren   de   jiang.
          ought.to we   these people receive award
          'It should be that we people get an award.'

       c. keneng   tamen yao canjia   bisai.
          be.possible they will participate.in competition
          'It's possible that they will participate in the competition.'

       d. hui-bu-hui[23]   ta xiang chuguo?
          be.likely-not-be.likely he want go.abroad
          'Is it likely that he wants to go abroad?'

Modals of the functional type in English do not allow this word order in declaratives. The word order is indeed required in *yes-no* questions, but the so-called subject–auxiliary inversion applies to modals and other auxiliaries alike. This is clearly not the case for Chinese. On the other hand, if the modals in Chinese are lexical verbs, the subsequent clause can be simply treated as the object of each modal verb, directly yielding (65).

In principle, the data in (62) and (65) plus the "default" use of the modals between the subject and the predicative VP can all be subsumed under a single structure (irrelevant details are ignored):

(66)

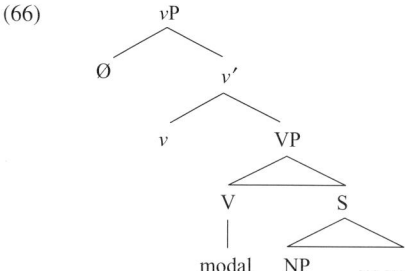

---

[23] For reasons unknown to us, *hui* must be in A-not-A form when appearing before the subject.

The modal is the lexical verb taking a clausal complement S. If no movement takes place, the modal is the first constituent from the left, yielding (65). If the whole S raises to the matrix subject position, marked "Ø," the modal becomes the last constituent one can hear and (62) results. If, on the other hand, only the subject NP of S raises to the higher subject position Ø, the modal occurs between the raised NP and the rest of S, i.e., the predicative *v*P-VP. The reason for raising a complement clause to the subject position has never been fully understood. Without getting into technicalities, we note that the three optional word order arrangements with respect to the modals in (60a) are by no means a language-specific oddity. Consider these English examples with the adjective *likely*:

(67) a. It is likely [for Shawn to go abroad].
      b. [For Shawn to go abroad] is likely.
      c. Shawn is likely [to go abroad].

The bracketed constituent is known to be a non-finite clause (cf. Chomsky 1981 and the references cited there), which stays in the complement position of *likely* in (67a), and raises to the subject position of the whole sentence in (67b). In (67c), only the subject of the non-finite clause raises, leaving the clause itself in situ. Except for the fact that English has a semantically empty pronoun *it*, called an *expletive*, to overtly fill up the subject position in the first case, (67) patterns with the Chinese examples examined so far.

In comparison, the modals in (60b) occur only between the subject and *v*P. Though this fact may classify such modals as functional words like *can* and *should* in English, we would like to highlight the fact that the modals in (60b) seem to assign a theta-role to the subject NP before them. In the framework adopted in this book, this fact has non-trivial implications. For ease of discussion, we refer to the lexical modals in (64a) as *raising modals* and the group in (64b) as *control modals*, for the reason to be made clear below.

To begin with, a control modal imposes a selective restriction on the semantics of the subject NP. A raising modal has no such restriction, accepting any subject NP that is compatible with the verb after the modal. Since the specific restrictions from the control modals vary, the examples below are meant to be illustrative but not exhaustive:

(68) Raising modals
      a. wo yinggai/keneng/keyi/hui   chang yi-shou xiaoqu.
         I   should/will.possibly/be.allowed.to/be.likely.to sing   one-CL   ditty
         'I should/will possibly/am allowed to/am likely to sing a ditty.'
      b. zhe-shou xiaoqu yinggai/keneng/keyi/hui   chang yi-dian.
         this-CL ditty should/will.possibly/be.allowed.to/be.likely.to long a-bit
         'This ditty should/will possibly/is allowed to/is likely to be a bit longer.'

(69)   Control modals
  a. wo gan/ken/neng/hui   chang yi-shou xiaoqu.
      I   dare/be.willing.to/be.able.to/be.able.to sing   one-CL   ditty
      'I dare/am willing to/am able to/am able to sing a ditty.'
  b. *zhe-shou xiaoqu gan/ken/neng/hui   chang yi-dian.
       this-CL   ditty   dare/be.willing.to/be.able.to/be.able.to long   a-bit
       *'This ditty dares/is willing to/is able to/is able to be a bit longer.'

Especially worth noting is that (68b) is acceptable with *hui* only when the modal has the probability reading; the sentence becomes bad when *hui* has the ability reading in (69b).

Intuitively, this contrast between the two groups of modals is easy to understand – a control modal has the intrinsic semantics that requires the subject to have certain qualities such as sentience and free will. In modern syntax, such restrictions on arguments are typically attributed to a thematic relation, namely that the modal assigns a theta-role to the subject. Then according to the theta-criterion, the NP subject preceding the modal in, say, (69a), must not be the actual subject of the verb *chang* 'sing' for the simple reason that otherwise, *wo* 'I' would receive two theta-roles, from the modal and *chang*, simultaneously. Put differently, *wo* could not have originated as the subject of *chang* and then raised to its sentence-initial position before the modal. In fact, there is only one basic structure for (69a):

(70) $[NP_i \text{ modal } [_X \text{ Pro}_i \text{ V} \ldots]]$

where Pro is coreferential with the NP subject of the modal. In syntax, the relation between a Pro and its c-commanding antecedent is called *control*, which is why we referred to this group of modals as control modals.

3.4   Summary

In brief, these initial chapters provide the foundation for the following ones. Chapter 1 examined the definitions of various categories, arguing for a feature-based theory that not only is capable of accommodating enough different classes of words and morphemes for syntactic analysis but also offers a way to capture certain shared properties among such classes. Chapter 2 explored the nature of theta-roles, the type of semantic relations between a verb and its arguments that form the basis for combining words into a sentence. Chapter 3, focusing on the internal structure of VP, investigates how a verb combines with phrases of various other categories, revealing different patterns among those that receive theta-roles from the verb and those that do not. Overall, we hope to have shown that sentence-formation follows rigorous patterns, the discovery of which has allowed us to understand a wide range of linguistic facts. The subsequent chapters are built on this foundation, each of them studying a particular phenomenon in Chinese syntax in great detail.

4

Passives

In Mandarin, passive sentences typically take either of the two forms illustrated in (1) and (2):

(1) Zhangsan bei Lisi da-le.
     Zhangsan BEI Lisi hit-LE
     'Zhangsan was hit by Lisi.'

(2) Zhangsan bei da-le.
     Zhangsan BEI hit-LE
     'Zhangsan was hit.'

Both forms involve the passive morpheme *bei*. In (1) *bei* is followed by an NP (the Agent) and a VP. In (2) *bei* is followed directly by the VP. In the latter case, the existence of an Agent is not expressed, but implied. We shall refer to these two forms of the passive construction as the "long passive" and the "short passive," respectively.[1]

A natural question arises as to whether these forms are to be derivationally related, and if so, how. For example, it may be natural to regard the short passive as being derived from the long passive by omission of the Agent phrase. This chapter will argue that this analysis, however intuitive it may be, is flawed. In Sections 4.1 and 4.2, we shall discuss the long and short passives in turn and argue that they involve somewhat different processes in derivation. In Section 4.3, we turn our attention to two types of "indirect" passives and argue that they should be analyzed

---

[1] There is another type of sentence with the semantics of a passive, where both the Agent argument and the passive morpheme *bei* are missing:

(i) yifu   xi-ganjing   le.
     clothes wash-clean   LE
     'The clothes have been washed clean.'

We take this type of passive to be an example of the middle construction, akin to English sentences like *The book sold well*. See Cheng and Huang (1994) for an analysis of (i) as a middle construction and arguments in its support.

on a par with "direct passives," in terms of the analyses proposed in Sections 4.1 and 4.2.

In what follows, "passive" will be used to refer to the long passive mostly, unless reference to the short passive is clear from context. This is because the long passive is the most robust form of the passive construction, exhibiting properties with which the bulk of this chapter will be concerned.

4.1   The Mandarin long passive

4.1.1   Two competing traditions

From the early days of generative linguistics, two competing lines of research have existed in the analysis of Chinese passives. One line of research assumes that they are derived as an instance of NP-movement as typical English passives are derived, according to which an underlying object moves to a surface subject position in the presence of the morpheme *bei*. The other line denies the existence of such movement, but postulates a structure of VP complementation according to which *bei* is a matrix verb taking an embedded clause whose object is deleted under identity with the matrix subject. These two approaches have existed side by side for nearly thirty years, with P. Wang (1970) being an early proponent of the movement approach and Hashimoto (1969) being the most prominent early advocate of the complementation approach. More recent adherents of the movement approach include A. Li (1985, 1990), Travis (1984), and Koopman (1984). The complementation approach has also been defended at length in more recent works such as Hashimoto (1987) and Wei (1994).

According to recent versions of the movement hypothesis, the passive morpheme *bei* has the property of *suppressing* (or *dethematizing*) the subject argument of the main verb, and *absorbing* its Accusative Case feature, which would normally be assigned to its Theme object. The Case-less Theme object then undergoes movement to the non-thematic subject position. The Agent argument is realized as part of an adjunct PP headed by the passive morpheme *bei*, assumed to be a P.

(3)   Passive as NP-movement
   a. Subject argument is suppressed.
   b. Accusative Case is absorbed.
   c. Theme object undergoes NP-movement to subject position.
   d. *bei* and the Agent NP form a PP adjunct.

Thus an active sentence like *Lisi da-le Zhangsan* 'Lisi hit Zhangsan' is turned into a passive with the structure shown in (4), where IP (Inflectional Phrase) represents the clause:

(4)

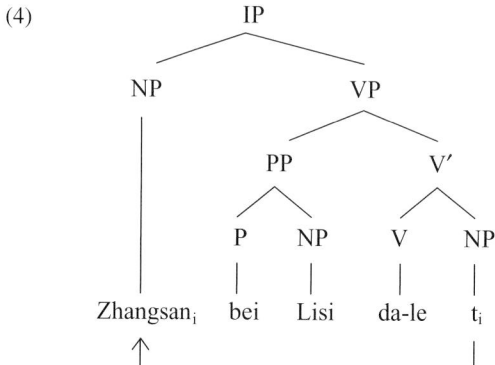

Zhangsan_i   bei   Lisi   da-le   t_i

Because passives are derived by NP-movement, it is correctly predicted that the theme subject is necessarily related to an empty category – an NP-trace coindexed with it – in the object position. The ungrammaticality of the following sentences is therefore explained in Chinese, as it is in English.[2]

(5)   a. *Zhangsan bei Lisi da-le   ta.
           Zhangsan BEI Lisi hit-LE him
           'Zhangsan was hit (*him) by Lisi.'

       b. *Zhangsan bei Lisi da-le   ziji.
           Zhangsan BEI Lisi hit-LE self
           'Zhangsan was hit (*self) by Lisi.'

       c. *Zhangsan bei Lisi da-le   Wangwu.
           Zhangsan BEI Lisi hit-LE Wangwu
           'Zhangsan was hit (*Wangwu) by Lisi.'

       d. *Zhangsan bei Lisi lai-le.   (no object at all)
           Zhangsan BEI Lisi come-LE
           *'Zhangsan was arrived by Lisi.'

The NP-movement hypothesis entails the existence of an NP-trace in the object position, from which the subject originated. Example (5d) is ungrammatical because it does not have an object position, and (5a–c) because the object

---

[2] The status of (5a–b) in relation to the analysis of passives was discussed in Huang (1982b) and A. Li (1990). As will be seen below, sentences of the sort represented by (5c–d) may be acceptable in some languages, each with a strong sense of "adversity," e.g., Zhangsan was adversely affected by Lisi's hitting Wangwu or by Lisi's arrival. Some speakers of Mandarin find (5c–d) marginally acceptable under the adversative reading.

position is filled by a distinct NP, and so the subject could not have originated there.

There are several difficulties with this NP-movement approach, however. First, this approach claims that the subject position of passives is a non-thematic position, but the following sentences suggest that the subject does not always play a pure Patient or Theme role which it inherits from the NP-trace; it may receive a thematic role of its own. This is evidenced by passive sentences containing subject-oriented adverbs like *guyi* 'deliberately, intentionally':[3]

(6)   Zhangsan guyi   bei da-le.
       Zhangsan intentionally BEI hit-LE
       'Zhangsan intentionally got hit.'

(7)   Zhangsan guyi   bei Lisi da-le.
       Zhangsan intentionally BEI Lisi hit-LE
       'Zhangsan intentionally got hit by Lisi.'

Subject-oriented adverbs impose selectional restrictions and are predicated on their subjects but not their objects. So for *guyi* only an NP denoting an Agent or Experiencer can qualify as its subject. This means that the subject of (6)–(7) cannot simply bear whatever theta-role it would bear in the object position following *da* 'hit,' i.e., Theme or Patient, but must be an Agent or Experiencer also. Under the NP-movement analysis, the subject would acquire its theta-role solely by inheriting it from the object, but being a Theme or Patient does not meet the selectional requirements of *guyi*. In other words, the occurrence of subject-oriented adverbs suggests that the subject of *bei* sentences may be base-generated and receive its theta-role in situ, instead of acquiring its subject status and theta-role through movement. In this respect, Chinese passives behave on a par with *get* passives in English, but differently from *be* passives (Lasnik and Fiengo 1974: 552f.), a difference that does not follow if both passive constructions are treated in the same way under NP-movement.

(8)   a. *The pedestrian deliberately was hit.
       b. The pedestrian deliberately got hit.

(9)   a. *Rodman intentionally was fouled by Ewing.
       b. Rodman intentionally got fouled by Ewing.

---

[3] These sentences would be most natural if *guyi* is put in focus, e.g., as part of a cleft sentence:

(i)   Zhangsan shi guyi   bei (Lisi) da-le.
       Zhangsan be intentionally BEI (Lisi) hit-LE
       'Zhangsan intentionally got hit (by Lisi).'

Second, since the *bei*-NP sequence is treated as a prepositional phrase (on a par with a *by*-phrase), it is expected to behave as a PP. But there is never any evidence that it behaves as a PP, or even as a constituent. For one thing, it cannot move (as a constituent) across a time phrase or prepose to a sentence-initial position (unlike the PP *by Bill* in the English translation):

(10) a. Zhangsan zuotian   *bei Lisi* da-le.
          Zhangsan yesterday BEI Lisi hit-LE
          (cf. John was hit by Bill yesterday.)

  b. *Zhangsan *bei Lisi* zuotian   da-le.
          Zhangsan BEI Lisi yesterday hit-LE
          (cf. John was hit yesterday by Bill.)

  c. **bei Lisi* Zhangsan zuotian   da-le.
          BEI Lisi Zhangsan yesterday hit-LE
          (cf. It was by Bill that John was hit yesterday.)

Other putative PPs are normally movable (see Chapter 1, example (42)):

(11) a. wo *gen Zhangsan* hen   chu-de-lai.
          I   with Zhangsan very get-along
          'I get along well with Zhangsan.'

  b. *gen Zhangsan* wo hen   chu-de-lai.
          with Zhangsan I   very get-along
          'I get along well with Zhangsan.'

(12) a. Zhangsan *dui Lisi* hen   keqi.
          Zhangsan to   Lisi very polite
          'Zhangsan is very polite to Lisi.'

  b. *dui Lisi* Zhangsan hen   keqi.
          to   Lisi Zhangsan very polite
          'Zhangsan is very polite to Lisi.'

(13) a. wo bai-le yi-pen hua   *zai zhuozi-shang*.
          I   put-LE one-pot flower on table-top
          'I put a pot of flowers on the table.'

  b. wo *zai zhuozi-shang* bai-le yi-pen   hua.
          I   on table-top   put-LE one-pot flower
          'I put a pot of flowers on the table.'

  c. *zai zhuozi-shang* wo bai-le yi-pen hua.
          on table-top   I   put-LE one-pot flower
          'I put a pot of flowers on the table.'

Thirdly, the following coordination test shows that the Agent NP forms a clausal constituent with the VP that follows it, to the exclusion of the preceding *bei*:[4]

(14)   (?)ta bei *Lisi ma-le   liang-sheng, Wangwu ti-le   san-xia.*
        he BEI Lisi scold-LE twice   Wangwu kick-LE three-times
        'He was scolded twice by Lisi and kicked three times by Wangwu.'

This shows that *bei + NP* does not form a constituent that excludes the following VP, and is hence not a PP.

A fourth argument against the PP analysis of the *bei*-NP comes from anaphor binding (see Chapter 9 for details), in particular the referential interpretation of a reflexive pronoun like *ziji* 'self.' It is now widely known that the reflexive *ziji* is "subject-oriented," i.e., it must take a subject as its antecedent (see Tang 1989, Cole, Hermon, and Sung 1990, Huang and Tang 1991, Y. Li 1993a, inter alia). This is illustrated by (15) below, where *ziji* must have *Zhangsan* but not *Lisi* as its antecedent:

(15)   a. Zhangsan gen Lisi taolun-le   ziji de xiangfa.
           Zhangsan with Lisi discuss-LE self DE opinion
           'Zhangsan$_i$ discussed with Lisi$_j$ his$_{i/*j}$ opinion.'

        b. Zhangsan tongzhi-le   Lisi ziji de fenshu.
           Zhangsan informed-LE Lisi self DE grade
           'Zhangsan$_i$ informed Lisi$_j$ of his$_{i/*j}$ grade.'

In the following passive sentences, however, *ziji* can refer to *Zhangsan* or to *Lisi*, suggesting that they are both subjects. In particular, the Agent NP *Lisi* is not a prepositional object, but a subject of an embedded clause:[5]

---

[4] Coordination is also possible with *bei* repeated in the second conjunct. But this fact is irrelevant to the point being made. Sentences like the following are generally considered to be cases of right-node raising (RNR). RNR is often used to identify the constituency of the raised phrase, but not that of the remnant. In (i), RNR establishes that *kanjian le* is a (VP) constituent.

        (i)   ta you bei Zhangsan, you bei Lisi, kanjian le.
               he also BEI Zhangsan also BEI Lisi, see   LE
               'He was seen both by Zhangsan and by Lisi.'

[5] See Xu (1993) and Cole and Wang (1996) for additional examples. For many speakers there is a strong preference for *ziji* to be bound by *Zhangsan* in (16), but the possibility for binding by *Lisi* should not be totally excluded if the contexts are appropriate (e.g., if the sentence is used to recount an event that all parties already know about). Binding by the Agent NP is clearly acceptable (in fact obligatory) in (17), where the subject 'that letter,' being inanimate, cannot antecede the reflexive.

(16)   Zhangsan bei Lisi guan zai ziji de jiali.
        Zhangsan BEI Lisi lock at self DE home
        'Zhangsan was locked by Lisi in self's home.' (ZS' or LS')

(17)   nei-feng xin   bei Lisi dai-hui   ziji de jia   qu-le.
        that-Cl letter BEI Lisi bring-back self DE home go-LE
        'That letter was brought back to self's (Lisi's) home by Lisi.'

Thus considerations of thematic relations, constituency, and anaphora jointly call into question an NP-movement analysis of passives.[6]

These considerations favor a complementation analysis, according to which *bei* is treated as the main verb, a two-place predicate meaning 'undergo,' 'experience,' etc., which selects an Experiencer as its subject and an Event as its complement. The object of the Event complement clause is obligatorily deleted under identity with the matrix subject. Recent proponents of this approach include Hashimoto (1987) and references cited there, and Wei (1994).[7] Under the complementation analysis, a long passive like (1) has the following structure:

(18)

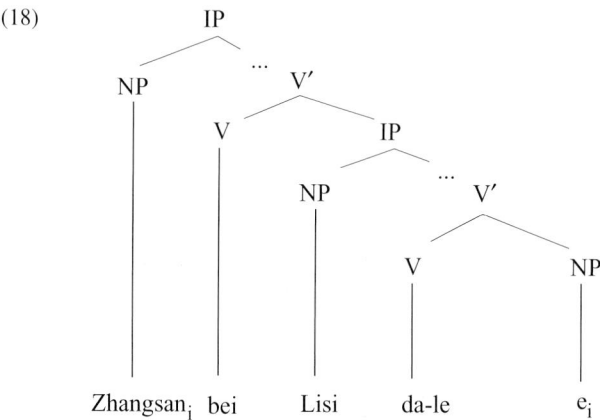

'Zhangsan underwent Lisi's hitting [him].'

---

[6] There is also a difficulty with treating *bei* as a P which arises from the way the subject argument is suppressed and the object Case is absorbed. It is assumed (e.g., Travis 1984) that both argument suppression and Case absorption are triggered by *bei*. But general considerations do not allow the head of an adjunct PP to affect the argument structure or Case property of a main verb.

[7] The complementation approach goes back to Hashimoto (1969). The third argument above, concerning the clausal constituency of NP-VP following *bei*, was presented by Wei (1994) to show that *bei* was clearly a verb taking a clausal complement in historical Chinese. The above point here establishes that the same constituency status of NP-VP remains for Modern Chinese. Since Wei was dealing with a historical stage where the Theme subject could still be related to an overt pronoun in postverbal position (unlike in Modern Chinese, as shown in (5a–c)), Wei's argument really only established the complementation structure of the historical stage that concerned him.

This approach is particularly attractive when we consider the four problems just noted for the movement approach. First, because *bei* is a two-place predicate with its own subject argument, a subject-oriented adverb may be naturally accommodated. If a passive sentence expresses an undergoing by an Experiencer, then it is entirely normal that an Experiencer may intentionally undergo some event. Second, as indicated by the tree diagram above, *bei* and the Agent NP do not form a constituent, let alone a PP constituent. Hence the *bei* + NP sequence does not behave as a PP, as shown above. Third, in (18) the Agent forms an IP with the VP that follows it, predicting the coordination fact indicated above. Finally, the problem of reflexive binding is also explained. According to (18), both the Experiencer *Zhangsan* and the Agent *Lisi* are subjects (matrix and embedded subjects, respectively), so in (17) the reflexive may be bound by *Lisi* and, in (16), by either *Lisi* or *Zhangsan*. Every problem that arose under the NP-movement approach disappears under the complementation approach.

A problem arises, however, concerning the obligatoriness of deleting the embedded object. As indicated in (18), the embedded null object would be an empty pronoun (a pro in the sense of Chomsky 1981). Whether a true pro is possible in object position is still controversial at best (see Huang 1984a, 1989, and references cited). Even if it is possible, the question remains as to why it cannot be replaced by an overt pronoun or reflexive. As we know, an embedded object can normally take the form of an overt pronoun or anaphor:

(19)   a. Zhangsan shuo Lisi da-le   ta.
          Zhangsan say   Lisi hit-LE him
          'Zhangsan said Lisi hit him.'

       b. Zhangsan shuo Lisi da-le   ziji.
          Zhangsan say   Lisi hit-LE self
          'Zhangsan said Lisi hit self.'

Except for the choice of their main verbs, these sentences have the same structures as the passive structure in (18). The question that the complementation theory raises is why a change from the verb *shuo* 'say' to the verb *bei* 'undergo' makes complement object deletion obligatory, and this seems a difficult question to answer. The question does not arise, of course, under the NP-movement approach, according to which the empty postverbal element is an NP-trace, an empty category which cannot be replaced by lexical material.

We have thus come to a situation where both the movement approach and the complementation approach seem to be correct and incorrect at the same time. In fact these two approaches seem to complement each other, so the problems that arise under one approach seem to provide evidence for the other, and vice versa.

4.1.2   *The analysis: A′-movement and predication*

The situation just described has persisted since the earliest generative studies of Chinese syntax, with scholars adhering to their favorite analyses but unaware of, or ignoring, problems associated with them. An analysis that came close to a solution to the dilemma was first proposed by Feng (1995). A number of other works have since appeared either employing or giving additional evidence in support of Feng's proposal, including Chiu (1995), Cheng, Huang, Li, and Tang (1993, 1996), and Ting (1995, 1996). The essential spirit of Feng's proposal is that Chinese passives should be analyzed on a par with current treatments of the *tough* construction in English. In the standard Principles-and-Parameters literature following Chomsky (1981), the complement of *tough* is analyzed as involving null operator (NOP) movement and predication:

(20)   This problem$_i$ is easy [$_{CP}$ NOP$_i$ for you to solve t$_i$].

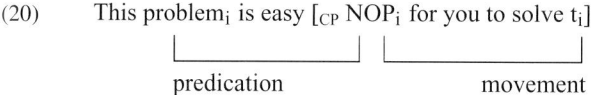

Derivationally, the object of the embedded clause is a null category that moves to the Specifier position of the embedded clause CP (Complementizer Phrase), from where it is then predicated on the matrix subject. The relation between the NOP and the embedded object position is one of movement; its relation with the matrix subject is one of predication, or control. The "*tough*-movement" analysis of (1) is as depicted in (21):

(21)

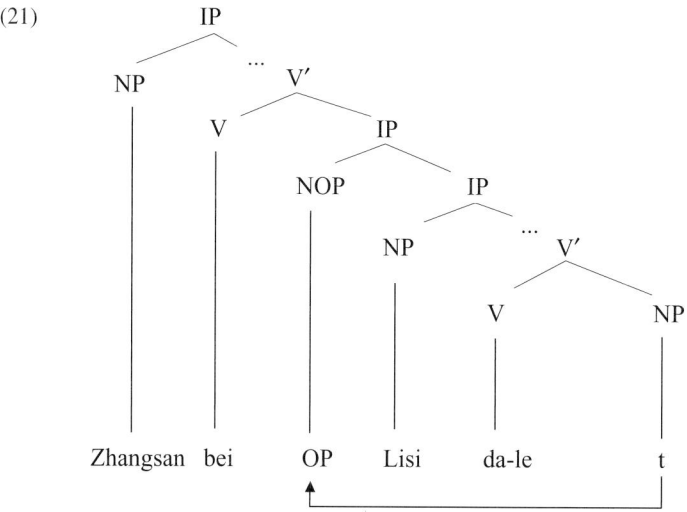

'Zhangsan was hit by Lisi.'

According to this analysis, the structure of a passive involves both complementation and movement. It involves complementation, as *bei* selects an NP as its subject and a clausal category as its complement (which we shall assume to be an IP). It also involves movement of the embedded null object (which we assume to be adjunction to IP). This analysis thus incorporates a combination of the two approaches we discussed in the preceding section. It should be noted, however, that the NOP movement assumed here is an instance of A′-movement (movement to a clause-peripheral, non-argument position) and therefore differs crucially from the NP-movement assumed in the earlier approach, which is a case of A-movement (movement to subject, an argument position).

An immediate argument for (21) is that it has the virtues of both the NP-movement analysis (as represented by (4)) and the complementation analysis (as represented by (18)), but none of their problems. Recall that an important property of the passives is the obligatoriness of an empty category in object position. This property follows from the NOP analysis as much as it does from the NP-movement analysis, because both assume the existence of an object that moves away.[8] The other properties, which pose problems for the NP-movement analysis, do not pose a problem for the NOP analysis. In fact they follow from the NOP analysis as much as they do from the complementation analysis. For example, since the subject is assigned a theta-role of its own (Experiencer), a subject-oriented adverb can be used in a Chinese passive sentence. The analysis also claims that the NP following *bei* is a subject that forms a clausal constituent with the following VP, but does not form a constituent with the morpheme *bei*. It thus explains why the *bei* + NP sequence cannot move like a PP or serve as a nominal modifier. The coordination test confirms the hypothesis embodied in (21) that the NP-VP sequence forms a constituent. Finally, the fact that the Agent NP may antecede the subject-oriented anaphor *ziji* follows because the Agent is a subject of the embedded IP. Note that the combination of these properties follows from the NOP analysis, but not from the NP-movement or the complementation analysis alone.

---

[8] With respect to this property, the passive bears resemblance to sentences like the following:

(i)   zhe-ben shu   hen zhide (ni)   kan.
       this-CL book very worth (you) read
       'This book is worth (your) reading.'

(ii)   zhe-dong fangzi xuyao xiuli.
       this-CL   house need repair
       'This house needs repairing.'

In both cases the matrix verb is followed by a transitive predicate whose object is obligatorily null. It would seem that these examples could be analyzed as NOP constructions as well. Whether or not this may work out remains to be seen.

Note that the structure (21) differs from (18) in how the coindexing relation between the subject of *bei* and the null object of the lower verb is established. According to the pure complementation approach represented by (18), this relation is established directly, so that the subject of *bei* directly binds the embedded null object. According to the NOP analysis, this relation is established indirectly: the null object is first adjoined to IP and it is from this IP-adjoined position that it gets bound by the matrix subject, as an instance of predication. Is the NOP analysis just a syntactic trick to obtain the facts reviewed so far? We shall now show that the NOP analysis is in fact supported by important semantic and historical considerations as well, in addition to a host of other independent syntactic motivations.

What semantic difference does it make to say that one structure involves NOP movement but not the other? We suggest that an NOP structure is a *predicate* denoting a property, whereas a normal clausal complement is an *argument* denoting an entity (an event, proposition, etc.). The structure (18) shows that the verb *bei* is a two-place (transitive) predicate selecting two arguments. In particular, in addition to the Experiencer subject, it selects an Event as its internal argument (complement), and uses an IP to realize that internal argument. The meaning of *bei* in this case is then approximately that of 'undergo' or 'experience.' On the other hand, the claim being made about (21) is that *bei* does not select an argument as a complement. Instead, it selects a predicate, which denotes a property. The *bei* in (21) is thus intransitive, with only one argument. There are two predicates, the primary predicate *bei*, and the *secondary* predicate realized by the NOP structure. By coindexing the NOP with the matrix subject (a case of prediction or "strong binding" of Chomsky 1986a), the NOP structure is interpreted as the secondary predicate of that subject.

How does NOP movement turn a propositional (IP) argument (as in (18)) into a predicate (as is claimed in (21))? The answer comes from the general conception of NOP movement as the syntactic correlate of "lambda-abstraction" commonly assumed in the semantic literature. An expression like 'Zhangsan hit him' (where *him* may be expressed by a null pronoun as in (18)) is a closed category with no open argument positions, and it denotes a proposition (or a truth value). A lambda-abstracted expression containing exactly one free variable is equivalent to an intransitive predicate, where exactly one argument position is unsaturated. Thus, the lambda expression $\lambda x (\dots x \dots)$, which can be informally read as "is an x such that $\dots x \dots$," denotes the set of individuals $\{x\}$ such that "$\dots x \dots$" is true. Any NP denoting the individual that fits this description is said to be the (semantic) subject of this predicate. We can turn a proposition into a predicate describing the property of one of its arguments by substituting into the argument's position a variable bound by the lambda operator. The NOP movement has exactly this effect. Thus the embedded IP in (18) expresses the *proposition* that

Lisi hit him, but the NOP clause in (21) expresses "the *property* of being an x such that Lisi hit x." General requirements of predication (e.g., that a predicate must be related to a subject, cf. Williams 1980, Chomsky 1982, 1986a) and general locality conditions (e.g., Minimal Distance Principle, see p. 143) ensure that the null operator is coindexed with the matrix subject, and the embedded predicate headed by the null operator is said to be a secondary predicate of the matrix subject.

Now, if *bei* in (18) has the meaning of 'undergo [an event],' an appropriate paraphrase of the *bei* in (21) would be 'get, acquire, or end up with the property of . . . ' According to (18), Zhangsan underwent an event in which Lisi hit him. According to (21), Zhangsan ended up with the property of being an x such that Lisi hit x. What is the difference between these two paraphrases? Not much as far as informal paraphrasing goes, but in a theory of syntax–semantics interface they correspond to, or are mapped from, different syntactic representations that are motivated by both synchronic and diachronic considerations. The two different syntactic structures (18) and (21) make different claims about the "lexical strength" (i.e., transitivity) of the verb *bei*. In (18) *bei* is a transitive verb with two arguments. In (21) *bei* is an intransitive with one argument and a secondary predicate. In the latter case, we may consider *bei* and the secondary predicate to make up an intransitive complex predicate which compositionally selects the subject as its single argument.[9] On the other hand, in (18) *bei* is treated as a true transitive main verb with a clausal complement. The different syntactic structures make different predictions concerning the properties of passive sentences, and as we have seen, (21) but not (18) correctly predicts the obligatoriness of a null object in passive constructions like (1). We shall see shortly below that (21) makes several other correct predictions that (18) does not.

In addition to synchronic considerations, distinguishing between the two structures (18) and (21) is also diachronically justified. There is good reason to believe that these structures reflect two different stages of grammaticalization in the historical development of the passive construction. In particular, as documented by Wei (1994), the (long) passive has undergone a gradual development through the grammaticalization of *bei* that can be traced through historical texts. Sentences with *bei-NP-VP* structure started out without the requirement that the VP contain any item anaphoric to the subject of *bei*, and then developed into a stage where the VP regularly contained an overt pronoun during the Medieval Period, as described in Wei (1994) and Peyraube (1996), and finally reached the stage (post-Tang Dynasty) where the pronoun became impossible, as we have observed

---

[9] In this case, because of its light functional load, *bei* comes close to having the status of an auxiliary (or light verb), giving the NOP clause the status of the main predicate.

in Modern Chinese. Some passive sentences from Medieval Chinese (of the Jin Dynasty) are given below:

(22)   bei Shalifo   hua   huo zhe   zhi.   (from *Bianwen*)
        BEI Sariputra transform fire cover him
        '(He) was covered [him] by the transformed fire of Sariputra.'

(23)   tiannü bei chi-zhu   jian zhi.   (from *Bianwen*)
        fairies BEI pool-owner see them
        'The fairies were seen [them] by the pool-owners.'

These examples contrast with (1) and (5a–b), repeated below:

(1)   Zhangsan bei Lisi da-le.
        Zhangsan BEI Lisi hit-LE
        'Zhangsan was hit by Lisi.'

(5a–b) *Zhangsan bei Lisi da-le   ta/ziji.
        Zhangsan BEI Lisi hit-LE him/self
        *'Zhangsan was hit by Lisi.'

It seems that (18) would be an appropriate analysis of passive sentences in Medieval Chinese as represented by (22)–(23), except that the coreference between the embedded object and the matrix subject is simply established by pronominal anaphora, but (21) is the proper analysis for the passives in Modern (possibly also Pre-Modern) Chinese with an obligatory null object. The *bei* sentences in Medieval Chinese are just experiential sentences involving a two-place experiential predicate *bei*, but the *bei* sentences in Modern Chinese are true passives with an intransitive complex predicate.

In short, the postulation of the structure (21) as distinct from (18) is justified not only on syntactic and semantic grounds, but also on historical considerations. Inasmuch as we need the structure (18) to describe the earlier language, we also need the structure (21) to bring out the difference of the modern language.

4.1.3   Further evidence for the NOP analysis

In addition to solving all the problems associated with either the NP-movement approach or the complementation approach, the analysis embodying NOP movement receives important independent evidence from the following facts.

4.1.3.1 Long-distance passives

First, Chinese passives exhibit "unbounded" dependency. As observed by Huang (1974), passives of the following sort are well-formed in Chinese, quite unlike English passives.[10]

(24)   Zhangsan bei Lisi pai   jingcha zhua-zou-le.
        Zhangsan BEI Lisi send   police arrest-LE
        'Zhangsan was "sent-police-to-arrest" by Lisi.'

(25)   nei-feng xin   bei wo jiao Lisi qing Wangwu tuo   ta   meimei ji-zou-le.
        that-CL letter BEI me tell Lisi ask Wangwu entrust his sister send-LE
        'That letter was "told-LS-to-ask-WW-get-his-sister-to-send" by me.'

According to (24), for example, Zhangsan was arrested by the police, but it was
Lisi who sent the police to arrest him. So the true Agent of the entire event is
Lisi, with the police being the Agent of a subevent of the event that Zhangsan
underwent. A more idiomatic translation of (24) into English might be 'Zhangsan
underwent Lisi's sending the police to arrest him' (and the police were successful
in making the arrest). Similarly, in (25) the Patient is the letter, but the Agent of
the entire event that the letter underwent is *wo* 'I,' not 'his sister,' the sender.

As is well known, unbounded dependencies are a characteristic property of
A′-movement. Given NOP movement as a case of A′-movement, long-distance
passivization is entirely expected. It is also well known that English *tough* sentences
also exhibit long-distance dependencies:

(26)   This problem is too easy for me to ask the teacher to help me solve.

4.1.3.2 Island sensitivity

A second piece of evidence in favor of the NOP movement analysis is
that Chinese long-distance passives exhibit island effects, thus passing another
diagnostic for A′-movement (cf. Chomsky 1977).

(27)   Zhangsan bei wo tongzhi Lisi ba zanmei *(ta) de shu   dou mai-zou-le.
        Zhangsan BEI me inform Lisi BA praise (him) DE book   all buy-away-LE
        'Zhangsan had me inform Lisi to buy up all the books that praise [him].'

The sentence is ungrammatical with a gap in the object position following *zanmei*
'praise,' the verb of the relative clause modifying *shu* 'book,' though it is well-
formed with a resumptive pronoun in that position. There is no similar deletion
analysis that would account for this distribution of an empty object by allowing

---

[10] Long-distance passivization was first observed by Huang (1974), who proposed that the
movement was directly into the subject position of the main clause, as the notion of NOP
movement was not available at the time. It was not until Feng (1995) that an explicit NOP
movement account was proposed. Huang also developed an account involving reanalysis
without an intermediate step of NOP movement. It seems that both NOP movement and
reanalysis are necessary in order to capture a mismatch between Case and thematic
properties of the passives.

long-distance dependency but not into a complex NP. This distribution is strongly symptomatic of A′-movement.

4.1.3.3   The particle *suo*

A third piece of additional evidence comes from the distribution of the particle *suo*. As observed in Chiu (1995), in somewhat literary speech a passive sentence may include the particle *suo* before the lower verb:

(28)   zhexie shiqing bu neng bei tamen **suo** liaojie.
these   thing   not can   BEI they   SUO understand
'These things cannot be understood by them.'

(29)   ni   zuijin dui ta   de xingwei kongpa hui bei wairen **suo** chixiao.
you   recent to him DE behavior afraid   will BEI others SUO laugh-at
'I'm afraid your recent behavior toward him will be laughed at by others.'

It is generally accepted that this *suo* is a remnant of Classical Chinese. It is also well known that the only other construction that involves this particle *suo* is the relative clause, specifically only when an object is relativized. An example of Modern Chinese relativization with *suo* is given below:

(30)   xiaotou **suo**ᵢ meiyou   touzou tᵢ de naxie shu   zai zhuozi-shang.
thief   SUO not-have steal   DE those book at   table-top
'The books that the thieves have not stolen are on the table.'

A widely accepted analysis of *suo* in the traditional literature treats *suo* on a par with an (object) relative pronoun since *suo* literally means 'location,' which is often used to refer to the "objective entity." Whether *suo* should be equated with a relative pronoun in English-type languages (where it occurs in Spec, CP) is controversial. What is uncontroversial is that such Chinese relative clauses exhibit A′-dependency involving an empty object position. The fact that the passive construction is the only other construction with *suo* and an accompanying empty object position then provides striking support for the idea that Chinese passives involve A′-movement of the object. In fact, Chiu (1995) argues strongly that the *suo* is triggered by the existence of *wh*-movement in both cases (see also Ting 2003 for related discussion).

4.1.3.4   Resumptive pronouns

Finally, the distribution of resumptive pronouns in Chinese passives also puts them together with relative clauses as instances of A′-movement. Earlier we highlighted the requirement that the passive must contain an object position with null content. Although this empty object requirement is true with simple sentences of the sort we have considered above, it is in fact possible to use a pronoun instead, when the object occurs within a somewhat more complex environment. We have just seen an example where such a pronoun is used, in (27), to avoid an island violation. The following example (of the sort cited in Feng 1995) allows a pronoun in the object position bound by the subject.

(31)   Zhangsan bei Lisi da-le   ta   yi-xia.
        Zhangsan BEI Lisi hit-LE him   once
        'Zhangsan was hit once by Lisi.'

Under the NP-movement approach, the grammaticality of (31) would be entirely unexpected.[11] Under the A′-movement approach, however, the overt pronoun is simply a resumptive pronoun, which is locally A′-bound but locally A-free. Note that (31) differs from the ungrammatical (5a), repeated below, only in that the verb phrase in (31) is longer than that in (5a).[12]

(5)   a. *Zhangsan bei Lisi da-le ta.
           Zhangsan BEI Lisi hit-LE him
           'Zhangsan was hit (*him) by Lisi.'

We do not know exactly why the additional material in (31) makes a pronoun possible, but we do know that the same effect can be observed with relative clauses. Thus simple object (or subject) relativization requires the gap strategy, whereas a resumptive pronoun strategy may be used when the relativized NP is surrounded by more materials.[13]

(32)   ??Lisi da-le   ta   de nei-ge ren   lai-le.
        Lisi hit-LE him   DE that-CL person come-LE
        Lit: 'The person who Lisi hit him came.'

---

[11] According to Chomsky's (1981) Binding Theory, an NP-trace is an anaphor which must be bound in its governing category. A pronoun in place of the NP-trace would require it to be also free in its governing category, an impossible requirement to satisfy. Hence NP-traces cannot alternate with overt pronouns at all. In fact, there is a more general property of the NP-trace, namely that it cannot alternate with any overt category, and this property comes from Case-theoretic considerations, independently of the Binding Theory.

[12] Feng (1995) highlighted the grammaticality of (31) as evidence that Chinese passives do not require an empty object position, but he ignored the ungrammaticality of simple sentences like (5a), where a resumptive pronoun is prohibited. His argument thus remained incomplete because the requirement of a null object in simple everyday passives was left unexplained.

[13] The literature on relativization strategies in Chinese is somewhat controversial. Sanders and Tai (1972) claim that the "gap" strategy is required only when the relativized NP is the matrix subject of the relative clause; all other relativized NPs can, or must, take the "pronoun" strategy. K. Mei (1978a) claims that direct object relatives also require the gap strategy, though indirect objects may employ the pronoun strategy. Our judgment agrees with that of Mei's. The more relevant point here is that (33) with *yi-xia* 'once' is better than (32) without it. The grammatical (33) and (31) would be on a par with

(33)   Lisi da-le ta   yi-xia de nei-ge ren   lai-le.
        Lisi hit-LE him once DE that-CL person come-LE
        'The person who Lisi hit [him] once came.'

Note that the contrast between (32) and (33) parallels that between (5a) and (31).
This parallelism is quite extensive and complete. For example, an optional resumptive pronoun is possible when an embedded subject is passivized or relativized:

(34)   Zhangsan bei Lisi huaiyi (ta) tou-le   qian.
        Zhangsan BEI Lisi suspect (he) steal-LE money
        'Zhangsan was suspected (by Lisi) [he] to have stolen the money.'

(35)   Lisi huaiyi (ta) tou-le   qian   de nei-ge ren   zou-le.
        Lisi suspect (he) steal-LE money DE that-CL person leave-LE
        'The person that Lisi suspected [he] stole the money has left.'

And when an object immediately following *ba* (or any element traditionally
analyzed as a preposition) is passivized or relativized, a resumptive pronoun is
required:

(36)   Zhangsan bei Lisi ba ta   pian de tuantuanzhuan.
        Zhangsan BEI Lisi BA him cheat DE run-around
        'Zhangsan was pushed around like a fool by Lisi.'

(37)   Lisi ba ta   pian de tuantuanzhuan de nei-ge ren   zou-le.
        Lisi BA him cheat DE run-around   DE that-CL person leave-LE
        'The person that Lisi pushed around like a fool has left.'

It is well known that the option of using the resumptive pronoun strategy is a property of A′-movement, not of A-movement.[14] The fact that passivization parallels
relativization so neatly in this respect lends important support to the A′-movement
analysis of the passives.

---

cases of indirect object relativization and passivization, respectively, where the "indirect
object" may be a Benefactor or an Affectee:

(i)   Lisi song-le ta   liang-ben shu   de na-ge ren   zou-le.
       Lisi give-LE him two-CL   book DE that-CL person leave-LE
       'The person who Lisi gave [him] two books left.'

(ii)   Lisi tou-le   ta   liang-ben shu   de na-ge ren   zou-le.
       Lisi steal-LE him two-CL   book DE that-CL person leave-LE
       'The person who Lisi stole two books from left.'

(iii) Zhangsan bei Lisi tou-le   ta   liang-bai   kuai   qian.
       Zhangsan BEI Lisi steal-LE him two-hundred dollar money
       'Zhangsan had 200 dollars stolen [from him] by Lisi.'

[14] In addition to Case, (36) would also be excluded by Binding Theory under an
A-movement approach. The resumptive pronoun *ta* would be A-bound by *Zhangsan*
in this case in its governing category, a configuration otherwise excluded by Binding
Theory.

In summary, an NOP analysis of Chinese (long) passives has the merits of both the NP-movement and the pure complementation approaches but none of their problems, and it receives independent motivation from considerations of long-distance dependency, island sensitivity, and the distribution of resumptive pronouns and the particle *suo*.

4.2   The Mandarin short passive

In the literature on Chinese syntax, one common assumption about the short passive (as in (2), repeated below) has been that it is derived from the long form (as in (1)) via deletion of the Agent NP (see, for example, Hashimoto 1987 and references cited there).

(1)   Zhangsan bei Lisi da-le.
       Zhangsan BEI Lisi hit-LE
       'Zhangsan was hit by Lisi.'

(2)   Zhangsan bei da-le.
       Zhangsan BEI hit-LE
       'Zhangsan was hit.'

While this seems an easy way to relate the two constructions, there are numerous reasons to reject such an analysis. Huang (1982b) pointed out that this analysis is inappropriate on both interpretive considerations and independent syntactic grounds. Wei (1994) argued that deriving the short passive in this way would be excluded by crucial historical evidence. Comparison with properties of the long passives also leads to the same conclusion (as briefly alluded to in Cheng, Huang, Li, and Tang 1993 and argued independently in Ting 1995, 1996). Let us consider these arguments in turn.

4.2.1   Against the Agent-deletion analysis

4.2.1.1   Accessibility

First, note that the Agent is located in a position that is generally inaccessible to deletion. This is true regardless of whether *bei* is analyzed as a preposition or as a verb. As a preposition, *bei* would permit no deletion of the Agent NP, given the general prohibition against preposition stranding, as illustrated in (38)–(39):

(38)   Zhangsan, zhe-jian shi   gen   *(ta)   mei-you guanxi.
        Zhangsan this-CL   thing with   *(him)   not-have relation
        'Zhangsan, this thing has nothing to do with him.'

(39)   zhe-jian shi   gen *(ta)   mei-you guanxi de na-ge   ren   zou-le.
        this-CL thing with *(him) not-have relation DE that-CL person leave-LE
        'The person such that this thing has nothing to do with him has left.'

As a verb, the environment in which *bei* occurs (a V-NP-V configuration) also
does not allow the Agent NP to be deleted (whether the NP is a constituent of the
higher clause or the subject of the lower clause), as illustrated below:[15]

(40)   *Zhangsan, wo shi   __ shengqi le.
        Zhangsan I   cause __ angry   LE
        'Zhangsan, I have caused to be angry.'

(41)   *Li Xiaojie, wo bi   __ gaijia   le.
        Miss Li   I   force __ re-marry LE
        'Miss Li, I have forced to re-marry.'

If the short passive were derived from the long passive by deletion of the Agent,
it would constitute an unexplained exception to the otherwise general prohibition.

4.2.1.2 Chronology of emergence

Independently arguing against Hashimoto's Agent deletion hypothesis,
Wei (1994) pointed out that the short passive was used as early as 300 BC (e.g.,
in the text of *Han Feizi*), much earlier than the long passive form, which was not
attested until 500 years later, in Han texts (ca. AD 200). Two examples of the short
form are found in the following quote from *Han Feizi*:

(42)   jin   xiongdi bei qin,   bi   gong zhe,   lian   ye;
        now   brothers BEI attack, must   attack person, straight SFP;
        zhi   you   bei ru,   sui   chou zhe,   zhen ye.
        know friends BEI insult, along angry person, loyal SFP
        'Now those who will attack when their brothers are attacked are straight;
        those who, when their best friends are insulted, will be likewise angry,
        are loyal.'

Since the long passive form did not exist at this stage, any attempt to derive
the short passives from underlying long passives would be extremely unsatis-
factory.

---

[15] In the speech of some speakers from northern China, sentences with *rang* 'let' excep-
tionally allow extraction in the context of (40)–(41):

(i)   Zhangsan, wo rang __ ca   chuanghu qu-le.
       Zhangsan I let   wipe   window   go-LE
       'Zhangsan, I had him go and wipe the windows.'

4.2.1.3   Obligatory null object

A related point has to do with the requirement of a null object. As indicated in connection with (22)–(23), the long passive developed from experiential sentences through grammaticalization of the experiential verb *bei*. Prior to its current form represented by (1), many earlier examples of the passive construction involved an overt pronoun in the embedded clause bound by the subject of *bei*. Additional Medieval Chinese examples are given below (from Jin texts cited in Feng 1998):

(43)   (Li Zi'ao) bei ming-he   tun   zhi.   (from *Soushenji*)
       Li Zi'ao   BEI chirping-cranes wallow him
       'Li Zi'ao was swallowed (him) by the chirping crane.'

(44)   Jindan ruo bei zhuwu   fan   zhi . . .   (from *Baopuzi*)
       Jindan if   BEI everything attack him
       'If Jindan was attacked (him) by everything . . .'

The requirement of a null object is in fact a relatively recent property of the long passive. On the other hand, the short passive has always involved an obligatory null object position from the very start in 300 BC. Needless to say, this makes deriving the short passive from the long passive synchronically even less plausible.

4.2.1.4   Adverbial positions

From a purely synchronic viewpoint, a number of differences also exist between the long and the short passives that argue against the Agent deletion analysis. One is that although sentential adverbials as well as VP-adverbials are allowed with long passives, only VP-adverbials may occur with the short form. Thus, (45) shows that both manner and place adverbials may occur with the long form, whereas (46) shows that the short form admits only manner adverbials:

(45)   a. Zhangsan bei Lisi momingqimiao de pian-zou-le.
          Zhangsan BEI Lisi confused   DE abduct-LE
          'Zhangsan was abducted in a state of confusion by Lisi.'

       b. Zhangsan bei Lisi zai xuexiao pian-zou-le.
          Zhangsan BEI Lisi at   school   abduct-LE
          'Zhangsan was abducted at school by Lisi.'

(46)   a. Zhangsan bei momingqimiao de pian-zou-le.
          Zhangsan BEI confused   DE abduct-LE
          'Zhangsan was abducted in a state of confusion.'

       b. *Zhangsan bei zai xuexiao pian-zou-le.
          Zhangsan BEI at   school   abduct-LE
          'Zhangsan was abducted at school.'

This suggests that while the long passive contains an IP following *bei*, the short passive contains a VP in that position. An analysis employing Agent deletion from the long passive would entail an IP containing a null subject position, but then it would be unclear why such a structure could not accommodate a locative adverbial.

4.2.1.5 Long-distance possibilities

Earlier we saw that the long passives exhibit unbounded dependencies subject to island constraints (as in (47)). By contrast, short passives are strictly local, disallowing any cross-clausal dependency (48):

(47) a. Zhangsan bei Lisi pai   jingcha zhua-zou le.
          Zhangsan BEI Lisi send police   arrest   LE
          'Zhangsan was "sent-police-to-arrest" by Lisi.'

      b. nei-feng xin   bei wo jiao Lisi qing Wangwu tuo   ta meimei ji-zou le.
          that-CL letter BEI me tell Lisi ask Wangwu request his sister   send LE
          'That letter was "told-LS–ask-WW–have-his-sister-send" by me.'

(48) a. *Zhangsan bei pai   jingcha zhua-zou le.
          Zhangsan BEI send police   arrest   LE

      b. *nei-feng xin   bei jiao Lisi qing Wangwu tuo   ta meimei ji-zou le.
          that-CL letter BEI tell Lisi ask Wangwu request his sister   send LE

We saw that unbounded dependencies and island sensitivity constitute an important diagnostic for A′-movement in the analysis of long passives. The lack of such unbounded dependencies with the short passive suggests that it does not involve A′-movement and hence argues against the hypothesis that the short passive is simply obtained by Agent deletion.

4.2.1.6 The particle *suo*

We saw above that, in some semi-literary styles, long passives may contain the particle *suo* (as in (28)–(29), repeated below), a property they share with relative clauses. This is taken to provide evidence for A′-movement.

(28)   zhexie shiqing bu   neng bei tamen **suo** liaojie.
         these thing   not can BEI they SUO understand
         'These things cannot be understood by them.'

(29)   ni   zuijin dui ta   de xingwei kongpa hui bei wairen **suo** chixiao.
         you recent to him DE behavior afraid will BEI others SUO laugh-at
         'I'm afraid your recent behavior toward him will be laughed at by others.'

By contrast, the short passive disallows *suo* in both spoken and literary styles:[16]

(49)   *zhexie shiqing bu   neng bei __ **suo** liaojie.
        these   thing   not can   BEI __ SUO understand
        'These things cannot be understood.'

(50)   *ni   zuijin dui ta   de xingwei kongpa hui bei __ **suo** chixiao.
        you recent to   him DE behavior afraid   will BEI __ SUO laugh-at
        'I'm afraid your recent behavior toward him will be laughed at.'

This contrast again would be unaccounted for under a simple Agent deletion analysis.

4.2.1.7   Resumptive pronouns

Finally, the long and short passives also contrast with respect to the distribution of resumptive pronouns. A long passive may employ the pronoun strategy in cases like (31), repeated below:

(31)   Zhangsan bei Lisi da-le   ta   yi-xia.
        Zhangsan BEI Lisi hit-LE him once
        'Zhangsan was hit once by Lisi.'

But a short passive does not admit any resumptive pronoun under similar circumstances:[17]

(51)   *Zhangsan bei da-le   ta   yi-xia.
        Zhangsan BEI hit-LE him once
        'Zhangsan was hit once.'

This suggests again that the derivation of the short passive must be very different from that of the long passive.

[16]   A related construction in Classical Chinese involving *wei* rather than *bei* is grammatical with *suo* but without the Agent phrase: *bu wei suo dong* 'was not moved [by it].' Though this looks like a "short passive" with *suo*, it should be noted that this "short passive" differs from the pattern under discussion in the text. This example involves true deletion of the Agent NP whose reference is clear in context, and so it is better translated as 'was not moved by it,' not 'was not moved,' which would be appropriate for a short passive we are considering in the text. See Wei (1994) for related remarks.

[17]   The following Agentless short passive does allow a resumptive pronoun within a "retained object":

(i)   Zhangsan bei qiang-zou-le   ta   zui   xihuan de wanju.
       Zhangsan BEI take-away-LE he most   like   DE toy
       'Zhangsan had the toy he liked most taken away.'

We argue below that passive forms like this involve the passivization of an "outer object" of a V′ phrase, in this case the phrase *qiang-zou-le ta zui xihuan de wanju*. In other words, the pronoun *ta* in (i) is anaphoric to the moved "outer object," but is not directly related to *Zhangsan* as its resumptive pronoun.

4.2.2   Analysis of the short passive

In view of the large number of arguments presented above, it is clear that a short passive cannot be treated as an Agent-deleted version of the long passive. Two possibilities for analyzing the short passive come to mind: it could involve NP-movement in some fashion, or it could be derived without any movement.

Some of the contrastive properties we have just seen – those concerning (the lack of) unbounded dependencies, resumptive pronouns, and *suo* – suggest that although the short passive does not involve A′-movement, an analysis in terms of A-movement of the sort used in English *be* passives might be appropriate. This is in fact the analysis adopted by Ting (1995, 1996), according to whom the surface subject of the short passive is derived via movement of the underlying object into the Spec of IP position. However, such an analysis ignores the fact that both the long and the short passives, but not the English *be* passive, may contain a subject-oriented adverb like *guyi* 'intentionally,' as we saw in (6) and (7) as repeated below, which suggests that the subject is base-generated in place and receives an independent thematic role from *bei*.

(6)   Zhangsan guyi   bei da-le.
       Zhangsan intentionally BEI hit-LE
       'Zhangsan intentionally got hit.'

(7)   Zhangsan guyi   bei Lisi da-le.
       Zhangsan intentionally BEI Lisi hit-LE
       'Zhangsan intentionally got hit by Lisi.'

For this reason, a more reasonable analysis might take the form depicted in (52) (following Hoshi's (1991, 1994a, b) analysis of English *get* passives and Japanese "*ni* passives"):[18]

(52)

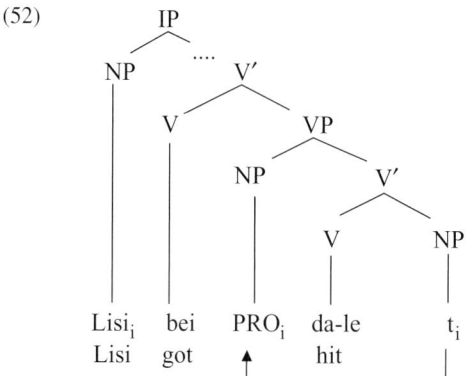

---

[18] Hoshi indicates that this was an adaptation of a similar analysis of *be* passives in English proposed earlier by Saito and Murasugi (1989).

According to this analysis, *bei* has the status of a deontic modal auxiliary or light verb, selecting an Experiencer as its subject and a predicate (a property) as its complement, and subcategorizing for a VP as the structural realization of the predicate complement. Following the Predicate Internal Subject Hypothesis (Contreras 1987, Sportiche 1988, Fukui and Speas 1986, Kitagawa 1986, Kuroda 1988, etc.), a VP contains a subject position of its own. The VP itself is a passive structure with internal NP-movement as shown above, with the underlying Patient argument moved into the non-thematic [Spec, VP] position, binding a trace. The moved Patient is itself an empty category, a PRO, which is controlled by the base-generated subject *Lisi*. Thus the short passive has a structure somewhat parallel to that of the long passive, except that while the long passive involves the A'-movement of an NOP which is then coindexed with the matrix subject under predication, the short passive involves the A-movement of a PRO which is then controlled by the subject. It is easy to see that all the properties considered so far of the short passive follow from this analysis.

First, because we assume that the auxiliary-like *bei* selects a VP (rather than IP), it follows that only manner adverbs (which can be adjoined to V' or VPs) may occur in short passives, to the exclusion of sentential adverbs (which must be adjoined to I' or IP). Second, because it assigns an independent Experiencer role to its subject, it follows that adverbs like *guyi* 'intentionally' are allowed. Third, because the short passive involves NP-movement, unbounded dependencies, resumptive pronouns, and *suo* are correctly excluded. Furthermore, because it does not involve deletion of an Agent phrase from the embedded subject position, the problem of accessibility does not arise. And finally, since this structure is postulated independently of the NOP structure of the long passive, the relative chronology of these two passive forms again poses no problem for our analysis.[19]

While this NP-movement-plus-control analysis seems quite elegant for the cases of the short passive we have considered, it is not the only possible analysis for the Agentless passive. It has been noted by Shen (1992) and Ting (1996), among others, that certain short passives must be derived by a lexical process, illustrated by (53):

(53)   Zhangsan bei bu-le.
        Zhangsan BEI arrest-LE
        'Zhangsan was arrested.'

---

[19] Another argument for not relating the long and short passives by derivation comes from dialectal comparison. For example, (spoken) Cantonese and Taiwanese, whose passives are formed with a different morpheme than that corresponding to Mandarin *bei*, have no equivalents of the short passive. For more details see Huang (1999) and Tang (1999).

(54)   dijun   bei fu-le.
        enemy BEI capture-LE
        'The enemy troops got captured.'

In these cases, the verb directly following *bei* is a bound morpheme. Contrast *bei bu* with *bei daibu*:

(55)   a. jingcha daibu-le   Zhangsan.
           police   arrest-LE Zhangsan
           'The police arrested Zhangsan.'

        b. Zhangsan bei jingcha daibu-le.
           Zhangsan BEI police arrest-LE
           'Zhangsan was arrested by the police.'

        c. Zhangsan bei jingcha mimide daibu-le.
           Zhangsan BEI police secretly arrest-LE
           'Zhangsan was secretly arrested by the police.'

        d. women xuexiao bei jingcha daibu-le   liang-ge xuesheng.
           our   school BEI police arrest-LE two-CL student
           'Zhangsan had two students arrested by the police.'

(56)   a. *jingcha bu-le   Zhangsan.
           police   arrest-LE Zhangsan

        b. *Zhangsan bei jingcha bu-le.
           Zhangsan BEI police arrest-LE

        c. *Zhangsan bei jingcha mimide bu-le.
           Zhangsan BEI police secretly arrest-LE

        d. *Zhangsan bei jingcha bu-le   liang-ge xuesheng.
           Zhangsan BEI police arrest-LE two-CL student

Cases like (53)–(54) must therefore be derived by a lexical process that directly combines *bei* with a verb to make a "passive verb."

It seems clear that the reason why the short passive has both a lexical and a phrasal form has to do with its history dating back, as indicated, to late Archaic Chinese, when the language was highly monosyllabic. At first, *bei* was used as an alternative for the passive marker *jian* (which soon gave way to *bei*):

(57)   wu chang jian xiao   yu dafang   zhi jia.   (from *Zhuangzi*)
        I   often get laughed by large-expertise DE[20] scholar
        'I often got laughed at by the great experts.'

(58)   wan-sheng   zhi guo bei wei   yu Zhao.
        10,000-vehicle DE state BEI surround by Zhao
        'A state of ten thousand chariots got surrounded by Zhao.'

---

[20] Classical Chinese *zhi* is glossed as DE here insofar as the specific instances are equivalent to the prenominal modifier marker *de*.

These sentences in Archaic Chinese could be related to their Modern counterparts in the following ways. On the one hand, *bei*, like *jian*, could be an auxiliary taking a VP complement whose subject theta-role is suppressed. These sentences would be like the English *get* passives, properly analyzed as in (52) above (à la Hoshi). The main difference between the Archaic (57)–(58) and the Modern (52) is that historically the Agent appeared as a postverbal PP headed by *yu*, but is completely missing in the Modern short passive. We can say that the Modern short passives are directly inherited from Archaic passives, and the absence of a postverbal Agent phrase is simply part of an independent historical development of the language – the disappearance of adjunct PPs from postverbal position.[21] This leaves the question of why some short passives are phrasal while others are lexical in Modern Chinese. We believe that this situation is the result of another well-known historical development whereby the language became highly disyllabic (and highly analytic in other ways). If the verb became disyllabic (as in *daibu* 'arrest'), it continued to head a VP structure under the auxiliary *bei*, and kept the template available for later development as a full phrasal short passive. If the verb remained monosyllabic, it needed to combine with the auxiliary *bei* (for prosodic reasons, see Feng 1994, 2000) to form a disyllabic unit, with the result that *bei* became the first element of a V-V compound or a prefix to the verb, as in *bei bu* 'get arrested,' *bei fu* 'get captured' in (53) and (54). When the monosyllabic forms of these verbs fell into disuse (and were replaced by *daibu* 'arrest' and *fulu* 'capture'), they became bound morphemes and could not appear in the environments in (56). In other words, the modern lexical short passives are frozen forms of historical phrasal passives.[22]

Whether or not the details of its history are correct, it seems quite certain that the short passive is not simply an Agent-deleted version of a long passive. The short passive in Modern Chinese is handed down from the Archaic passive construction. The phrasal short passive seems to retain the NP-movement properties of Archaic passives whereas the lexical passive appears to have been fossilized from Archaic forms that were once phrasal.

Summarizing, we have argued that there are (at least) two ways to derive passive sentences in Chinese. The long passive involves the main verb *bei* with a clausal complement which undergoes null-operator movement and type-shifts into

---

[21] See Sun (1996) and references cited therein for indication that the postverbal adjunct PPs did not "move" historically to the preverbal position; they simply fell into disuse in postverbal position.

[22] Logically, for a monosyllabic free form like *da* 'hit,' a simple passive like *ta bei da le* 'He got hit' could involve either lexical or phrasal passive, though *ta bei da de hen teng* 'He was hit (and was) severely (hurt)' and *ta bei tongkuai de da-le* 'He was soundly beaten' require a phrasal analysis.

a property predicated on the Experiencer subject. The short passive involves an auxiliary-like *bei* with a VP complement whose PRO object is NP-moved and controlled by the Experiencer subject.

(59)   Zhangsan$_i$ bei   [$_{IP}$ OP$_i$ [$_{IP}$ Lisi da-le   t$_i$]]

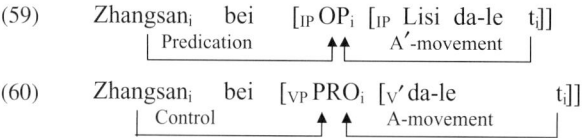

(60)   Zhangsan$_i$ bei   [$_{VP}$ PRO$_i$ [$_{V'}$ da-le   t$_i$]]

Both passive forms thus have the dual character of both movement and control predication.[23] In this respect, Chinese passives are similar to *get* passives in English, unlike *be* passives which involve NP-movement only. An appropriate analysis of an English *get* passive would be (61), as opposed to (62) for a corresponding *be* passive:[24]

(61)   John$_i$ got   [$_{VP}$ PRO$_i$ [$_{V'}$ blamed   t$_i$ for the failure]]

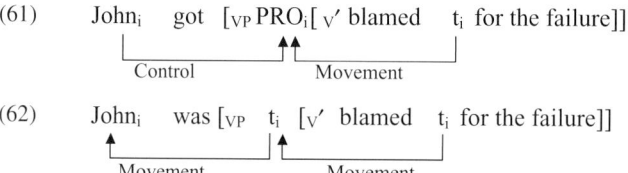

(62)   John$_i$ was [$_{VP}$ t$_i$ [$_{V'}$ blamed   t$_i$ for the failure]]

Because they involve predication/control, Chinese passives are different from the more familiar passives in English and other Western languages. This also seems to be the most prominent property of passives in other East Asian languages.

---

[23] Predication and control are clearly of the same or similar nature. In Williams (1980), control is simply treated as a special case of (secondary) predication.

[24] The difference between *get* and *be* passives is then the difference between control and raising verbs. As the following examples show, the distinction between *get* and *be* with respect to the distribution of subject-oriented adverbs and idiom chunks is clearly also found with familiar control vs. raising predicates.

(i)   a.   *John intentionally was cheated.
       b.   John intentionally got cheated.

(ii)   a.   *John is intentionally likely to win.
       b.   John is intentionally eager to win.

(iii) a.   Advantage was taken of John.
       b.   *?Advantage got taken of John.

(iv)   a.   The shit is likely to hit the fan.
       b.   *The shit is eager to hit the fan.

4.3   The analysis of indirect passives

4.3.1   *Direct vs. indirect passives*

Another prominent property of passives in East Asian languages is the existence of "indirect passives."[25] In the previous examples we have seen, the subject of a passive sentence is coindexed with the direct object of the main verb.[26] Such are the "direct passive" sentences. But the passive may also be "indirect," where the subject may be related to something other than the direct object, or not to any apparent syntactic position in the main clause at all. Borrowing Washio's (1993) terminology, we may distinguish between two kinds of indirect passives: "inclusive" and "exclusive." In the first, the subject is related to some other position than the object within the predicate (such as the possessive position):

(63)   Zhangsan bei Lisi daduan-le   yi-tiao tui.
Zhangsan BEI Lisi hit-break-LE one-CL leg
'Zhangsan had a leg [of his] broken by Lisi.'

(64)   Zhangsan bei tufei   qiang-zou-le san-jian xingli.
Zhangsan BEI bandit rob-away-LE 3-CL   luggage
'Zhangsan had 3 pieces of [his] luggage robbed by the bandits.'

In the second, the subject is not apparently related to any position in the predicate at all. The "exclusive" indirect passives are also known as "adversative passives," because of the strong sense of adversity they convey on the part of the referents of

---

[25] The direct–indirect distinction has figured prominently from the early days of generative study in Japanese syntax, though it has not attracted much attention in Chinese syntax. The analysis of the various passive forms in Japanese has been a topic of considerable controversy among researchers. A major item of debate has been whether the various passive forms should be analyzed in a uniform manner or not. The uniform approach (championed by Kuroda 1965 and many others in subsequent work) postulates clausal complementation for all passive forms, with deletion of the embedded object in the case of direct passives. The non-uniform approach (Kuno 1973 inter alia) postulates clausal complementation for the indirect passives but analyses the direct passives in terms of NP-movement. As far as the direct passives are concerned, these two approaches parallel the two competing traditions in the analysis of Chinese long passives as discussed in the preceding sections. For important recent discussions on the analysis of passives in Japanese, see Kitagawa and Kuroda (1992) and Hoshi (1994a, 1994b) and references cited there. For related discussion, see Huang (1999).

[26] Or that of a complement verb in cases of long-distance passivization. The one exception is (55d), which is an example of the "indirect passive" under discussion here.

their subjects, as illustrated below:[27]

(65)   wo you   bei ta zi-mo-le.
        I   again BEI he self-touch-LE
        'I again had him 'self-draw' [on me].'
        (Said of a Mahjong game where one converts by drawing the last matching
        tile by oneself, rather than converting on an opponent's discarded tile.)

(66)   Lisi you   bei Wangwu jichu-le yi-zhi   quanleida.
        Lisi again BEI Wangwu hit-LE   one-CL   home-run
        'Lisi again had Wangwu hit a home run [on him].'

(67)   wo bei ta zhemo yi   zuo, jiu   shenme   dou kan-bu-jian-le.
        I   BEI he thus   one sit   then everything all can-not-see-LE
        'As soon as I had him sitting this way [on me], I couldn't see anything at all.'
        (Said of a concert, when someone tall sits in front of me and blocks my view.)

We have analyzed the direct passives as involving both movement (A or A′) and
control/predication. How should the indirect passives be analyzed? Considerations
of theoretical economy would lead us to expect that they may be subject to the same
or a similar analysis, involving both movement and control/predication. However,
although such an analysis can be entertained for the inclusive indirect passives,
it is not obvious how it can be implemented. Furthermore, for the adversative
passives with no missing NP position in the main predicate, an analysis in terms
of movement and control/predication seems apparently out of place. Let us take
up each of these two forms in turn.

4.3.2   The inclusive indirect passive

One sort of inclusive indirect passive is the "possessive passive," exemplified in (63)–(64), and (68) below.

(68)   Zhangsan bei tufei   dasi-le baba.   (Mandarin)
        Zhangsan BEI bandits kill-LE father
        'Zhangsan had his father killed by the bandits.'

Similar examples are commonly found in Taiwanese and other East Asian
languages:

(69)   goa ho   i   that-tio pakto   a.   (Taiwanese)
        I   PASS him   kick   stomach SFP
        'I was "kicked [my] stomach" by him.'

---

[27] Example (67) is from Shen (1992). It is the case, though, that Mandarin adversative
passives are considerably less widespread than, say, Japanese adversative passives. Thus,
while *wo bei ta ku le for 'I was affected by him crying' is not generally acceptable in
Mandarin, its Japanese counterpart is perceived to be quite natural.

(70)   John-ga   Mary-ni   kodomo-o sikar-are-ta.   (Japanese)
        John-NOM   Mary-DAT   child-ACC scold-PASS-PAST
        'John had his child scolded by Mary.'

(71)   haksayng-i sensayngnim-eykey son-ul   cap-hi-ess-ta.   (Korean)
        student-NOM teacher-DAT   hand-ACC catch-PASS-PAST-DECL
        'The student had his hand caught by the teacher.'
        (The student was caught by the hand by the teacher.)

Assuming that there is indeed a null possessive phrase in the predicate co-indexed with the subject of the passive verb in each of these sentences, the question arises as to how this anaphoric relationship is established. One possibility would be that the possessive phrase directly undergoes NOP movement. (To simplify discussion, we shall consider only long passives. Hence, the question will mainly concern how the sentences might be analyzed in terms of NOP movement and predication.) This "possessive raising" hypothesis must be ruled out, however, for the following reasons. First, movement out of a possessive phrase is prohibited, as this would violate Ross' (1967) Left Branch Condition (LBC). A similar problem arises with respect to the Complex NP Constraint (CNPC) in the following sentence, where the supposed movement would have originated from within a relative clause:

(72)   Lisi bei wo mai-zou-le   [[e] zui   xihuan de na-ben shu].
        Lisi BEI me buy-away-LE   most like   DE that-CL book
        'Lisi was affected by the fact that I bought up the book that [he] liked.'

Second, such a movement hypothesis would leave unexplained contrasts like the one between (68) and the following marginal sentence:

(73)   ??Zhangsan$_i$ bei tamen kanjian-le e$_i$ baba le.
        Zhangsan BEI they   scc-LE   father LE
        'Zhangsan was affected by the fact that they saw [his] father.'

If the possessive of *baba* 'father' were allowed to be moved out in (68), the same movement should be allowed in (73), but (73) is considerably less natural than (68).

It has been suggested in Huang (1992), inter alia, extending an idea of Thompson (1973), that sentences like (68)–(69) should be analyzed as involving a complex predicate with an "outer object" that controls the null possessor. The possessor is not a trace, but a Pro controlled by the outer object. What is moved is the outer object itself.

(74)

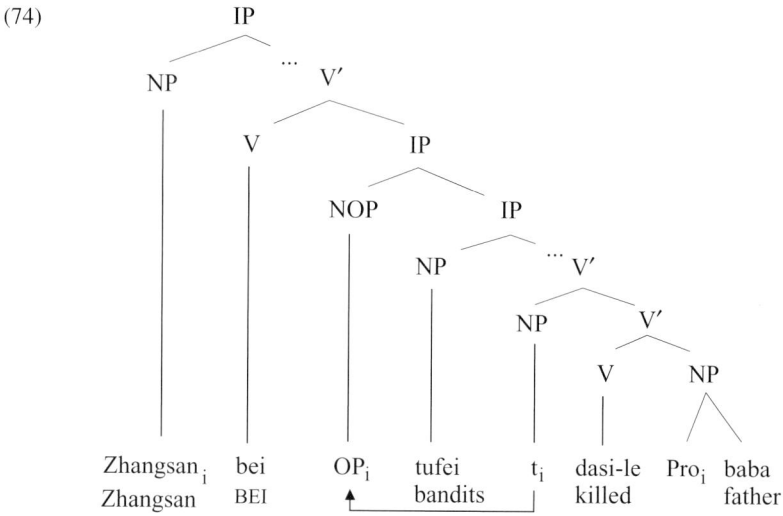

'Zhangsan was "father-killed" by the bandits.'

In this structure, the verb *dasi* 'kill' takes the NP *baba* 'father' as its immediate object. The verb and this object form a complex predicate V′ that takes another object, the "outer object." The outer object controls the possessor Pro and is in turn NOP-moved to IP, where it is coindexed with *Zhangsan* under predication. (Both predication and control are subject to a Minimal Distance Principle of the sort first proposed by Rosenbaum (1970), as part of the Generalized Control Theory of Huang (1984a, 1992), inter alia.) We take the standard view that theta-role assignment is compositional. The inner object receives the Patient/Theme role from the verb *dasi*, and the outer object receives the Affectee role from the V′ *dasi-le Pro baba*.

It is easy to see that the two problems encountered by the "possessive raising" hypothesis immediately disappear under the "outer object" hypothesis. First, since movement does not take place directly from the possessive position or from within a relative clause, neither the LBC nor the CNPC is violated. Secondly, the contrast between (68) and (73) receives a natural explanation. The complex predicate meaning 'kill one's father' can be semantically transitive (taking an Affectee as an outer object) as the event can indeed affect someone (the inalienable possessor of the father). On the other hand, the complex predicate meaning 'see one's father' (as in (73)) denotes an event that (under normal circumstances) can hardly affect anyone and hence is hard to construe as being semantically transitive.[28] The

---

[28] Unless *Zhangsan* has purposely hidden his father somewhere, in which case (73) is acceptable.

marginality of (73) therefore follows from the fact that the subject *Zhangsan* is not related to an Affectee of the event. The contrast observed below can be similarly explained:

(75)   zhuozi$_i$ bei wo da-duan-le   yi-tiao [e$_i$] tui.
        table   BEI I   hit-break-LE one-CL   leg
        'The table had one of its legs broken by me.'

(76)   *zhuozi$_i$ bei wo kanjian-le yi-tiao [e$_i$] tui.
         table   BEI I   see-LE   one-CL   leg
        *'The table had one of its legs seen by me.'

Assume that an entity can be "affected" in the linguistically relevant sense if it can be altered physically or psychologically by the event in question. Example (75) is therefore good because a table can be physically affected by one of its legs being broken, but (76) is bad because one can neither physically or psychologically affect a table by seeing it. (With an animate subject, (76) would range from marginal to acceptable, depending on the situation.) In other words, given a complex predicate analysis, we can say that the complex predicate meaning 'see a leg of' places a selectional restriction on its outer object that it be animate. This property is not one of the V *kanjian* 'see' alone, but that of the V′ complex.

What we have argued up to now is that, if inclusive indirect passives are to be derived via movement of something (NOP or PRO) into a position for predication or control, then movement must take place from an outer object position, not from a possessive position or from within a syntactic island. But is there evidence that movement actually takes place? One might contend, for example, that these sentences involve a relation of control, i.e., that the subject directly binds an empty category in a possessive position or within a relative clause. With the notion of a complex predicate, the subject can receive the Affectee theta-role compositionally, with no need for mediation or movement by an outer object.

Although this alternative view cannot be ruled out *a priori*, there is additional empirical evidence for the existence of an outer object (and hence movement). The first is theory-internal, bearing on the Minimal Distance Principle (MDP) alluded to above, which requires a PRO or NOP to be controlled by, or predicated on, the closest c-commanding NP. According to the MDP, the empty subject Pro in (72) (for example) is controlled by the Agent *wo*, not by the subject *Lisi*. But this is not the intended reading of this inclusive indirect passive. With the postulation of an outer object between *wo* and the complex predicate V′, the correct interpretation is obtained.

The existence of an outer object can also be detected from sentences like (77):

(77)   Zhang Zhenxing bei jianchaguan   qiu-xing   qi-nian.
        Zhang Zhenxing BEI district-attorney ask-for-jail-term seven-year
        'Zhang Zhenxing had the DA requesting a jail term of seven years for him.'

Although all argument positions seem to be filled already in the main predicate, note that the active IP below *bei* is itself incomplete:

(78)   *jianchaguan   qiu-xing   qi-nian.
         district-attorney ask-for-jail-term seven-year
         'The DA requested a jail term of seven years.'

This sentence gives a strong sense of being an incomplete transitive sentence whose object nevertheless does not seem to fit anywhere within the complex predicate. An outer object in the form of an NP-trace in (77) provides that missing object and renders the sentence grammatical. In fact, for some speakers the following is quite acceptable with the outer object case-licensed by *ba*:

(79)   jianchaguan   ba Zhangsan qiu-xing   qi-nian.
        district-attorney BA Zhangsan ask-for-jail-terms seven-year
        'The DA requested a jail term of seven years for Zhangsan.'

In Korean, evidence for an outer object comes directly from the existence of double accusative marked sentences like the following:

(80)   Mary-ka   John-ul   tali-lui   cha-ess-ta.
        Mary-NOM John-ACC leg-ACC kick-PAST-DECL
        'Mary kicked John in the leg.' [Lit. 'Mary "leg-kicked" John.']

The status of *John* as an outer object in (80), rather than as a possessive specifier of *tali* 'leg,' is confirmed by the ungrammaticality of (81), with a complex predicate denoting an event of leg-seeing:

(81)   *Mary-ka   John-ul   tali-lui   po-ess-ta.
         Mary-NOM John-ACC leg-ACC see-PAST-DECL
         Lit. 'Mary "leg-saw" John.'

The existence of "double accusative" constructions in Korean thus provides overt evidence for the outer object occurring in situ. As for why other languages do not also generally exhibit in situ outer objects, we can assume that these languages lack an appropriate device to Case-license them in their base position.

For Japanese, evidence for the outer object has been presented by Homma (1995), who independently made the same arguments regarding the notion of a natural transitive predicate and Korean double accusative constructions. In addition, citing Kayne (1975), Homma shows that certain Romance inalienable possessive constructions include an Affectee argument which must be accommodated in what we have dubbed the "outer object" position.

Hiroto Hoshi (personal communication) pointed out another piece of support for this hypothesis from quantifier floating:

(82)   gakusei-ga   sensei-ni   san-nin t kino   [sakubun-o home]-rare-ta.
         student-NOM teacher-DAT 3-CL   yesterday essay-ACC praise-PASS-PAST
         'Three students had their essays praised by the teacher yesterday.'
         Lit. 'Three students were "essay-praised" by the teacher yesterday.'

Note that the quantifier phrase (QP) *san-nin* '3-classifier,' which is related to *gakusei* 'student,' is stranded in the matrix clause, not as part of a possessive phrase modifying *sakubun* 'essays.' This shows that there must be a position in construction with the floated quantifier that is external to the complex predicate *sakubun-o home* 'praise the essays' but internal to the main VP headed by *rare*, and this is the position of the outer object.[29]

Summarizing, the complex predicate analysis for the "inclusive" indirect passive is supported by several independent considerations: (a) the theory of movement constraints; (b) contrasts between natural and unnatural "transitive complex

---

[29] The conclusion that certain cases of non-local (i.e., long-distance) passivization are reduced to the local passivization of an Affectee outer object raises the question of whether all apparent long-distance cases are so reducible. We think this is neither necessary nor empirically possible. For one thing, note that A′-movement cannot be dispensed with: even the locally moved outer objects have to be A′-moved, since the subject of IP is already filled. Since A′-movement can typically go long-distance (while respecting island constraints), it would be unnecessary, in fact undesirable, to suppose that all apparent cases of long-distance passivization are local passivization of the outer object. Furthermore, there are many grammatical passive sentences that can be derived by A′-movement using the resumptive pronoun strategy which could not be derived by the local movement of an outer object. We have seen with (74) that *dasi baba* 'kill father' can be a complex predicate taking an Affectee as an outer object. This is further evidenced by the fact that the Affectee can appear following *ba* in a *ba* construction:

(i)   tufei   ba Zhangsan [dasi-le Pro baba].
        bandit BA Zhangsan kill-LE Pro father
        'The bandits "father-killed" Zhangsan.'

predicates"; (c) distribution of quantifier floating; and (d) the overt existence of outer objects in some languages (e.g., Korean and Romance). Note that this analysis applies not only to long passives which involve NOP movement, but also to short passives involving PRO movement. The following are a few *indirect* short passives:

(83)   Beida bei daibu-le san-ge   xuesheng.
        PKU   BEI arrest-LE three-CL students
        'Peking University had three students arrested.'

(84)   tamen bei qiang-zou-le zui   xihuan de wanju.
        they BEI rob-away-LE most   like   DE toy
        'They had the toys that [they] liked most robbed [from them].'

Note crucially that in a *ba* construction of this sort, where *Zhangsan* is clearly an outer object, the Pro possessor of *baba* 'father' cannot be replaced by a pronoun:

(ii)   *tufei   ba Zhangsan [dasi-le ta baba].
        bandit BA Zhangsan kill-LE his father
        'The bandits "killed-his-father" Zhangsan.'

This prohibition does not apply to passivization, however. Thus both (iii) (=74) and (iv) are well-formed:

(iii)   Zhangsan bei tufei   dasi-le baba.
        Zhangsan BEI bandits kill-LE father
        'Zhangsan had his father killed by the bandits.'

(iv)   Zhangsan bei tufei   dasi-le ta-de baba.
        Zhangsan BEI bandits kill-LE his   father
        'Zhangsan had his father killed by the bandits.'

This difference between the passive and the *ba* construction can be accounted for if we say that (iv) is derived not by movement of an outer object, but by establishing an A'-dependency directly with the possessor using the resumptive pronoun strategy. The following contrast also shows the same point.

(v)   *Zhangsan ba Lisi da-le   ta   yixia.
        Zhangsan BA Lisi hit-LE him   once
        'Zhangsan hit Lisi once.'

(vi)   Lisi bei Zhangsan da-le   ta   yixia.
        Lisi BEI Zhangsan hit-LE him   once
        'Lisi was hit once by Zhangsan.'

Example (v) shows that the outer object *Lisi* cannot serve as the antecedent of the overt pronoun. The grammatical (vi) therefore cannot be derived by A'-movement of an outer object; an A'-dependency must be established with the possessor directly using the resumptive pronoun strategy.

If our analysis that the short passives involve PRO movement is correct, then something must be moved into the Spec of VP below *bei*. Given the above considerations, it is the hypothesized outer object that is moved, but not the Possessor of *san-ge xuesheng* 'three students' in (83) or the subject of the relative clause. The structure of (84), for example, is:

(85)

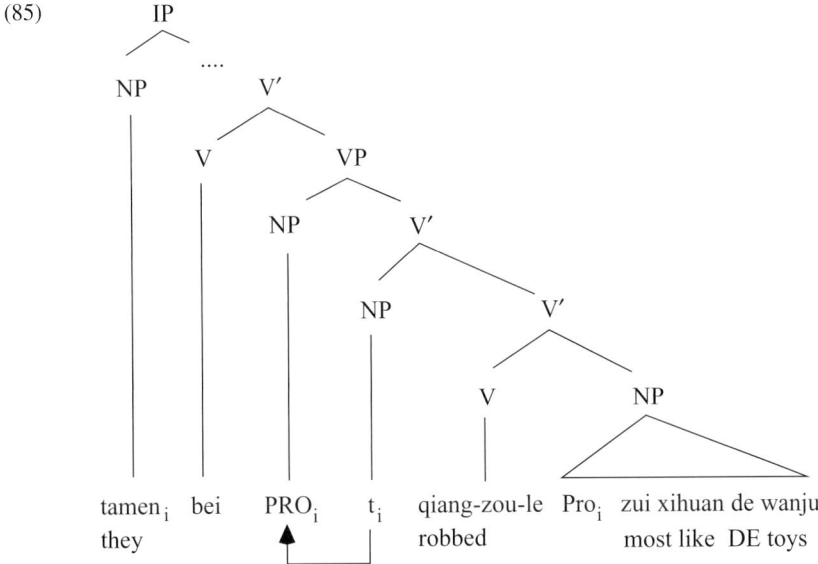

4.3.3   *The adversative passive*

We have argued that inclusive indirect passives should actually be analyzed as direct passives, i.e., as involving the promotion of some object, albeit an outer object. Like the direct passives, they involve both complementation and movement. Now what about the exclusive, adversative passive? The standard assumption in the literature is that this construction does not involve any movement or coindexation of any sort. The adversative passive sentence is just like a normal experiential sentence, except that the usual cases involve a neutral Experiencer, but *somehow* when the passive verb is used it displays a strong sense of adversity. The subject is completely "excluded" in the real sense.

This standard assumption, however, is not obviously the best assumption. Our suggestion is that the adversative passives, too, can and should be treated as involving an outer object of some kind – one that is even more remote from the verb than the outer object involved in the inclusive indirect passive. For lack of a better term, let us call this adversely affected object the "outermost object," and assume that it bears the theta-role Indirect Affectee. We also propose that whereas the (direct) Affectee is an object of a V′, the Indirect Affectee is an object of the VP.[30] Still assuming the Predicate Internal Subject Hypothesis, an adversative passive like (66) has the following structure:

(86)

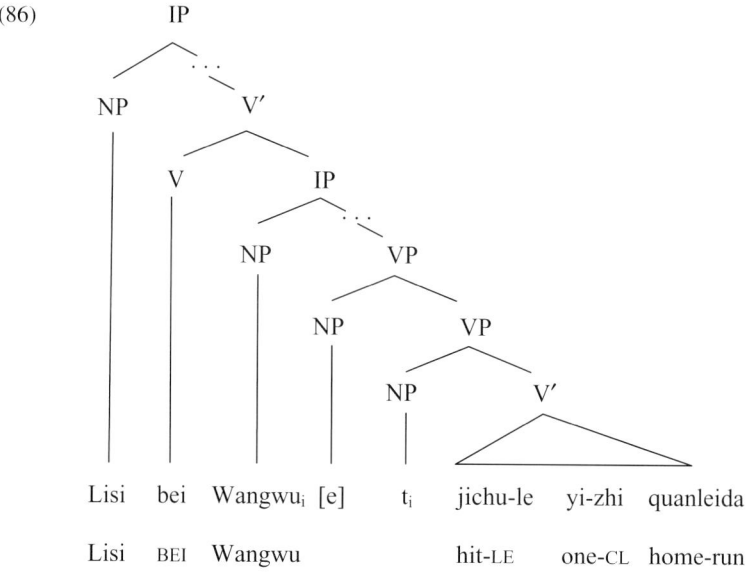

Lisi	bei	Wangwu$_i$ [e]		t$_i$	jichu-le	yi-zhi	quanleida
Lisi	BEI	Wangwu			hit-LE	one-CL	home-run

'Lisi had Wangwu hit a home run on him.'

In this structure, [e] is the "outermost object." It is seen as an object of the VP whose subject has raised to IP. The outermost object undergoes NOP movement and is coindexed with the subject *Lisi*.

The assumption that the "outer object" is an object of the V′ and the "outermost object" the object of the VP very elegantly characterizes the two meanings of the following Taiwanese sentence:

(87)   goa ho i   yong-tiao nengpa kho   khi-a.
        I PASS him use-up   200   dollars away-SFP
        a. 'I had [my] 200 dollars used up by him.'
        b. 'I am affected by his using up [his own] 200 dollars.'

---

[30] In a more fine-grained event structure where the verb is fully decomposed, both the "object of VP" and the "object of V′" are each in fact the Spec of a light verb with the elementary semantics of '(indirectly) affect.'

The first reading is the "inclusive indirect" reading, and the second reading is the adversative, (so-called) exclusive reading.[31] The inclusive reading is obtained when the "outer object" is adjoined to V′, where it can control the Pro possessor of *nengpa kho* '200 dollars.' The adversative reading is obtained with the "outermost object" adjoined to VP, where it is too far away to control the Pro possessor. (Instead, the trace of the embedded subject *i* 'him' controls the possessor.)

The proposal to represent the adversely affected NP as the "outermost object" of a predicate thus provides us with a structural account of the distinction between a neutral experiential sentence and an adversative experiential sentence and explains adversity as a property of the exclusive indirect passives. A sentence is passive if its subject has prototypical object properties. The most prototypical object is the NP bearing the Patient role. Such a situation automatically obtains when indeed a direct object that bears the Patient role is passivized. The less directly involved one is in an event, the harder it is for one to qualify as the reference of object, unless it is understood to be affected in some way, most typically in an adverse way. Thus when an outer object is passivized to form an inclusive indirect passive, adversity adds to its naturalness. And when an outermost object is passivized, adversity becomes a requirement. The amount of adversity required for a sentence to sound natural is inversely proportionate to the proximity of the passivized argument to the main verb.

We have thus treated all forms of the passive as inclusive passives. In fact, they are all "direct" passives in the sense that they all involve the passivization of an object (inner, outer, or outermost object). At least as far as the cases we have dealt with are concerned, we have a highly uniform characterization of the East Asian type of passives: they possess basically the same properties – involving both movement and complementation. If this is correct, there ceases to be any ground for the traditional debates between uniform and non-uniform approaches.

The postulation of an "outermost object" is not only justified on theoretical considerations but also supported by empirical evidence. Although in Mandarin there seems to be no grammatical active counterpart to the adversative passive, in Taiwanese it is common to use the *ka* construction (often said to be the Tai-wanese counterpart of the Mandarin *ba* construction) to make an active adversative sentence. In the following active sentences, the NP immediately following *ka* fits

---

[31] The inclusive reading comes more readily than the adversative reading, but the latter is still possible. Some speakers find the adversative reading difficult to get. This is natural, for pragmatic reasons. In general, the availability of a direct passive reading of a sentence will pretty much exclude an indirect reading; and the availability of an inclusive indirect reading is much more accessible than an exclusive reading.

perfectly the description of our "outermost object":

(88)   yi ka goa tsao-khi   a.
        he KA I   run-away SFP
        'He ran away on me.'

(89)   yin ka lan yiaN kui-a   tiuN   khi   a.
        they KA we   win   several games away SFP
        'They won several games away on us already.'

(90)   goa kinazit be khimo, be   lai   ka i   thetsa hapan.
        I   today   not happy will come KA him earlier take-off
        'Today I'm not happy, so I will quit early for the day on him [e.g., my boss].'

(91)   i   chhittsa-petsa to   ka goa hapan, ho   goa kiong beh khisi.
        He so-early   then KA me take-off, cause me almost will anger-death
        'He left for the day so early on me, it almost angered me to death.'

Note that in each case the NP following *ka* is completely dispensable for the completeness of the sense of its predicate. The *ka*-NP is simply added by brute force, so to speak, to what seems to be already a complete predicate, and it is understood that the reference of the *ka*-NP is psychologically affected, most generally in an adverse way.[32]

As shown in the translation for each of (88)–(91), English expresses adversity by putting the Indirect Affectee within an *on*-PP. The status of the *on*-PP in English has never, as far as we know, been made clear in the literature, but in light of the Taiwanese data it seems quite reasonable to treat it as an "outermost object" of VPs.[33]

French, too, seems to provide good evidence for the existence of an "outermost object." All the following sentences convey some degree of passivity:

(92)   a. Jean s'est fait broyer par un camion.
            'Jean *se* got crushed by a truck.'

        b. Jean s'est fait broyer la jambe par un camion.
            'Jean *se* had his leg crushed by a truck.'

---

[32] Sometimes a benefactive, rather than adversative, sense is present, but often with a sarcastic tone. For example, suppose someone has been bragging about his cooking, and we decide to do him a favor by accepting his invitation to dinner. The following sentence is acceptable:

(i)   lan lai   ka i   chia chit-waN.
       let's come KA him eat   one-bowl
       'Let's eat a bowl on him.'

[33] As expected from Case-theoretic considerations, the Indirect Affectee must appear within a PP. The choice of preposition *on* is determined by thematic-role considerations (*to* for a Goal argument, and *on* for an Indirect Affectee, etc.).

   c. Jean s'est fait broyer sa voiture par un camion.
     'Jean *se* had his car crushed by a truck.'

   d. Jean s'est fait broyer la voiture de son amie par un camion.
     'Jean *se* had his friend's car crushed by a truck.'

   e. Jean s'est fait broyer la voiture de Marie par un camion.
     'Jean *se* had Marie's car crushed by a truck.'

Note that each sentence above contains the reflexive clitic *se*. Thus, although (92a) is directly translatable as 'Jean got crushed by a truck,' a more faithful translation might be 'Jean got himself crushed by a truck,' with the reflexive treated as the Indirect Affectee. The case for an "outermost object" is even more compelling in (92b–e). Here the reflexive clitic cannot have originated as a direct argument of any verb or as a possessor of a larger NP because all syntactic positions for such functions are already lexically filled. As a result the reflexive may be felt to be an unnecessary element that should be deleted. But the reflexive is crucially needed for the passive reading to be present – without it, these sentences would only have a causative reading. We can solve this problem by analyzing the reflexive as the "outermost object" denoting the Indirect Affectee. It is the presence of an outermost object that gives rise to passivity. And since the outermost object is only indirectly affected, a sense of adversity normally accompanies this kind of passive.[34]

    In short, we have seen that the "outermost object" analysis of the adversative passive is justified on several important considerations: (a) the speakers' intuition about the active–passive contrast; (b) the existence of overt outermost objects (in Taiwanese, English, and French); and (c) the fact that it explains adversity, tying it to the notion of prototypical objecthood. An additional advantage of the analysis is that it enables us to treat all passive forms uniformly, as direct passives formed by complementation and movement.

4.4   Summary

    In this chapter we have argued for a unifying approach to the various passive forms in Chinese. All of the various passives are derived by complementation *and* movement. The long passives are formed by clausal complementation and A'-movement of an NOP which is then predicated on the matrix subject of *bei*. The short passives are formed by VP complementation and A-movement of

---

[34] See Authier and Reed (1992) and references cited for the treatment of "affected datives." Their treatments of the reflexive clitic in (92) corresponds to what we analyze here as an "outermost object."

a PRO, subject to control by the matrix subject. Contrary to earlier analyses of indirect passives, we have proposed that they are derived in a fashion similar to the direct passives. The difference between them lies in which object undergoes movement: a direct passive involves the movement of the inner object, while an indirect passive is formed by moving the outer or outermost object.

5

The *ba* construction

The basic facts about *ba* are deceptively simple:

(1) a. Lisi sha-le na-ge   huaidan.
   Lisi kill-LE that-CL scoundrel
   'Lisi killed that scoundrel.'

   b. Lisi ba na-ge   huaidan   sha-le.
   Lisi BA that-CL scoundrel kill-LE
   'Lisi killed that scoundrel.'

(2) a. Linyi qi-lei-le   ma.
   Linyi ride-tired-LE horse
     i. 'Linyi rode a horse and made it tired.'
     ii. 'Linyi became tired from riding a horse.'

   b. Linyi ba ma   qi-lei-le.
   Linyi BA horse ride-tired-LE
   Intended reading: same as (2ai).

The object of *ba* is typically, though not always, the object of a verb. In some intuitive sense this object is "disposed" or "affected" in the event described.[1] For instance, the NP *ma* 'horse' after *ba* in (2b) must be made tired from the event of horse-riding, effectively excluding the second reading found with (2a).

As simple as the *ba* construction appears, the difficulty lies in how best to characterize the properties of the *ba* construction to achieve the maximal degree of empirical adequacy. Beyond the straightforward examples readily accepted by all speakers is a wide range of extended cases that are more or less acceptable in various dialects. The complexity of the data has generated such an amount of work in Chinese linguistics that it simply is impossible to list all of them. The reader is referred to, among many others, Bender (2000), Bennett (1981), Chao (1968), Cheng (1986), Cheung (1973), Frei (1956), Goodall (1987, 1990), Hashimoto (1971), Huang (1982b), Koopman (1984), F. Li (1997), J.-I. Li (1997),

---

[1] The term *disposal* was used in L. Wang (1954) and Chao (1968) to describe the characteristic interpretation of the post-*ba* NP that something is done to the entity it denotes. In current syntax and syntactico-semantics, such an NP is more commonly said to be *affected*.

Li and Thompson (1981), Y. Li (1995), A. Li (1990, 2005), Y.-C. Li (1974), S.-F. Lin (1974), T.-H. Lin (2001), Liu (1997), K. Mei (1978b), Peyraube (1996), Shi (2000), Sun (1996), Sybesma (1999),[2] Teng (1975), Tiee (1986), Travis (1984), H. Wang (1984), L. Wang (1954), M. Q. Wang (1987), P. Wang (1970), M. Wu (1982), Yang (1995), and Zou (1995) for a glimpse of the properties of *ba* and the variety of the relevant theories and approaches they represent.

Despite all of this attention, there has not been a clear consensus on how best to characterize the properties of the *ba* construction. The limited space here unfortunately prevents us from doing justice to the vastness of the relevant literature. We shall therefore focus only on works in the generative literature. Through the following discussion, we hope to clarify what issues have found resolution and what other problems remain, perhaps simply beyond the scope of grammatical studies. We will consider certain important grammatical properties of the *ba* construction and show how their characterization has remained murky to the present day.

For reasons that will become clear shortly, we start with a comparison of the *ba* construction with the passive *bei* construction.

5.1   *ba* and *bei* constructions

The *ba* and *bei* constructions have often been brought together because they are generally regarded as two closely related patterns serving special functions. The *bei* construction has been said to carry a "pejorative" meaning (see L. Wang 1954, Chao 1968: 703 about Chinese passives "usually of unfavorable meanings") describing an unfortunate event,[3] although contemporary Chinese does not require such a pragmatic constraint in all cases.[4] The *ba* construction expresses an object being affected, dealt with, or disposed of, although these terms are very difficult

---

[2] Sybesma (1999) is an extensive revision of Sybesma (1992) and includes many of his other works. We will mainly quote from Sybesma (1999). See Sybesma (1999: 220–221) for other related references.

[3] L. Li (1980) and H. Wang (1984), among others, noted that the unfortunate event does not have to be from the perspective of the subject. It can be in regard to the speaker or other elements in the sentence or discourse.

[4] However, according to a recent corpus study by Xiao, McEnery, and Qian (2006), passives are no longer restricted to verbs with an inflictive meaning in Chinese. Their study of the LCMC corpus includes thirty-one verbs with a negative meaning (e.g., *bang* 'truss up,' *jie* 'rob,' *pian* 'cheat,' and *sha* 'kill'), six verbs with a positive meaning (e.g., *pingwei* 'choose . . . as,' *yuwei* 'honour . . . as,' *tisheng* 'promote,' and *feng* 'confer (a title)'), and twenty-four verbs that are neutral (e.g., *chengwei* 'call,' *renming* 'appoint,' and *anpai* 'arrange'). Many other works noted the possibility of non-negative meaning in passives, such as Liang (1958) and Shao and Zhao (2005). Zhang (2001) uses the notion of direct and indirect causer/affectee (shi-yin-zhe/shou-dong-zhe) to distinguish the *ba* and *bei* constructions.

to define clearly and accurately to allow all acceptable sentences and rule out the unacceptable ones.[5] These two constructions are variations of the canonical SVO order: in the *bei* construction, what would ordinarily be the object becomes the subject of the sentence; in the *ba* construction, it surfaces as the object of *ba*. That is, the subject of *bei* generally corresponds to the object of *ba*.[6] In addition, the presence of *ba* and *bei* provides an extra position for an argument: the subject of *bei* and the object of *ba* can generally accommodate an argument that is one too many to occupy an argument position in a canonical sentence. The corresponding patterns are illustrated in (3), whose verb cannot be followed by two objects, and (4), whose semantic object appears as the possessor of the object of the complex verb *mian-zhi* 'relieve (someone of his) job':

(3)   a. *wo zhuang-man-le kache daocao.
          I   load-full-LE   truck hay

        b. kache bei wo zhuang-man-le daocao.
           truck BEI me load-full-LE   hay
           'I loaded the truck with hay.'

        c. wo ba kache zhuang-man-le daocao.
           I   BA truck load-full-LE   hay
           'I loaded the truck with hay.'

(4)   a. wo mian-le   Lisi de zhi.
          I   relieve-LE Lisi DE job
          'I fired Lisi.'

        b. Lisi bei wo mian-le   zhi.
           Lisi BEI me relieve-LE job
           'Lisi was fired by me.'

        c. wo ba Lisi mian-le   zhi.
           I   BA Lisi relieve-LE job
           'I fired Lisi.'

Nonetheless, the loosening of the restriction is only obvious in the cases when an inner object is passivized. The structures provided in the previous chapter for the three types of *bei* constructions only allow the cases with an inner object not to involve an affected object. The other two types, an outer object and an outermost object, are assigned an "affected" theta-role.

[5] See Sybesma (1999: 132) for a brief summary of the terms used to describe the *ba* construction. The important ones are: the "disposal construction" (L. Wang 1954, Chao 1968, Li and Thompson 1981, Tiee 1986), "the executive construction" (Hashimoto 1971), the "accusative construction" (Teng 1975), and "a highly transitive construction," where "transitivity" is defined as "the carrying over of an activity from an agent to a patient" (M. Q. Wang 1987: 72).

[6] The discourse functions of topic or focus have been attached to the subject of *bei* and the object of *ba*. Tsao (1977) argues that the object of *ba* is a secondary topic. Shao and Zhao (2005) use the notion of focus or highlighting to express these objects.

Both *bei* and *ba* constructions are limited by a number of factors. For instance, verb types affect acceptability. The following examples are some instances that are not acceptable in the *ba* and *bei* patterns.

(5)　a. *Lisi bei wo renshi-le hen jiu　le.
　　　　Lisi BEI me know-LE very long LE
　　　　'Lisi has been known for a very long time by me.'

　　　b. *wo ba Lisi renshi-le hen jiu　le.
　　　　I　BA Lisi know-LE very long LE
　　　　'I have known Lisi for a very long time.'

(6)　a. *zhe-ge wenti　bei ta　xihuan-le.[7]
　　　　this-CL question BEI him like-LE
　　　　'This question has been liked by him.'

　　　b. *wo ba zhe-ge wenti　xihuan-le.
　　　　I　BA this-CL question like-LE
　　　　'I liked this question.'

(7)　a. *ta bei women baifang-le henduo ci.
　　　　he BEI us　visit-LE　many　times
　　　　'He was visited many times by us.'

　　　b. *women ba ta　baifang-le henduo ci.
　　　　we　BA him visit-LE　many　times
　　　　'We visited him many times.'

Moreover, both constructions generally are not possible with verbs in the bare form. They require complex verb phrases.[8] The following examples briefly

---

[7] This cannot be ruled out by the requirement of "pejorative" meaning because the fact of his liking the question might be unfortunate to the speaker, similar to *zhe-ge wenti bei ta jie chulai le* 'the problem was solved by him' – his solving the problem was regarded as unfortunate by the speaker. The semantic/pragmatic constraint on the use of the *bei* construction is as difficult to characterize as for the *ba* construction. See Sections 5.5–5.6.

[8] There are many classifications made regarding the types of possible complex verb phrases. For instance, Lü (1955, 1980) classified thirteen patterns for the *ba* construction, which has been the foundation of many subsequent works, such as Sybesma (1999: 135–9), who combined them into ten classes, and Liu (1997: 68–71), who listed nine patterns (see Section 5.6 and A. Li 2006 for a review).

For the short passive cases with *bei* immediately followed by a V, the verb can be a bare one (see L. Yang 2006), such as:

(i)　a. ta bu xihuan bei ma.
　　　　he not like　bei scold
　　　　'He does not like being scolded.'

　　　b. ta xianxie bei da.
　　　　he almost BEI hit
　　　　'He was almost hit.'

illustrate this restriction:

(8)   a. *Lisi bei women ma.
           Lisi BEI us   scold
           'Lisi was scolded by us.'

        b. *women ba Lisi ma.
           we   BA Lisi scold
           'We scolded Lisi.'

(9)   a. Lisi bei women ma-le.
           Lisi BEI us   scold-LE
           'Lisi was scolded by us.'

        b. women ba Lisi ma-le.
           we   BA Lisi scold-LE
           'We scolded Lisi.'

(10)   a. Lisi bei women ma(-le) yi-dun.
           Lisi BEI us   scold-LE one-while
           'Lisi was given a scolding by us.'

        b. women ba Lisi ma(-le) yi-dun.
           we   BA Lisi scold-LE one-while
           'We gave Lisi a scolding.'

(11)   a. Lisi bei women ma de hen lihai.
           Lisi BEI us   scold DE very serious
           'Lisi was scolded seriously by us.'

        b. women ba Lisi ma de hen lihai.
           we   BA Lisi scold DE very serious
           'We scolded Lisi seriously.'

Despite the many similarities, the *ba* and *bei* constructions differ in some important ways. Mainly, they differ in the following respects.

First, the *ba* construction accepts fewer types of verbs than the *bei* construction. The following are examples with perception verbs.

(12)   a. ta bei women kandao/tingjian-le.
           he BEI us   see/hear-LE
           'He was seen/heard by us.'

In these instances, the bare verb and *bei* form a phonological unit. For the *ba* construction, a bare verb is also possible when it has more than one syllable:

(ii)   ni bu yinggai ba tamen daibu, you   mashang   shifang.
        you not should BA they arrest again immediately release
        'You should not arrest them and release (them) immediately.'

See Feng (1995) for the effect of prosody on the *bei* construction.

  b. *women ba ta kandao/tingjian-le.
    we BA him see/hear-LE
    'We saw/heard him.'

(13) a. ta-de mimi bei women faxian-le.
    his secret BEI us discover-LE
    'His secrets were discovered by us.'

  b. *women ba ta-de mimi faxian-le.
    we BA his secret discover-LE
    'We discovered his secret.'

It has been pointed out that it is not simply the verb types that affect the acceptability of *ba* and *bei* constructions (see W.-X. Zhang 2001, among others). It is the notion of whether something (entity or event) is affected. Thus, even though the following *ba* and *bei* sentences are not quite acceptable, the *bei* construction can be made acceptable by changing the subject to an NP that can be affected by the event, as in (15).

(14) a. *wo ba lan-tian kanjian-le.
    I BA blue-sky see-LE

  b. *lan-tian bei wo kanjian-le.
    blue-sky BEI I see-LE

(15) ta bei wo kanjian-le.
    he BEI I see-LE
    'He was seen by me.'

The restrictions on the use of the *ba* construction have largely been attributed to a requirement on the NP following *ba* – referred to as the post-*ba* NP – being an affectee. Only those that have been afflicted upon, or "dealt with" are acceptable as post-*ba* NPs (recall the terms of "disposal," "executive," and "strong transitivity" listed in note 5). Indeed, Zhang (2001) notes that the two main differences between *ba* and *bei* constructions are (i) direct or indirect influence and (ii) direct or indirect cause. We briefly describe the first difference:[9] *ba* sentences require

---

[9] The second difference discussed by Zhang can be illustrated by the following pair of examples (adapted from his (19a–b)):

(i) a. wo chouyan, diyi kou jiu ba wo qiang de lianlian kesou.
   I smoke first mouth then BA I choke DE continuously cough
   'I smoked; the first try immediately choked me and kept me coughing.'

  b. *wo chouyan, jiu bei diyi kou qiang de lianlian kesou.
   I smoke then BEI first mouth choke DE continuously cough
   'I smoked and was immediately choked by the first try, keeping me coughing.'

According to Zhang, *diyi kou* is not a direct causer. A direct causer integrates with a result (*zhijie shiyin chengfen he jieguo rong wei yi-ti*). Readers are referred to Zhang's article for more examples based on these notions.

the post-*ba* NP to be directly affected by an action. In contrast, *bei* sentences may just express an indirect effect of an action. What is affected need not be expressed as an argument in the sentence. The following pairs of sentences provide further illustrations (see note 4) (Zhang's examples (13) and (16)):

(16) a. *wo ba na-ge   xiaoxi zhidao-le.
         I   BA that-CL news   know-LE

      b. na-ge   xiaoxi bei wo zhidao-le.
         that-CL news   BEI I   know-LE
         'The news became known to me.'

(17) a. *laoshi   ba ta-de zhi-tiao kanjian-le.
         teacher BA his   scrip   see-LE

      b. ta-de zhi-tiao bei laoshi   kanjian-le.
         his   scrip   BEI teacher see-LE
         'His scrip was seen by the teacher.'

According to Zhang, the NP following *ba* must be the one that is directly affected. Because what is seen or known cannot be affected, the *ba* sentences above are not acceptable. However, the subject NP of *bei* need not be the one that is affected. What is affected is an indirect participant, such as *ta* in (17b) and someone who might be affected by the event of the news becoming known to me in (16b). Nonetheless, as will be shown later in this chapter, the notions of "affectee" or "affected" are very vague and difficult to characterize. Moreover, having an Affectee does not guarantee the acceptability of a *ba* sentence. Notably, the *ba* counterpart to the third type of *bei* sentences discussed in the last chapter – the adversative passive – is generally much less acceptable:[10]

(18) a. Linyi you   bei Wangwu jichu-le yi-zhi   quanleida.
         Linyi again BEI Wangwu hit-LE   one-CL home-run
         'Linyi again had Wangwu hit a home run [on him].'

      b. ??Wangwu you   ba Linyi jichu-le yi-zhi   quanleida.
         Wangwu again BA Linyi hit-LE   one-CL home-run
         'Wangwu again hit a home run on Linyi.'

(19) a. wo bei ta zheme yi   zuo, (wo) jiu   shenme   dou
         I   BEI he thus one sit   I   then everything all
         kan-bu-jian le.
         can-not-see LE
         'As soon as I had him sitting this way [on me], I couldn't see anything at all.' [Said of a concert, when someone tall sits in front of me and blocks my view.]

---

[10] Because of the influence of the *ka* construction in Taiwanese, Taiwan Mandarin speakers accept the third type more generously than the Northern Mandarin speakers.

b. ??ta   ba   wo   zheme   yi   zuo,   (wo)   jiu   shenme   dou
    he   BA   I   thus   one   sit   I   then   everything   all
    kan-bu-jian   le.
    can-not-see   LE
    'He sat this way [on me]; I could not see anything.'

These examples indicate that the possibilities for the *ba* construction are more limited than for the *bei* construction. Nonetheless, there are other cases showing that the *bei* construction is more restricted. An instance showing such different restrictions is the loss of interpretive possibilities in the *bei* construction. The *ba* sentence below has several interpretations (Y. Li 1995, 1999); however, the *bei* construction loses the interpretation according to which the subject of *bei* is both an Affectee and an Agent.

(20) a. xiaohai ba mama   zhui-lei-le.
      child   BA mother chase-tired-LE
      i. 'The child chased the mother and the mother became tired.'
      ii. 'The child got the mother tired from chasing him.'

    b. mama   bei xiaohai zhui-lei-le.
      mother BEI child   chase-tired-LE
      i. 'The child chased the mother and the mother became tired.'
      ii. *'The child got the mother tired from chasing him.'

In the following case, even though the *ba* sentence is ambiguous, the *bei* sentence must have the interpretation according to which the subject of *bei* is also the subject of the result complement.

(21) wo ba tamen da-de shou dou zhong-le.
    I   BA them hit-DE hand all   swollen-LE
    i. 'I hit them such that my hands got swollen.'
    ii. 'I hit them such that their hands got swollen.'

(22) tamen bei wo da-de shou dou zhong-le.
    They BEI I hit-DE hand all   swollen LE
    i. 'They were hit by me such that their hands got swollen.'
    ii. *'They were hit by me such that my hands got swollen.'

When the subject of the *ba* sentence, not the post-*ba* NP, is the subject of the result complement, the *bei* counterpart is unacceptable.

(23) a. wo ba fan   chi-bao, jiu   lai.
      I   BA meal eat-full   then   come
      'I will come when I eat my fill (finish my meal).'

    b. *fan   bei wo chi-bao, (wo) jiu   lai.
      meal BEI I   eat-full (I)   then   come
      'When the meal is eaten-full by me, I will come.'

These examples suggest that it is the subject of the *bei* sentence, not the NP following *bei*, that can be thematically related to the complement of the main verb (the result complement 'tired' in (20), 'hands swollen' in (21)–(22) and 'full' in (23)). In contrast, either the subject of the *ba* sentence or the NP following *ba* can be thematically related to the complement. The restriction on the *bei* construction might be related to the fact that an operator is involved in this construction and this operator must be controlled by the subject of *bei* (see the analysis of the *bei* construction in the previous chapter).[11] The contrast between *ba* and *bei* constructions in this respect suggests that the structure for the *ba* construction must be different from the one for the *bei* construction. Indeed, there is evidence that, in contrast to the *bei* construction, the *ba* construction does not exhibit the properties characteristic of operator movement. Unlike the *bei* construction, the *ba* construction neither occurs with *suo*, nor allows a resumptive pronoun in the typical object of verb position, when the post-*ba* NP is interpreted as the object of the verb.[12] These facts are illustrated below.

[11] This might be related to Visser's Generalization, i.e., subject control verbs generally do not passivize (see, for instance, Bresnan 1982, Sag and Pollard 1991 for extensive discussions).

[12] The long-distance dependency relation demonstrated in Section 4.1.3.1 of the previous chapter seems to be somewhat likely with the *ba* construction:

  (i)   Zhangsan bei Lisi pai   jingcha zhua-zou-le.
         Zhangsan BEI Lisi send police arrest-LE
         'Zhangsan was "sent-police-to-arrest" by Lisi.'

  (ii)   Zhangsan bei wo jiao Lisi qing Wangwu dai dao xuexiao.
         Zhangsan BEI I   tell Lisi ask Wangwu bring to school
         'Zhangsan was "told-LS-to-ask-WW-to bring to school" by me.'

  (iii) ?Zhangsan ba Lisi pai   jingcha zhua-zou-le.
         Zhangsan BA Lisi send police arrest-LE
         'Zhangsan sent police to arrest Lisi.'

  (iv) ?wo ba Zhangsan jiao Lisi qing Wangwu dai dao xuexiao.
         I   BA Zhangsan tell Lisi ask Wangwu bring to school
         'I told Lisi to ask Wangwu to bring Zhangsan to school.'

Further note that the use of a resumptive pronoun in such cases seems to make the *ba* sentences less acceptable:

  (v)   *wo ba Zhangsan$_i$ jiao Lisi qing Wangwu dai   ta$_i$
         I   BA Zhangsan ask Lisi invite Wangwu bring him
         dao xuexiao.
         to   school
         'I asked Lisi to invite Wangwu to bring Zhangsan to school.'

Thus, the relative acceptability of (iii) and (iv) does not seem to argue for a long-distance dependency relation in the *ba* construction. An outer object can still be assigned by the complex VP. Addressing this issue clearly would require identifying and formulating more precisely the conditions governing the distribution of outer objects.

(24)   tamen ba zhexie shiqing (*suo) zuo-wan-le.
        they BA these thing   SUO do-finish-LE
        'They finished doing these things.'

(25)   Linyi ba ta   (*suo) pian-de   tuantuanzhuan.
        Linyi BA him   SUO cheat-till run-around
        'Linyi pushed him around like a fool.'

The following examples show that the *ba* construction does not allow a resumptive pronoun coindexed with the NP following *ba*:

(26)   Lisi ba Linyi da-le (*ta) yi-xia.
        Lisi BA Linyi hit-LE him once
        'Lisi hit Linyi once.'

The facts above demonstrate that the *ba* and *bei* constructions differ in whether or not they involve an operator movement process. The latter is derived by an operator moved to the periphery of the clause embedded under the (modal) verb *bei*, predicated of the subject of *bei* (see the previous chapter). On the other hand, the *ba* construction does not seem to involve an operator.

Briefly summarizing, the facts above demonstrate that the *ba* and *bei* constructions, although quite similar in carrying special meanings and providing an additional argument position, are subject to some different constraints. The *ba* construction should not be derived in the same way as the *bei* construction. The *bei* construction is analyzed as a pattern containing the verb (or modal) *bei* assigning a thematic role to its subject and taking an IP or VP as its complement. An operator is moved to the periphery of the complement and is controlled by the subject of *bei*. *Ba* might also take a VP as a complement. However, it does not seem to assign a theta-role to its subject or take an IP as its complement. Nor does it have the same operator movement as in the *bei* construction. These important characteristics of the *ba* construction (vs. the *bei* construction) will help characterize this structure. We turn to the analysis of *ba* by first considering some of its morpho-syntactic properties.

5.2   What is *ba*?[13]

Ba seems to have been analyzed in every possible way in the literature.

5.2.1   *The categorial status of* ba

Historically, *ba* was a lexical verb meaning 'take, hold, handle' (see Bennett 1981, H. Wang 1957, L. Wang 1954, for instance). It also occurred in

---

[13] This section and Sections 5.5–5.6 are adapted from A. Li (2006).

the so-called serial verb construction [V1 + NP + V2 + XP],[14] with *ba* as V1 [*ba* + NP + V + XP]. The pattern can mean 'to take NP and do [V XP] (to it).' Such a historical origin remains detectable in many contemporary *ba* sentences.[15] For instance, the following question and answer pairs in Modern Chinese look like serial verb constructions:

(27) a. ni   ba juzi   zenmeyang-le?
         you BA orange how-LE
         'What did you do to the orange?'

      b. wo ba juzi bo-le   pi   le.
         I   BA orange peel-LE skin LE
         'I peeled the skin off the orange.'

(28) a. ni yao ba ta   zenmeyang?
         you want BA him how
         'What do you want to do to him?'

      b. wo yao ba ta   da-duan   tui.
         I   want BA him hit-broken leg
         'I want to break his leg.'

These sentences bear great similarity in form to the serial verb construction [Subject + V1 + NP + V2 + XP]. They are interpreted as 'Subject takes NP and does [V + XP] to it; what the subject does to NP is [V + XP]': (27b) means 'what I did to the orange was to peel its skin' and (28b) means that 'what I want to do to him is to break (his) leg.'

However, *ba* in Modern Chinese has lost standard verbal properties, according to most of the works on this construction (see Zou 1995 for an extensive review of relevant works). It has become "grammaticalized"[16] and does not behave like a verb according to traditional verbhood tests: (i) it cannot take an aspect marker (29b); (ii) it cannot form an alternative V-not-V question (29c) (however, see note

[14] A "serial verb construction" is not a unified structural notion. It refers to all constructions with the surface form of more than one verb phrase occurring consecutively. Structurally, the series of VPs can be analyzed as different types of coordination or subordination structures. See Li and Thompson (1981, Chapter 2), among many others. Other more recent works include A. Li (2006).

[15] In modern Shanghai and Wuhan dialects, it is possible in some cases to use *ba* in the pattern [*ba* NP1 V NP2] with NP2 being a pronoun coreferential with NP1 (Bingfu Lu, Yuzhi Shi, personal communication).

[16] Several West African languages, such as Twi and Fong, have similar constructions involving the grammaticalization of a morpheme like *ba*; see Zou (1995) for discussions on cross-linguistic comparisons of such structures and the grammaticalization process.

18); and (iii) it cannot serve as a simple answer to a question (29d) (see, e.g., Chao 1968, Li and Thompson 1981).[17]

(29) a. ta ba ni   hai-le.
          he BA you hurt-LE
          'He hurt you.'

      b. *ta ba-le ni   hai(-le).
          he BA-LE you hurt(-LE)
          'He hurt you.'

      c. (*)ta ba-mei/bu-ba ni   hai(-le).[18]
          he BA-not-BA   you hurt-LE
          'Did he hurt you?'

      d. *(mei/bu-)ba
          (not-)BA

However, such morpho-syntactic tests are not quite satisfactory. There is a very small number of verbs in Chinese that simply do not behave like standard verbs according to these tests; nonetheless, they are clearly verbs. *Shi* 'make, cause' is such an example. It behaves like *ba* with respect to verbhood tests; however, no linguist has raised doubts as to the verbal status of *shi*:

(30) a. ta shi   ni   hen kuaile.
          he make you very happy
          'He made you happy.'

      b. *ta shi-le   ni   hen kuaile.
          he make-LE you very happy
          'He made you happy.'

      c. *ta shi-mei/bu-shi ni   hen kuaile?
          he make-not-make you very happy
          'Did he make you happy?'

      d. *(mei/bu-)shi
          (not-)make

---

[17] There have also been proposals claiming that *ba* is a "coverb" (see, among others, L. Wang 1954, Lü 1955, Li and Thompson 1974, 1981: Chapter 9, 15). A coverb is a special category created in Chinese grammatical studies to represent the group of words which were verbs but have gradually lost their verbal properties. They are so labeled because they are no longer verbs and yet they have not become true prepositions, either: they don't fully behave like lexical verbs or typical prepositions. The morphemes that fill light verb positions (Huang 1997, T.-H. Lin 2001) have the same status.

[18] There are speakers who find *ba* in the V-not-V question form acceptable (see, for instance, M. Wu 1982). Using the V-not-V form as a test for verbhood does not seem to be deterministic, even though it has frequently been applied in the literature. For some speakers, a preposition, an adjective, and an adverb such as *jingchang* 'usually' etc. can also occur in the "V-not-V" form, which should be more correctly labeled as a general A-not-A question form, not just V-not-V.

Nevertheless, what is clear is that the NP following *ba*, the post-*ba* NP, can be the object of the following verb, as in (29a). When the post-*ba* NP is understood as the object of the following verb (V), the object position of the V must be empty. It cannot be occupied by a pronoun or a reflexive coreferential with the post-*ba* NP, as in (31a–c). These properties of *ba* and the post-*ba* NP do not hold for typical verbs and their objects.

(31) a. *ta ba Lisi$_i$ hai-le   ta$_i$.
          he BA Lisi hurt-LE him
          'He hurt Lisi.'

     b. *ta ba Lisi$_i$ hai-le   ziji/taziji$_i$.
          he BA Lisi hurt-LE self/himself
          'He hurt Lisi.'

Example (31b) should be contrasted with (31c), which allows *shi* 'make, cause' to precede a verb and a reflexive:

(31) c. ta shi   Lisi$_i$ hai-le   ziji/taziji$_i$.
          he make Lisi hurt-LE self/himself
          'He made Lisi hurt himself.'

The contrast between (31a–b) and (31c) shows that *ba* in Modern Chinese is different from lexical verbs.

5.2.2   *The analysis of* ba

Although *ba* has become "grammaticalized" and does not behave like a lexical verb, questions arise as to what it means to be grammaticalized. What morpho-syntactic properties does the "grammaticalized" *ba* have? There have been so many proposals that the logical possibilities seem to have been exhausted:[19]

(32) a. *Ba* as a lexical verb (Hashimoto 1971)
      b. *Ba* as a preposition (Chao 1968, Lü 1980, Travis 1984, Cheng 1986, A. Li 1985, 1990)
      c. *Ba* as a dummy Case assigner (Huang 1982b, Koopman 1984, Goodall 1987)
      d. *Ba* as a dummy filler, inserted to fill the head of a CAUSE phrase when verb raising does not take place (Sybesma 1999)
      e. *Ba* as the head of a base-generated functional category (Zou 1995)

Recall that *ba* does not behave like a verb according to the verbhood tests or like the special set of verbs such as *shi*, as just described in the previous section, which

---

[19] All these possibilities allow *ba* to assign Case to the following NP and the *ba* construction carries a special meaning, which might be captured in different ways, as shown in this chapter. See Y. Li (1990, 1995, 1999) for *ba* as a Case assigner and the special meaning of the *ba* construction (causer role).

makes the first option less attractive. Proposal (32b) on the one hand and (32d–e) on the other can be distinguished by one major difference: constituency. According to (32b), the post-*ba* NP alone (without *ba*) and the VP should not constitute a unit. In contrast, (32d–e) take *ba* as the head of a CAUSE phrase or some other functional projection; the post-*ba* NP should form a constituent with the following VP, not with *ba*. As a dummy Case assigner (32c), *ba* may be subsumed under (32b) or (32d) with respect to constituency.

The fact is that the post-*ba* NP and the VP can form a constituent, as illustrated by the coordination test (see M. Wu 1982).[20]

(33)   ta ba [men xi-hao],   [chuanghu ca-ganjing]-le
        he BA door wash-finish   window   wipe-clean-LE
        'He washed the door and wiped the windows clean.'

This suggests that (32d–e) are more adequate. However, there is a subset of *ba* sentences which indicates that *ba* can form a constituent with the post-*ba* NP, suggesting the inadequacy of solely relying on the analyses established on (32d–e).[21] This subset of sentences is the type that Sybesma (1999) refers to as "canonical *ba* sentences" (expressing that somebody (animate Agent) does something to some entity, in contrast to his "causative *ba* sentences" whose subjects are generally inanimate causers).[22] Let us use another simple example such as (34a): *ba* and the post-*ba* NP can be preposed as a unit to the sentence-initial position, as in (34b). That is, such "canonical *ba* sentences" not only allow the post-*ba* NP to form a constituent with the following VP but also allow *ba* and the post-*ba* NP to form a constituent.[23]

---

[20] It is acceptable if *ba* also occurs in the second conjunct, i.e., *ba*, the *ba*-NP, and the following VP can form one constituent.

[21] The preposing is not possible when it is a "causative" sentence (i.e., the type of sentence whose subject bears a causer theta-role). See Section 5.4 for the analysis of two different *ba* structures.

(i)   a. zhe-ping   jiu   ba ta   zui-dao-le.
          this-bottle wine   BA him   drunk-fall-LE
          'This bottle of wine made him very drunk.'

       b. *ba ta,   zhe-ping jiu   zui-dao-le.
          BA him   this-bottle wine drunk-fall-LE

[22] L. Wang (1954) suggests the terms "disposal" and "causative," which are Sybesma's "canonical" and "causative," respectively.

[23] It was observed by Zou (1995), for instance, that *ba* and the *ba*-NP cannot form a constituent and be preposed. However, we found that it is not that difficult to prepose the *ba* phrase in some instances, though this pattern occurs only in casual informal speech. It seems that preposing of the *ba* phrase is the best in the contexts where the

(34) a. ni   xian ba zhe-kuai rou   qie-qie ba!
         you first BA this-CL meat cut-cut SFP
         'Cut the meat first.'

      b. [ba zhe-kuai rou], ni   xian qie-qie ba!
          BA this-CL   meat you first cut-cut SFP
         'Cut the meat first.'

Compare:

      c. ni   ba [zhe-kuai rou   qie-qie], [naxie cai   xixi] ba!
         you BA this-CL meat cut-cut   those vegetable wash SFP
         'You cut the meat and wash the vegetable.'

Sentences like (34b) show that it is not always sufficient to just take *ba* as the head of a CAUSE phrase or the head of some other functional projection not forming a constituent with the following NP.

In sum, *ba* in Modern Chinese does not behave like a lexical verb. The coordination test illustrated in (33) and (34c) shows that the structure [*ba* NP VP] can be analyzed as [*ba* [NP VP]]. In addition, when a *ba* sentence is of the "canonical" type, meaning that somebody does something to some entity, the constituent structure seems to have the possibility of being analyzed as [[*ba* NP] VP], because *ba* and the post-*ba* NP can be preposed as a unit (34b). The former observation is in line with the approaches that treat *ba* as the head of a projection taking [NP VP] as its complement, such as (32d–e). The latter observation might go along with a verbal analysis in (32a) or a preposition analysis in (32b), with *ba* and the NP forming a unit modifying the following VP. We will first focus on the structures along the line of (32d–e) and return to the variation at the end of Section 5.4.

The discussion above describes the categorial status of *ba*. Thematically, it can be shown that *ba* does not assign a theta-role to its subject, in contrast to *bei*. There is also no evidence that it assigns a theta-role to the NP following it. These properties are elaborated below.

5.3   *ba* not a theta-role assigner

Note that *ba* must be immediately followed by an NP. This collocation requirement can be captured by Case assignment. If Case is assigned by *ba* to the NP following it, the necessity of this linear order emerges naturally from the fact

---

interpretation of doing something to the *ba*-NP is clearest. A command sentence is a very good example. However, it does not have to be a command:

(i)   ba na-dui   wenzhang, wo zao jiu gai-hao-le.
       BA that-pile article   I   early then correct-finish-LE
       'I corrected that pile of articles long ago.'

that Case assignment follows an adjacency condition in Chinese (Stowell 1981, A. Li 1985, 1990). Accordingly, it is plausible to claim that *ba* is a Case-assigning head category. Does this head also assign a theta-role to the NP that receives Case from it, and does it assign a theta-role to the subject of the sentence?

5.3.1   ba *and the subject*

The single reason for suspecting that *ba* assigns a theta-role to the subject is such examples as (35), showing the type of construction labeled as "causative" *ba* with an inanimate causer as subject:

(35) a. na   san-da-wan   jiu   ba Lisi he-zui-le.
          that three-big-bowl wine   BA Lisi drink-drunk-LE
          'Those three big bowls of wine got Lisi drunk.'

      b. shi-shou xiaoqu ba Linyi chang-de kouganshezao.
          ten-CL   ditty   BA Linyi sing   DE mouth.thirsty.tongue.dry
          'Singing ten folk songs made Linyi dry in his mouth.'

      c. Lisi-de xiaohua ba Linyi xiao de duzi teng.
          Lisi-DE joke   BA Linyi laugh DE belly hurt
          'Lisi's jokes made Linyi laugh so much that his belly hurt.'

      d. Lisi tuntuntutu de yangzi ba Linyi ji-si-le.
          Lisi hesitant   DE manner BA Linyi anxious-die-LE
          'Lisi's hesitant way of talking made Linyi anxious to death.'

Common to all these examples is that the post-*ba* NP is (or can be) the thematic subject of the first verb in the verb complex. For instance, *Lisi he-zui-le* 'Lisi drink-drunk-LE' is a standalone clause in which *Lisi* did the drinking and became drunk as a result. But if the first verb already assigns its subject theta-role to *Lisi*, then the real subject of (35a), *na san-da-wan jiu* 'those three big bowls of wine,' will have to receive its theta-role from somewhere else in order to satisfy the theta-criterion. It seems natural, then, that *ba* is the source of the theta-role. In addition, the sentence has the clear interpretation that the wine made Lisi drunk. This would follow if *ba* functions as a causative verb comparable to the causative use of *make* in English. Example (36) below schematically illustrates this option:

(36)   [those three big bowls of wine MAKE Lisi drink-drunk]

where MAKE may be realized as *ba*. So at least in examples like (35a–d), it seems that *ba* needs to have the ability to assign a subject theta-role. This theta-role is not Agent because 'the wine' in (35a) is not even animate. In the literature, it is typically labeled as Cause.

We believe this conclusion to be misleading. First of all, the data in (35a–d) really fall into two groups, (35a–b) on the one hand and (35c–d) on the other. We start with the first group.

In these first examples, the subject is thematically related to the verb *he* 'drink' in (35a) and *chang* 'sing' in (35b): they are the logical objects of these verbs. The relation can be illustrated by the non-*ba* counterpart:

(37) a. Lisi he   na   san-da-wan   jiu   he-zui-le.
         Lisi drink that three-big-bowl wine drink-drunk-LE
         'Lisi drank those three big bowls of wine and got drunk.'

      b. Linyi chang shi-shou xiaoqu chang de kouganshezao.
         Linyi sing ten-CL   ditty sing DE mouth.thirsty.tongue.dry
         'Linyi sang ten folk songs and got dry in his mouth.'

In these cases, every NP has its own theta-role from the lexical verb. The comparison between (35a–b) and (37a–b) would allow us to claim that the subjects of the *ba* sentences in (35a–b) each receive their thematic role from the lexical verb. Indeed, if we replace the subject in (35a–b) with an NP that cannot be thematically related to the verb, the sentence becomes unacceptable:[24]

(38)   *yumen   de xinqing ba Lisi he-zui-le.
          depressed DE mood   BA Lisi drink-drunk-LE
          Intended reading: 'The depressed feeling made Lisi drunk from drinking.'

Not surprisingly, the non-*ba* counterpart of (38) is not acceptable:

(39)   *yumen   de xinqing he-zui-le   Lisi.
          depressed DE mood   drink-drunk-LE Lisi
          Intended reading: 'The depressed feeling made Lisi drunk from drinking.'

---

[24] What is important to our discussion is that a *ba* sentence always has a non-*ba* counterpart. Therefore, *ba* does not assign a thematic role. Note that a wide range of thematic relations is possible. The following sentence illustrates a case of benefactive theta-role to the subject in *ba* and non-*ba* form (see Chapter 2 for the discussion on possible theta-roles in subject and object positions; also see Shen 2004 for sentences like those below):

   (i)   zhe-chang pailian   ba women chang-lei-le.
         this-CL   rehearsal BA us   sing-tired-LE
         'This rehearsal made us tired from singing.'

   (ii) zhe-chang pailian   chang-lei-le   women.
         this-CL   rehearsal sing-tired-LE   us
         'This rehearsal made us tired from singing.'

   Compare:

   (iii) women gei zhe-chang pailian   chang (ge).
         we   for this-CL   rehearsal sing   song
         'We sing a song for this rehearsal.'

The similarity between these *ba* and non-*ba* sentences points to the lack of thematic contribution by *ba*. Further note that replacing *ba* with a causative verb *shi* 'make' renders (38) acceptable:

(40)   yumen   de xinqing shi   Lisi he-zui-le.
         depressed DE mood   make Lisi drink-drunk-LE
         'The depressed feeling made Lisi drunk from drinking.'

The sets of examples in (35a–b) and (38) only differ in the choice of words for the subject NP, but they contrast sharply in acceptability. Replacing *ba* with a true causative verb *shi* 'make' turns the sentences from unacceptable to acceptable. The contrasts among these three sets of sentences indicate that the subject of the *ba* sentence must be thematically related to the theta-assigning verbs in the sentence. *Ba* itself does not assign a theta-role, unlike the causative verb *shi* 'make.' The contrast between *ba* and *shi* in assigning a theta-role to the subject can be further supported by the contrast between the following examples:

(41)   a. Linyi chi-bao-le.
          Linyi eat-full-LE
          'Linyi was full from eating.'

       b. *Lisi ba Linyi chi-bao-le.
           Lisi BA Linyi eat-full-LE
           Intended reading: 'Lisi made Linyi full from eating.'

       c. Lisi shi   Linyi chi-bao-le.
          Lisi make Linyi eat-full-LE
          'Lisi made Linyi full from eating.'

(42)   a. jinyu   you   de kanbujian-le.
          goldfish swim DE out.of.sight-LE
          'The goldfish swam out of sight.'

       b. *haizi ba jinyu   you   de kanbujian-le.
           child BA gold-fish swim DE out.of.sight-LE
           Intended reading: 'The child made/let the goldfish swim out of sight.'

       c. haizi shi   jinyu   you   de kanbujian-le.
          child make gold-fish swim DE out.of.sight-LE
          'The child made/let the goldfish swim out of sight.'

The (b) and (c) sentences above contrast in acceptability. Moreover, *shi* and *ba* contrast sharply in the following cases where there is a pronoun in the object position.

(43)   a. Zhangsan$_i$ shi   wo dashang ta$_i$.
          Zhangsan make me hurt   him
          'Zhangsan made me hurt him.'

    b. *Zhangsan$_i$ ba   wo dashang ta$_i$.
       Zhangsan make me hurt   him
       'Zhangsan made me hurt him.'

The object in (43b) must be related to the post-*ba* NP and cannot be an overt pronoun. However, the object in (43a) need not be related to the NP following *shi* and can be a pronoun. The fact that the pronoun can be coindexed with the subject of *shi* indicates that the sentence is a bi-clausal structure.[25]

The facts observed above are expected if the causative verb *shi* 'make' assigns a theta-role to its subject, in contrast to *ba*. The subject NPs in (42b) and (43b) are not assigned a theta-role from anywhere, a violation of the theta-criterion. Therefore, *ba* does not assign a theta-role to the subject of the *ba* sentence.

Next, we turn to the cases in (35c–d). It is notable that the verbs *xiao* in (35c) and *ji* in (35d) can be alternatively transitive and intransitive:

(44) a. zui xiao-ren   de shi Lisi jingran mei dai   xinyong ka.
        most laugh-person DE be Lisi even   not bring credit   card
        'What made people laugh most was that Lisi didn't even bring his credit card.'

      b. zhei shi   zhen ji-ren!
        this thing really make.anxious-person
        'This thing really makes people anxious!'

In each of these examples, *xiao* and *ji* are causativized (without overt morphology) and take the object *ren* 'person,' as reflected through the English translations. The transitive usage is further illustrated by the following examples:

(45) a. ni ji   shenme?[26]
        you anxious what
        'What are you anxious about?'

      b. ni xiao shenme?
        you laugh what
        'What are you laughing about?'

Because *xiao* and *ji* can be transitive, (35c–d) fall into the most typical pattern of the *ba* construction, like those in (35a–b), or sentences with transitive verbs such as *da* 'hit' or *ma* 'scold' as in *wo ba ta da/ma le* 'I *ba* him hit/scolded = I

---

[25] Recall that the main distinction between *shi* and *ba* is that *shi* is a lexical verb that can have an external argument (subject) and a clausal complement. *Ba* is part of a verb complex and is not a lexical verb itself.

[26] Each of these sentences also has a reading according to which 'what' is interpreted like 'why': 'why are you anxious?' and 'why are you laughing?'

hit/scolded him.' In addition, (35c–d) have well-formed non-*ba* counterparts:

(46)   a. Lisi-de xiaohua xiao   de Linyi duzi   teng.
          Lisi-DE joke   laugh DE Linyi belly hurt
          'Lisi's jokes made Linyi laugh so much that his belly hurt.'

        b. Lisi tuntuntutu de yangzi ji-si-le   Linyi.
          Lisi hesitant   DE manner anxious-die-LE Linyi
          'Lisi's hesitant way of talking made Linyi anxious to death.'

Were the subject of the *ba* sentence in (35c–d) dependent on *ba* for thematic assignment, the acceptability of (46a–b) would not be expected.

5.3.2   ba *and the post-*ba *NP*

The discussion above demonstrates the fact that a *ba* sentence always has an acceptable non-*ba* counterpart. This suggests that none of the arguments in the relevant sentences depends on *ba* for thematic assignment, including the post-*ba* NP. Recall that the *ba* construction is generally acceptable with the patterns corresponding to the *bei* structures with an inner object and with an outer object. An inner object receives a theta-role from the relevant verb. An outer object, generally related to the complement of the verb, has an "affected" theta-role, according to the analysis in the previous chapter.

If there is a reason to argue for the ability of *ba* to assign a theta-role to the post-*ba* NP, it is the widely accepted observation that the *ba* construction carries a special meaning, as embodied in the terms of "disposal," "executive," and "strong transitivity" (see notes 1 and 5). However, given the possibility of a complex predicate assigning an "affected" theta-role to an outer object, *ba* would not be needed to assign a theta-role to the post-*ba* NP. Recall that the *ba* and *bei* constructions differ in the types of verbs that can occur in these patterns. Some representative examples ((12) and (13)) are repeated here:

(47)   a. ta bei women kandao/tingjian-le.
          he BEI us   see/hear-LE
          'He was seen/heard by us.'

        b. *women ba ta   kandao/tingjian-le.
          we   BA him see/hear-LE
          'We saw/heard him.'

(48)   a. ta-de mimi bei women faxian-le.
          his   secret BEI us   discover-LE
          'His secrets were discovered by us.'

        b. *women ba ta-de mimi faxian-le.
          we   BA his   secret discover-LE
          'We discovered his secret.'

The two constructions accept different types of verbs. However, the effect of verbs on the acceptability of these constructions is only demonstrated in the cases where an inner object is relevant: when an inner object is passivized or serves as the post-*ba* NP. When an outer object is available, the two constructions essentially carry the same meaning and have a similar range of possibilities (except for cases such as (20)–(22), which we return to shortly). It is possible to pursue the option that the observed difference between these two constructions can be traced to an "affectedness" requirement on the post-*ba* NP. While the *bei* construction allows an inner object to be passivized, the *ba* construction requires the post-*ba* NP to have originated as an outer object and nothing else. That is, the post-*ba* NP is always the outer object, which is assigned an "affected" theta-role by the complex verb phrase following the post-*ba* NP. In the case of inner objects, the post-*ba* NP still originates as an outer object but is related to an empty argument in the inner object position. Regardless of whether this option should be adopted, it remains that *ba* does not assign a theta-role to the post-*ba* NP.

Further support for the lack of theta-assigning capability of *ba* may be found in the unacceptability of the sentences with an argument solely interpreted as "affected," such as those corresponding to the third type of *bei* constructions discussed in Chapter 4 ((66) and (67); the outermost object), repeated below:

(49)   ??Wangwu you   ba Linyi jichu-le yi-zhi   quanleida.
         Wangwu again BA Linyi hit-LE   one-CL home-run
         'Wangwu again hit a home run on Linyi.'

(50)   ??ta ba wo zhemo yi   zuo, jiu   shenme   dou kan-bu-jian-le.
         he BA I   thus   one sit   then everything all   can-not-see-LE
         'He sat this way [on me]; I could not see anything.'

Were *ba* able to assign a theta-role to the post-*ba* NP, it is not clear how these sentences could be ruled out. Take (49) for instance: *ba* is followed by a post-*ba* NP and a verb phrase, like a typical *ba* sentence such as:

(51)   wo ba Linyi qiang-zou-le   maozi.
         I   BA Linyi snatch-away-LE hat
         'I afflicted Linyi by snatching away (his) hat.'

That is, structurally, the post-*ba* NP is followed by a VP in both (49) and (51). It is puzzling why one is acceptable and the other is not. However, if an outer object is always an argument in the complement clause of the verb or related to the argument of the verb (by being a possessor of an object NP, for instance), the NP *Linyi* in (49) is not an outer object, but the same NP in (51) is. The post-*ba* NP in (49)–(50) does not qualify as an outer object, nor is it assigned a theta-role by *ba*. These cases are not possible because the post-*ba* NP does not have a theta-role.

In short, it is plausible to claim that *ba* does not assign a theta-role to the post-*ba* NP or the subject of the *ba* sentence. The only contribution *ba* makes seems to be assigning Case to the post-*ba* NP. The following summarizes the properties of the *ba* construction:

(52) a. A *ba* sentence is possible only when there is an inner object or an outer object. The post-*ba* NP is an inner or outer object – but not the outer*most* object.

   b. Although *ba* assigns Case to the post-*ba* NP and no element can intervene between them, they only form a syntactic unit in "canonical" *ba* sentences, not in "causative" *ba* sentences.

   c. *ba* does not assign any theta-roles: neither the subject of the sentence nor the post-*ba* NP receives a theta-role from *ba*.

   d. The *ba* construction does not involve operator movement.

We began this chapter by comparing the *ba* construction with the *bei* construction. The two constructions share some properties but also differ in significant ways. We saw in the last chapter that *bei* is a verb (or modal) that has the capability to assign a theta-role to the subject. It also requires its complement to contain an operator.[27] In contrast, *ba* does not assign a theta-role and does not exhibit the properties of operator movement. In addition, *ba* does not accept the third type of *bei* constructions involving the outermost object. The last property not only provided further support for *ba*'s inability to assign a theta-role but also requires us to disallow an IP with an outermost object as complement of *ba*; i.e., the structures of the *ba* construction should be defined restrictively. The following section will focus on the structures of the *ba* construction.

5.4   Structures

An adequate characterization of the structure for the *ba* construction must be able to accommodate the generalizations in (52) and capture the contrast between the *ba* and *bei* constructions.

5.4.1   A preliminary analysis

The word *ba* is not a phrase; therefore it is an X^0 category. The constituency tests provided in Section 5.2.1 show that in most cases, *ba* and the post-*ba* NP do not form a constituent. Instead, the post-*ba* NP and the following verb phrase form a constituent. Because *ba* is neither a true verb nor a true P, but does assign

---

[27] However, *bei* is like *ba* in the behavior of verbhood: it does not pass the commonly used verbhood tests, such as A-not-A questions and short answers (see Section 5.2.1 for the relevant tests on *ba*). In this respect, *bei* is identical to *ba*.

Case, the only possibility left is to group *ba* with the light verbs (Huang 1997, Lin 2001).[28] In regard to the post-*ba* NP, it is generally the "affected" outer object, the one assigned a theta-role by a complex predicate consisting of a verb and its complement. The comparison with the *bei* construction further indicates that the *ba* construction does not involve the movement of an operator, as no properties of operator movement are evident in this structure. Accordingly, a straightforward logical possibility of the structure of *ba* sentences is the one below:

(53)

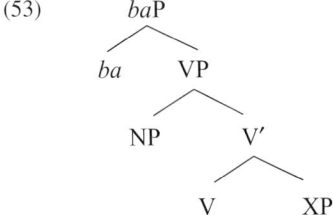

In this structure, the NP in the Spec of VP is the post-*ba* NP. It is the outer object assigned a theta-role by V′. If the post-*ba* NP in some cases should originate as an inner object, it is then raised to the Spec of VP position (see the discussion in the previous section for the option of taking the post-*ba* NP as the outer object in all cases).

The structure also captures the fact that *ba* follows the aspectual morphemes *you* and *zai*, which are argued to head ASPP below IP but above VP (cf. Section 3.3.1 in Chapter 3, especially the diagram in (52)).

(54) a. Lisi mei-you ba laohu da-si.
          Lisi not-have BA tiger beat-die
          'Lisi didn't kill the tiger.'

     b. *Lisi ba laohu mei-you da-si.
          Lisi BA tiger not-have beat-die

(55) a. Linyi zai ba yifu   bao-cheng yi-ge   da bao.
          Linyi at BA clothes wrap-into one-CL big bundle
          'Linyi was wrapping the clothes into a big bundle.'

     b. ??Linyi ba yifu   zai bao-cheng yi-ge   da bao.
          Linyi BA clothes at wrap-into one-CL big bundle

---

[28] There might be another possibility: some functional category to be defined (see Chapter 1). Ignited by Pollock's (1989) seminal work on projecting such functional categories as Tense and Agreement in a clausal structure, much recent literature quite generously postulates various functional categories and makes use of them in syntactic analyses (for recent representative works, see Cinque 1999, Rizzi 2002). Ultimately, what functional categories exist in UG and how they are integrated in syntactic structures is an empirical question.

The structure in (53) resembles very much the *v*P structure discussed extensively in Chomsky (1995) or the VP-shell structure proposed by Larson (1988) for double object structures, if *ba* is the head of a higher VP or *v*P. Indeed, if the label *ba*P is replaced by *v*P or VP, the structure is a regular verb phrase like Chomsky's *v*P structure or Larson's VP shell structure. Let us consider the adoption of Chomsky's *v*P structure in the representations and keep in mind that, if Larson's VP shell structures are used, each *v*P will be replaced by VP and each *v* by V, to which we return shortly.

(56)

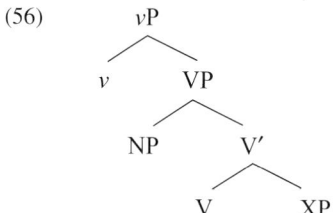

If *ba* appears in the *v* position, the verb is in the V position and a *ba* sentence is derived like the one below.

(57)   wo ba beizi na   gei-ta.
        I   BA cup   take to-him
        'I took the cup and gave it to him.'

Alternatively, *ba* need not appear in the *v* position. In that case, the verb moves up to the *v* position, deriving a non-*ba* sentence (see Sybesma 1999, Chapter 6):

(58)   wo na   beizi gei-ta.
        I   take cup   to-him
        'I took the cup and gave it to him.'

In other words, *ba* may be taken as the spell-out of a small *v*. When *v* is spelled out as *ba*, V-to-*v* raising does not apply, deriving [*ba* NP V XP]. When *ba* does not occur, V-to-*v* raising takes place, deriving [V NP XP] (see Huang 1993, Tang 1998 for V-to-*v* raising in Chinese).

5.4.2   *Revision*

The structure in (53) seems to capture the properties in (52). We saw how *ba* sentences and their non-*ba* counterparts are derived. *Ba* heads a projection and nothing can intervene between *ba* and the post-*ba* NP since *ba* assigns Case to the post-*ba* NP and Case assignment obeys an adjacency condition (Stowell 1981). *Ba* is part of a verb complex and does not assign theta-roles independently.

This structure also accommodates the contrast between the *ba* and *bei* sentences with regard to the role played by operator movement: no operator exists in the structure.

However, (53) is not quite adequate. It is especially problematic with respect to the placement of adverbials. Take a manner adverb for illustration. In a *ba* sentence, a manner adverb can occur before or after *ba*:

(59) a. wo xiaoxin-de ba beizi na-gei-ta.
          I   carefully   BA cup   take-to-him
          'I gave the cup to him carefully.'

      b. wo ba beizi xiaoxin-de na-gei-ta.
          I   BA cup   carefully   take-to-him
          'I gave the cup to him carefully.'

Because of the acceptability of (59a–b), a manner adverb should be able to adjoin to either V′ or some node higher than the *ba*P in (53). Such adverb placement possibilities would predict that the non-*ba* counterpart, after V raises to v, should be acceptable. Such a minimal pair is shown in (60a–b). However, (60b) is not acceptable.[29]

(60) a. wo xiaoxin-de na   beizi gei-ta.
          I   carefully   take cup   to-him
          'I gave the cup to him carefully.'

      b. *wo na   beizi xiaoxin-de gei-ta.
          I   take cup   carefully   to-him
          'I gave the cup to him carefully.'

The contrast between (59b) and (60b) casts doubt on the adequacy of a structure like (53), with v spelled out as *ba* or as the landing site of V-to-v raising.

The distribution of adverbs illustrated in (59) and (60) indicates that *ba* must be higher than the landing site of the raised main verb; i.e., higher than the vP in

---

[29] One may argue that the distribution of adverbs can be captured by an analysis that assumes adverbs must be licensed by a lexically filled head. When *ba* occurs, an adverb can be licensed by the main verb occurring in the lower V position or by *ba* in the higher v position. When V-to-v raising takes place, the lower V is an empty category and cannot license an adverb within the lower VP. Such an approach would require cross-linguistic parameterization, because V-raising does not always prevent an adverb from occurring in the lower position, as shown in the study of French by Pollock (1989). Moreover, if the analysis by Huang (1993), Soh (1998), and S.-W. Tang (1998) concerning V-raising is correct, an empty verb in Chinese can license a Duration/Frequency Phrase.

(53), as in the one below:

(61)

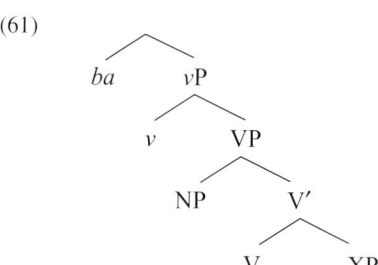

In such a structure, an adverb is adjoined to *v*P (or an intermediate projection *v*′, or some other node higher than *v*P). For a non-*ba* sentence, an adverb appears to the left of the main verb after the main verb is raised from V to *v*. In a *ba* sentence, an adverb may appear to the right of *ba* (as well as to the left if the adverb is adjoined to a node higher than the *ba* projection).

The structure in (61) solves the problem with adverb placement noted in (59)–(60). However, it raises the question of where the post-*ba* NP is positioned. It certainly cannot be the NP immediately dominated by the VP in (61). The post-*ba* NP and *ba* can never be separated by any element. The structure in (61) would wrongly allow the main verb to occur between *ba* and the post-*ba* NP. An NP position must exist adjacent to *ba*. One possibility is to identify the post-*ba* NP as the Specifier of *v*P:

(62)   [*ba* [*v*P NP [*v*′ *v* [VP V XP]]]]

This structure captures most of the properties presented so far. However, there still remains one important problem: *ba* seems to be able to form a unit with the post-*ba* NP in canonical *ba* sentences, although not in causative *ba* sentences (see Section 5.2.2). It is plausible to suggest that *ba* in canonical *ba* structures retains the verbal property with the meaning of 'handle, deal with.' The verbal property allows the relevant *ba* sentences to be analyzed as [[VP *ba* NP] [VP]], with the [VP *ba* NP] functioning like a VP modifying the following VP, much like the expressions *yong dao, mai hua* in the following examples:

(63)   a. ta yong dao   sha-le   henduo ji.
            he use   knife kill-LE many chicken
            'He used a knife and killed lots of chicken (He killed lots of chickens with a knife).'

        b. wo yao   mai hua   song gei ta.
            I   want buy flower give to   him
            'I will buy flowers to give to him.'

The expressions *yong dao, mai hua* behave as a unit and can be preposed:

(64) a. yong dao   ta   sha-le henduo ji.
          use   knife he   kill-LE many   chicken
          'Using a knife, he killed lots of chickens.'

    b. mai hua   wo yao   song gei ta.
        buy flower I   want give to   him
        'Buying flowers, I will give [them] to him.'

The ambiguity of structures for canonical *ba* sentences, not for causative sentences, also provides an answer to a range of facts regarding the interpretation of an empty pronoun in the result complement clause. For instance, a sentence like (65) is ambiguous with regard to the interpretation of the possessor of the subject in the result complement clause ('my hands' or 'their hands,' see the discussion regarding the sentence (21) in Section 5.1):

(65)   wo ba tamen da de shou dou zhong-le.
        I   BA them   hit DE hand all   swollen-LE
        i. 'I hit them such that my hands got swollen.'
        ii. 'I hit them such that their hands got swollen.'

The two possible interpretations follow from the ambiguous structures. There is an empty pronoun in the complement result clause (the owner of the hands). The empty pronoun is identified with the closest c-commanding NP (see the discussion on Generalized Control in the next chapter). Because *ba* may or may not form a unit with the post-*ba* NP, the empty pronoun may or may not search past the post-*ba* NP for a c-commanding NP as its antecedent. This predicts that, if the *ba* NP can be preposed, the ambiguity found in (65) will no longer exist. This is true, as illustrated by the following example.

(66)   ba tamen, wo da de shou dou zhong-le.
        BA them   I   hit DE hand all   swollen-LE
        i.   'I hit them such that my hands got swollen.'
        ii. *'I hit them such that their hands got swollen.'

Moreover, causative *ba* sentences do not have the verbal interpretation 'handle, deal with,' because they do not have the alternative structure. Accordingly, causative *ba* sentences do not allow preposing of *ba* and the post-*ba* NP, nor do they allow the interpretation according to which an empty pronoun in the result complement clause is coindexed with the subject of *ba*. These predictions are borne out, as illustrated here in (67) and (68), respectively.

(67)   *ba wo zhe-ben shu   kan de yanjing dou lei-le.
         BA I   this-CL book read DE eye   all tired-LE

(68) a. zhe-ben shu   ba wo kan de yanjing dou lei-le.
         this-CL book BA I   read DE eye   all tired-LE
         'I read the book such that my eyes got tired.'

      b. *zhe-ben shu   ba wo kan de fengmian dou huai-le.
          this-CL book BA I   read DE cover   all ruined-LE
          'I read the book such that the cover of the book got ruined.'

Further note that, even though *bei* is also a verb, the expression *bei* + NP cannot be preposed as a constituent:

(69) a. wo bei ta   pian-le.
          I   BEI him cheat-LE
          'I was cheated by him.'

      b. *bei ta   wo pian-le.
          BEI him I   cheat-LE

The difference between *bei* as a verb in passives and *ba* as a verb in canonical *ba* sentences lies in the structure: *bei* is the main verb of a passive structure sub-categorized for a clausal complement. In contrast, *ba* is a verb taking an NP as its object and forming a VP with the object to modify the following VP.

To complete the discussion on the structure of *ba* sentences, we would like to bring forth a related issue: Where should a subject be in a structure like (61)? Recall from Chapter 3 that a subject is placed in the Spec of *v*P position. When a *ba* phrase appears in the sentence, where is the subject? The distribution of the distributive or totalizing marker (Lee 1986) *dou* 'all' seems to suggest that the subject should not be lower than the *ba* phrase in the structure. *Dou* generally occurs with an associated plural NP to its left and the two must be close to one another (we refer to the relation between *dou* and the associated NP as a licensing relation). For instance, when the associated NP is in the subject position of a sentence, *dou* can be separated from it by an adverbial generally regarded as modifying an element larger than a VP (such as a reason/time/location adverbial modifying a Tense Phrase or Aspect Phrase), but not a manner adverbial, which generally is an adverbial modifying a VP.

(70) a. tamen yinwei   shengbing dou bu lai-le.
          they   because sick   all not come-LE
          'They all won't come because they are sick.'

      b. tamen zai xuexiao dou hen   renzhen.
          they   at   school   all very diligent
          'They are all very diligent at school.'

      c. tamen na   yi-tian dou shengbing-le.
          they   that one-day all   sick-LE
          'They all got sick that day.'

(71) a. *tamen hen jin   de dou bao-zhe   qiu.
          they   very firm DE all hold-ZHE ball

      b. tamen dou hen jin de bao-zhe   qiu.
         they   all very firm DE hold-ZHE ball
         'They were all holding balls firmly.'

In sentences with negation, *dou* can appear after the negation and be associated with the subject on the left of the negation:

(72) a. tamen bu   dou xihuan zhe-ge gushi.
         they   not all like   this-CL story
         'They do not all like the story.'

      b. tamen mei dou zuo-wan   gongke.
         they   not all do-finish homework
         'They didn't all finish the homework.'

The locality condition observed by *dou* and its associated NP can be captured in terms of a domain condition on *dou* licensing. Suppose every adverbial should be licensed by a head (Travis 1988). *Dou* can be licensed by a V head or an I head. Taking the Tense Phrase and Aspect Phrase among the phrases within the I domain (assuming a split inflection projection), *dou* in (70) is licensed by an I and can be associated with an NP within the I domain, which may be the subject. In contrast, *dou* in (71) occurs after the manner adverb and is not licensed in the I domain. It does not license the subject NP in the I domain. Another important property of the licensing of an NP by *dou* is the directionality requirement. Generally, the NP associated with *dou* occurs to its left (see for instance, Aoun and Li 1993a, Cheng 1995, S. Huang 1996, Lee 1986, X. Li 1997, Lin 1998, Liu 1997, Wu 1999), as illustrated by the following contrast:

(73) a. naxie shu, ta dou xihuan.
         those book he all like
         'Those books, he likes all.'

      b. *ta dou xihuan naxie shu.
         he all like   those book
         'He likes all those books.'

Pertinent to our discussion, *dou* and the associated NP cannot be separated by a *ba* phrase.

(74) a. tamen dou ba Linyi da-le   yixia.
         they   all BA Linyi hit-LE once
         'They all hit Linyi once.'

      b. *tamen ba Linyi dou da-le   yixia.
         they   BA Linyi all hit-LE once

Further note that the trace of the associated NP should be able to satisfy the domain requirement (see A. Li 1992a; also see Cheng 1995 using the notion of resumptive pronouns). The following examples demonstrate the licensing of traces derived by topicalization and subject-raising (*dou* and the associated NPs are bold-faced).

(75)   a. ***tamen** shuo Linyi **dou** lai-le.
            they   say   Linyi all   come-LE

       b. **tamen dou** shuo Linyi lai-le.
            they   all   say   Linyi come-LE
            'They all said Linyi came.'

       c. **tamen**$_i$, Linyi shuo e$_i$ **dou** lai-le.
            they   Linyi say   all   come-LE
            'They$_i$, Linyi said e$_i$ all came.'

(76)   **tamen**$_i$ bu keneng e$_i$ **dou** zuo   na-jian shi.
            they   not likely all   do   that-CL matter
            'They are not all likely to do that work.'

The facts above suggest that a subject should not originate from a position lower than *ba* or inside the projection of verb phrases that contain the *ba* phrase and manner adverbials. Then, where is the internal subject? An answer is to generate the internal subject outside the licensing domain of *dou*, to the left of *ba*. A straightforward option is to situate the internal subject in the Spec of the *ba* phrase:

(77)   [$_{baP}$ Subject [$_{ba'}$ *ba* [$_{vP}$ NP [$_{v'}$ *v* [$_{VP}$ V XP]]]]].

Dou following the post-*ba* NP must be within *vP*. The impossibility of such a *dou* associated with the subject in the Spec of *ba* phrase may be captured if *ba* and *v* constitute different domains in regard to *dou* licensing or a minimality condition is relevant to the licensing. The minimality condition can be phrased as the following: *dou* must be associated with the closest NP. Such a restriction on *dou* licensing can be demonstrated by the following instance:[30]

(78)   Zhangsan he Lisi, wo (*dou) hen xihuan zhe liang-ge ren.
        Zhangsan and Lisi I   all   very like   this two-CL   person
        'Zhangsan and Lisi, I like (these two people) both.'

---

[30] Note that the following sentence is possible with *dou* associated with the topic NP:

(i)   Zhangsan he Lisi, wo dou hen xihuan.
        Zhangsan and Lisi I   all very like
        'Zhangsan and Lisi, I like them both.'

In this case, *Zhangsan he Lisi* is moved from the object through a position close to *dou* and licensed accordingly.

This sentence can be ruled out if the topicalized phrase is not within the licensing domain of *dou* or if the subject *wo* is the closer NP to be licensed by *dou*.

The adoption of the structure in (78), where *ba* is lower than the internal subject, might also help us understand the lack of a post-*ba* NP as the outermost object. Recall the comparison between *ba* and *bei* constructions. Even though the subject of *bei* often corresponds to the object of *ba*, a significant systematic difference between the two lies in the fact that the subject of *bei* can be interpreted as an affected object of an IP but not the object of *ba*. The structure in (77) indicate that *ba* is too low in the clausal structure to take an IP as its complement. Accordingly, a post-*ba* NP cannot be assigned an affected theta-role by an IP.

The account presented above is adequate for the varieties of acceptable and unacceptable *ba* sentences in Mandarin Chinese. It may very well be the analysis that should be adopted considering the similarities between the *ba* and *bei* constructions. Nonetheless, there is an alternative if we compare the *ba* construction with its counterpart in Taiwanese. The comparison would indicate that there is an alternative to capturing the lack of the *ba* counterpart of the adversative passive, which would also suggest the possibility of an accompanying change of the analysis of the adversative passive. For simplicity, we will refer to the *ba* counterpart of the adversative passive as the adversative *ba* in the following sections.

The *ba* construction can be productively compared with the *ka* construction in Taiwanese. *Ka* is quite similar to *ba* in interpretation and syntactic behavior. In particular, the two constructions behave exactly alike with respect to the placement of adverbials in relation to *ba/ka* and the distribution of *dou/long* 'all.' Thus, all the *ba* sentences discussed in this section can be translated into *ka* sentences without change of acceptability. However, the two do differ in an important respect. *Ka* does allow the counterpart to the adversative passive. Thus, the *ka* sentences corresponding to the unacceptable *ba* sentences in (18b) and (19b) are both acceptable. Quite generally, as long as there is an "affected" interpretation, a *ka* sentence is acceptable, regardless of whether the post-*ka* NP is related to the verb of the sentence at all. The following sentence is an instance with a clear intransitive stative verb (adjective) 'small.'

(79)   li-e syaNim na ka gua se-ka   bolang thiaN-u,   gua
        you voice   if KA me small-extent nobody hear-have I
        tio   ka li   si   thaolo.
        will KA you fire job
        'If your voice is so small that nobody can hear you (at my cost),
        I will fire you.'

Because the *ka* construction generally is like the *ba* construction except for the possibility of an adversative *ka* contrasting with the impossibility of an adversative *ba*, we cannot claim that the lack of adversative *ba* follows from the structural position of *ba*, as just indicated. After all, a *ka* sentence with an outer object or an inner object still behaves like a *ba* sentence. That is, both *ka* and *ba* take a verb phrase as their complement. It is not clear why *ka* can also take an IP as its complement (adversative *ka*) but *ba* cannot. We can assume that these are the idiosyncratic subcategorization properties of *ka/ba* and do not need to pursue them further. Alternatively, we may explore the option that the basic difference between *ka* and *ba* lies in their ability (or inability) to assign theta-roles to the NP following them. We elaborate on this option below.

Note that there is an important difference in the *ba/ka/bei* cases between inner objects and outer objects on the one hand, and outermost objects on the other. An inner object and an outer object are thematically related to the sentence directly without *ba/ka/bei*: an inner object is assigned a theta-role by the verb and an outer object is associated with an NP in the complement of the verb (possessor or an argument in the complement clause). Structures involving these types of objects can all have well-formed non-*ba/ka/bei* counterparts. On the other hand, the presence of an outermost object is closely related to the presence of *ka/bei*. This can be illustrated by the possibility of an inner object or an outer object, but not an outermost object, being a topic.

(80) a. juzi$_i$,   wo xihuan e$_i$ – inner object
        orange, I   like
        'Oranges, I like.'

     b. juzi$_i$,   wo bo-le   e$_i$ pi le. – outer object
        orange, I   peel-LE skin LE
        'An orange, I peeled (the skin).'

     c. *Linyi, Wangwu jichu-le yi-zhi   quanleida.
        Linyi Wangwu hit-LE   one-CL home-run
        Intended reading: 'Linyi$_i$, Wangwu hit a home run [on him$_i$].'

Raising structures do not allow an outermost object, either:

(81)   *Linyi keneng Wangwu jichu-le yi-zhi   quanleida.
        Linyi likely Wangwu hit-LE   one-CL home-run
        Intended reading: 'Linyi$_i$ is likely to have Wangwu hit a home run [on him$_i$].'

A possible reason for the unacceptability of (80c) and (81) is that the additional NP is not assigned a theta-role directly or indirectly (by association with a theta-bearing element). In other words, the adversative *ba* is not possible in Mandarin because the post-*ba* NP, which should have originated as the outermost object, is not directly or indirectly assigned a theta-role. This means *ba* does not assign a theta-role to post-*ba* NP, either (as we suggested in Section 5.3). In contrast, *ka* in Taiwanese assigns a theta-role to the NP. Therefore, the adversative *ka* is possible. *Ka* in this sense is analyzed like a head subcategorized for two complements: one is the post-*ka* NP and the other is the verb phrase that follows the NP. The thematic relation is between *ka* and the post-*ka* NP, not an outermost object assigned a theta-role by an IP. This view of the contrast between *ka* and *ba* adversative constructions in terms of their theta-assigning capabilities suggests a similar option for analyzing the adversative passive. It might not be an outermost object that is assigned a theta-role from an IP. Instead, it might be that *bei* is subcategorized for an IP and also has an external argument. The external argument, the subject NP, receives a theta-role from *bei*, whose complement is an IP. The adversative passive would not need to contain an operator. The sentence of the form [NP *bei* IP] would simply mean the NP suffers from the event expressed by IP.

In brief, the *ba* construction in Mandarin can be viewed as a more grammaticalized and emptier version of the *ka* construction in Taiwanese. The two minimally differ in their theta-assigning capabilities, which accommodate the contrast between the possibility of an adversative *ka* in Taiwanese and the impossibility of an adversative *ba* in Mandarin. Moreover, in the same way the *ba* and *ka* constructions contrast with each other, the different theta-assigning capabilities might also be responsible for the systematic contrast between the *bei* construction and the *ba* construction in regard to the (un)acceptability of the cases involving an outermost object.

The *ba* construction has also been compared with the *bei* construction in other respects. Aside from the fact that different types of verbs may affect the *bei* and *ba* constructions differently due to the special interpretations generally denoted by these constructions, the *bei* construction loses some interpretations possible with the *ba* construction, such as those in (20)–(23). In these specific instances, both the subject of *ba* and the post-*ba* NP can be thematically related to the result complement; however, only the subject of the *bei* sentence can be so related. We traced these differences to the identification of the operator involved in *bei* constructions and the ambiguous structures possible in canonical *ba* sentences (vs. causative *ba* sentences). We should note that, even though the judgments regarding the effects of different verbs in *ba* and *bei* sentences may be uncertain and the choice of arguments easily influences the acceptabilities (see the discussions regarding (12)–(17)), the cases that have been reduced to structural factors, such as the contrast in the interpretive possibilities of *ba* and *bei* sentences and the lack of the *ba* sentences with an outermost object, are clearer-cut. The uncertain part generally has much to do with how the relevant sentences are interpreted or the context in which they are used. We next turn to this very issue.

5.5   "Affected"

In the attempt to distinguish acceptable and unacceptable *ba* sentences, we have relied heavily on the notion of an "affected" theta-role, assigned to an outer object by a complex verb phrase. We even suggested that the *ba* sentences with the post-*ba* NP originating in the inner object position might be reduced to those having an outer object with an "affected" interpretation. However, we did not attempt to define what "affected" is. Nor were we able to firmly establish the range of acceptable and unacceptable *ba* sentences. Our failure to clarify these issues is due to the limitations of what grammar can accommodate adequately. There are many uncertainties about the use of the *ba* construction and speakers' judgments also vary with context. Accordingly, we would like to suggest that, grammatically, the analysis of *ba* sentences is as presented in the previous section. However, the notion of "affectedness" will be left to such additional factors as discourse and pragmatics (including speakers' intention).

A great majority of the literature on the *ba* construction has focused on the usage of *ba* sentences by expounding on such notions as "affectedness/disposal," which state that the post-*ba* NP is the NP that is disposed of, dealt with, or manipulated in some way. These notions are responsible for the requirements on the types of arguments and predicates in this pattern. Such an approach seems to capture the basic intuition about this construction and the canonical interpretation of a *ba* sentence. In the clearest cases like *wo ba cai chao de hen lan* 'I stir-fried the vegetable very mushy,' we know that the vegetable is affected by the cooking, the result being that it is mushy. In cases like the unacceptable *wo ba Li xing le* 'I take the surname Li (my surname is Li),' our intuition tells us that this is an impossible use because, in the common world, a surname cannot be affected or manipulated by someone's having that surname. However, when we go beyond the clear cases, the picture becomes fuzzy. It is not always easy to determine when a post-*ba* NP is indeed affected. Li and Thompson (1981: 469) note some very interesting examples. A few are adapted below.

(82)   ta ba ni   xiang de fan   dou bu-ken   chi.
       he BA you miss DE food even not-willing eat
       'He misses you so much that he won't even eat his meals.'

(83)   ta ba xiao-mao ai de   yao si.
       he BA small cat love DE want die
       'He loves the kitten so much that he wants to die.'

(84)   wo ba ta   hen le xin   dou tong-si-le.
       I   BA him hate DE heart all pain-dead-LE
       'I hate him so much that (my) heart aches extremely.'

It is not clear how missing/loving/hating someone would affect the person being missed/loved/hated. Take (82) for instance. It is the subject, not the post-*ba* NP, that cannot eat because of the missing of the post-*ba* NP. Moreover, the post-*ba* NP might not even know that he was being missed. For instance, (84) can be very naturally followed by a sentence like the one below.

(85)   keshi ta bu zhidao.
            but he not know
            'But he does not know (it).'

Liu (1997) notes that an example like (86) questions the adequacy of an account for the well-formedness of *ba* sentences based on the notion of affectedness:

(86)   ta ba yi-ge da-hao jihui cuo-guo-le.
            he BA one-CL big-good opportunity wrong-GUO-LE
            'He let a great opportunity pass.'

Nonetheless, Li and Thompson (1981) try to relate such cases to the notion of affectedness. They note that the use of the postverbal expression in (82)–(83) greatly exaggerates the degree of his missing/loving you/the cat. It is as if one cannot help thinking that you or the cat is affected in some way when he misses you to such an extent that he can't even eat or he loves the cat to such a degree that he wants to die. The added expression *yao si* '(he) wants to die' in (83) hypothetically creates an image that such intense love must have some effect on the small cat. Accordingly, the "affected" interpretation is implied by the verb and the other elements in the verb phrase. Li and Thompson suggest that the notion of "affectedness" should be relaxed to include non-physical or imaginary situations. Such a modification adds a great deal of uncertainty to any account based on the notion of "affectedness." It becomes more difficult to see "affectedness" as an "explanation" for the (un)acceptabilities of *ba* sentences. For instance, what is the difference between hating someone for life (87a) and fearing someone for life (87b) that makes one better than the other as a *ba* sentence? What is the difference between missing someone extremely and resembling someone extremely that makes one acceptable as a *ba* sentence and the other unacceptable as a *ba* sentence? Under both situations, the *ba* NP, the one that is missed or taken after, does not need to be aware that he/she is missed/taken after.

(87)   a. wo hui ba ta hen yi-beizi.
          I will BA him hate one-life
          'I will hate him for life.'

        b. ??wo hui ba ta pa yi-beizi.
            I will BA him fear one-life
           'I will fear him for life.'

(88) a. xiaohai ba ta   xiang-de yao si.
           child BA him miss-DE want die
           'The child misses him extremely.'

      b. *xiaohai ba ta   xiang-de   yao si.
           child BA him resemble-DE want die
           'The child resembles him extremely.'

Compare:

      c. xiaohai xiang   ta   xiang-de   yao si.
           child resemble him resemble-DE want die
           'The child resembles him extremely.'

Of course, one can always create an "explanation" to accommodate the difference. For instance, if I am in fear of him (87b), he is probably the one that is more in control. He might not be the affected one even in the non-physical, imaginary sense. However, such an "explanation" will always be fuzzy, uncertain, unpredictable, and even circular in many cases. Nevertheless, this does highlight the fuzziness and uncertainty of some uses of this construction. It is not surprising that speakers often disagree on their judgments of atypical *ba* sentences. The same speaker may also make different judgments according to different contexts. The difficulty in clearly defining the conditions when a *ba* sentence is acceptable leads some linguists to claim that the acceptability of *ba* sentences need not be viewed as absolute; there are just relatively better or worse *ba* sentences. This conception can be best summarized by Li and Thompson's (1981: 487) conditions on the use of the *ba* construction as a continuum:

(89)	*ba*	*ba*	*ba*	*ba*
	impossible		likely	obligatory
	---
	indefinite or nonreferential object		definite and highly prominent object	
	no disposal			strong disposal

A definite and highly prominent object is an object that is "more obvious in the speech context and more immediate to our discussion" (p. 484). The table in (89) takes into account the role of the post-*ba* NP (definiteness, prominence) and the disposal meaning of the *ba* sentence. Li and Thompson further provide support for their continuum in (89) on the basis of statistics: the more elements that are added to elaborate the nature of disposal, the more likely are the sentences to appear in the *ba* form. For instance, in their corpus study that produced 83 *ba* sentences, none of them contained verbs that were reduplicated or only followed by *zhe* (which have little "disposal" meaning added, according to them).[31] Only six or seven percent out of the eighty-three *ba* sentences ended with just V-*le*. They also suggest that the continuum may capture the fact that speakers tend to disagree on the acceptability of certain *ba* sentences, especially those that are less clear on their disposal nature, i.e., those in the middle of the continuum.

Regardless of whether a table like (89) adequately describes the contexts in which *ba* sentences are acceptable, central to the account is still some notion of "affectedness" which remains undefined. Not surprisingly, this reliance on the vague notion of "affectedness" has been challenged. Attempts have been made to characterize the *ba* construction in different terms with the hope of more accurately describing the properties of the *ba* construction. Indeed, there have been proposals claiming that the notion of "affectedness/disposal" is not necessary. Under such proposals, the *ba* construction is not unique and can be subsumed under other regular structures. The constraints on the *ba* construction can be derived from some better-defined structural or semantic characterizations. These alternative proposals offer insight into this construction from different perspectives and contribute to our understanding of the complex properties of this pattern. Unfortunately, it is the complexity of this pattern, reflected by the continuum in (89), that makes precise structural accounts for this pattern fall short empirically. Above all, there exist many minimal pairs with identical grammatical structures that exhibit different degrees of acceptability as a *ba* sentence because of the different contextual information involved. It is difficult to make such contextual information precise in grammatical terms. We will review some of these alternatives and demonstrate the difficulty in clearly defining the range of (un)acceptable *ba* sentences in the suggested structural terms.

5.6   Alternatives

Briefly, we will discuss two important analyses in the recent literature and show that the empirical concerns would make it difficult to adopt these analyses

---

[31] This does not mean that there are no acceptable *ba* sentences with V-*zhe*. It is generally the progressive *zhe* that is not compatible with the *ba* sentence, as in (i). A "resultative" *zhe* is possible in a *ba* sentence, as in (ii):

(i)   ta zheng xie-zhe   xin.   *ta zheng ba xin   xie-zhe.
        he right write-ZHE letter   he right BA letter write-ZHE
        'He is writing letters.'

(ii)   ta na-zhe   shu. ta ba shu   na-zhe.
        he hold-ZHE book he BA book hold-ZHE
        'He is holding the book.'

the way they are. The analyses in question are Liu's (1997) aspectual approach and Sybesma's (1992, 1999) event-structural approach.

Liu argues that a *ba* construction is essentially a construction expressing a bounded event and that constraints on the *ba* construction are due to the aspectual properties of this pattern. She suggests that the predicate of a *ba* sentence must denote a bounded event or situation – "bounded situations" are as defined below:[32]

(90)   Bounded situations do not have internal stages that are static or stages that can be viewed as such.

The constraints on possible types of NPs and VPs in a *ba* sentence are manifestations of obligatorily expressing a bounded event/situation. Using the term "event" to refer to denotations of predicates, presented in perfective or imperfective aspect, and "situation" to refer to denotations of uninflected predicates, Liu argues that the notion of boundedness can be expressed in two ways: it can be bounded on the basis of the situation denoted by the uninflected predicate (situation type or situational aspect, see Vendler 1967, Dowty 1979, Tai 1984, S.-H. Teng 1985, Chen 1988, Smith 1991, Yong 1993), or it can be bounded when a situation of an appropriate type is presented in a certain aspect (viewpoint aspect). If the terminal point or resultative state is included in the meaning of the uninflected predicate, then the situation alone will guarantee boundedness. If, however, the terminal point or resultative state is included only when the situation is presented in an appropriate aspect, then a bounded event depends on both the situation and the aspect in which it is presented.

Sybesma (1992, 1999) incorporates the interpretation of and the semantic (pragmatic) constraints on the *ba* construction into the syntactic structure, representing the best syntactic structural effort to account for the properties of the *ba* construction. According to him, *ba* sentences are always CAUSE-sentences in some abstract sense. The VP (comprising the V after the *ba* NP and the embedded XP) does not have an external argument. The subject of the sentence (NP1 in (91) below) bears the role of the causer; in other words, it bears a semantic relation to the head CAUS (not to the VP).

---

[32] This definition was based on the notion of boundedness by Dahl (1981), repeated below.

(i)   A class of situations or a characterization of a situation (e.g., a sentence) is bounded if and only if it is an essential condition on the members of the class or an essential part of the characterization that a certain limit or end-state is attained.

(91)

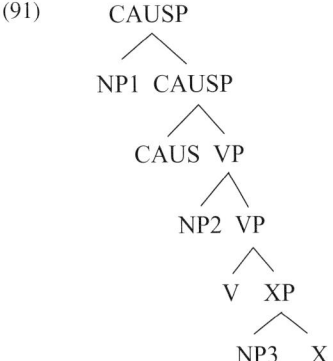

In this structure, NP1 is the subject of the sentence. NP2 and NP3 are related by NP-movement, with NP3 being the trace of NP2. The head of the CAUSP (for CAUS Phrase) is either phonologically filled by way of insertion of *ba* or by movement of the head of VP (Sybesma 1999: 170). The latter derives a non-*ba* sentence with an accomplishment VP. The former derives a *ba* sentence. Because *ba* is only a phonological filler, interpretations are the same for structures derived by verb-raising or *ba*-insertion. That is, a *ba* sentence does not carry a special meaning. It is just like a non-*ba* sentence with an accomplishment predicate. Both express a result or an endpoint: the VPs embedded under CAUS must be unaccusatives, which are "characterized by the fact that they involve an end point" (p. 178). The *ba* NP is the subject of the underlying result clause (the end point) and is the theme that undergoes a change of state or location.

This structure, according to Sybesma, can be paraphrased as "the subject causes the *ba* NP to undergo the event denoted by the VP." Revised slightly to be distinct from the lexical causative cases, such as those with causative verbs *shi* 'make' or *rang* 'let,' the structure is interpreted as "the subject of the sentence (the causer) brings about a new state of affairs which results from the event denoted by V" (p. 178). Importantly, the *ba* NP is not independently mentioned and is only semantically dependent on the embedded predicate. It is part of the resulting state. This is a departure from the "affected/disposal" tradition: a *ba*-sentence is no longer viewed as primarily aimed at disposing of the *ba* NP. The paraphrase applies to all causatives and accomplishments (or simply, all are accomplishments). That is, the structure in (91) is the structure for both *ba* and accomplishment sentences, and the *ba* construction is simply a subcase of this accomplishment structure. When verb-raising takes place, it is an accomplishment sentence; when *ba* is inserted, it is a *ba*-sentence.

This structure derives the constraints on the *ba* construction, according to Sybesma. The "affectedness" of the post-*ba* NP follows from the fact that the structure expresses a bounded event. "An event is bounded if it contains an object which is affected and quantificationally closed" (p. 173). The relevant factor for the "affectedness" of the post-*ba* NP is the "change of state" (p. 175).

Sybesma's contribution is to approach the *ba* construction with its specific interpretation and constraints from an event structural perspective. The *ba* construction is simply realization of a CAUS head in the CAUSP of an event structure. The event structure has a CAUS head subcategorized for a VP that is an unaccusative (without a subject, necessarily involving an end point). When the unaccusative verb is not raised to the CAUS head, it is spelled out as *ba*. The *ba* construction is not unique at all. It is just a variation of a construction with an accomplishment verb phrase and the verb-raising process is replaced by *ba*-insertion. The constraints on possible types of NPs and VPs in a *ba* sentence follow from the event structure (bounded event, cf. Liu's analysis in the previous section).

The brief descriptions of Liu's and Sybesma's analyses show that the two share the notion of "boundedness." Unfortunately, as we have seen time and time again, the contexts allowing the use of the *ba* construction are too complicated to fall neatly within a precise syntactic or semantic notion.[33] First of all, "boundedness" does not rule out all the unacceptable *ba* sentences and does not allow all the acceptable ones. There are unbounded cases that allow the use of the *ba* structure. Consider Liu's example (59a) (pp. 70–71):

(92)   ta zhengzai   ba dongxi wang   wuli   ban.
        he in-progress BA things   toward room-in move
        'He is in the process of moving things into the room.'

Although Liu translated the predicate as 'moving things into the room,' a more appropriate translation would be 'moving things toward the room.' *Wang* 'toward' simply expresses direction, rather than reaching a destination like 'into.' Such a predicate is not compatible with the time expression 'in X-amount of time' (test in Liu 1997 for a bounded situation):

(93)   *ta zai yige-zhongtou-nei ba dongxi wang   wuli   ban.
        he   at   one-hour-in   BA things toward room-in move
        'He moved things toward the room in an hour.'

That is, the adverbial phrase does not make the predicate express a bounded situation, yet the predicate is acceptable in the *ba* form. Other examples are available. For instance, (94) below shows the predicate 'carefully interrogate them' expresses

---

[33] For more examples and relevant discussions, see A. Li (2006).

an unbounded event; it is also possible in the *ba* form, as in (95):

(94) *ta zai yige-zhongtou-nei zixide   shenwen   tamen.
       he at   one-hour-in   carefully interrogate them
       'He interrogated them carefully in an hour.'

(95)   ni bu ba tamen zixide   shenwen, zen hui cha-chu wenti?
       you not BA them carefully interrogate how will find-out question
       'If you don't interrogate them carefully, how can you find problems?'

On the other hand, a bounded event is not always possible in the *ba* form, illustrated below.

(96) *ta ba zhexie wenzhang dou kan de hen shengqi.
       he BA these article   all read DE very angry
       'He got angry from reading all these articles.'

(97) *wo ba zhe-ping-jiu he-zui-le.
       I   BA this-CL-wine drink-drunk-LE
       'I have drunk the wine drunk.'

(98) a. *tufei   ba ta   baifang-le fuqin.
          bandit BA him visit-LE   father
          'The bandit visited his father.'

      b. *women ba ta   tanlun-le xiaohai.
          we   BA him discuss-LE child
          'We discussed his child.'

(99) *wo ba ta   renshi san-nian   le.
       I   BA him know   three-year LE
       'I have known him for three years.'

(100) a. *ta ba na-difang likai-le.
          he BA that-place leave-LE
          'He left that place.'

      b. *ta ba qiu-sai   canjia-le.
          he BA ball-game   participate-LE
          'He participated in the ball game.'

      c. *ta ba na-ge canting   baifang-le.
          he BA that-CL restaurant visit-LE
          'He visited that restaurant.'

      d. *ta ba wode mingling fucong-le.
          he BA my   order   obey-LE
          'He obeyed my order.'

One cannot attribute the unacceptability of these sentences to the lack of a result true of the post-*ba* NP. As illustrated by the examples reproduced here, the subject of the result need not be the post-*ba* NP. It can refer to the matrix subject.

(82)   ta ba ni   xiang de fan   dou   bu-ken   chi.
        he BA him miss DE food even not-willing eat
        'He misses you so much that he won't even eat his meals.'

(83)   ta ba xiao-mao ai de   yao   si.
        he BA small cat love DE want die
        'He loves the kitten so much that he wants to die.'

(101)   ta ba wo hen de ya   yang-yang de.
        he BA I   like DE tooth itchy-itchy SFP
        'He hated me so much that his teeth became itchy.'

In (102a) below, the subject of the result clause is coreferential with the matrix subject. The result expression *dong* in (102b) should take the matrix subject as its subject, rather than the *ba* NP; the *ba* NP is the object of the result expression: *ta dong-le wenzhang le* 'He understood the article.' The result expression *tou* 'thorough' in (102c) is more like a degree modifier of the verb, the hatred being thorough, rather than being a predicate of the *ba* NP. Similarly, the "result" expression *hen zixi* 'very carefully' in (102d) modifies the verb, rather than functioning as the predicate of the *ba* NP. If *hen zixi* can have a subject at all, it is the action, not the *ba* NP, that functions as the subject: *ta de kaolu hen zixi* 'his thinking is careful,' compare *zhe shi hen zixi* 'this thing is careful.'

(102) a. wo ba ta   ma   de wo-ziji dou shou-bu-liao!
            he BA him scold DE myself all   put-not-up
            'I scolded him so much that I could not stand it myself.'

      b. xian rang ta   ba wenzhang nian-dong   yihou zai
         first let him   BA article   read-understand after then
         wen ta   wenti   ba!
         ask him question SFP
         'Let him first understand the article and then ask him questions.'

      c. ta yiding   hui ba ni   hen-tou   de.
         he definitely will BA you hate-thorough SFP
         'He will definitely hate you thoroughly.'

      d. wo ba zhe-shi   kaolu de hen   zixi.
         I   BA this matter think DE very carefully
         'I thought about the matter carefully.'

5.7   Summary

The *ba* construction is one of the most studied topics in the grammatical study of Chinese. However, its complex properties elude a clear analysis.

Structurally, it is clear what the constituents are, what positions they occupy and how they are related to each other. We argued that a structure like (77), repeated here, appropriately represents a *ba* sentence.

(77)   [$_{ba}$P Subject [$_{ba'}$ *ba* [$_{v}$P NP [$_{v'}$ *v* [$_{VP}$ V XP]]]]].

Adverbials can be adjoined to *ba*P or VP (or *ba'* and *v'* if intermediate projections allow adjunctions). The comparison with the *bei* construction helped characterize the morpho-syntactic properties of *ba*. *Ba* assigns Case, but not a theta-role. However, the difficult issue in characterizing the *ba* construction has been its usage: we have demonstrated repeatedly that identical structures can produce acceptable and unacceptable *ba* sentences. The traditional wisdom of "affectedness/disposal" seems to capture the function of the *ba* construction intuitively. However, only the core cases submit easily to the characterization. Our account did not address this difficult issue. We simply referred to an "affected" theta-role, following the analysis for the passives. As a conclusion, we would like to discuss briefly the role of the "affected" theta-role in the direction of a c(ause)-role in the style of Y. Li (1990, 1995, 1999).

Leaving aside the exact definition of affectedness or disposal, the following generalization is largely true with a typical *ba* sentence, although causer and disposal are normally not part of the thematic structure of the main verb in a *ba* sentence:

(103)   Though *ba* has no theta-role for the subject or the object after it, the subject of a *ba* sentence is associated with a causer reading and the post-*ba* NP tends to be associated with a disposal reading.

Moreover, in the typical cases of the arguments in a clause having the causer and disposed readings, the subject is the causer and the object the disposed. Recall in Chapter 2 the discussion on thematic hierarchy. It is plausible that there is a causal hierarchy:

(104) a. Causal hierarchy: {Causer {Disposed}}
       b. Condition on causal alignment:
           The causal hierarchy must be aligned with the syntactic hierarchy.

Causer and Disposed in (104a) can be regarded as semantic additions to arguments in a structural environment such as the *ba* construction and are not part of the theta-grid of verbs. This separate layer of interpretive structure helps define the additional interpretations imposed on the *ba* construction despite our claim that *ba* does not play a role thematically. It is the role of a Causer–Disposed interpretive hierarchy like (104) independent of the thematic properties of the verb that coerces the interpretation of the subject of a *ba* sentence to be a causer and the post-*ba* NP to be the one that is disposed. Because conformity to (104) may require coercion, different degrees of deviations from the norm create different degrees of acceptability. In other words, two options can be entertained to encode the "affected" interpretation of *ba* sentences: one is to resort to the assignment of an affected theta-role by a complex verb phrase and the other is to separate theta-roles from the "c(ause)-roles" (104) imposed on constructions. We leave the choice between these two for further research.

6

Topic and relative constructions

Chapter 4 discussed constructions derived by movement: the passive *bei* construction can be derived by movement of an NP to an argument position (short passives) or by movement of an operator to the peripheral non-argument position of an embedded clause (long passives). The former is an instance of A-movement and the latter an instance of non-A or A′-movement. In the generative literature, there are many constructions that have been shown to be derived by A′-movement. They are typically labeled as "*wh*-movement" structures because they are well represented by *wh*-interrogative constructions in English like (1a–b), which move *wh*-phrases to the clause-peripheral position.

(1) a. Who$_i$ do you like t$_i$?
     b. I wonder who$_i$ you like t$_i$.

Many other constructions have been shown to behave like *wh*-interrogatives.[1] An example is the construction containing a relative clause – the relative construction, illustrated below.

(2) the man who$_i$ you like t$_i$

In this example, the relative pronoun *who* originates in the object position of the relative clause and ends up in the peripheral position of the relative clause.

Another case is the construction containing a nominal phrase fronted to the beginning of a sentence – topicalization:[2]

(3) John$_i$, I like t$_i$.

---

[1] See Chomsky (1977) and Browning (1987), among many others.
[2] Other constructions that have been claimed to involve "*wh*-movement" or "A′-movement" are cleft structures, pseudo-clefts, comparatives, etc. in English (see the references in note 1). It is not clear Chinese has a pseudo-cleft construction, distinct from a relative structure. Nor is it clear that A′-movement is involved in all these structures in Chinese. We leave these issues aside.

As A′-movement structures, topics and relative clauses share several properties with *wh*-constructions. The following are characteristics of A′-movement:

(4) a. A gap exists and has an A′-antecedent – the peripheral *wh*-phrase in (1)–(2) or non-*wh*-phrase in (3).

    b. The antecedent–gap relation can cross multiple clause boundaries – unbounded dependency.

    c. The dependency relation is sensitive to locality conditions such as Subjacency and the Condition on Extraction Domain.

Condition (4b) is illustrated by the relative structure in (5a) and the topic structure in (5b) in English.

(5) a. This is the girl [whom$_i$ I think [that John believes that [Bill likes t$_i$]]].

    b. That girl, I think that John believes that Bill likes.

Condition (4c) is demonstrated by the unacceptability of the dependency relation crossing an "island" (in the sense of Ross 1967), such as a complex NP island in (6), an adjunct island in (7), a subject island in (8), and a *wh*-island in (9):

(6) Complex NP island: no extraction from within a complex NP

    a. *the girl who$_i$ you bought [the books that criticize t$_i$]

    b. *that girl$_i$, you bought [the books that criticize t$_i$]

(7) Adjunct island: no extraction from within an adjunct clause

    a. *the girl who$_i$ you got jealous [because I praised t$_i$]

    b. *that girl$_i$, you got jealous [because I praised t$_i$]

(8) Subject island: no extraction from within a subject

    a. *the girl whom$_i$ you said [[that John likes t$_i$] is important]

    b. *that girl$_i$, you said [[that John likes t$_i$] is important]

(9) *Wh*-island: no extraction from within an embedded *wh*-interrogative clause

    a. ?the gift which$_i$ you remember [where I bought t$_i$][3]

    b. ?that gift$_i$, you remember [where I bought t$_i$]

That is, complex NPs, embedded *wh*-questions, subjects, and adjuncts all constitute islands out of which movement cannot take place. In Chomsky (1973, 1981) and subsequent works, the constraints against extraction from complex NPs and *wh*-islands are subsumed under the Subjacency Condition. In Huang (1982b), prohibitions of extraction from subject and adjunct phrases are accounted for by the Condition on Extraction Domain (CED). According to the "diagnostics" in (4), an antecedent–gap relation that may obtain over unbounded domains but is otherwise constrained by Subjacency and the CED is a relation of movement.

---

[3] Violation of a *wh*-island is not as pronounced, so it has been called a "weak island" (see Chomsky 1981, Cinque 1990, Rizzi 1990, for instance).

In addition to the null operator movement in passive constructions discussed in Chapter 4, Chinese has been noted to show other A′-movement structures, such as *wh*-interrogative, topic, and relative structures, illustrated by (10), (11), and (12), respectively:

(10)   ni   xihuan shei?
        you like   who
        'Who do you like?'

(11)   yuyanxue, wo zui   xihuan.
        linguistics I   most like
        'Linguistics, I like the most.'

(12)   [ni   xihuan de [haizi]]
        you like   DE child
        'the child that you like'

We will leave the *wh*-interrogative construction to the next chapter. It has been observed that topic structures are closely related to relative constructions: some have argued that when an element is relativized, it is derived from a topic position (see Kuno 1973, Jiang 1990). However, this is somewhat controversial (see Ning 1993). What, then, are the syntactic properties characterizing topic and relative structures in Chinese? Section 6.1 will focus on the topic structure and Section 6.2 will focus on the relative structure.

6.1   Topic structures

Topic structures have been extensively investigated in the literature on Chinese grammar. Chinese has been claimed to be a topic-prominent language, in contrast to English, which is claimed to be subject-prominent (Li and Thompson 1976, 1981). What is a topic? Word order is a good clue. In addition to the typical SVO word order, Chinese allows variations of SOV and OSV.

(13)   Canonical order:
        wo hen   xihuan yinyue.   – SVO
        I   very like   music
        'I like music.'

(14)   Variations:
        a. wo yinyue hen   xihuan.   – SOV
            I   music   very like
            'I, music, like.'

        b. yinyue, wo hen   xihuan.   – OSV
            music   I   very like
            'Music, I like.'

The variations contrast with the canonical SVO order in several respects. For instance, the object in the SOV and OSV patterns (preverbal object) generally does not allow an indefinite non-specific expression, but the object of SVO (postverbal object) easily allows it:

(15) a. wo zai zhao yi-ben xiaoshuo.
          I   at seek one-CL novel
          'I am looking for a novel.'

      b. *wo yi-ben xiaoshuo zai zhao.
          I   one-CL novel   at   seek

      c. *yi-ben xiaoshuo, wo zai zhao.
          one-CL novel   I   at   seek

Similarly, when a bare nominal appears preverbally, it generally is interpreted as definite.[4]

(16) a. shu, wo hui kan.
          book, I   will read
          'The book(s), I will read.'

      b. wo shu   hui kan.
          I   book will read
          'I, the book(s), will read.'

Compare:

      c. wo hui kan shu.
          I   will read book
          'I will read books.'

Examples (16a–b) contrast with (16c). Only the last one allows the object *shu* 'book' to be interpreted as indefinite.

The preverbal and postverbal objects also differ in how they relate to other elements in the sentence. For example, a negative polarity item can be licensed by the sentential negation *mei* when it occupies the object position in the SVO pattern, but not in the SOV or the OSV structure.

(17) a. ta mei xie   shenme/renhe shu.
          he not write what/any   book
          'He did not write any book.'

      b. *ta shenme/renhe shu   mei xie.[5]
          he what/any   book not write

      c. *shenme/renhe shu, ta mei xie.
          what/any   book he not write

---

[4] A generic or kind interpretation (Carlson 1977, Krifka 1995) is also possible. See Chapter 8 on the interpretation of different types of nominal expressions.

[5] The sentences in (17b) and (17c) are acceptable if the adverb *dou* or *ye* occurs after the subject. *Dou* and *ye* license the negative polarity item to their left.

Although SOV and OSV patterns share properties that distinguish them from the SVO construction, the two are not identical. The object in the SOV structure requires a contrastive or focus interpretation, but the one in the OSV structure does not (cf. Ernst and Wang 1995, Lu 1994, Qu 1994, Shyu 1995). This contrast is illustrated below:

(18)   ta   Zhang xiaojie$_i$ bu xihuan t$_i$.[6]
        him Zhang Miss   not like
        'Miss Zhang does not like him.'
        '??He does not like Miss Zhang.'

The contrastive interpretation is clearer with a clause highlighting the contrastive usage of the preposed object, as in (19):

(19)   Q: ta hui zhui Zhang xiaojie ma?
           he will court Zhang Miss   Q
           'Will he court Miss Zhang?'

        A: ta Zhang xiaojie$_i$ bu xiang zhui t$_i$, Li xiaojie$_j$ cai   hui zhui t$_j$.
           he Zhang Miss   not want court   Li Miss   only will court
           'He does not want to court Miss Zhang; (he) only will court Miss Li.'

SOV and OSV structures also have different syntactic properties. For instance, only OSV, not SOV, allows a coindexed pronoun in the postverbal object position:

(20)   a. *wo Zhang xiaojie$_i$ bu xiang zhui ta$_i$, Li xiaojie$_j$ cai   hui zhui ta$_j$.
           I   Zhang Miss   not want court her Li Miss   only will court her
Compare:
        b. Zhang xiaojie$_i$, wo bu xiang zhui ta$_i$.
           Zhang Miss   I   not want court her
           'Miss Zhang, I don't want to court her.'

---

[6] When the object is an inanimate expression, such as in (i), the SOV order does not require a contrastive interpretation (however, see Tsai (1994a: 138), for the claim that the object in SOV must be contrastive):

(i)   ni   gongke   zuo-le t$_i$ ma?
        you homework do-LE   Q
        'Did you do homework?'

A "no-ambiguity" constraint may play a role. As noted by Tsao (1977), Qu (1994), and Shyu (1995), if the two NPs can switch theta-roles and make good sentences, [NP1 NP2 V] is always interpreted as OSV, not SOV. The latter is possible only when the object is used contrastively. If they cannot switch theta-roles (e.g., *shu hen xihuan wo 'the book likes me'), the SOV order is acceptable without a contrastive interpretation.

Furthermore, only the OSV order allows the object to move across a tensed-clause boundary.

(21)   *ni   shu$_i$ renwei ta   kan-wan-le   t$_i$ ma?
        you   book   think   he   read-finish-LE   Q
        Lit: 'Do you, the book, think he finished reading?' [Intended reading:
        'Do you think he finished reading the book?'].

(22)   shu$_i$,   ni   renwei ta   kan-wan-le   t$_i$ ma?
        book   you   think   he   read-finish-LE   Q
        'The book, do you think he finished reading?'

These differences, as suggested by Qu (1994) and Shyu (1995), among others, can be accounted for if the SOV structure is derived by A-movement and the OSV structure by A′-movement. A-movement is generally limited within the minimal domain containing a subject, whereas A′-movement allows long-distance operations (cf. the short and long-distance passives in Chapter 4). The SOV construction has generally been regarded as a contrastive or a focus structure and OSV as a topic structure. What follows will concentrate on the topic structure.

In general, a topic structure refers to a sentence that has a phrase "preposed" to the position before the subject [XP + Subject . . .]. The use of the term "preposed" is suggestive of movement. However, this is a point of contention in the literature. We turn to the properties of topic structures below.

6.1.1   Movement or not?

There has been considerable debate on whether topic structures are derived by movement. The controversy concerns the relevance of the locality conditions governing movement constructions to topic structures. Another point of contention is whether topic structures need to be derived in two different ways: base-generation and movement.

First, consider the issue of whether both movement and base-generation are necessary to derive topic structures. As has often been observed, there are topics not related to a gap in the clause. Examples like the following ones do not contain a gap (see Chao 1968, Li and Thompson 1976, 1981, Tang 1979, Teng 1975, Tsao 1977, among many others):

(23)   nei-chang huo, xingkui   xiaofangdui lai   de kuai.
        that-CL   fire   fortunately   fire-brigade come   DE fast
        '(As for) that fire, fortunately the fire brigade came fast.'

(24)   shuiguo, wo zui   xihuan xiangjiao.
        fruit   I   most like   banana
        '(As for) fruits, I like bananas most.'

There have been two views regarding such "gapless" topic structures. One view takes these sentences as evidence for the existence of base-generated topic structures, as opposed to topic structures derived by movement (making a distinction between discourse topics and contrastive topics; see Tsai 1994a, for instance).[7] The alternative to having two ways of deriving topic structures is to adopt a movement approach for all topic structures and claim that sentences like (23)–(24) are derived by movement and subsequent deletion (see Shi 1992). Take (24) for example. It might be derived from something like (25) below:

(25)   shuiguo, wo zui   xihuan [(shuiguo zhong de) xiangjiao].
        fruit   I   most like   fruit   among DE banana
        '(As for) fruits, I like bananas (among fruits) most.'

The topic *shuiguo* 'fruit' is moved from within the nominal expression containing *xiangjiao* 'banana' and the parenthesized phrase is then elided. However, it is doubtful that such a movement from within a nominal expression is available in Chinese. If it were available, a sentence like (26) should be acceptable, contrary to fact.

(26)   *Zhangsan, wo zui   xihuan [(Zhangsan de) baba].
        Zhangsan I   most like   Zhangsan DE father
        'Zhangsan, I like Zhangsan's father the most.'

Moreover, the topic and the relevant nominal expression in (25) can be separated by island boundaries (see further discussion later in this chapter and the next chapter).[8]

(27)   shuiguo, wo zui   xihuan [[bu pa   chi xiangjiao de] ren].
        fruit   I   most like   not afraid eat banana   DE person
        '(As for) fruits, I like the most the people who are not afraid to eat bananas.'

Accordingly, we adopt a base-generation approach to the "gapless" topic structures in (24)–(25). A gapless topic construction is interpreted according to an "aboutness" relation: the comment clause is about the topic.

---

[7] There are many works on East Asian languages arguing for the base-generation of topic and relative constructions based on "gapless" structures. See, among others, Hoji (1985), Saito (1985), Ishii (1991), Murasugi (1991, 2000a,b).

[8] The acceptability of (27) indicates that the whole–part relation between 'fruits' and 'bananas' can be established without a gap of the whole at a position adjacent to the part. This contrasts with the inalienable possession relation between 'Zhangsan' and 'father' in (26). There must be a gap adjacent to 'father' coindexed with 'Zhangsan.' Example (26) is ruled out by the impossibility of the gap coindexed with 'Zhangsan' according to the identification rules applying to empty pronouns.

When base-generation is possible, it is tempting to conclude that all topic structures in Chinese are generated in the same manner. That is, all topic structures are instances of an "aboutness" relation and no movement ever applies. However, such a claim is neither logically necessary nor empirically supported. Consider the sentences below:

(28) a. Zhangsan$_i$, ta$_i$ zou-le.
        Zhangsan he leave-LE
        'Zhangsan$_i$, he$_i$ left.'

     b. *Zhangsan$_i$, ta$_i$ bu renshi.
         Zhangsan he not know
        *'Zhangsan$_i$, he$_i$ doesn't know.'

In (28a), the pronoun *ta* 'he' may be understood to be coreferential with the topic, but in (28b) the coreference relation is not allowed. If all topic structures are base-generated and do not contain gaps (empty categories), the difference in interpretation between these sentences is not easily captured. Note that the ungrammaticality of (28b) is related to the fact that the pronoun *ta* cannot be coindexed with *Zhangsan* in (29):

(29)   *ta$_i$ bu renshi Zhangsan$_i$.
         he not know Zhangsan
        'He$_i$ doesn't know Zhangsan$_i$.'

A theory that postulates movement in the derivation of (28b) from something like (29) can easily capture the facts in (28). The ill-formedness of (28b) follows from whatever principle also rules out the relevant interpretation in the source structure (29), such as one of the Binding Principles (Chomsky 1981):[9]

(30) a. An anaphor is bound in its governing category.
     b. A pronominal is free in its governing category.
     c. An R(eferential)-expression is free.

In particular, because *Zhangsan* in (29) is a referential expression, by Principle C in (30c) it must not be A-bound or coindexed with a c-commanding NP in an A-position. But in (29) *Zhangsan* is A-bound by the subject *ta*; the sentence is ruled out by Principle C. Example (28b) can be ruled out in the same way, if it is assumed that *Zhangsan* is put back (reconstructed) in the object position from which it originates. Alternatively, we may seek explanation from a property of the empty category in the object position, represented in (31). It is a variable bound

---

[9] For more discussions on the Binding Principles, see Chapter 9.

by an A′-element (the topic). A variable is also an R-expression and subject to Binding Principle C. It therefore cannot be A-bound:

(31)   *Zhangsan$_i$, ta$_i$ bu renshi e$_i$.
         Zhangsan   he not know
         'Zhangsan$_i$, he$_i$ does not know (him$_i$).'

Similarly, the contrast below can be accounted for by the fact that (32b) but not (32a) contains an empty category coindexed with both the topic and the subject *ta*:

(32)   a. Zhangsan$_i$, ta$_i$ shuo Lisi zou-le.
            Zhangsan   he say   Lisi leave-LE
            'Zhangsan$_i$, he$_i$ said that Lisi left.'

        b. *Zhangsan$_i$, ta$_i$ shuo Lisi kanjian-le e$_i$.
            Zhangsan   he say   Lisi see-LE
            *'Zhangsan$_i$, he$_i$ said that Lisi saw e$_i$.'

Example (32b) is ruled out, again by Principle C, on a par with (33) and the cases involving "strong crossover" like (34):

(33)   *ta$_i$ shuo Lisi kanjian-le Zhangsan$_i$.
         he say   Lisi see-LE   Zhangsan
         *'He$_i$ said that Lisi saw Zhangsan$_i$.'

(34)   *Who$_i$ did he$_i$ say that I saw t$_i$?

A different kind of contrast points to the same conclusion:

(35)   a. *ziji$_i$-de shu, Zhangsan$_i$ dou shui-zhao-le.
            self's   book Zhangsan   even fall-asleep-LE
            *'Self$_i$'s book, even Zhangsan$_i$ fell asleep.'

        b. [ziji$_i$-de shu]$_j$, Zhangsan$_i$ bu xiang kan e$_j$.
            self's   book Zhangsan   not want read
            'His$_i$ own book, Zhangsan$_i$ did not want to read.'

Example (35a) is ill-formed because the reflexive anaphor *ziji* 'self' is not bound within its governing category in accordance with Principle A of Binding Theory (30a).[10] Example (35b), on the other hand, exhibits the "reconstruction effect." Although *ziji* is not c-commanded by *Zhangsan* in this sentence, it can be placed

---

[10] The ill-formedness of (35a) cannot be attributed to a violation of the "aboutness requirement." In talking about an extremely boring book, the following sentence, where the topic does not contain the anaphor *ziji*, is well-formed:

(i)   nei-ben shu, Zhangsan dou shui-zhao-le.
        that-CL book Zhangsan even fall-asleep-LE
        '(As for) that book, Zhangsan is about to fall asleep.'

back in the gap and interpreted accordingly. Alternatively, the fact that the topic containing *ziji* is coindexed with an empty category c-commanded by *Zhangsan* allows us to count the anaphor as being "bound" in some extended sense. It can satisfy Principle A without being placed back in the object position. This is the notion of "chain-binding" proposed in Barss (1986). The preposed topic and its original object position form a chain. As long as a member in the chain containing an anaphor is c-commanded by an A-element, this A-element can bind the anaphor.

Alternatively, we may also claim that the anaphor is put back into the object position (reconstructed). There are many interesting works in the literature debating the merits of "chain-binding" and "reconstruction." We will not discuss them here, except to note a one-way implication: if reconstruction (chain-binding) is possible, movement must have taken place (see Aoun and Li 2003).

Taking reconstruction effects as a test, we may conclude that (36a), in contrast to (36b), is derived by movement. The two differ minimally in the use of an overt pronoun:

(36)　a.　[ziji$_j$-de baba]$_i$,　Zhang xiaojie$_j$　hen　zunzhong t$_i$.
　　　　　self's　father　Zhang Miss　　very respect
　　　　　'Self's father, Miss Zhang respects (him).'

　　　b.　*[ziji$_j$-de baba]$_i$,　Zhang xiaojie$_j$　hen　zunzhong ta$_i$.
　　　　　self's　father　Zhang Miss　　very respect　him
　　　　　'Self's father, Miss Zhang respects him.'

Other reconstruction effects can be demonstrated. For instance, an idiom is regarded as one unit in the lexicon. If some part of an idiom is separated from the rest of it, movement must have applied: the moved part should be reconstructed back to become one unit with the rest of the idiom. Topic structures show such reconstruction effects:

(37)　a.　zhe zhong cu,　　ni　qianwan chi-bu-de.
　　　　　this kind　vinegar　you　certainly　eat-not-obtain
　　　　　Lit: 'This kind of vinegar, you definitely should not eat.'
　　　　　'You definitely should not be jealous of this.'

　　　b.　ta-de dao,　wo bu-gan　kai.
　　　　　his　knife I　not-dare open
　　　　　Lit: 'His knife, I dare not open.'
　　　　　'I dare not operate on him.'

In short, the contrasts illustrated above show that topic structures involve move-ment. A non-movement approach to all topic structures, represented by Li and Thompson (1976), cannot be adopted.

The contrasts demonstrated here also argue against the views of Xu and Langendoen (1985) and Xu (1986). Xu and Langendoen agree with Li and

Thompson and argue that Chinese topic structures are not formed by movement at all. Unlike Li and Thompson, who do not postulate the existence of gaps, Xu (1986) advocates for the view that a sentence like (28b) above does contain an empty category. Nonetheless, the empty category is a "free empty category" (FEC). It may be freely interpreted as an anaphor, a pronominal, or an R-expression (variable) as long as the "aboutness requirement" and other Gricean principles of cooperation are met. Thus, according to Xu (1986), (28b) should be well-formed because it contains an object FEC, which, if coindexed with the subject *ta*, can be admitted as an anaphor. Example (32b) should be well-formed because the object FEC can be coindexed with *ta* and interpreted as a pronominal. In other words, (28b) and (32b) should be as good as their (a) counterparts and as good as the sentences below:

(38)   Zhangsan$_i$, ta$_i$ renshi ziji$_i$.
        Zhangsan   he know   self
        'Zhangsan, he knows himself.'

(39)   Zhangsan$_i$, ta$_i$ shuo Lisi bu renshi ta$_i$.
        Zhangsan   he say   Lisi not know   he
        'Zhangsan, he said that Lisi didn't know him.'

The unacceptability of (28b) and (32b) suggests that the FEC analysis is not adequate.

In brief, not all topic structures are derived in the same manner. Some topics are derived by movement and related to gaps in the comment clause. Some other topics are not associated with any gaps, and are interpreted according to an "aboutness" relation. Movement derives the former, and base-generation the latter.

If the topic structure containing a gap is derived by movement, we should expect the distribution of gaps to be sensitive to the locality conditions on movement. More generally, topic structures with gaps should exhibit the properties listed in (4). The facts are largely as predicted. Exceptions are due to the possibility of base-generating an empty pronoun in certain contexts, as shown next.

6.1.2   *Island conditions*

To begin with, note that, as in (4b) (an unbounded antecedent–gap relation), it is possible to topicalize an element that is deeply embedded in a complement clause:

(40)   Zhangsan$_i$, wo zhidao Lisi juede nimen dou hui xihuan e$_i$.
        Zhangsan I   know   Lisi feel   you   all will like
        'Zhangsan, I know that Lisi feels that you will all like.'

However, extraction is not possible from within certain domains. One such extraction-blocking domain is the complex NP island shown in (41) below.

(41)   a. *Lisi$_i$, wo renshi [henduo [[e$_i$ xihuan] de] ren].
              Lisi   I   know   many   like   DE   person
              '*Lisi$_i$, I know many people who e$_i$ likes.'

        b. *Lisi$_i$, wo hen   xihuan [[[e$_i$ chang ge]   de] shengyin].
              Lisi   I   very   like   sing   song DE   voice
              '*Lisi$_i$, I like the voice with which e$_i$ sings.'

These sentences become acceptable if the gap [e$_i$] is replaced by a resumptive pronoun, indicating that the ill-formed sentences are not semantically or pragmatically anomalous. The reason for the ill-formedness of (41a–b) is a bona fide instance of island violation – it is an effect of Ross' (1967) Complex NP Constraint (CNPC), a special case of Chomsky's Subjacency.

That topicalization in Chinese is constrained by the CNPC has been noted by a number of linguists (see, among many others, Tang 1977). This is expected, of course, if topicalization is derived by movement when a gap occurs. In fact, we predict that other island constraints, including the CED, which subsumes the Adjunct Condition (AC) and the Subject Condition (SC), and the Left Branch Condition (LBC), which prohibits extraction from the left branch, should all apply in Chinese as well. The prediction is borne out for the LBC and AC:

(42)   Left Branch Condition (LBC)
        *Zhangsan$_i$, wo kanjian-le [e$_i$ baba].
         Zhangsan   I   see-LE   father
         'Zhangsan$_i$, I saw [his$_i$] father.'

(43)   Adjunct Condition (AC)
        *Lisi$_i$, zhe-jian shi   [gen e$_i$ mei lai]   mei you   guanxi.
         Lisi   this-CL   matter with   not come not   have relation
         'Lisi$_i$, this matter is not related to [his$_i$] not having come.'

Regarding the SC, although some previous studies have shown that extraction out of a sentential subject may lead to ungrammatical strings (see Huang 1982b, Paris 1979, Tang 1977), it is actually not difficult to find acceptable examples that violate the SC (see Huang 1982b, 1984a):

(44)   zhe-ge xuesheng$_i$, [[e$_i$ qu canjia   zhe-ge bisai]   zui   heshi].
        this-CL student   go participate this-CL competition most appropriate
        'This student$_i$, for [him$_i$] to participate in this competition is most appropriate.'

The LBC seems also violated in some cases:

(45)   Zhangsan$_i$, [[e$_i$ baba] hen youqian].
        Zhangsan   father very rich
        'Zhangsan$_i$, [his$_i$] father is rich.'

In fact, other islands also seem violable. The following sentences apparently violate the CNPC and AC, but are perfectly acceptable:

(46)   Zhangsan$_i$, [[e$_i$ xihuan de] ren]   hen   duo.
        Zhangsan   like   DE person very many
        'Zhangsan$_i$, people who [he$_i$] likes are many.'

(47)   Lisi$_i$, yinwei e$_i$ piping-le   Zhangsan, (suoyi) meiren yao   ta.
        Lisi because   criticize-LE Zhangsan so   nobody want him
        '(As for) Lisi$_i$, because [he$_i$] criticized Zhangsan, nobody wants him.'

More generally, island effects seem to be nullified when a given island occurs in a subject or pre-subject position. Why are there these exceptions? Huang (1984a and subsequent works) shows that an important difference between Chinese and English lies in which empty pronoun (pro or PRO) is available.[11] Chinese allows an empty pronoun in all argument positions (pro), in contrast to English, which only allows an empty pronoun in a Caseless position (PRO, such as the subject of an infinitival clause). The distribution of a pro or a PRO is governed in part by a Generalized Control Rule, generalizing the control rule for the reference of PRO in English:

(48)   The Generalized Control Rule (GCR):
        An empty pronoun is coindexed with the closest nominal.

The apparent island violations in the cases discussed above can be solved in the following way. Assuming that the GCR may coindex an empty pronoun with either an antecedent in an A-position or with one in an A'-position, all the apparent island violations can be shown to arise from the independent possibility of having a pro properly coindexed with an A'-binder in accordance with the GCR in Chinese, i.e., from the possibility of using pro as a resumptive pronoun in this language. Because the GCR only looks for the closest antecedent and, unlike movement, is not subject to Subjacency, the CED, or other island constraints, no real violation of these constraints has occurred.

---

[11] Generally, a PRO is in a position not assigned Case while pro appears in a position that is assigned Case. In the framework of Government and Binding (Chomsky 1981), pro, not PRO, can be in a governed position.

To illustrate, consider an example in which topicalization out of a complex NP appears possible. In particular, consider the contrast below:

(49)   a. Lisi$_i$, [[e$_i$ chang ge   de] shengyin] hen   haoting.
          Lisi   sing song DE voice   very good
          'Lisi$_i$, the voice with which [he$_i$] sings is very good.'

       b. *Lisi$_i$, wo hen   xihuan [[e$_i$ chang ge   de] shengyin].
          Lisi   I   very like   sing song DE voice
          'Lisi$_i$, I like the voice with which [he$_i$] sings.'

In each case above, the binding relationship between the empty category [e] and the topic cannot be established by movement, because the process of movement involved would violate Subjacency. However, Chinese allows a pro; such an empty category may be base-generated. Its reference is determined by the GCR. The nominal phrase minimally c-commanding the empty category is the topic in (49a), so by the GCR the pro is coindexed with the topic, and we have a case of a topic properly binding a pro within a complex NP. Because the GCR is subject only to the notion of "closest," not to island constraints, the binding relation does not violate any principle of grammar. The empty category is admitted in (49a) not as a trace of movement, but as a pro – an empty resumptive pronoun.

Now consider (49b). Because of Subjacency, the empty category cannot be created as a trace by movement. It can be base-generated as a pro. The GCR does not allow its coindexation with the topic, however. The closest antecedent c-commanding the empty category is the subject *wo* 'I' of the comment clause, not the topic *Lisi*. Because the empty category cannot be related to the topic, either as a trace or as a pro, the sentence is ill-formed under the intended reading. More specifically, the sentence must yield the reading '(As for) Lisi, I like my own voice of singing,' which does not make sense because the topic is not related to the comment.

The GCR correctly predicts that an element may be topicalized out of a complex NP if the complex NP occurs in subject position, but not if it occurs in object position. It also correctly captures the fact that, if an object complex NP is preposed before the subject, extraction from the complex NP becomes possible.

Similarly, the GCR also accounts for the asymmetry we saw earlier with respect to the LBC and the AC. Nor is it surprising that the subject of a sentential subject can be topicalized. We will not elaborate on the details here. Readers are referred to Huang (1984a).

The problem left is why it is possible to extract not only a subject but also an object out of a clause-initial island, such as the sentences in (44) and (46), and also in (50a–b) below:

(50)   a. zhe-ge xiaohai$_i$, [[Lisi zhaogu e$_i$] zui   heshi].
          this-CL child   Lisi care   most appropriate
          'This child$_i$, that Lisi takes care of [him$_i$] is most appropriate.'

b. Zhangsan$_i$, [[e$_j$ piping   e$_i$ de ren$_j$]   hen duo].
　　Zhangsan   criticize   DE person very many
　　'Zhangsan, people who criticize [him] are many.'

Huang suggests that topicalization of the object has applied first within the embedded clause, resulting in a pro occurring at the peripheral position of the sentential subject. This can be schematically represented below:

(51)　　Topic$_i$, [$_{Clause}$ [$_{Subject}$ pro$_i$ . . .   t$_i$] . . .]
　　　　　　└───── GCR ─────┘└ Move ─┘

The additional mechanism creates new challenges, which are addressed in A. Li (2007). Nonetheless, island effects are indeed relevant to topic structures. Topic structures can be derived by base-generation or movement. The latter is sensitive to island conditions. What appears to be an island violation actually involves a pro, which is identified with the Topic by the GCR. The relevance of island conditions on all topic structures containing gaps also argues against a clear-cut distinction between a discourse topic structure being derived by base-generation and a contrastive topic structure being derived by movement. Regardless of interpretive possibilities, what matters is the presence or the absence of an empty category and the nature of the empty category (trace or pro).[12]

The study of topic structures strengthens the claim in the generative grammatical theory that movement is sensitive to island conditions. In turn, island conditions can be taken as diagnostics for movement. Moreover, as shown earlier, "reconstruction effects" also help to identify movement. If a structure exhibits reconstruction effects, movement must have taken place. These properties of islandhood and reconstruction are further illustrated by the relative construction, which is usually associated with topicalization. We turn to relative structures next.

---

[12] A distinction has been made by some linguists concerning the O of OSV as a discourse topic or a contrastive topic (Tsai 1994a, Shyu 1995, for instance; see Hoji 1985 for Japanese topic structures). The former is base-generated and the latter is derived by movement. Because of the possibility of movement, a contrastive topic can be an indefinite expression, in contrast to a definite discourse topic. An indefinite contrastive topic is illustrated by sentences such as (i) below (Tsai 1994a: 138, example (31b)).

(i)　　yi-pian lunwen, we hai keyi yingfu. (liang-pian, na jiu tai duo le.)
　　　　one-CL paper   I   still can handle   two-CL   that then too much LE
　　　　'One paper, I can still handle. (Two papers, that's too much.)'

It is not clear, however, that this is an indefinite expression. A. Li (1998) suggests that 'one paper' may be analyzed as a quantity expression. A quantity expression can be regarded as a definite expression or irrelevant to the definiteness requirement. See Chapter 8 and A. Li (1998) for the distinction between a quantity-denoting expression and an individual-denoting expression.

6.2   Relative structures

Topic and relative structures have generally been understood as sharing many properties. Both constructions belong to the group of structures subsumed under *wh*-constructions, as mentioned at the beginning of this chapter. To capture the similarity between topic and relative structures, Kuno (1976) proposed the "Thematic Constraint," according to which a relative clause construction is well-formed just in case there is a corresponding well-formed topic structure, in which the head modified by the relative clause is used as the topic and the relative clause as a comment about the topic. In the same spirit, Tang (1979) proposed that in the formation of a relativized construction in Chinese, an argument is first topicalized within the relative clause. The relativized argument is always a topic in the relative clause. Jiang (1990) made the same claim. Nevertheless, there are important differences between topicalization and relativization that cannot be captured under this hypothesis. Some topic structures are acceptable without corresponding relative structures and vice versa.

We saw in the previous section that a topic structure in Chinese does not require an element in the comment clause be coindexed with the topic; there are sentences such as those in (23)–(24) licensed by an "aboutness relation" that holds between the topic and comment. However, such an aboutness relation is not sufficient to license a relative construction:

(52)   *[[xingkui   xiaofangdui lai   de kuai de] nei-chang huo]
          fortunately fire-brigade come DE fast DE that-CL   fire
          'the fire such that fortunately the fire brigade came fast'

(53)   *[[wo zui   xihuan xiangjiao de] shuiguo]
          I   most like   banana   DE fruit
          'the fruit such that I like bananas'

This contrast between topic and relative structures can be further illustrated below. The verb *fasheng* 'happen' has both an unaccusative and a transitive use. Example (54) illustrates the unaccusative use with one argument (Theme), and (55) the transitive use with an additional argument (Experiencer):

(54)   yiwai   fasheng-le.
         accident happen-LE
         'An accident happened.'

(55)   tamen fasheng-le yiwai   le.
         they happen-LE accident LE
         'They had an accident.'

Both (54) and (55) may occur in a topic construction:

(56)   tamen, yiwai   fasheng-le.
         they   accident happen-LE
         '(As for) them, an accident happened.'

(57)   tamen_i, e_i fasheng-le yiwai   le.
         they   happen-LE accident LE
         '(As for) them, they had an accident.'

However, only (57), not (56), has a well-formed relativized counterpart:

(58)   *[[yiwai   fasheng-le de] neixie ren]
            accident happen-LE DE those person
            'the people such that an accident happened'

(59)   [[e_i fasheng-le yiwai   de] neixie ren_i]
             happen-LE accident DE those person
            'the people who had an accident'

Were a topic structure the source of relativization, (56) and (58) should not differ in acceptability.

In other respects, a relativized construction may be well-formed even though its corresponding topic structure is not. For example, although an adjunct can be relativized, it often cannot be used as a topic (Ning 1993).

(60)   a. ta chang ge   de shengyin hen hao   ting.
            he sing   song DE voice   very good hear
            'The voice with which he sings is nice to listen to.'

         b. *nei-ge shengyin, ta chang ge.
             that-CL voice   he sing   song

(61)   a. ta duidai Lisi de fangshi hen bu hao.
            he treat   Lisi DE style   very not good
            'The manner in which he treated Lisi is very bad.'

         b. *zhei-ge fangshi, ta duidai Lisi.
             this-CL manner he treat   Lisi

(62)   a. ta xiu che de chechang
            he fix car DE garage
            'the garage where he fixed cars'

         b. *zhe chechang, ta bu   xiu che.
             this garage   he not fix car
             'This garage, he does not fix cars.'

(63)   a. ta xiu hao na-bu che de fangfa
            he fix well that-CL car DE way
            'the way he fixed that car'

         b. *na-ge fangfa, ta xiu hao le na-bu   che.
             that-CL way   he fix well LE that-CL car
             'That way, he fixed that car.'

(64)   a. ta bu xiu che de yuanyin
            he not fix car DE reasons
            'the reason he does not fix cars'

        b. *na-ge   yuanyin, ta bu xiu che.
            that-CL   reason   he not fix car
            'That reason, he does not fix cars.'

Thus, the well-formedness of a topic structure is neither necessary nor sufficient
for the acceptability of a corresponding relative structure, suggesting that relative
clause structures are not derived from topic structures. If this is the case, what
is a relativized phrase and what is the process of relativization? We turn to these
questions next.

6.2.1   Distribution and interpretation

A nominal phrase has specific constituents and certain ordering requirements. While Chapter 8 will focus on the internal structure of nominal expressions,
this section will sketch the basics in order to lay the groundwork for the discussion
on relative constructions.

The basic component of a nominal phrase is a noun, such as *mao* 'cat.' A noun
can appear with a number to express quantity. In Chinese, the presence of a number
requires a classifier to specify the unit with which the entity denoted by the noun is
counted or measured. A demonstrative (and other words that are in complementary
distribution with demonstratives, such as the quantifier *mei* 'every') may occur
before the number. The order of these constituents can be summarized in (65):

(65)   Demonstrative + Number + Classifier + Noun
        zhe/na   yi/san   zhi/bei   mao/shui
        this/that   one/three   CL/cup   cat/water
        'this/that (one) cat; these/those three cups of water'

A relative clause may appear in the positions indicated by the roman numerals
I–III in (66), illustrated by the examples in (67a–c) respectively.

(66)   Demonstrative + Number + Classifier + Noun
        I   II   III

(67)   a. [[ta xihuan de] na   (yi)-ge haizi][13]
            he like   DE that one-CL child
            'the child that he likes'

---

[13] We have seen quite a few examples of classifiers in the previous chapters and always
      put a hyphen before a classifier. This is because a classifier and the preceding number
      form a phonological unit. A classifier is like a clitic or part of a compound consisting of
      number and a classifier.

b. [zhe [Zhangsan shuo chulai de] yi-ju   hua] bi
   this Zhangsan speak out   DE   one-CL word compare

  [na [Lisi xie   chulai de] yibai-ju   hua] hai   you yong.
   that Lisi write out   DE   one.hundred-CL word more have use
  'This one sentence that Zhangsan uttered is even more useful than those
  hundred sentences that Lisi wrote.'

c. [na   (yi)-ge [ta xihuan de] haizi]
   that one-CL he like   DE   child
  'the child that he likes'

As indicated by the more complex example in (67b), position II (between a demonstrative and a number) is not the most natural position for a relative clause. We put this aside (see Lu 1998). The contrast between I and III, illustrated by (67a) and (67c), has been extensively discussed in the literature, including the cases when the demonstrative does not appear, as in (68).

(68)   Number + Classifier + Noun
      I   III

The distinction between these two positions for relatives has been cast in various ways in the literature. The relative occurring in position I is "restrictive" and the one in position III is "non-restrictive" (see, for instance, Chao 1968, Hashimoto 1971, Huang 1982b). Del Gobbo (2003) extensively discusses the differences between restrictive and non-restrictive (also known as appositive) relatives. Some of them are repeated below.

(69) a. In terms of categories, the antecedent of an appositive can be any maximal projection (Sells 1985, among others).

     b. Sentential adverbs of modification can appear only inside appositives, not inside restrictives (Ogle 1974).

     c. A quantified NP cannot be the antecedent of an appositive (Ross 1967).

     d. No quantifier in the matrix clause can have scope over a pronoun in the appositive clause (Safir 1986).

     e. Appositives are affected by the presence of negation in the main clause (Demirdache 1991).[14]

She shows that the so-called non-restrictive relative in Chinese is not like an appositive in English. It actually behaves like a restrictive in English. For lack of space, we will not repeat all the arguments and examples, except for sketching some of the points listed above with a few illustrations.

---

[14] More specifically, if a noun is modified by an appositive, it cannot be in the scope of a negation in the matrix clause.

Consider (69c). The elements modified by quantifiers such as *every*, *any*, and *no* cannot usually serve as antecedents of an appositive clause; the following example is from Ross (1967):

(70) a. Every student that wears socks is a swinger.
      b. *Every student, who wears socks, is a swinger.

In Chinese no difference arises if the relative clause is in position I or III, as pointed out by Lin (1997):

(71) a. [mei   yi-ge [$_{Op}$ chuan wazi   de xuesheng]] dou shi tiaowu de.
          every one-CL   wear socks DE student   all   be   dancers DE
          'Every student who wears socks is a dancer.'

      b. [$_{Op}$ chuan wazi de [mei   yi-ge   xuesheng]] dou shi tiaowu de.
              wear   socks DE every one-CL student   all   are dancers DE
          'Every student who wears socks is a dancer.'

Condition (69d) prohibits a quantifier in the matrix clause from binding a pronoun in the appositive clause:

(72) a. *Every Christian$_i$ forgives John, who harms him$_i$.
      b.   Every Christian$_i$ forgives a man who harms him$_i$.   (Safir 1986: 672)

Again, according to Del Gobbo, such binding possibilities are demonstrated in both types of relatives in Chinese.

(73) a. [mei   yi-ge   xuesheng]$_i$ dou yuanliang naxie [cengjing shanghai tamen$_i$
          every one-CL student   all forgive   those formerly harm   them
          de]   ren.
          DE   people
          'Every student forgives those who have harmed him before.'

      b. [mei   yi-ge   xuesheng]$_i$ dou yuanliang [cengjing shanghai tamen$_i$ de]
          every one-CL student   all forgive   formerly harm   them   DE
          naxie ren.
          those people
          'Every student forgives those who have harmed him before.'

Finally, consider (69e). Demirdache (1991), following Sells (1985), points out that appositives – but not restrictive relatives – are affected by the presence of negation in the main clause. No phrase modified by an appositive can be in the scope of a negative marker in the matrix clause:

(74)   *Every rice-grower in Korea doesn't own a wooden cart, which he uses when he harvests the crop.

Chinese behaves differently, regardless of where a relative clause is:

(75) a. mei-ge   nongfu dou mei-you yi-liang [yong-lai shouge de] chezi.
         Every-CL farmer all   not-have one-CL use-for   harvest DE cart
         'Every farmer doesn't have a cart that he uses for harvesting.'

      b. *mei-ge   nongfu dou mei-you [yonglai shouge de] yi-liang chezi.
         every-CL farmer all not-have use-for harvest DE one-CL cart

The relative in position III, as in (75a), is quite acceptable. The unacceptability of (75b) has to do with the fact that a modifier in position I of (68) (before the number, without a demonstrative) makes the expression specific or definite.[15]

In brief, relatives in position I and III are not the equivalents of English restrictive and appositive (non-restrictive) clauses. According to Del Gobbo, citing Huang (1982b), a more appropriate distinction can be made in terms of modification scope: a relative clause modifies what follows it (the scope of modification is the elements to the right of the modifier). A relative in position I modifies [(Demonstrative) + Number + Classifier + Noun]; a relative in position III modifies [Noun].[16] The demonstratives in these two patterns function differently. In the pattern [Demonstrative + Number + Classifier + Relative + Noun], the demonstrative is a deictic expression. It refers to a designated definite entity ('this one,' 'that one'). The said entity has the property expressed by the relative. In the pattern [Relative + Demonstrative + Number + Classifier + Noun], the demonstrative is an "anaphoric" expression. It is identified by the preceding relative. This distinction can also be understood in terms of a descriptive vs. identificational/referential use of the relative, as proposed by Lu (1998). Lu notes that position I (his pre-Q) modifiers help identify the referent of a nominal expression, and position III (his post-Q) modifiers contribute to the description of the property.

---

[15] The terms "strong" and "weak" quantifiers are used by Del Gobbo. Weak quantifiers have a non-specific interpretation. Strong quantifiers (*every, all*) and expressions with a demonstrative (definite expressions) do not occur in contexts where a specific or definite expression is disallowed. An existential sentence is such a case:

(i)   *you meigeren/na-ge ren/zai nian shu de san-ge   ren   zai zher.
         have everyone/that-CL person/at read book DE three-CL person at here
         'There was everyone/that person/the person that was reading at this place.'

Lu (1998) notes that a nominal expression with a modifier in position I is generally definite, unless the modifier carries a contrastive stress or the whole expression refers to a certain quantity, not individual entities (A. Li 1998). Also see Hsieh (2004) for the claim that a modifier in position I of (68) (without a demonstrative) is necessarily contrastive, which is not the case with a modifier in position I of (66) (with a demonstrative).

[16] Stacking of modifiers makes some relatives in position III modify [Modifier + Noun], not simply a noun.

To capture the fact that a modifier modifies the elements to its right, Huang (1982b) proposes a modification structure in Chinese like the one below, with Mod modifying its sister constituent:

(76)

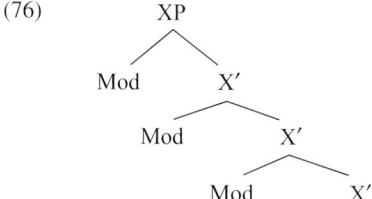

The XP can be a nominal phrase – NP. A modifier is "adjoined" to N′ (an adjoined element is neither a specifier nor a complement). N′ can be repeated as many times as the number of modifiers. Although the theoretical framework and the conceptions of nominal structures change over time (see Chapter 8), the insight of such an adjunction structure and the scope of modification remain, as we see in the following sections on the structure and derivation of relatives.

6.2.2   Movement

Do relatives behave like topic structures with regard to movement? It has been argued in Chiu (1995) that the morpheme *suo* in Chinese relatives is an indication of movement. Specifically, *suo* occurs only when the object of a verb (accusative object) is relativized. The object position must be empty. The following examples illustrate this generalization. Only (77), which relativizes an accusative object, is acceptable with *suo*. The sentences in (78)–(92) do not relativize an accusative object and do not accept *suo* (examples are from Chiu 1995: 78–81).

(77)   [Lisi (suo) mai __ de] neixie shu   – accusative object relativization
        Lisi suo buy   DE those book
        'the books that Lisi bought'

(78)   [__ (*suo) lai-guo   de] neixie ren   – subject relativization
             suo come-GUO DE those people
        'those people who came'

(79)   [Lisi (*suo) gen   ta   zhu-guo de] neige   ren   – object of P
        Lisi   suo with him live-GUO DE that-CL person
        'the person that Lisi lived with'

(80)   a. [Lisi (*suo) kandao Zhangsan __ de] difang   – where
           Lisi   suo see   Zhangsan   DE place
           'the place where Lisi saw Zhangsan'

        b. [Lisi (*suo) kandao Zhangsan __ de] shihou   – when
           Lisi   suo see   Zhangsan   DE time
           'the time when Lisi saw Zhangsan'

In addition, a pronoun in place of the gap in the object position makes *suo* unacceptable.

(81)   [wo *suo* kanguo (*ta)   de] neige   ren
         I   SUO see-GUO him DE that-CL person
         'the person that I saw (him)'

These examples show that relatives are like topic structures: movement applies and derives a gap. The appearance of a pronoun indicates the absence of movement. *Suo* is a clue to relativizing an accusative object by movement. The postverbal object position (where an accusative object is) must be empty when *suo*, referred to as an object clitic by Chiu, appears before the verb.

In what follows, we will show that relativization, even in the cases without *suo*, is indeed derived by movement when the relativized position is a gap. If a pronoun appears, movement has not taken place. The distinction is supported by reconstruction tests. A relative clause is adjoined to the nominal expression that it modifies. For convenience, we will refer to the nominal expression modified by the relative clause as the Head (of the relative construction).

When movement takes place, island conditions must be relevant. We saw in Section 6.1.2 how island conditions constrain topicalization. They apply in exactly the same manner to derive relatives that contain gaps. Indeed, all the examples given in Section 6.1.2 can have the relativization counterpart with identical acceptability judgments, illustrated below.

(82) a. *[[wo renshi henduo [[e$_i$ xihuan] de] ren   de] na-ge   nuhai$_i$]
          I   know   many   like   DE person DE that-CL girl
          'the girl that I know many people who e$_i$ likes'

      b. *[[wo hen xihuan [[[e$_i$ chang ge] de] shengyin] de] na-ge   nuhai$_i$]
          I   very like   sing song DE voice   DE that-CL girl
          'the girl that I like the voice with which e$_i$ sings'

(83)   *[wo kanjian-le [e$_i$ baba] de] na-ge   nuhai$_i$
         I   see-LE   father DE that-CL girl
         'the girl that I saw [her] father'

The preposing of [e$_i$ *baba*] makes both topic and relative structures acceptable, due to the availability of a properly identified *pro* (the GCR).

(84)   [[e$_i$ baba] wo kanjian-le de] na-ge   nuhai$_i$
         father I   see-LE   DE that-CL girl
         'the girl whose father I saw'

In brief, relative and topic structures are very much alike with respect to their sensitivity to island conditions. That is, when a gap is present, they exhibit island effects. Even though there are cases where the island conditions appear to be violated, they can be accommodated by the GCR.

The movement derivation is further supported by the relevance of reconstruction effects.[17] The following examples show that the reflexive contained in the Head can be interpreted as if it were inside the relative clause. Example (85a) shows that the binding of *ziji* 'self' by the c-commanding 'everyone' is possible. When the expression containing *ziji* is relativized, binding is still possible, as in (85b).

(85) a. wo jiao Zhangsan quan   meigeren$_i$ kai   ziji$_i$ de chezi guolai.
          I   ask Zhangsan persuade everyone drive self DE car   come
          'I asked Zhangsan to persuade everyone to drive self's car over.'

      b. [[wo jiao Zhangsan quan   meigeren$_i$ kai   t guolai de] ziji$_i$ de chezi]
           I   ask Zhangsan persuade everyone drive   come DE self DE car
          'self's car that I asked Zhangsan to persuade everyone to drive over'

Reconstruction effects are also exhibited in the following cases containing bound pronouns in a relativized Head. Example (86a) shows that the binding of the pronoun by 'every student' is possible. Example (86b) illustrates that the relativization of the expression containing the pronoun can still be bound by 'every student' inside the relative clause.

(86) a. wo xiwang mei-ge   xuesheng$_i$ dou neng ba wo gei ta$_i$ de
          I   hope   every-CL student   all can BA I give him DE
          shu   dai   lai.
          book bring come
          'I hope every student$_i$ can bring the book that I gave to him$_i$.'

      b. ni   hui kandao [[wo xiwang mei-ge   xuesheng$_i$ dou neng dai   t lai
          you will see   I   hope   every-CL student   all can bring come
          de] wo gei   ta$_i$ de shu].
          DE I   give him DE book
          'You will see the book that I gave to him$_i$ that I hope every student$_i$ will bring.'

Relatives containing idioms show the same reconstruction effects. Parts of an idiom can be separated, with one part in the relativized Head position and the rest inside the relative clause.

(87) a. [[ta chi e$_i$ de] cu$_i$]   bi   shei dou da.
           he eat   DE vinegar compare who all big
          Lit: 'The vinegar he eats is greater than anyone else's.'
          'His jealousy is greater than anyone else's.'

      b. wo ting-bu-dong   [[ta you e$_i$ de] mo$_i$].
          I   listen-not-understand   he hu-   DE -mor
          Lit: 'I do not understand the -mor that he hu-ed.'
          'I do not understand his humor.'

---

[17] The following discussion is based on Aoun and Li (2003, Chapters 5–6).

6.2.3   Base generation

In addition to movement, a relative construction can also be base-generated, just like some topic structures. Consider the following examples. An overt pronoun occurs where the Head is interpreted in the relative clause; i.e, the overt pronoun is a resumptive pronoun in the relative clause:

(88)   a. wo xiang kan [[ni   shuo meigeren$_j$ hui dai   (*ta$_i$) huilai de]
            I   want   see   you   say   everyone   will bring   him back   DE
            [ziji$_j$ de pengyou]$_i$].
            self   DE friend
            'I want to see self's friend that you said that everyone would bring back.'

        b. *wo xiang kan [[ni   shuo meigeren$_j$ hui dai   (*ta$_i$)
            I   want   see   you   say   everyone   will bring   him
            huilai de] [wo jieshao-guo   gei ta$_j$ de pengyou]$_i$].
            back   DE   I   introduce-GUO to   him   DE friend
            'I want to see the friend that I have introduced to him that you said everyone would bring back.'

These cases demonstrate that the binding of the anaphor or the bound pronoun contained in the Head by 'everyone' within the relative clause is not acceptable when a resumptive pronoun is present.

As expected, the use of a resumptive pronoun renders island conditions irrelevant. A pronoun may occur in contexts inaccessible to movement:

(89)   wo xiang kan [[ni   [yinwei   ta$_i$ bu hui lai]   hen shengqi
        I   want   see   you   because he   not will come very angry
        de] [na-ge   xuesheng]$_i$].
        DE   that-CL student
        'I want to see the student that you are angry because he would not come.'

The acceptability of sentences like (89) requires a base-generation strategy to derive the relative construction.

The discussion so far has shown that, just like topic structures, relatives can be derived by movement or base-generation. The two derivations are distinguished by the appearance of a gap vs. a pronoun. When the relativized position inside the relative clause is a gap, the relative is sensitive to island constraints and exhibits reconstruction effects. When a pronoun replaces the gap, island conditions are irrelevant and reconstruction effects are absent.

6.2.4   Relative operator

Gaps and pronouns are good indications of how a given relative construction is derived. However, there are instances without gaps where movement is still relevant. An example is the relativization of 'how' and 'why' expressions, as noted by Ning (1993).

Weishenme 'why' and *zhenme* 'how' have an interesting use in Chinese relatives. They can occur "resumptively" within the relative clause when the Head is *yuanyin/liyou* 'reason' (which occurs with 'why'), *fangfa* 'method,' or *yangzi* 'manner' (the latter two occurring with 'how'). This contrasts with other *wh*-words that cannot be used in this manner, such as *shei* 'who' and *shenme shihou* 'when.' The "resumptive" 'how' and 'why' are optional (i.e., a gap may appear instead).

(90) a. ?ta (**ruhe**$_i$/**zenme**$_i$) xiu che de fangfa$_i$, meiren zhidao.
          he how   fix car DE method nobody know
          'Nobody knows the way (how) he fixed the car.'

      b. ta (**weishenme**$_i$) bu lai   de yuanyin$_i$, meiren zhidao.
          he why   not come DE reason nobody know
          'Nobody knows why he didn't come.'

      c. ni kandao ta$_i$/*shei$_i$ mama de xiaohai$_i$
          you see he/who mother DE child
          'the child whose mother you saw'

      d. *ni zai shenme shihou$_i$ lai de shihou$_i$
          you at what time   come DE time
          'the time when you came at what time'

A resumptive *wh*-word inside a relative can be related to the Head noun across clausal boundaries:

(91) a. ?zhe jiu shi [[ta juede [ni yinggai (**ruhe**$_i$/**zenme**$_i$) xiu che] de] fangfa$_i$].
          this exactly is he feel you should how   fix car DE method
          'This is the way$_i$ (how$_i$) he feels you should fix the car t$_i$.'

      b. zhe jiu shi [[women yiwei [ta (**weishenme**$_i$) mei lai] de] yuanyin$_i$].
          this exactly is we thought he why   not come DE reason
          'This is the reason$_i$ why$_i$ we thought he did not come t$_i$.'

However, the distribution of resumptive *wh*-words is sensitive to island conditions:

(92) a. *zhe jiu shi [[[ruguo ta (**weishenme**$_i$) shengqi] wo hui bu
          this exactly is if he why   angry I will not
          gaoxing] de] yuanyin$_i$].
          happy DE reason
          *'This is the reason I will not be happy if he gets angry why.'

      b. *zhe jiu shi [[[ruguo ta (**zenme**$_i$) xiu che] wo hui bu
          this exactly is if he how   fix car I will not
          gaoxing] de] fangfa$_i$].
          happy DE method
          *'This is the way I will not be happy if he fixes cars how.'

These facts seem to suggest that movement has applied during the relativization of 'how' and 'why' relatives (referred to as adjunct relatives), even when these *wh*-words appear inside the relative clause. The movement is sensitive to island conditions. What movement is this, where an apparent "resumptive" *wh*-phrase is allowed? The answer may lie in where movement takes place or what properties characterize *wh*-words in Chinese. The former has to do with the distinction of overt and covert movement. The latter concerns the indeterminate use of *wh*-phrases (see Cheng 1997, Huang 1982b, Kim 1989, 1991, Kuroda 1965, A. Li 1992b, Nishigauchi 1986, Tsai 1994a). The properties of *wh*-words and movement will be the subject of the next chapter.

Putting aside the possible alternatives and specific mechanisms, let us entertain the option that the generation of these adjunct relatives involves the movement of an operator equivalent to *why* in English.[18] That is, these relatives have a structure like (93) in English at some level in the grammar, with the relative operator at the peripheral position of the relative clause.

(93)   I heard the reason$_i$ [**why**$_i$ he would not come here e$_i$].

That a relative operator is present can be supported by the unacceptability of sentences like the one below, which disallows an interrogative *wh*-phrase inside the relative.

(94)   *ta tingdao-le [[ni (weishenme) jiao shei   xiu che] de yuanyin]?
        he heard-LE   you why   ask whom fix car   DE reason
        *'He heard the reason you asked whom to fix the car?'

The unacceptability of (94) can be captured by a familiar "minimality" effect prominent in the Minimalist Program (Chomsky 1995, for instance). As will be shown in the next chapter, *shei* needs to be associated with an operator. The linking to an operator generally shows a "minimality" effect: the link has to be the shortest possible (cf. the notion of Attract Closest defined in Chomsky (1995: 296) or the Minimal Binding Requirement in Aoun and Li (1993a)). Because sentence (94) is an interrogative, the *wh*-phrase is interpreted in the matrix clause. That is, *shei* should be related to an operator in the matrix clause to make a question (the relevant operator being a question operator). However, the relative operator in the peripheral position of a relative clause intervenes, resulting in unacceptability. Example (94) minimally contrasts with (95), which does not contain an interrogative *wh*-phrase and is acceptable:

(95)   ta tingdao-le [[ni (weishenme) jiao ta   xiu che] de yuanyin].
        he heard-LE   you why   ask him fix car   DE reason
        'He heard the reason you asked him to fix the car.'

---

[18] The relative containing *the way how* is not quite acceptable in English. Nonetheless, such a relative is still derived by movement of a relative operator.

Similar "minimality" effects can be found in (96) and (97), which relativize an argument. The only difference between the (a) sentences in (96) and (97) and the (b) sentences lies in the presence vs. absence of an interrogative *wh*-phrase in the relative clause.

(96) a. *ta xihuan [[shei dasuan qing ta$_i$ lai   yanjiang de] zuojia$_i$]?
         he like   who plan   ask him come talk   DE author
         *'He likes the author that who planned to ask him to come to talk?'

     b. ta xihuan [[Zhangsan dasuan qing ta$_i$ lai   yanjiang de] zuojia$_i$].
         he like   Zhangsan plan   ask him come talk   DE author
         'He likes the author that Zhangsan planned to ask him to come to talk.'

(97) a. *ta yao jian [[shei xiang zhao tamen$_i$ lai   zher de] xuesheng$_i$]?
         he want see who want seek them   come here DE student
         *'He wants to see the students that who wants to bring them here?'

     b. ta yao jian [[laoshi xiang zhao tamen$_i$ lai   zher de] xuesheng$_i$].
         he want see teacher want seek them   come here DE student
         'He wants to see the students who the teacher wants to bring here.'

As in the adjunct relative case, such a contrast indicates that the unacceptable sentences contain a relative operator at the peripheral position of the relative clause, which intervenes between the interrogative *wh*-phrase inside the relative clause and a question operator in the matrix clause.

Importantly, when the resumptive pronoun coindexed with the Head is replaced by a gap, the unacceptable (a) sentences in (96)–(97) become better:

(96) c. ta xihuan [[shei dasuan qing Ø$_i$ lai   yanjiang de] zuojia$_i$]?
         he like   who plan   ask   come talk   DE author
         'He likes the author that who planned to ask him to come to talk?'

(97) c. ta yao jian [[shei xiang zhao Ø$_i$ lai   zher de] xuesheng$_i$]?
         he want see who want find   come here DE student
         'He wants to see the students that who wants to bring them here?'

Why does such a contrast exist between the cases containing a resumptive pronoun and those with a gap in regard to the "minimality" effect? Note that our minimality account for the (a) sentences in (96)–(97) is based on the presence of a relative operator in the peripheral position of the relative clause. Logically, then, the improvement shown by the (c) sentences is an indication of the absence of the relative operator. This is the analysis proposed by Aoun and Li (2003: Chapters 4–6) on the two types of relative constructions: one type contains a relative operator and the other involves the raising of the relativized nominal to the Head position. The latter is the pattern relativizing an argument (argument relative) and yielding a gap. The former has two constructions: adjunct relatives and argument relatives with a pronoun. Argument relatives with a gap are derived by directly raising the nominal without resorting to a relative operator. Adjunct relatives are not derived by directly raising the relativized phrase: the nominal Head of an adjunct relative must be base-generated. Moreover, as shown earlier, relatives containing a pronoun instead of a gap are not derived by movement either.

That such a contrast in derivation exists is supported by the differences with respect to reconstruction effects. A Head derived by raising shows reconstruction effects, but a base-generated Head does not. In the (a) cases of (96)–(97), a resumptive pronoun appears and no movement has applied. In the (c) cases, the gap indicates derivation by movement. Accordingly, the former pattern does not show reconstruction effects whereas the latter does. This difference is illustrated by the unacceptability of (98a–b) and the acceptability of (99a–b).

(98) a. *wo xiang kan [[ni   shuo meigeren$_j$ hui dai   ta$_i$ hui-lai de]
          I   want see   you say everyone   will bring him back   DE
          [ziji$_j$ de pengyou]$_i$].
          self DE friend
          'I want to see self's friend that you said that everyone would bring back.'

      b. *wo xiang kan [ni   shuo meigeren$_j$ hui dai   ta$_i$ huilai de
          I   want see you say everyone   will bring him back   DE
          [wo jieshao-guo   gei ta$_j$ de pengyou]$_i$].
          I   introduce-GUO to   him DE friend
          'I want to see the friend that I have introduced to him that you said everyone would bring back.'

(99) a. wo xiang kan [[ni   shuo meigeren$_j$ hui dai Ø$_i$ huilai de] [ziji$_j$ de pengyou]$_i$].
          I   want see   you say everyone   will bring back DE   self DE friend
          'I want to see self's friend that you said that everyone would bring back.'

      b. wo xiang kan [[ni   shuo meigeren$_j$ hui dai   Ø$_i$ huilai de]
          I   want see you say everyone   will bring   back DE
          [wo jieshao-guo   gei ta$_j$ de pengyou]$_i$].
          I   introduce-GUO to   him DE friend
          'I want to see the friend that I have introduced that you said everyone would bring back.'

The following generalizations emerge:

(100) a. Relatives with a gap in argument positions:
          A relative can be derived by directly raising the nominal to be relativized to the Head position. The Head is related to the trace in an argument inside the relative.

      b. Relatives with the Head related to an adjunct or a pronoun in an argument position:
          The Head of the relative is base-generated. The Head–relative clause relation is via a relative operator at the peripheral position of the relative clause.

The two types of relatives can be further distinguished by another interesting property: the possibility of a null Head. Relative constructions of the type in

(100a) allow the Head to be null but those involving an operator (100b) do not. The following examples illustrate the nominal and adjunct contrast:

(101) a. lai   zher de Ø
         come here DE
         'the one that came here'

      b. ta zuo de Ø
         he do DE
         'the thing that he did'

      c. *ta xiu che de Ø
          he fix car DE
          'the (way) that he fixed the car'

      d. *ta likai de Ø
          he leave DE
          'the (reason) that he left'

A null Head in relatives with resumption is not possible:

(102) a. *wo xiang kan [[ni   shuo Zhangsan hui dai   ta₁   huilai de] Ø₁].
          I   want see you say Zhangsan will bring him back   DE
          'I want to see the one that you said that Zhangsan would bring back.'

      b. *wo xiang kan [[ni   [yinwei ta₁ bu lai] hen shengqi de] Ø₁].
          I   want see you because he not come very angry   DE
          'I want to see the one that you are angry because he would not come.'

      c. *wo xiang kan [[ni   yaoqing [dai   ta₁ lai de ren]   lai   zher de] Ø₁].
          I   want see you invite   bring him over DE person come here DE
          'I want to see the one that you invited the person over that brought him over.'

Note that it is not the case that expressions of 'how' and 'why' cannot appear in the null form. This prohibition against a null Head is in effect only when a relative clause is present.

(103) a. [[ta xiu che de] fangfa] bi   [[wo xiu che de] *(fangfa)] hao.
          he fix car DE method compare I   fix car DE   method good
          'The way he fixes cars is better than the way I fix cars.'

      b. [[ta xiu che de] fangfa] bi   [[wo de] (fangfa)] hao.
          he fix car DE method compare I   DE   method good
          'The way he fixes cars is better than mine.'

Example (103a) contrasts with (103b): when the modifier is a nominal phrase, not a relative clause, the modified Head can take a null form. The following examples are further illustrations:

(104) a. [[ta bu neng lai   de] yuanyin] wo zhidao le; [[ni   bu neng
          he not can come DE reason I   know LE   you not can
          lai   de] *(yuanyin)] ne?
          come DE   reason   Q

'The reason that he cannot come, I know; how about the reason you cannot come?'

b. [[ta bu neng lai   de] yuanyin] wo zhidao le; [[ni   de] (yuanyin)] ne?
   he not can come DE reason   I know LE you DE reason   Q
   'The reason that he cannot come, I know; how about yours?'

(105) a. ni   yinggai ba ta **ruhe/zenme**ᵢ xiu che de *(fangfa) gaosu women.
    you should BA he how   fix car DE method tell us
    'You should tell us the (way) (how) he fixed the car.'

b. ni   yinggai ba ta **weishenme**ᵢ bu lai   de *(yuanyin) gaosu women.
   you should BA he why   not come DE reason tell us
   'You should tell us the (reason) why he didn't come.'

Because the unacceptable cases are those involving an operator, it is possible that such a contrast is due to some requirement on the relative operator: a relative operator needs to be identified in the sense that some content (restriction) needs to be provided for the operator to be interpreted. A null form does not have enough content to identify the null operator. Alternatively, it is possible to claim that a relative clause is licensed when the relative operator and the Head match in features, including phi-features (person, number, gender) and substantive features such as [human], [place], [time]. However, an empty Head does not have lexical content and does not have these features. In contrast, for relatives derived by directly raising a nominal to the Head position, a null form (not an operator) can be base-generated and moved there. No operator needs to be identified. A null Head, therefore, is acceptable in such cases.

Summing up, the brief discussion in this section is meant to demonstrate that a relative clause can be derived by directly raising a phrase to the Head position. It may also involve a relative operator in the peripheral position of the relative clause and a base-generated Head. The former always leaves a gap in the relativized position within the relative clause. The latter allows a pronoun or an (optional) "resumptive" adjunct *wh*. The difference in derivation and the relevance of a relative operator is supported by the interaction with an interrogative *wh*-phrase inside the relative clause, the presence or absence of reconstruction effects, and the possibility of a null Head.

Relatives are interesting not only in the complexities of their possible derivations but also in the range of structures that they exhibit.[19] For lack of space, we will only briefly discuss in the next section one important aspect of the syntactic representation of relatives.

[19] For a more extensive and detailed discussion on the properties and accounts of different types of relatives, see Aoun and Li (2003: Chapters 4–7). Also see Åfarli (1994), Munn (1998), and Sauerland (2000, 2003) for the two different derivations discussed in this section. Additionally, Winkler and Schwabe (2003) provide an extensive review.

6.2.5   NP adjunction

We understand that the function of a relative clause is to modify the Head. Structurally, there are many different representations of the relative construction in the literature, and they do not always intuitively capture the modification relation. Two main approaches are (i) an adjunction structure (see Schachter 1973 and Vergnaud 1974, for instance) and (ii) a complementation structure (Kayne 1994). An adjunction structure adjoins a relative clause to its Head. If a relative clause appears prenominally, it is adjoined to the left of the Head (left-adjunction): [$_{NP}$ Relative CP + Head NP]. If the relative occurs postnominally, it is right-adjoined: [$_{NP}$ Head NP + Relative CP]. A complementation structure, such as the one proposed in Kayne (1994), takes the relative clause to be the complement of a determiner (D). Such an analysis crucially makes a distinction between NP and DP, to be discussed in Chapter 8. We will jump ahead and bring up the relevant points here.

A determiner such as *the* in English, for instance, heads a functional projection. This is known as a D projection. The D head can take an NP as its complement. A nominal expression such as *the big boy* in English therefore has the structure [$_{DP}$ [$_D$ *the*] [$_{NP}$ *big boy*]]. In the case of relatives, the functional projection D is subcategorized for a clause, CP, according to Kayne. The Head noun is raised to the Spec of CP:

(106)   [$_{DP}$ D [$_{CP}$ DP$_i$ [C [$_{IP}$ . . . e$_i$ . . .]]]]

According to Bianchi (1999), such a structure is supported by the following generalizations:[20]

(107) a. Because the relative CP is the complement of D, the presence of a relative CP entails the presence of D.

   b. A selection relation between D and CP exists.

   c. D does not form a constituent with the Head NP, which is in Spec of CP.

Without elaborating on the details, we simply focus on (107a) because of its direct implications for the structure of a relative construction in Chinese.

Important facts illustrating (107a) involve coordination structures.[21] Generally, English allows *and* to conjoin DPs, NPs, and NPs modified by adjectives.

(108) a. He saw [[an actor] and [a producer]].   – DP coordination
   b. He is an [[actor] and [producer]].   – NP coordination
   c. He is a [[great actor] and [brilliant producer]].   – Adj + NP coordination

---

[20] See Alexiadou, Law, Meinunger, and Wilder (2000) for different approaches to relatives in various types of languages and Aoun and Li (2003: Chapter 4) for a summary and the varieties in English.

[21] The following discussion is based on Aoun and Li (2003: Chapter 5).

However, when a relative clause occurs with a conjunct, the conjunct must contain a determiner, suggesting that what are conjoined must be DPs (see Longobardi 1994).

(109) a. *He is an [[actor that wants to do everything] and [producer that wants to please everyone]].

    b. He is [[an actor that wants to do everything] and [**a** producer that wants to please everyone]].

    c. He is an [[actor] and [producer]] that wants to please everyone.

    d. He is [[an actor] and [[a producer] that does not know how to produce]].

The contrast between (109a) and (109b) demonstrates the obligatoriness of a determiner when a relative clause occurs. The relative clause in (109c) must modify both of the conjuncts, not just one of the conjuncts. Nonetheless, a relative clause can, in principle, modify only one conjunct. If the conjunct has a determiner, the modification of that single conjunct is acceptable (109d). These facts support the necessity of a DP projection when a relative clause occurs.[22] However, relatives in Chinese behave differently, as we will soon see.

First, jumping ahead, we assume that Chinese also distinguishes a DP from an NP; a typical nominal expression thus can be expressed as [$_{DP}$ Demonstrative [$_{NumP}$ Number [$_{ClP}$ Classifier [$_{NP}$ N]]]] (see Chapter 8). The element following the classifier is an NP. The phrase containing the demonstrative is a DP. When a number and a classifier appear, the projection must be larger than an NP (a NumP or DP). Semantically, a DP is an individual-denoting expression; an NP, property-denoting.

With respect to conjunction, just as English allows the conjunction of two NPs, as in (110), Chinese can do the same, as in (111).

(110) He is a [secretary and typist].

(111) ta shi [mishu   jian daziyuan].
      he is   secretary and typist
      'He is a secretary and typist.'

The expression *secretary and typist* describes the dual roles of one individual. In Chinese, a number and classifier expression *yi-ge* 'one-CL,' which functions more or less like an indefinite determiner in English, can also occur before the conjunction:

(112) ta shi yi-ge [mishu   jian daziyuan].
      he is one-CL secretary and typist
      'He is a secretary and typist.'

---

[22] Smith (1964) argues that a relative clause is part of the determiner. Larson (1991) developed the idea further by placing the determiner and the relative clause under one bigger node [NP [Det + Rel Clause]] from where the determiner undergoes movement, deriving the word order [Det + NP + Rel Clause].

Further examples illustrate conjunctions describing one individual:

(113)   wo xiang zhao yi-ge   [mishu   jian daziyuan]. – one person being sought
         I   want find one-CL secretary and typist
         'I want to find a secretary and typist.'

Relevant to our discussion is the use of the conjunction *jian* in such examples. In contrast to *and* in English, which can be used to conjoin like phrases of basically any category, Chinese has a rich set of conjunctions used to conjoin different types of like categories. For instance, if two individual-denoting expressions are conjoined, the connector is *he* or *gen*, which contrasts with *jian*, a connector used exclusively to conjoin two properties pertaining to one individual.

Example (113) should be contrasted with the following sentences where the conjunction of two individuals requires *he/gen* and is indicated by the addition of a number + classifier expression to the second conjunct as well as the first.

(114)   wo xiang zhao [[yi-ge   mishu] he/gen [yi-ge   daziyuan]].
         I   want find one-CL secretary and   one-CL typist
         'I want to find a secretary and a typist.'

Not only can number + classifier + noun expressions denoting individuals be conjoined by *he/gen*, but also other individual-denoting expressions such as proper names, pronouns, and expressions with demonstratives:

(115) a. wo hen   xihuan [[zhe-ge xuesheng] he/gen [na-ge   xuesheng]].
         I   very like   this-CL student   and   that-CL student
         'I like this student and that student.'

      b. wo hen   xihuan [[ta]   he/gen [Zhangsan]].
         I   very like   him and   Zhangsan
         'I like him and Zhangsan.'

Such conjunction of individual-denoting expressions is not possible with *jian*:

(116)   *wo xiang zhao [[yi-ge   mishu]   jian [yi-ge   daziyuan]].
         I   want find   one-CL secretary and one-CL typist
         'I want to find a secretary and a typist.'

(117) a. *wo hen xihuan [[zhe-ge xuesheng] jian [na-ge   xuesheng]].
         I   very like   this-CL student   and that-CL student
         'I like this student and that student.'

      b. *wo hen xihuan [[ta]   jian [Zhangsan]].
         I   very like   him and   Zhangsan
         'I like him and Zhangsan.'

Jian, as already shown, can be used to conjoin two properties describing one individual. It can also conjoin two activities for one individual. That is, it can conjoin two VPs:[23]

(118)   Zhangsan [[nian-shu] jian [zuo-shi]], hen   mang.
         Zhangsan   study   and   work   very busy
         'Zhangsan studies and works; (he is) busy.'

When two clauses are conjoined, none of the above conjunctions (*he*/*gen*/*jian*) is used. Instead, *erqie* is used.

(119) a. [[wo xihuan ta]   erqie [Zhangsan ye   xihuan ta]].
         I   like   him and   Zhangsan also like   him
         'I like him and Zhangsan also likes him.'

      b. [[wo xihuan ta]   erqie [Zhangsan hui   zhaogu ta]].
         I   like   him and   Zhangsan will care   him
         'I like him and Zhangsan will take care of him.'

The function of conjunctions can be summarized below:

(120) a. The connector *jian* conjoins two properties of a single individual or two activities performed by one individual. In terms of categories, *jian* can conjoin NPs or VPs.[24]

      b. The conjunction *he*/*gen* conjoins two individual-denoting expressions, i.e., two DPs, which can be proper names, pronouns, expressions containing demonstratives, or expressions containing number and classifier expressions.

      c. The conjunction *erqie* conjoins two non-nominal categories, including clauses, adjective phrases, and VPs not expressing dual properties/activities of one individual.

      d. These conjunctions are not interchangeable.

The unique distribution of conjunctions provides us with an important test for the categorial status of complex nominals. Suppose that the complementation structure [DP D CP] advocated by Kayne were an appropriate structure for Chinese relative constructions; then we would expect the conjunction of the relative clause with

---

[23] Two VPs conjoined by *jian* express dual activities performed by one person or simultaneous activities. Otherwise, the connector is *erqie*, which can be used to conjoin any non-nominal expressions. The conjuncts connected by *jian* cannot contain aspect markers (or negation or any other functional categories above VP):

   (i)   *ta nian-zhe/-le/-guo   shu,   jian zuo-zhe/le/guo   shi.
          he read-PROG/LE/GUO   book, and   do-PROG/LE/GUO   work

[24] Such a requirement of *jian* may have to do with the fact that *jian* can be a verb meaning doing something simultaneously with another, as indicated by the V-O compound *jian-chai* 'Jian-job=do part-time work, do jobs simultaneously.'

the Head (excluding D) to be possible with the CP conjunction *erqie*. This expectation is not met:

(121)   *wo xiang zhao yi-ge   [[fuze   Yingwen de mishu]   **erqie**
         I   want find one-CL   charge English DE secretary and
         [jiao   xiaohai de jiajiao]].[25]
         teach kid   DE tutor
         'I want to find a secretary that takes care of English (matters) and tutor that
         teaches kids.'

Indeed, such sentences can only be made acceptable by replacing *erqie* with *jian*, the conjunction of dual properties to a single individual. Neither *he* nor *gen* is possible:

(122)   wo xiang zhao yi-ge   [[fuze   Yingwen de mishu]   **jian** [jiao
         I   want find one-CL   charge English DE secretary and   teach
         xiaohai de jiajiao]].
         kid   DE tutor
         'I want to find a secretary that takes care of English (matters) and tutor that
         teaches kids.'

(123)   ??wo xiang zhao yi-ge   [[fuze   Yingwen de mishu]   **he/gen** [jiao
         I   want find one-CL   charge English DE secretary and   teach
         xiaohai de jiajiao]].
         kid   DE tutor
         'I want to find a secretary that takes care of English (matters) and tutor that
         teaches kids.'

Not surprisingly, just as (114) is acceptable with *he/gen*, which requires a number + classifier expression in the second conjunct, (123) can be rescued in the same way:

(124)   wo xiang zhao [[yi-ge   fuze   Yingwen de mishu]   **he/gen**
         I   want find   one-CL charge English DE secretary and
         [yi-ge   jiao xiaohai de jiajiao]].
         one-CL teach kid   DE tutor
         'I want to find a secretary that takes care of English (matters) and a tutor that
         teaches kids.'

The acceptability of (124) is expected since the conjuncts are individual-denoting expressions (DPs). It is the use of *jian* in (122) that is significant. Recall that under

---

[25] Some speakers seem to accept such sentences, especially if the sentences are made more complicated. A remark made by one of such speakers is that they sound "interpretable but not logical" (Bingfu Lu, personal communication).

a complementation approach, a complex nominal in English is always a DP and the category inside D is a CP. However, Chinese relative constructions can only be conjuncts of *jian*, the NP conjunction, not the CP conjunction *erqie*, or the DP conjunction *he/gen*. This suggests that the conjoined categories are NPs, not CPs or DPs. Indeed, if a complex nominal were always a DP, we would not expect the conjuncts of NP conjunction to contain any relative clause. This contrasts with English, which does require a D for a relative construction. Some of the relevant examples are repeated here:

(125) a. *He is an [[actor that wants to do everything] and [producer that wants to please everyone]].

   b. He is [[an actor that wants to do everything] and [**a** producer that wants to please everyone]].

Summarizing, the contrast between the Chinese (122) and the English (125) clearly argues for the different categorial status of a relative construction in these two languages: it can be an NP in Chinese, but it must be a DP in English. Moreover, because a relative clause can be adjoined to an NP Head and still be conjoined by the NP-conjunction *jian*, the relative construction should have a left-adjunction structure [$_{NP}$ CP NP].

A puzzle still remains. Chinese allows a relative clause in at least positions I and III in (126a–b):

(126) a.   Demonstrative + Number + Classifier + Noun
          I   II   III
     b.   Number + Classifier + Noun
          I   III

What we have suggested only generates a relative clause in position III. How is a relative clause in position I to be derived? It is possible that a relative clause in I is derived by moving the relative clause in III upward, after the number and classifier expressions are merged with the NP. The motivation for movement may be (contrastive) focus (see Hsieh 2004, Zhang 2004) or referentiality (Lu 1998). Readers are referred to these works for detailed discussions.

6.3   Gapless structures

To complete the paradigm of relative constructions, we would like to briefly discuss the so-called gapless relative structures in Chinese – those without a gap or a resumptive pronoun in the relative clause. This is illustrated by the following examples:

(127) a. zhe jiu   shi [[ta kao-shi   de] jieguo].
          this exactly is   he take-exam DE   result
          'This is the result of his exam-taking.'

      b. zhe jiu   shi [[ta chang-ge de] shengyin].
          this exactly is   he sing-song DE   voice
          'This is his singing voice.'

      c. zhe jiu   shi [[ta zuo-e   de] houguo].
          this exactly is   he do-evil DE   consequence
          'This is the consequence of his evil-doings.'

      d. zhe jiu   shi [[ta sha zhe-ge xiaohai de] jiama].
          this exactly is   he kill this-CL child   DE   price
          'This is the price for him killing the child.'

In such instances, the relative Head cannot be related to any position within the relative clause. Most importantly, such relative clauses are much more limited. The Head noun must be related to the entire relative clause; it cannot be merely related to an embedded clause within the relative. Therefore, (128a) is not acceptable because 'the voice' is unable to be related to the embedded clause. Neither is (128b) acceptable because 'the consequence' is unable to be related to the embedded clause.

(128) a. *zhe jiu   shi [[wo xihuan [ta chang-ge] de] shengyin].
          this exactly is   I   like   he sing-song DE   voice
          'This is the voice of my liking him singing.'

      b. *zhe jiu   shi [[wo ting-shuo [ta zuo-e] de] houguo].
          this exactly is   I   hear-say   he do-evil DE   consequence
          'This is the consequence of my hearing him do evil.'

This type of "relative clause" may not be the typical relative clause with which we are familiar. More precisely, this pattern, rather than being a counterpart of the English [Head + Relative clause], is more like a Head noun with a preposition and XP (a PP) in English, such as [*the price* [*for him killing the boy*]], [*the sound* [*of his singing*]], [*the consequence* [*of his evil doings*]]. Just like these English cases where the entire PP bears a direct modification relation to the Head noun, the Head noun in (127)–(128) must also be modified by the entire "relative clause," rather than a subpart of it (such as an embedded clause, as in (128)).[26] Examples (128 a–b)

---

[26] It is not surprising that the Chinese counterpart of the English [NP [P XP]] is [XP *de* NP]. The prepositions in question are generally quite empty: *the result **of** his exam, the consequence **of** his evil doing*, etc. Chinese rarely uses such empty prepositions within nominal expressions (except for *dui*, which occurs with some complements). Chinese

can be contrasted with (129a–b), which also contain embedded clauses but are acceptable. They are acceptable because the voice is related to the voice of my imagination (of his singing) and the consequence is related to my liking him to do evil:[27]

(129) a. zhe jiu   shi [[wo xiangxiang ta chang-ge de] shengyin].
          this exactly is   I   imagine   he sing-song DE voice
          'This is the sound of my imagining him singing.'

    b. zhe jiu   shi [[wo xihuan ta zuo-e   de] houguo].
          this exactly is   I   like   he do-evil DE consequence
          'This is the consequence of my liking him to do evil.'

These properties of the so-called gapless relatives lead us to propose that they are in fact not relatives, but rather *complements* of the nouns that follow them. The nouns in each case are used in their relational sense where their denotations do not exist independently. Thus a 'consequence' (*houguo*) does not exist by itself, but only as a consequence *of something*. Similarly, a *jiama* 'price' does not exist by itself, but only as a price of something. This is similar to nouns denoting "inalienable posession" like *baba* 'father,' *didi* 'younger brother,' and *jiao* 'foot' (kinship terms and body parts). Under this view, a "gapless relative" is in fact an argument of the head noun. Since it is not a relative, no gap is expected.

---

    always has modifiers to the left of N, in contrast to English, which may have modifiers to the right of N. *De* appears after a modifier within a Chinese nominal expression. See Fu (1994) for relevant discussions.

[27] Murasugi (1991) notes a locality condition on "gapless" relative clauses in Japanese, which is similar to the one for Chinese.

7

Questions

Like other languages, Chinese has several types of interrogative sentences, including *yes-no* questions, disjunctive questions, and constituent questions:

(1)   ni   renshi ta   ma?
         you know him Q
         'Do you know him?'

(2)   ni   xiang chu-qu kan dianying haishi zai jia   da   majiang?
         you want go-out see movie   or   at home play mahjong
         'Would you like to go out to see a movie or play mahjong at home?

(3)   ni   xiang gen   shei shangliang zhe-jiang shi?
         you want with who discuss   this-CL   thing
         'Who would you like to discuss this matter with?'

These question types are also known as particle questions, alternative questions, and *wh*-questions, respectively. In addition to these three types, researchers have generally recognized a special question form, termed A-not-A questions in the Western linguistics literature:

(4)   ni   renshi ta   bu renshi ta?
         you know him not know him
         'Do you know him or not?'

While an A-not-A question translates like a *yes-no* question, most researchers have agreed that A-not-A questions should be viewed as a special type of disjunctive question. Semantically, an A-not-A question requests the addressee to choose between a positive and a negative alternative provided in the question, while a *yes-no* question asks for a confirmation or denial of a single proposition, which itself may be positive or negative. Thus, a *yes-no* question may take a positive form as in (1), asking for the addressee's truth-evaluation of the proposition "you know him," or it may take a negative form:

(5)   ni bu renshi ta   ma?
         you not know him Q
         'Don't you know him?'

Pragmatically, *yes-no* questions may be used to express the speaker's skepticism, and so (5) may be uttered with the expectation that the answer will confirm in the positive that you do know him. An A-not-A question is entirely neutral, however, conveying no expectation from the speaker as to which alternative is more likely to be correct.[1] This difference is syntactically realized by the distributional difference between two attitudinal adverbs, *nandao* and *daodi*: *nandao* occurs only with a *yes-no* question, whereas *daodi* occurs with an A-not-A or *wh*-question, but not with a *yes-no* question:[2]

(6)   ni   nandao/*daodi (bu) renshi ta   ma?
       you actually/truly   not know him Q
       'Is it actually the case that you (don't) know him?'

(7)   ni   daodi/*nandao renshi ta   bu renshi ta?
       you truly/actually know him not know him
       'Let me get to the answer now: do you know him or not?'

Another syntactic difference is that A-not-A questions may optionally end with the Q(uestion)-particle *ne*, whereas *yes-no* questions must end with *ma*:

(8)   ni   renshi ta   bu renshi ta   ne/*ma?
       you know him not know him Q
       'Do you know him or not?'

(9)   ni   renshi ta   ma/*ne?
       you know him Q
       'Do you know him?'

In all these respects, A-not-A questions behave on a par with disjunctive questions and, in some respects, also with *wh*-questions:

(10)   ni   daodi/*nandao xiang kan dianying haishi da   majiang ne/*ma?
       you truly/actually want see movie   or   play mahjong Q
       'Would you – please tell me! – rather go to the movie or play mahjong?'

---

[1] See Li and Thompson (1979) for this observation.

[2] The two items *nandao* and *daodi* are somewhat difficult to translate word-for-word. The full meanings of these expressions may be gleaned from their components. Literally, *nandao* means 'difficult-say,' and its full literal meaning might be something like 'Isn't it difficult to say/believe [that . . .]?' A more idiomatic translation would be 'Do you mean to say [that . . .]?' In other words, *nandao* marks incredulity on the part of the speaker. As for *daodi*, its literal meaning is 'reach-bottom,' i.e., 'Now, let me get to the bottom (of this question).' When used in a disjunctive, A-not-A, or *wh*-question, it expresses an urgent desire, even a sense of impatience, on the part of the speaker to get to the specific information being requested. Thus a *wh*-question containing *daodi* has a pragmatic flavor akin to questions containing *who the hell, who on earth, what the dickens*, etc., as indicated in the translation for (11). To save space, we have used 'actually' and 'truly' in our word-for-word glosses for these two attitudinal adverbs, but their full meanings must be kept in mind.

(11)   ni   daodi/*nandao xiang shuo shenme ne/*ma?
        you   truly/actually want   say   what   Q
        'What the hell are you trying to say?'

We shall then treat A-not-A questions as a type of disjunctive question in this chapter, though at the level of formal analysis, we shall end up with the surprising conclusion that some true A-not-A questions are treated on a par with normal *wh*-questions while others are treated as particle questions.

We shall start with a brief discussion of *yes-no* questions and normal disjunctive questions in Sections 7.1 and 7.2. This will be followed by a detailed analysis of A-not-A questions in Section 7.3. The syntax and interpretation of *wh*-questions will be discussed in Section 7.4. Section 7.5 is a brief summary.

7.1   *yes–no* questions

The formation of *yes-no* questions is quite straightforward in Chinese: it simply attaches the *yes-no* question marker *ma* to the end of a statement:

(12)   a. ta   zhu zher.
            he   live here
            'He lives here.'

        b. ta   zhu zher **ma**?
            he   live here Q
            'Does he live here?'

(13)   a. ta   bu   zhu zher.
            he   not live here
            'He does not live here.'

        b. ta   bu   zhu zher **ma**?
            he   not live here Q
            'Does he not live here?'

A *yes-no* question requests the addressee to indicate whether a given proposition is true or false. Rather than being entirely neutral, sometimes the speaker may have a certain belief about a given proposition. In such a case, a *yes-no* question is used to solicit the addressee's confirmation of that belief. Such a predisposition is signaled by an expression of the speaker's disbelief, either with appropriate intonation or with the incredulity marker *nandao* 'do you really mean to say':

(14)   a. nandao   ta shi laoshi ren   ma?
            actually he be   honest person Q
            'Do you really mean to say that s/he is an honest person?'

        b. ta nandao   shi laoshi ren   ma?
            he actually be   honest person Q
            'Is s/he actually an honest person?'

As shown above, *nandao* may precede or follow a subject. While the two versions are virtually identical in core meaning, they differ with respect to their focus, or scope – how much of a given proposition is being called into question. In (14a), the scope of the question includes the subject; in (14b), the subject is outside the scope of the question. With *nandao* preceding the subject, the focal point of the question may be about the identity of the subject referent, i.e., whether s/he is the person associated with the property of being honest. With *nandao* following the subject, the identity of the subject referent is presupposed, and the focal point of the question is whether this subject referent does have the property of being honest.

Taking the subject preceding *nandao* to be presupposed material falling outside of the focus of the *yes-no* question explains why focalized and asserted constituents – such as existential phrases and clefted constituents, as well as constituents associated with 'even,' 'only,' and negation – cannot appear before *nandao*:

(15) a. nandao you   ren   xihuan Lisi ma?
         actually exist person like   Lisi Q
         'Does someone/anyone actually like Lisi?'

     b. *you   ren   nandao xihuan Lisi ma?
         exist person actually like   Lisi Q

(16) a. nandao shi Lisi xian taozou de ma?
         actually be Lisi first escape DE Q
         'Is it actually Lisi who ran away first?'

     b. *shi Lisi nandao xian taozou de ma?
         be Lisi actually first escape DE Q

     c. *shi nandao Lisi xian taozou de ma?
         be actually Lisi first escape DE Q

(17) a. ta nandao shi zuotian   cai   chufa de ma?
         he actually be yesterday only-then depart DE Q
         'Was it actually not until yesterday that he departed?'

     b. *ta shi nandao zuotian   cai   chufa de ma?
         he be actually yesterday only-then depart DE Q

(18) a. nandao lian yi-ge ren   dou bu mai ma?
         actually even one-CL person all not buy Q
         'Is it actually the case that not even a single person wants to buy [it]?'

     b. *lian yi-ge ren   nandao dou bu mai ma?
         even one-CL person actually all not buy Q

(19) a. ni nandao bu xiang guo-lai   ma?
         you actually not want pass-come Q
         'Do you actually not want to come over here?'

     b. *ni bu nandao xiang guo-lai   ma?
         you not actually want pass-over Q

Note that since *nandao* selects a *yes-no* question as its complement, and because a *yes-no* question is restricted to be the matrix clause, it follows that *nandao* cannot occur in an embedded clause:[3]

(20) a. nandao ni   xiangxin ta shi laoshi ren   ma?
         actually you believe   he be   honest person Q
         'Do you actually believe that he is an honest person?'

      b. ni   nandao xiangxin ta shi laoshi ren   ma?
         you actually believe   he be   honest person Q
         'Do you actually believe that he is an honest person?'

      c. *ni   xiangxin nandao ta shi laoshi ren   ma?
          you believe   actually he be   honest person Q

      d. *ni   xiangxin ta nandao shi laoshi ren   ma?
          you believe   he actually be   honest person Q

It was mentioned briefly above that while *nandao* occurs with a *yes-no* question, the adverb *daodi* occurs with an information-seeking question (a *wh-*, disjunctive, or A-not-A question). Like *nandao*, *daodi* is also an attitudinal adverb. While *nandao* expresses incredulity, *daodi* conveys impatience on the part of the speaker (see note 2).

(21)   Zhangsan daodi mai-le zhe-ben shu   haishi na-ben shu?
         Zhangsan truly buy-LE this-CL book or   that-CL book
         'Let me get to the truth: did Zhangsan buy this or that book?'

(22)   ni   daodi ai-bu-ai   ta?
         you truly love-not-love him
         'Truly, do you love him or not?'

---

[3] The following acceptable sentences should be analyzed as direct quotations under the matrix expression: '[What do] you think':

   (i)   ni   xiang nandao ta shi laoshi ren   ma?
          you think   actually he be   honest person Q
          'You think: is he actually an honest person?'

   (ii)   ni   xiang ta nandao shi laoshi ren   ma?
          you think   he actually be   honest person Q
          'You think: is he actually an honest person?'

A pause is preferred following the main verb *xiang* 'think.' A third person replacing the second person *ni* 'you' in the matrix subject position makes the quotative reading more difficult and the acceptability decreases unless there is a very clear pause:

   (iii) ta xiang: ni   nandao shi laoshi ren   ma?
          he think   you actually be   honest person Q
          'He thinks: are you an honest person?'

(23)   ta daodi ai-shang-le shei le?
        he truly love-on-LE who LE
        'Who the hell has he fallen in love with?'

In addition to expressing the speaker's attitude as above, *daodi* can also be used to express the attitude of the matrix subject referent – the "internal speaker." This is the case with embedded questions:

(24)   Lisi bu xiaode [ni   daodi mai-bu-mai nei-ben shu].
        Lisi not know   you truly buy-not-buy that-CL book
        'Lisi doesn't know whether you truly want to buy that book.'

(25)   ta xiang-zhidao [ni   daodi qu-le nar].
        he wonder   you truly go-LE where
        'S/he wonders where on earth you have been.'

This property of being embeddable distinguishes *daodi* from *nandao*. This difference is not surprising, of course: it simply follows from the fact that while information questions may be direct or indirect questions, *yes-no* questions are always direct questions. A real difference does exist between them: when *daodi* occurs in an embedded clause, it may (like the question constituent in the embedded clause) have matrix scope – thus marking the attitude of the speaker:[4]

(26)   Lisi shuo [ta daodi shenme shihou hui jia]?
        Lisi say   he truly what   time   go home
        'When on earth did Lisi say that he will go home?'

Just as *nandao* must occur in a position c-commanding the focus of a *yes-no* question, in syntactic structure *daodi* must c-command the focus of an information question – the disjunctive or A-not-A constituent or the *wh*-constituent.

(27)   a. daodi shei shi zheli de hai-qun-zhi-ma?
            truly who be here DE black-sheep
            'Who on earth is the black sheep here?'

        b. *shei daodi shi zheli de hai-qun-zhi-ma?
            who truly be here DE black-sheep

In addition, although presupposed materials may appear before *daodi*, focalized and asserted material cannot:

(28)   a. daodi you yi-ge   ren   mai-le shenme?
            truly exist one-CL person buy-LE what
            'What on earth did someone buy?'

        b. *you yi-ge   ren   daodi mai-le shenme?
            exist one-CL person truly buy-LE what

---

[4] For further discussion of the syntax of *daodi*, see Kuo (1996) and Huang and Ochi (2004).

(29)   a. daodi ta weishenme lian yi-ben shu dou mai-bu-qi?
          truly he why   even one-CL book all buy-not-up
          'Why on earth can't s/he afford to buy a single book?'

       b. *lian yi-ben shu daodi ta weishenme dou mai-bu-qi?
          even one-CL book truly he why   all buy-not-up

(30)   a. ta daodi bu xiang mai shenme?
          he truly not want buy what
          'What the hell does he truly not want to buy?'

       b. *ta bu daodi xiang mai shenme?
          he not truly want buy what

7.2   Disjunctive questions

Chinese disjunctive questions are formed with two or more constituents conjoined by *haishi* 'or.'[5] A variety of constituent types can enter into the formation of disjunctive questions:

(31)   Zhangsan zai jiali shuijiao haishi Lisi zai gongsi shangban?   (S or S)
       Zhangsan at home sleep   or   Lisi at firm   work
       'Is it that Zhangsan is sleeping at home or that Lisi is working at the firm?'

(32)   Zhangsan zai jiali shuijiao haishi zai gongsi shangban?   (VP or VP)
       Zhangsan at home sleep   or   at firm   work
       'Is Zhangsan sleeping at home or working at the firm?'

(33)   Zhangsan zai jiali   haishi zai gongsi shangban?   (PP or PP)
       Zhangsan at home or at   firm work
       'Does Zhangsan work at home or at the firm?'

---

[5] Chinese distinguishes *haishi* from *huoshi* and *huozhe* (all of which translate as 'or') in that while the first is used in disjunctive questions, the latter two are used in declaratives. So a more accurate translation of *haishi* would be '(whether) . . . or,' and of *huoshi* and *huozhe*, '(either) . . . or.' In other words, *haishi* is *huoshi* or *huozhe* plus [+wh]. Thus substitution of *haishi* with *huozhe* in each of (31)–(35) would result in a declarative, e.g.:

(i)   Zhangsan huozhe Lisi zai jiali shangban.
       Zhangsan or   Lisi at home work
       'Either Zhangsan or Lisi works at home.'

Sometimes, *haishi* and *huozhe* are interchangeable, as in (ii):

(ii)   juzi haishi/huozhe pingguo dou xing.
       orange or/or   apples all okay
       'Either oranges or apples will do.'
       'Whether it's oranges or apples, [both possibilities] will do.'

This is because the sentence can be analyzed in either way, as involving either a choice between two NPs or a choice between two propositions that may serve as answers to a (concealed) embedded question.

(34)   Zhangsan haishi Lisi zai jiali   shangban?   (NP or NP)
        Zhangsan or   Lisi at   home work
        'Does Zhangsan or Lisi work at home?'

(35)   Zhangsan xihuan haishi taoyan Lisi?   (V or V)
        Zhangsan like   or   detest Lisi
        'Does Zhangsan like or detest Lisi?'

A disjunctive question may also be formed without the conjunction *haishi*. In the following examples, two phrasal constituents appear to be simply juxtaposed without a conjunction (sometimes called "asyndetic coordination"), and each sentence is interpreted as a disjunctive question:

(36)   ni   jintian chi fan chi mian?
        you today   eat rice eat noodles
        'Would you like to eat rice or eat noodles today?'

(37)   ni   mai biao   xiu   biao?
        you sell watch repair watch
        'Do you sell watches or repair watches?'

(38)   ni   xihuan Zhangsan xihuan Lisi?
        you like   Zhangsan like   Lisi
        'Do you like Zhangsan or (do you) like Lisi?'

(39)   ni   xihuan Zhangsan taoyan Zhangsan?
        you like   Zhangsan detest Zhangsan
        'Do you like Zhangsan or (do you) detest Zhangsan?'

Such cases of "juxtaposed choice questions" are not as freely constructed as the normal *haishi*-questions. Huang (1988b, 1991) observed that the two alternatives being juxtaposed must retain certain degrees of phonetic or phonological similarity. Thus in both (36) and (38) the juxtaposed VPs contain the same verbs, and in both (37) and (39) the two VPs contain the same objects. Crucially, when both verbs and objects are different, a disjunctive question without *haishi* is ungrammatical:

(40)   *ni   mai shu   xiu   biao?
        you sell book repair watch
        Intended reading: 'Do you sell books or repair watches?'

(41)   *ni   xihuan Zhangsan taoyan Lisi?
        you like   Zhangsan detest Lisi
        Intended reading: 'Do you like Zhangsan or detest Lisi?'

Sentences (40)–(41) are acceptable but, without *haishi*, each must be construed as a conjunctive declarative sentence: 'You sell books *and* repair watches,' 'You like Zhangsan *but* dislike Lisi.' The precise nature and reason for this partial identity requirement is not clear to us, and will not be dealt with here. But one thing that seems clear is that the identity is phonological/prosodic (or phono-syntactic?), but not semantic in nature. This is shown by the fact that the identity displayed in (39) cannot be satisfied by replacing the second occurrence of *Zhangsan* with a coreferential pronoun:

(42)   *ni   xihuan Zhangsan taoyan ta?
        you like   Zhangsan detest him
        Intended reading: 'Do you like Zhangsan or (do you) dislike him?'

Most questions of this sort involve the juxtaposition of whole VPs (in part because of the need to repeat identical portions). For convenience we shall refer to these juxtaposed VP disjunctive questions as "VP VP Questions," to be distinguished from the *normal* disjunctive questions with *haishi*.

7.3   A-not-A questions

Typical disjunctive questions involve two choices, A and B, in either the form [A or B] with *haishi*, or the form [A B] without, as just indicated. If B is realized in the form of not-A, then we have either an "A or not-A" question as illustrated in (43), or an "A-not-A" question as illustrated in (44b–d).[6]

(43)   a. Zhangsan mai shu   haishi Zhangsan bu   mai shu?
           Zhangsan buy book or   Zhangsan not buy book
           'Does Zhangsan buy books or doesn't he buy books?'

        b. Zhangsan mai shu   haishi bu   mai shu?
           Zhangsan buy book or   not buy book
           'Does Zhangsan buy books or not buy books?'

        c. Zhangsan mai haishi bu   mai shu?
           Zhangsan buy or   not buy book
           'Does Zhangsan buy or not buy books?'

        d. Zhangsan mai shu   haishi bu   mai?
           Zhangsan buy book or   not buy
           'Does Zhangsan buy books or not buy [them]?'

(44)   a. ??Zhangsan mai shu   Zhangsan bu   mai shu?
            Zhangsan buy book Zhangsan not buy book
            'Does Zhangsan buy books or doesn't he buy books?'

        b. Zhangsan mai shu   bu   mai shu?
           Zhangsan buy book not buy book
           'Does Zhangsan buy books or not buy books?'

        c. Zhangsan mai bu   mai shu?
           Zhangsan buy not buy book
           'Does Zhangsan buy or not buy books?'

---

[6] As indicated by the contrast between (43a) and (44a), when the conjuncts are full sentences, *haishi* is required.

d. Zhangsan mai shu   bu   mai?
Zhangsan buy book not buy
'Does Zhangsan buy books or not buy [them]?'

These examples show that these questions allow various degrees of reduction of their constituents. Early syntactic treatments, represented by Wang (1967), considered these various forms to belong to the same paradigm, being derived from the successive optional application of a deletion process. Thus (44) results from the omission of *haishi*. Furthermore, the various reduced forms result from the (successive) application of a single rule of Conjunction Deletion, which deletes one of two identical constituents in either (forward or backward) direction. For example, in (44b) and (44d) respectively, an identical subject and object are reduced under forward deletion, while in (44c) an identical object has been backward-deleted.

7.3.1   Three types of A-not-A questions

Huang (1988b, 1991) argued for a "modular" approach to these various reduced forms, against the "one-rule approach" to the various reduced forms that had been followed since Wang (1967). In particular, he proposed (a) that the forms with *haishi* as in (43) and those without it as in (44) should be treated differently in a proper synchronic grammar – the former as special instances of normal [A or B] questions, and the latter as "true" A-not-A questions.[7] He further argued that two subtypes of A-not-A questions should be distinguished: the "V-not-VP" type and the "VP-not-V" type. The V-not-VP type is exemplified by (44c), in which the object is missing from the VP position preceding *not*, and the VP-not-V type is exemplified by (44d), in which the object is missing from the second VP.[8] The following are further examples illustrating the V-not-VP vs. VP-not-V distinction:

(45)   a. ta xihuan bu xihuan zhe-ben shu?   (V-not-VP)
he like   not like   this-Cl book
'Does he like or not like this book?'

---

[7] Even though they may very well have a historical relationship (as shown in T. Mei 1978).

[8] More generally, Huang (1991) distinguished between the A-not-AB type and the AB-not-A type, where A and B are variables. The V-not-VP type is a case of A-not-AB (with A = V, and B = object of VP) and the AB-not-A type is a case of VP-not-V. As for the cases in (44a) and (44b), with S-not-S and VP-not-VP, Huang considered them to be analyzable as either A-not-AB or AB-not-A (with A = VP or S, and B = zero).

b. ta xihuan zhe-ben shu   bu xihuan?   (VP-not-V)
   he like   this-Cl book not like
   'Does he like this book or not like [it]?'

(46) a. ni   renshi bu renshi zhe-ge ren?   (V-not-VP)
        you know   not know this-Cl person
        'Do you know or not know this person?'

      b. ni   renshi zhe-ge ren   bu renshi?   (VP-not-V)
        you know   this-Cl person not know
        'Do you know this person or not know [him]?'

In support of his first point, i.e., the need to distinguish between *haishi*-questions and *true* A-not-A questions, Huang pointed out that the true A-not-A questions exhibit systematic island properties with respect to their distribution and inter-pretation, whereas *haishi*-questions are free from island constraints. One property that A-not-A questions and *haishi*-questions have in common is that they may occur in an embedded clause, from where they may take either embedded scope (interpreted as indirect questions, as in (47)) or matrix scope (each interpreted as part of a direct question, as in (48)):

(47) a. Zhangsan bu xiaode [ni lai   haishi bu lai].
        Zhangsan not know   you come or   not come
        'Zhangsan does not know whether you will come or not.'

      b. Zhangsan bu xiaode [ni   lai   bu lai].
        Zhangsan not know   you come not come
        'Zhangsan does not know whether you will come or not.'

(48) a. ni   juede [ta hui haishi bu hui lai] (ne)?
        you feel   he will or   not will come Q
        'Do you think he will come or not?'

      b. ni   juede [ta hui bu hui lai]   (ne)?
        you feel   he will not will come Q
        'Do you think he will or will not come?'

However, when an A-not-A form is embedded in an island such as a sentential subject or relative clause, a direct-question reading is not possible:

(49)   *[ta lai   bu lai] bijiao hao   (ne)?
         he come not come more good Q
         Intended reading: 'Is it better that s/he comes or that s/he doesn't?'

(50)   *ni bijiao xihuan [lai   bu lai   de nei-ge   ren]   (ne)?
         you more like   come not come DE that-CL person Q
         Intended reading: 'Do you prefer the person that will come or the one who will not?'

For such embedding to be possible, an indirect-question interpretation is required, as when the island clauses are selected by appropriate verbs or nouns:

(51)   [ta lai   bu lai]   yidiar dou mei guanxi (*ne?).
        he come not come at-all all no matter   Q
        'Whether s/he comes or not does not matter at all.'

(52)   wo xiang taolun [ta lai   bu lai   de wenti]   (*ne?).
        I   want discuss he come not come DE question   Q
        'I would like to discuss the question of whether he will come or not.'

In contrast, a *haishi*-question in the context of (49) and (50) (as well as (51)–(52)) can readily be the focus of a direct question:

(53)   [ta lai   haishi bu lai]   bijiao hao (ne)?
        he come or   not come more good Q
        'Is it better that s/he comes or that he doesn't?'

(54)   ni bijiao xihuan [lai   haishi bu lai   de nei-ge ren]   (ne)?
        you more like   come or   not come DE that-CL person Q
        'Do you prefer the person that will come or the one who will not?'

Note incidentally that the property of island sensitivity applies to all forms of the true A-not-A questions, whether in the form of VP-not-VP, V-not-VP, or VP-not-V:

(55) a. *ni   bijiao xihuan [mai shu   bu mai shu   de ren]?   (VP-not-VP)
           you more like   buy book not buy book DE person
           'Do you prefer people who buy books or [those who] don't buy books?'

      b. *ni   bijiao xihuan [mai bu mai shu   de ren]?   (V-not-VP)
           you more like   buy not buy book DE person
           'Do you prefer people who buy or not buy books?'

      c. *ni   bijiao xihuan [mai shu   bu mai de ren]?   (VP-not-V)
           you more like   buy book not buy DE person
           'Do you prefer people who buy books or [those who do] not?'

Even the VP VP questions of the sort illustrated in (36)–(39) exhibit island restrictions in contrast to their *haishi* counterparts:

(56)   ni bijiao xihuan [chi fan *(haishi) chi mian   de ren]?
        you more like   eat rice or   eat noodle DE person
        'Do you prefer people who eat rice or [those who] eat noodles?'

McCawley (1994) provided an additional argument for distinguishing true A-not-A questions from those with *haishi*. He observed that when positive and negative items are conjoined by *haishi*, the order of these two conjuncts is free: both *A haishi Not-A* and *Not-A haishi A* are fine – just as both *A haishi B* and *B haishi*

A are fine. However, a true A-not-A question strictly requires A to occur before Not A:

(57) a. ta daodi lai   (haishi) bu lai?
          he truly come (or)   not come
          'Let me get to the answer: will he come or not?'

      b. ta daodi bu lai   *(haishi) lai?
          he truly not come or   come
          'Let me get to the answer: will he not come or come?'

In short, *haishi*-questions and true A-not-A questions differ with respect to their ability to escape syntactic islands and their ability to reorder their choice constituents.

In regard to his second point, the need to distinguish between V-not-VP and VP-not-V questions, Huang showed that these two constructions behave differently with respect to the Principle of Lexical Integrity (PLI) and the prohibition against P(repositon)-Stranding. In addition, Zhu (1991) cited dialectal considerations as further evidence for this distinction. We reproduce the relevant observations below.

First, in V-not-VP questions the element preceding 'not' may be something less than a word or zero-level category, whereas in VP-not-V questions the element following 'not' must be no less than a full word:

(58) a. ta xi-bu xihuan zhe-ben shu?
          he li-not like   this-CL book
          'Does he like or not like this book?'

      b. *ta xihuan zhe-ben shu bu xi-?
          he like   this-CL book not li-

(59) a. ni   jintian gao- bu gaoxing?
          you today   hap- not happy
          'Are you happy today or not?'

      b. *ni   jintian gaoxing bu gao-?
          you today   happy   not hap-

In (58a), what appears before *bu* 'not' is the first syllable of the verb *xihuan* 'like' (*xi-*, glossed as 'li-'), and in (59a) it is the first syllable of *gaoxing* 'happy' (*gao-*, glossed as 'hap-'). As shown in the (b) sentences, such meaningless syllables are totally unacceptable in the position after 'not' in VP-not-V questions. More examples illustrating this sharp contrast: *ni ren- bu renshi zhe-ge ren?* 'Do you know the person or not?' but *ni renshi zhe-ge ren bu ren-?*; *ta you- bu youmo?* 'Is s/he humorous or not?' but *ta youmo bu you-?*; etc.

Under the "one-rule approach" (following Wang 1967), the V-not-VP is derived via backward deletion of the material following the V, and the VP-not-V is derived via forward deletion. The contrasts we see here indicate that these questions behave differently with respect to the PLI, which prohibits phrase-level syntactic processes from affecting (e.g., extracting, deleting, etc.) any proper subpart of a word.[9] In particular, backward deletion seems to freely violate the PLI by deleting the second syllable of *xihuan* 'like,' *gaoxing* 'happy,' *renshi* 'know,' *youmo* 'be humorous,' etc. to produce V-not-VP questions, but forward deletion is not allowed to do so in forming VP-not-V questions.

A second, parallel distinction can be observed with respect to the prohibition against P-stranding, which is generally understood as a filter against a preposition taking an empty category as its object: *p [e] (see e.g., Hornstein and Weinberg 1981). In addition to prepositions, the morphemes *bei* and *ba* also cannot be stranded.

(60)   a. Boshidun Nan-zhan,   women mingtian jiu   cong *(nar) chufa.
         Boston   South-Station we   tomorrow then from   there depart
         'Boston South Station, we shall then depart from *(there) tomorrow.'

       b. nei-ge ren,   wo wu fa   gen *(ta)   hezuo.
          that-CL person, I no means with him cooperate
          'That person, I cannot cooperate with *(him).'

       c. nei-ben shu, wo ba *(ta) jie-gei-le   Lisi le.
          that-CL book I ba   it   loan-to-LE Lisi LE
          'That book, I already loaned (it) to Lisi.'

       d. nei-ge xiaohai, wo you   bei *(ta) pian le.[10]
          that-CL child   I   again BEI him cheat LE
          'That child, I was deceived by *(him) again.'

However, under the deletion approach, V-not-VP questions seem to systematically allow stranding, while this is again impossible with VP-not-V questions:[11]

(61)   a. nimen mingtian cong bu cong Nan-zhan   chufa?
          you   tomorrow from not from South-Station depart
          'Will you depart from South Station tomorrow or not?'

---

[9] See Huang (1984b) for more discussion in relation to the PLI.

[10] The sentence *?nei-ge xiaohai, wo you bei pian le* is marginally acceptable as a topic structure meaning '(As for) that child, I was deceived again,' but without the specific meaning that I was deceived by that child. In other words, the sentence must be interpreted as an Agentless short passive with no empty category following *bei*.

[11] Zhu (1991), in discussing Huang (1988b), pointed out that some Beijing speakers would accept apparent P-Stranding cases like the following:

(i)   ni gen ta shuo hua bu gen?
       you with him speak word not with
       'Do you speak with him or not?'

This in fact also sounds better to us than the examples with stranded *ba* and *cong*. It seems that the discrepancies arise because some prepositions that were historically derived from verbs have retained their verbal status to varying degrees.

b. *nimen mingtian cong Nan-zhan   chufa bu cong?
   you   tomorrow from South-Station depart not from
   'Will you depart from South Station tomorrow or not?'

(62) a. ni   ba bu ba nei-ben shu jie gei wo?
         you BA not BA that-CL book lend to me
         'Will you lend the book to me or not?'

      b. *ni   ba nei-ben shu jie gei wo bu ba?
          you BA that-CL book lend to me not BA

Zhu (1991) provided an additional argument in support of Huang's distinction between V-not-VP and VP-not-V questions. Based on an extensive survey, Zhu pointed out that while the VP-not-V questions are common among the northern dialects of Chinese, V-not-VP questions are primarily innovations of the southern dialects. For example, in the speech of elderly Beijing speakers, A-not-A questions are overwhelmingly VP-not-VP or VP-not-V. Furthermore, in Huojia, Luoyang, and Kaifeng, VP-not-VP and VP-not-V forms are used to the exclusion of V-not-VP. As for the V-not-VP questions, they are found in abundance in dialects and subdialects of the Yue, Wu, Min, and Kejia groups, all of southern China.

In short, three types of so-called A-not-A questions can be distinguished based on their different behaviors: the normal *haishi*-questions that happen to have A and not-A as their choices, the true A-not-A questions of the form V-not-VP, and those of the form VP-not-V.[12]

7.3.2   *A-not-A questions: a modular approach*

Based on the above and other considerations in Huang (1988b, 1991), McCawley (1994), and Zhu (1991), we adopt a modular approach to the paradigm in (43)–(44). To derive the various sentence types, it is assumed that three grammatical processes may be involved: (a) Conjunction Reduction, (b) Anaphoric Ellipsis, and (c) Reduplication.

First of all, we assume that *haishi*-questions are derived from full-size, bi-clausal underlying sources (as in (43a), repeated below), and shorter forms such as (43b–d) are obtained via one of two deletion processes:

(43) a. Zhangsan mai shu   haishi Zhangsan bu mai shu?
         Zhangsan buy book or   Zhangsan not buy book
         'Does Zhangsan buy books or doesn't he buy books?'

---

[12] The PLI and the prohibition against P-Stranding are irrelevant to the VP-not-VP questions (e.g., (44b)) and VP-VP questions (e.g., (36)). Based on cursory observations, those who prefer the V-not-VP form generally also do so over the VP-not-VP form. We shall take the VP-not-VP type to be in closer affinity to the VP-not-V type.

    b. Zhangsan mai shu   haishi bu mai shu?
       Zhangsan buy book or   not buy book
       'Does Zhangsan buy books or not buy books?'

    c. Zhangsan mai haishi bu mai shu?
       Zhangsan buy or   not buy book
       'Does Zhangsan buy or not buy books?'

    d. Zhangsan mai shu   haishi bu mai?
       Zhangsan buy book or   not buy
       'Does Zhangsan buy books or not buy [them]?'

In particular, Conjunction Reduction (CR) applies to the full-form source (43a) in the forward direction and deletes the second occurrence of *Zhangsan* to give (43b). A further application of CR to (43b) operates backward to delete the first occurrence of *shu* 'book,' giving (43c). We assume, following Ross (1967), that CR is subject to a Directionality Constraint (DC) that prevents it from applying in the forward direction to produce (43d).[13] We claim that the process responsible for producing (43d) is Anaphoric Ellipsis (AE), which applies forward to delete the object *shu* 'book' from the second conjunct.

Both CR and AE are independently needed mechanisms in UG and in Chinese grammar. CR also derives reduced [A *haishi* B] questions like (32)–(35) above, as well as other reduced coordinate structures involving 'and,' 'or,' 'but,' etc. AE is observed not only in coordinate structures (where deletion invariably applies forward), but also in other contexts:

(63)   ruguo ni   xiang kan zhe-ben shu, wo jiu   song gei ni.
        if   you want read this-CL book, I   then give to you
        'If you want to read this book, I will give [it] to you.'

(64)   ruguo ni   xiang kan, I jiu   ba zhe-ben shu song gei ni.
        if   you want read I then BA this-CL book give to you
        'If you want to read [it], I will give the book to you.'

While CR is subject to DC, AE obeys general conditions on anaphora (like pronominal binding and VP ellipsis, involving notions such as c-command and

---

[13] As first shown by Ross (1967), CR obeys DC such that deletion applies forward if identical elements occur on a left branch, but backward if identical elements occur on a right branch. Thus, given the underlying source *John sang and John danced*, where the identical subjects occur on a left branch of a tree, deletion applies forward to give *John sang and danced* (see also (43b) above). And for a conjoined VP like [*cooked the noodles and ate the noodles*], where the identical objects occur on a right branch, deletion applies backward to give *cooked and ate the noodles* (see also (43c)).

precedence). The independent existence of CR and AE means that they do not incur extra cost to our description of A-not-A questions.[14]

For the VP-not-V questions, we claim that they are derived by AE from base-generated VP-not-VP questions, much as (43d) is an elliptical form of (43b). We assume that a mechanism exists to base-generate a coordinate [[VP] [Not VP]] structure joined by a null *haishi* with appropriate formal features (e.g., +Q and +A-not-A), the latter ensuring that the choices must occur in the order *A > Not A* but not vice versa. This mechanism gives rise to the VP-not-VP question (44b). Applying AE to (44b) gives (44d):

(44) b. Zhangsan mai shu   bu mai shu?
          Zhangsan buy book not buy book
          'Does Zhangsan buy books or not buy books?'

      c. Zhangsan mai bu   mai shu?
          Zhangsan buy not buy book
          'Does Zhangsan buy or not buy books?'

      d. Zhangsan mai shu   bu mai?
          Zhangsan buy book not buy
          'Does Zhangsan buy books or not buy [them]?'

As for V-not-VP questions like (44c) and especially[15] examples like the following (repeated from (58a)–(59a), and (61a)–(62a)), we claim that they are not the results of deletion, but of reduplication.

(65)   ta xi- bu xihuan zhe-ben shu?
          he li- not like   this-CL book
          'Does he like or not like this book?'

(66)   ni   jintian gao- bu gaoxing?
          you today   hap- not happy
          'Are you happy today or not?'

(67)   nimen mingtian cong bu cong Nan-zhan   chufa?
          you   tomorrow from not from South-Station depart
          'Will you depart from South Station tomorrow or not?'

[14] One possible alternative to CR is to assume that the relevant reduced coordinate structures are base-generated by a general rule schema that generates coordinate structures of various sorts (either by the traditional XP → XP Conj. XP; X → X Conj. X; etc., or possibly along the lines of Munn (1993) and Zoerner (1995), according to which the coordinate structure is projected from the conjunction as its head). In this alternative, there would not be a process of CR. There are some minor negative consequences in taking this alternative, but we shall not go into them.

[15] We say 'especially' those examples that seem to violate the PLI but allow P-Stranding, because V-not-VP forms in which V is a full verb (e.g., (43c)) may have the alternative of being derived via (backward) CR from VP-not-VP sources like (44b).

(68)   ni   ba bu ba nei-ben shu jie   gei wo?
        you BA not BA that-CL book lend to   me
        'Will you lend the book to me or not?'

More specifically, we propose that for each of (65)–(68), the underlying source
is a simplex sentence with an interrogative functional head, located in the same
position where one would find the negation head of a negative sentence, as follows:

(69)

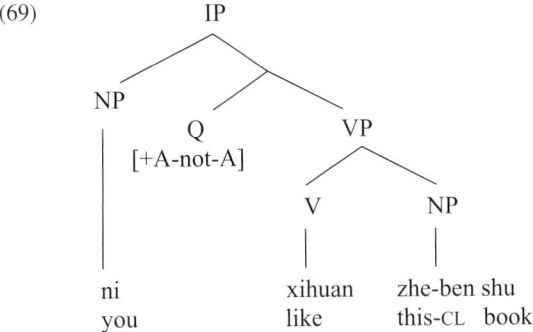

ni   xihuan   zhe-ben shu
you   like   this-CL book

The Q is realized morphologically in the following way: it first reduplicates an
initial portion of the VP constituent, and second turns the second of the identical
parts into its appropriate negative form. If the full verb *xihuan* is reduplicated,
we have [*xihuan bu-xihuan*] (as in (45a)). If only the initial syllable of *xihuan* is
reduplicated, we have [*xi bu-xihuan*] (as in (65)). And if the reduplicated portion
is a preposition or *ba*, *bei*, etc., we get forms like *ba-bu-ba*, *cong-bu-cong*, etc.
(as in (67)–(68)). What form the negative part will take depends on the aspectual
property of the verbal element. Thus, if the verb is an accomplishment verb like
kanjian 'see' or *kandong* 'read-understand,' the negative would take the form
mei (instead of *bu*): *kan-mei-kanjian, kanjian-mei-kanjian* 'see-not-see'; *kan-mei-
kandong, kandong-mei-kandong* 'understand-not-understand (from reading)':

(70)   a. ni   kan(jian)-mei-kanjian Lisi?
            you see-not-see   Lisi
            'Did you see Lisi or not?'

        b. ni   kan(dong)-mei-kandong   zhe-pian wenzhang?
            you understand-not-understand this-CL   article
            'Have you understood this article or not?'

And with a potential verb, we get results like *kandedong-kanbudong*:

(71)   ni   kandedong   kanbudong   zhe-ben shu?
        you can-understand cannot-understand this-CL book
        'Can you understand this book or not?'

To summarize, in our treatment of Chinese disjunctive questions we have distinguished between *haishi*-questions and true A-not-A questions, and among the latter we have distinguished between a V-not-VP and a VP-not-V type of question. The *haishi*-questions have a bi-clausal (or multi-clausal) source, and various reduced *haishi*-questions may be obtained by CR or AE. The true A-not-A questions have two sources: (a) a base-generated coordinate VP (in [VP (not)-VP] form) headed by an abstract conjunction with disjunctive semantics, whose second conjunct VP may be optionally reduced by AE; and (b) a simplex VP preceded by an interrogative functional head, which is morphologically realized by reduplication. We observed that these three question forms exhibited different behaviors. Given the analyses described here, we are ready to derive their differences.[16]

7.3.3   Explaining the differences

One major difference we observed between *haishi*-questions and true A-not-A questions was that the true A-not-A questions, but not the *haishi*-questions, exhibit a full range of island effects. Again following Huang (1991), we explain this difference by the hypothesis that while the *haishi*-questions have bi-clausal sources that give their underlying semantics and certain reduction processes (CR and AE) that derive their various surface forms, the true A-not-A questions are base-generated with an "A-not-A constituent" (an interrogative coordinate VP or an interrogative functional head) which is subject to interpretation for the assignment of its scope in Logical Form (LF). Following an LF movement approach (to be discussed in more detail in conjunction with *wh*-questions below; see also Chapter 3, Section 3.3.1.), we may assume that the A-not-A constituent moves to

---

[16]   Ambiguities exist as to the derivational source of certain forms. For example, when a VP consists solely of an intransitive verb (*lai, gaoxing,* etc.), the question (*lai bu lai, gaoxing bu gaoxing*) may be derived from a base-generated coordinate VP or via morphological reduplication (though the form *gaobu gaoxing* can only be derived by reduplication). We see no empirical consequence in this ambiguity. Another potential case of derivational ambiguity exists in the derivation of V-not-VP sentences where the initial V is a full verb (e.g., *xihuan bu xihuan zhe-ben shu*). Instead of reduplication, one might propose that it could originate as a base-generated coordinate VP but be reduced by CR. We again see no major empirical consequence here. As a third potential case, one might wonder whether VP-not-V questions could be derived by reduplicating an entire VP (thus base-generating all A-not-A questions with a simplex VP source) followed by AE. We rule out this possibility, however, for the reason that we take reduplication to be a morphological process, which cannot reduplicate phrasal categories nor be followed by syntactic deletion processes. Hence, we assume that the reduplicative process only generates V-not-VP questions where V is a full verb or less than a full verb.

an appropriate position in CP at LF, thus causing that CP to be interpreted as a question. Question (72a) has (72b) as its LF representation:

(72)   a. [$_{CP}$ [$_{IP}$ ni   gaoxing bu gaoxing] (ne)]?
                          you happy   not happy   Q

       b. [$_{CP}$ [$_{VP}$ gaoxing-bu-gaoxing]$_i$ [$_{IP}$ ni   t$_{VP}$] (ne)]
                          happy-not-happy   you   Q

The A-not-A constituent *gaoxing-bu-gaoxing* is then taken as a (non-objectual) quantifier ranging over two predicate meanings, {happy, not happy}:

       c. For which x, x ∈ {gaoxing, bu-gaoxing}, (ni x)

And the V-not-VP question *ni gao-bu-gaoxing* 'you hap-not-happy,' with the underlying structure (73a), will be represented as in (73b) and interpreted as in (73c):

(73)   a. [$_{CP}$ [$_{IP}$ ni Q$_{[+A\text{-}not\text{-}A]}$ gaoxing]]
       b. [$_{CP}$ Q$_{[+A\text{-}not\text{-}A]}$ [$_{IP}$ ni t$_{[+A\text{-}not\text{-}A]}$ gaoxing]]
       c. For which x, x ∈ {affirmative, negative}, (ni x gaoxing)

We noted earlier that an A-not-A constituent may occur in a complement clause, but in that position it can be interpreted as having either embedded scope (for an indirect A-not-A question (74)) or matrix scope (for a direct A-not-A question (75)):

(74)   wo bu   zhidao [ta xi-bu-xihuan ni] (*ne).
           I   not know   he li-not-like   you   Q
           'I don't know whether he likes you or not.'

(75)   ni   juede [ta xi-bu-xihuan ni] (ne)?
           you feel   he li-not-like   you Q
           'Do you think he likes you, or (do you think he does) not?'

The LF-movement hypothesis derives these two readings by raising the A-not-A constituent to the embedded or the matrix CP as determined by the matrix verb. The movement hypothesis also explains why the A-not-A constituent cannot occur in an island and be interpreted as having matrix scope:

(76)   a. [ta gao-bu-gaoxing] bu   zhongyao.
               he hap-not-happy   not important
               'Whether he is happy or not is not important.'

       b. *[ta gao-bu-gaoxing] bijiao hao?
               he hap-not-happy   more good
               Intended reading: 'Is it better that he is happy, or that he is not?'

(77)   a. women zai taolun [ta gao-bu-gaoxing de wenti].
               we   at discuss he hap-not-happy   DE question
               'We are discussing the question of whether he is happy or not.'

b. *nimen zai taolun [gao-bu-gaoxing de nei-ge ren]?
   you   at discuss hap-not-happy DE that-CL person
   Intended reading: 'Are you discussing the person who is happy or the
   one who isn't?'

(78)   ni   xiang-zhidao [shei gao-bu-gaoxing]?
        you wonder   who hap-not-happy

   a. OK: 'Who is the person x such that you are wonder whether x is happy or
      not?'
   b. Not: 'Are you wondering who is happy or are you wondering who is unhappy?'

Assuming that movement leaves a trace, the ungrammatical cases can be attributed
to the Empty Category Principle (ECP) of Chomsky (1981). As will be shown
in more detail in Section 7.4.1. below, the ECP prohibits the movement of a
non-argument (such as an A-not-A element or an adjunct) out of an island. The
following configuration is ill-formed:

(79)   *[A-not-A]$_i$ ...   [$_{island}$ ... t$_i$ ...] ...
         |_____x_____|

In our analysis, then, a true A-not-A question is treated as a constituent question
on a par with other constituent questions like *why*-questions: they are both subject
to LF movement whose outputs are constrained by the ECP. On the other hand, the
haishi-questions have full bi-clausal underlying sources which may be reduced by
a deletion process (CR or AE). Their interpretation does not involve movement,
and is therefore not subject to the ECP.[17]

Turning now to the differences between VP-not-V and V-not-VP questions,
recall that the latter, but not the former, seem to violate Lexical Integrity and
allow P-Stranding. Here it is useful to note that *haishi*-questions behave like VP-
not-V questions in both respects: they respect the PLI and disallow P-Stranding.
There is also a third difference between VP-not-V and V-not-VP: that they dis-
tribute differently among the various dialect groups. We can now see that these
differences directly follow from the hypothesis that while VP-not-V questions are
derived via Ellipsis, V-not-VP questions are formed by a morphological process
of reduplication.

First, the mere fact that they have different derivation sources makes their difference in dialect distribution a natural consequence rather than a mystery. According
to Zhu (1991), V-not-VP questions are primarily an innovation of the southern
dialects. It has also been pointed out that some dialects also employ questions

---

[17] We speculate that the omission of *haishi* is compensated by the creation of a null *or* with
a formal feature that makes movement necessary, and one that ensures the correct order
A > Not A, as observed by McCawley (1994).

formed with a preverbal particle, *ke* in Mandarin, *kam* in Taiwanese, *a* in Shang-hainese, etc.

(80) ni   ke ting-guo   zhe-zhong shi?   (Mandarin)
      You KE heard-GUO   this-CL   thing
      'Have you heard of this kind of thing before?'

(81) li   kam bat   jit-e   hakseng?   (Taiwanese)
      You KAM know this-CL student
      'Do you know this student?'

Now, in some such dialects, a preverbal particle may co-occur with a VP-not-V type of question (i.e., *ke VP not V?*), but is never found in any of the V-not-VP type (i.e., **ke V-not-VP?*). In other words, the particle *ke/kam* is mutually exclusive with the V-not-V constituent of a V-not-VP question:

(82) li   kam bat   jit-e   hakseng (a) m-bat?   (Taiwanese)
      you KAM know this-CL student (or) not-know
      'Do you know this student or not?'

(83) *li kam bat-m-bat   jit-e   hakseng?
      you KAM know-not-know   this-CL student

This fact may be naturally captured by our analysis of V-not-VP questions as being derived from the morphological realization of a preverbal Q-morpheme. According to our analysis, the Q-morpheme may be realized either with a Q-particle, or by morphological reduplication, but not both. But a preverbal Q-particle is in principle not incompatible with a VP-not-V question.

What about the difference with respect to Lexical Integrity? This comes from the fact that while AE (and CR for *haishi*-questions) is a syntactic, post-lexical phenomenon, the proposed reduplication is a morphological phenomenon. The PLI is a principle that governs syntactic and perhaps also post-syntactic operations. But a morphological process is not subject to the PLI. In fact, it is in the nature of a morphological process that it affects parts of a word.

Finally, the difference with respect to P-Stranding also follows straightforwardly. Both CR and AE are deletion processes that produce empty categories. The result of deleting an object of a preposition would be a case of P-Stranding. However, since V-not-VP questions are formed by reduplication, giving structures like *gen-bu-gen* and *cong-bu-cong*, no empty category is created, and no P-Stranding ever occurs.

7.3.4   *VP-neg questions*

In addition to VP-not-VP, VP-not-V, and V-not-VP questions, another alternative question form has been identified in the recent literature (see

Zhang 1990, Zhu 1991, and Cheng, Huang, and Tang 1996) as illustrated below:

(84)   a. ta mai shu   bu?
          he buy book not
          'Does he buy books or not?'

       b. ni   chi-le fan mei?
          you eat-LE rice not
          'Have you eaten or not?'

These questions have been termed "VP-neg" questions following Zhang (1990) and Zhu (1991). Both questions (84a) and (84b) end with a negative morpheme.[18] It is tempting to think of these forms as further elided forms of VP-not-V questions. While this may well have been the case in historical terms, it is important to note that the VP-neg questions differ from normal VP-not-V questions in important ways. For one thing, VP-neg questions can only be formed as direct, matrix questions. Unlike normal VP-not-V questions, they cannot occur in embedded clauses:

(85)   a. *wo bu xiaode [ta mai shu   bu].
          I   not know   he buy book not
          Intended reading: 'I don't know if he buy books or not.'

       b. *[ta mai shu   bu] bu zhongyao.
           he buy book not not important
          Intended reading: 'Whether he buys books or not is not important.'

       c. *women lai   taolun [ta mai shu   bu] de wenti.
          we   come discuss he buy book not DE problem
          Intended reading: 'Let us discuss the question of whether he buys books or not.'

Another notable characteristic is that although normal VP-not-V questions may optionally be followed by the Q-particle *ne*, VP-neg questions cannot:

(86)   a. *ta mai shu   bu ne?
          he buy book not Q

       b. *ni   chi-le fan mei ne?
          you eat-LE rice not Q

---

[18] A question ending with *meiyou* as in (i) has sometimes also been considered to be a VP-neg question:

(i)   ni   chi-le fan mei-you?
       you eat-LE rice not-have
       'Have you eaten or not?'

However, there is some controversy as to whether this is really a VP-neg question. Some speakers have different judgments with respect to the three properties noted in the text. We shall not deal with this here. For some discussion, see Hsieh (2001) and Hagstrom (2006).

These two facts can be jointly accounted for if we say that the VP-neg is not an A-not-A alternative question, but a particle question: the negative morphemes *bu* and *mei* are in fact Q-particles themselves occupying the C of a CP, rather than the negation found with the negative conjunct of an A-not-A question. This move immediately explains why VP-neg questions cannot take the Q-particle *ne* (because the C is already occupied by Neg). Given that Chinese Q-particles are not permitted in embedded clauses, the ungrammaticality of (85) also follows straightforwardly. A further fact in support of this analysis is that the examples in (84) are naturally uttered with the intonation pattern of a particle question.

This analysis of the Neg in VP-neg questions as a Q-particle amounts to treating VP-neg questions as equivalent to *yes-no* questions with the particle *ma*. While this is syntactically the case on the surface, it is still important to keep the following in mind. First, a VP-neg question is not a *yes-no* question, as it still retains the syntax, semantics, and pragmatics of an A-not-A choice question. For example, a VP-neg question is strictly neutral with respect to the answers expected of the addressee, and cannot accept short answers like *shide* 'yes.' In addition, a VP-neg question may occur with *daodi* 'to the bottom, truly' but not *nandao* 'is it really the case that':

(87) a. ni   daodi/*nandao chi-le fan   mei?
          you   truly/actually   eat-LE rice not
          'Let me get to the truth, have you eaten or not?'

      b. ni   *daodi/nandao yijing   chi-guo-le   ma?
          you   truly/actually   already eat-GUO-LE Q
          'Is it actually the case that you have eaten?'

A third fact concerning VP-neg questions is that the morphological form of the negation morpheme (*bu* or *mei*) is clearly determined by, or agrees with, the main verb in terms of its aspectuality class. This is different from normal Q-particles (*ma* and *ne*), which have invariable forms. This leads us back to the possibility that Neg occurs within the main predicate, but not in C.

To solve this paradox we tentatively follow the hypothesis made by Cheng, Huang, and Tang (1996), that the Neg of a VP-neg question originates in the IP underlyingly but ends up in C on the surface. One way to execute this idea is to posit that a preverbal Neg, triggered by an [+A-not-A] feature, moves to C. This might be seen as an alternative to the reduplication process.[19]

---

[19] Certain questions arise which we shall not deal with here. It has been pointed out that the VP-neg questions existed historically long before VP-not-V and V-not-VP questions were attested in most available written texts. This might be taken as an argument against deriving VP-neg from the newer forms. However, Zhu (1991) also indicated that in some newly excavated documents dated to Qin or pre-Qin periods, VP-not-VP and VP-not-V forms were already attested, though for unknown reasons these forms failed to be recorded in later texts until a whole thousand years later.

7.3.5   Summary

We conclude that there are several ways to form an alternative question with the semantics of an A-not-A question: (a) as a special case of a disjunctive question with *haishi*, (b) by base-generating a VP-not-VP constituent, (c) by reduplication, and (d) by moving Neg to C. These represent all the three general types of questions Chinese has: type (a) is treated as an alternative question and type (d) is a particle question, while types (b) and (c) are treated as constituent questions whose A-not-A constituents are subject to scope interpretation in LF. Both *haishi-* and VP-not-VP questions may obtain various reduced forms through independent reduction processes (CR and/or AE), which obey general constraints concerning directionality, anaphora, lexical integrity, and P-Stranding. The reduplicative A-not-A questions do not result from a reduction process, but have a simplex sentence source. The VP-neg question is formed by Neg-to-C raising, as an alternative to reduplication.

The syntax of A-not-A questions in Chinese continues to be an area of great interest with interesting consequences both for Chinese syntax and for general syntactic theory. The views expressed above have been taken up or scrutinized by many other scholars, including Cole and Lee (1997), Ernst (1994), Hsieh (2001), Wu (1997), and Zhang (1997). For the latest discussions on the subject, see Hagstrom (2006), Gasde (2004), Law (2006), and the references cited there.

7.4   *wh*-questions

A question may be formed through the use of an interrogative *wh*-phrase such as *shei* 'who,' *shenme* 'what,' *shenme shihou* 'when, what time,' *nar* 'where,' *zenme* 'how,' *weishenme* 'why,' *na-ge ren* 'which person,' *na-ge difang* 'which place,' and so forth. One of the most important (and familiar) typological features of Chinese *wh*-questions is that, whereas many other languages (e.g., English) form their *wh*-questions by moving a *wh*-word or phrase to a clause-initial position, Chinese *wh*-questions are formed by leaving such interrogative constituents in situ (in their underlying, clause-internal positions). We describe this situation by saying that English is a *wh*-movement language and Chinese a *wh*-in-situ language:

(88)   a. Who did John see?
         b. What does he like?

(89)   a. Zhangsan kanjian-le shei?
            Zhangsan see-LE   who
            'Who did Zhangsan see?'

         b. ta xihuan shenme?
            he like   what
            'What does he like?'

7.4.1   *A movement approach to* wh-*in-situ*

The phenomenon of *wh*-movement has been a central topic of research since the earliest days of generative grammatical studies, and research on *wh*-questions (in those languages employing *wh*-movement) has formed the basis of important theoretical constructs and principles that characterize generative syntactic theory as we know it. However, because Chinese *wh*-questions do not involve a visible movement process, the syntax of Chinese *wh*-questions seemed to fall outside of general interest and played little role in the development of the early generative theory of syntax.

Huang (1982a, b) argued that this need not be the case, and that Chinese *wh*-questions offered rich insights for the theory of movement, sometimes in ways that are otherwise less observable in *wh*-movement languages. Huang proposed that while Chinese does not move its *wh*-phrases in overt Syntax, it employs a covert movement process in the interpretive component Logical Form (LF), by which a *wh*-in-situ phrase is moved to an appropriate clause-peripheral position (e.g., Spec of CP) in a way similar to overt *wh*-movement in English. Thus the LF representation of (89a) would be as in (90):

(90)   [shei$_i$ [Zhangsan kanjian-le t$_i$]]?
         Who   Zhangsan see-LE

Huang provided a number of arguments for this LF-movement hypothesis by highlighting certain hidden similarities between Chinese-type and English-type *wh*-questions. One argument turns on the requirement of selection in syntax. Consider the following:

(91)   a.   What does John think Mary bought t?
         b.   *John thinks what Mary bought t.

(92)   a.   *What does John wonder Mary bought t?
         b.   John wonders what Mary bought t?

(93)   a.   What does John remember Mary bought t?
         b.   John remembers what Mary bought t.

The preposed *wh*-phrases in these sentences all originate as the object of the verb in the embedded clause:

(94)   John thinks Mary bought what

(95)   John wonders Mary bought what

(96)   John remembers Mary bought what

However, the verb *think* in (94) cannot have a question as its complement and the verb *wonder* in (95) must select a question as its complement. The verb *remember* in (96) can select either a question or a statement as its complement. These selection properties are reflected in where the *wh*-phrases can and cannot occur, as illustrated in (91)–(93).

The process of *wh*-movement not only captures selection properties, it also provides for a quantificational schema suitable for interpretation. A question such as (93a) or (93b) has the interpretation as indicated below, which is straightforwardly represented by the position of the preposed *wh*-phrase.

(97)   a. [[for which x: x a thing] [John remembers Mary bought x]]
       b. [John remembers [[for which x: x a thing] Mary bought x]]

Since Chinese *wh*-questions keep their *wh*–phrases in situ, their surface forms correspond to (94)–(96) but not (91)–(93).

(98)   Zhangsan yiwei Lisi mai-le shenme?
         Zhangsan thinks Lisi buy-LE what
         'What does Zhangsan think Lisi bought?'

(99)   Zhangsan xiang-zhidao Lisi mai-le shenme.
         Zhangsan wonder   Lisi buy-LE what
         'Zhangsan wonders what Lisi bought.'

(100)   Zhangsan jide   Lisi mai-le shenme(?)
         Zhangsan remember Lisi buy-LE what
         'Zhangsan remembers what Lisi   bought.'
         'What does Zhangsan remember Lisi bought?'

Despite their similar appearance, (98)–(100) are interpreted very differently. Example (98) must be interpreted as a direct question to which an answer is needed and (99) must be interpreted as a statement containing an embedded question, while (100) may be interpreted in either way. These restrictions are clearly the same ones just observed with the English sentences (91)–(93). The only difference is that whereas the restrictions are observed as a matter of form (i.e., grammaticality) in English, they present themselves as a matter of interpretation (e.g., presence vs. absence of ambiguity) in Chinese. A unified account is available if it is assumed that *wh*-phrases in Chinese-type languages, even though they do not move in overt Syntax, nevertheless undergo covert movement in LF. Assuming that *wh*-phrases undergo movement in LF as they do in overt Syntax, the structures below may be derived from (98)–(100).

(101) a. [shenme$_i$ [Zhangsan yiwei [[Lisi mai-le t$_i$]]]]?
           'For which x: x a thing, Zhangsan thinks Lisi bought x?'
       b. *[[Zhangsan yiwei [shenme$_i$ [Lisi mai-le t$_i$]]]].
           'Zhangsan thinks [for which x: x a thing, Lisi bought x].'

(102) a. *[shenme$_i$ [Zhangsan xiang-zhidao [[Lisi mai-le t$_i$]]]]?
           'For which x: x a thing, Zhangsan wonders Lisi bought?'
       b. [[Zhangsan xiang-zhidao [shenme$_i$ [Lisi mai-le t$_i$]]]].
           'Zhangsan wonders [for which x: x a thing, Lisi bought x].'

(103) a. [shenme_i [Zhangsan jide [[Lisi mai-le t_i]]]]?
           'For which x: x a thing, Zhangsan remembers Lisi bought t?'

       b. [[Zhangsan jide [shenme_i [Lisi mai-le t_i]]]].
           Zhangsan remembers [for which x: x a thing, Lisi bought x].

The non-ambiguity of (98) and (99) follows because they each correspond to only one LF representation that satisfies the selectional requirements of their matrix verbs. In particular, just as (91b) and (92a) are ungrammatical representations in overt Syntax, (101b) and (102a) are ruled out as ill-formed LF representations that fail to satisfy the selectional requirements of their main verbs. The similarities with respect to selection and interpretation of *wh*-questions between English and Chinese follow from the application of the same *wh*-movement process, although one is overt and the other is covert.

A second, perhaps more important, argument turns on the fact that the distribution and interpretation of *wh*-questions in Chinese exhibit certain restrictions that are typically associated with movement processes. Particularly relevant is the syntax of questions involving adjunct *wh*-phrases. Huang (1982a, b) showed that, in English, when an adjunct *wh*-phrase is extracted out of a syntactic island to form a direct question, such as a relative clause (104), an adjunct clause (105), or a sentential subject (106), severe ungrammaticality results.

(104)   *How_i do you like [the man who fixed the car t_i]?

(105)   *How_i did you feel satisfied [after he fixed the car t_i]?

(106)   *How_i would [for him to fix the car t_i] be nice?

In Chinese, a sentence with an adjunct *wh*-phrase like *weishenme* 'why' inside a syntactic island cannot be used to form a direct question about the adjunct:

(107)   *ni   zui   xihuan [weishenme mai shu   de ren]?
          you most like   why   buy book DE person
          'Why do you like [the person who bought the books t]?'

(108)   *ta [zai Lisi weishenme mai shu   yihou] shengqi le?
          he at Lisi why   buy book after angry LE
          'Why did he get angry [after Lisi bought the books t]?'

(109)   *[wo weishenme mai shu] zui   hao?
          I   why   buy book most good
          'Why is [that I buy the books t] best?'

A similar point can be made with an observed argument/adjunct asymmetry under extraction from within an indirect question (a *wh*-island). As illustrated in (110) and (111), it is substantially more difficult to move an adjunct out of a *wh*-island than it is to move an argument.

(110)   ??What_i did you wonder [how to fix t_i]?

(111)   *How_i did you wonder [what to fix t_i]?

In Chinese, although *wh*-phrases apparently do not move, we see a similar argument/adjunct asymmetry as illustrated below:[20]

(112)   ni   xiang-zhidao [wo weishenme mai shenme]?
      you wonder   I   why   buy   what

    a. 'What is the x such that you wonder why I bought x?'
    b. Not: 'What is the reason x such that you wonder what I bought for x?'

In particular, with the two *wh*-phrases *shenme* 'what' and *weishenme* 'why' embedded in situ, (112) can be interpreted as a direct question about 'what,' but not as a direct question about 'why.' This asymmetry mirrors that shown by (110) and (111), except that in one case it is an asymmetry in movement and in the other case it is an asymmetry in interpretation.

These parallel properties provide a strong argument for an LF-movement account of *wh*-in-situ. Huang (1982b) shows, in particular, that all the ungrammatical sentences in (104)–(109) and the asymmetries illustrated in (110)–(112) can receive a unifying account from the Empty Category Principle of Chomsky (1981), if all *wh*-phrases are assumed to move – if not overtly in Syntax, then covertly in LF. The ECP specifically applies to traces of movement only (and not to overt categories or null pronominals):

(113)   The Empty Category Principle (ECP)
    A non-pronominal empty category (i.e., trace) is properly governed.

"Proper government" is defined in terms of the notion "government": α governs β iff α c-commands β and no maximal phrase intervenes that contains β but not α. An empty category is properly governed if it is (a) governed by a lexical head, or (b) governed by its antecedent (the moved category).[21] A complement

---

[20] The behavior of *zenme* 'how' parallels *weishenme* 'why' in this respect:

    (i)   ni   xiang-zhidao [shei zenme xiuhao nei-bu che de]?
        you wonder   who how   fix   that-CL car   DE

      a. 'Who is the person x such that you wonder how x fixed the car?'
      b. Not: 'What is the method/manner x such that you wonder who fixed the car by x?'

However, when *zenme* is put in a relative clause or a sentential subject, the result is often milder, ranging from marginal to acceptable. See Rizzi (1990) for other differences between *why* and *how* in English, and Lin (1992) and Tsai (1994b) for discussion of different senses of *weishenme* and *zenme*.

[21] For our present purposes, we shall assume the classical, "disjunctive" version of the ECP. More recent formulations of the principle have reduced it to the basic notion of minimality, as properly defined. See Rizzi (1990), Chomsky (1995), etc., among others. For the most part these are theoretical improvements over the classical ECP, though they do not affect the point being made in the text.

is head-governed, but an adjunct is not. Therefore, in order to satisfy the ECP, an adjunct trace must be antecedent governed. For antecedent government to be possible, the moved category cannot go too far: it cannot cross the boundary of a syntactic island. The ungrammaticality of (104)–(106) and (111) thus falls under the ECP. Likewise, (107)–(109) and the reading (112b) are ruled out under the LF-movement hypothesis, because their respective LF representations would be in violation of the ECP.

The ECP and the LF-movement hypothesis together account for other asymmetries as well. As we indicated in the preceding section, A-not-A questions differ from normal disjunctive questions in that a sentence with an A-not-A constituent located in a syntactic island cannot be interpreted as a direct A-not-A question. This fact readily falls under the ECP if the A-not-A constituents are assumed to undergo LF movement. Another area of interest is the syntax of multiple questions in English. English multiple questions, for example, exhibit systematic "superiority effects," as illustrated below. Chomsky (1973) proposed the Superiority Condition (SC) to account for the subject–object asymmetry illustrated in (114), and Jaeggli (1981) argued that the SC readily reduces to the ECP if each of the unmoved *wh*-phrases does move in LF:

(114) a.   Who bought what?
       b.   *What did who buy?

Huang (1982b) further observed adjunct–complement contrasts like the following and argued that they, too, follow from the ECP applied at LF:

(115) a.   Why did you buy what?
       b.   *What did you buy why?

(116) a.   Tell me how you fixed which car.
       b.   *Tell me which car you fixed how.

In short, English and Chinese adjunct *wh*-questions are subject to the same island restrictions. The main difference is that whereas the restrictions are observed as a matter of form (i.e., grammaticality) in English, they present themselves as a matter of interpretation in Chinese. A unified account is available if covert LF movement is assumed for *wh*-in-situ. This hypothesis is further supported by similar behavior observed in multiple questions in an English-type language.[22]

---

[22] Other arguments have been adduced in the literature, including generalizations concerning Weak Crossover and the Specificity Condition. We shall omit these from discussion here and below.

7.4.2   *LF movement: some problems and alternatives*

The arguments we have reviewed in favor of LF movement hinge on the similarities observed between English and Chinese *wh*-questions, especially adjunct *wh*-questions. However, there are also significant differences between them, especially with respect to questions with *argument wh*-phrases. For instance, it is consistently unacceptable for a *wh*-phrase to be moved out of an island, whether it is an adjunct as in (104)–(106), or an argument as shown below:

(117)   *What$_i$ do you like [the man who fixed t$_i$]?

(118)   *What$_i$ did you feel satisfied [after he fixed t$_i$]?

(119)   *What$_i$ would [for him to fix t$_i$] be nice?

However, an argument *wh*-phrase inside an island in Chinese can easily be interpreted as being outside the island, even though an adjunct *wh*-phrase cannot be so interpreted (see (107)–(109)):

(120)   ni   zui   xihuan [mai shenme de ren]?
         you most like   buy what   DE person
         'What do you like [the person who bought t]?'

(121)   ta [zai Lisi mai shenme yihou] shengqi le?
         he at Lisi buy what   after   angry   LE
         'What did he get angry [after Lisi bought t?]'

(122)   [wo mai shenme] zui   hao?
         I   buy what   most good
         'What is [that I buy t] best?'

A similar point can be made with multiple questions in English. Thus, whereas adjunct *wh*-phrases are not permitted in situ (see (115)–(116)), an unmoved *wh*-argument within an island is quite easily interpreted out of the island. Compare the following contrasts:

(123) a. *Who did you buy the books that criticize t?
       b.   Who bought the books that criticized who?

(124) a. *Who did you get jealous because I praised t?
       b.   Who got jealous because I praised who?

(125) a. *Who did you say that pictures of t are nice?
       b.   Who said that pictures of who are nice?

(126) a. ?*What did you remember where I bought t?
       b.   Who remembers where I bought what?

In each (a) sentence above, overt movement of an argument across an island produces unacceptable results, but in each (b) counterpart, an argument left in situ within an island can be construed with the matrix *who* to form a direct question. Thus, although the behavior of adjunct *wh*-phrases in situ provides evidence for LF movement, the behavior of argument *wh*-phrases in situ seems to argue against it.

This paradoxical situation is resolved in Huang (1982b) by the assumption that movement constraints fall into two types with respect to their scope of application: the ECP constrains the output of movement at both S-Structure and LF, while the bounding conditions of Subjacency and the CED constrain only movement in overt Syntax. Thus, the English sentences in (117)–(119) are ruled out because they violate Subjacency or the CED in overt Syntax; their Chinese counterparts in (120)–(122) are acceptable because these bounding conditions do not apply in LF. When an adjunct is involved, however, extraction out of an island is ruled out by the ECP, regardless of whether extraction is overt (as in (104)–(106) in English) or covert (as in (107)–(109) in Chinese or the multiple questions (115b) and (116b) in English).[23]

Although Huang's proposal obtains the facts as desired, it begs the question of why Subjacency and the CED should differ from the ECP with respect to their scope of application, and why they do so in the way stipulated but not, say, the other way around. In the spirit of the LF-movement hypothesis, which claims that movement occurs throughout overt Syntax and LF, the question arises as to why overt and covert movement should even differ with respect to these constraints at all. Furthermore, the crucial reference to a point in derivation where a given principle becomes irrelevant is at odds with current minimalist assumptions that have eliminated S-Structure as a distinct level of representation. Empirically, there is also evidence suggesting that certain hypothesized LF-movement processes do in fact obey Subjacency. For example, it has been shown by several authors (Ito 1986, Barss, Hale, Perkins, and Speas 1991, and Cole and Hermon 1994) that the syntax of internally-headed relative clauses (as observed in such languages as Japanese, Navajo, and Imbabura Quechua) exhibits Subjacency and CED effects in the same way normal processes of (external) relativization do. Under the assumption that the internally headed relative clauses involve an LF head-raising operation, one must ensure that this process does not violate Subjacency or the CED.

Two general strategies have been followed in the literature in the analysis of *wh*-in-situ that do not suffer from the theoretical and empirical problems just noted. The first approach, taken by Nishigauchi (1986) and Fiengo, Huang, Lasnik, and Reinhart (1988) among others, maintains that LF movement obeys Subjacency and CED, but that due to possibilities of LF pied-piping, certain island effects are

---

[23] *When* and *where* behave like arguments when they are left in situ, both in Chinese and in English multiple questions. See Huang (1982a, b) for an analysis that brings out this difference between *when* and *where* on the one hand and *why* and *how* on the other.

invisible. The second approach, developed most fully by Aoun and Li (1993a, 1993b) and Tsai (1994a), maintains that *wh*-phrases in situ do not move in LF (hence they do not exhibit island effects), but are bound by an abstract operator – an "unselective binding" approach in the sense of Heim (1982). Other writers, most notably Pesetsky (1987) and Tsai (1994a), have adopted a mixed approach, maintaining that while some *wh*-phrases move (and possibly pied-pipe), others are "unselectively bound" in situ. In the rest of this chapter we shall review these strategies.

7.4.3   LF Subjacency and pied-piping

Nishigauchi (1986) hypothesized that Subjacency does apply to LF just as it does to overt Syntax. Under this hypothesis the theoretical problems that arise under Huang's (1982b) S-Structure Subjacency hypothesis immediately disappear. The main challenge of this hypothesis is to explain why argument *wh*-phrases in situ do not display familiar Subjacency/CED effects as observed with overt movement, though adjunct *wh*-phrases do. Nishigauchi proposes that the answer comes from the possibility of pied-piping an entire island when LF movement applies to a *wh*-argument contained in the island. Consider the well-formed (120) for example, with *shenme* 'what' contained in a complex NP. Under the pied-piping hypothesis, LF movement of *shenme* may pied-pipe the entire complex NP *mai shenme de ren* 'the person that bought what' and place it in [Spec, CP], giving the following LF representation:

(127)   [$_{CP}$ [mai shenme de ren]$_i$ [$_{IP}$ ni zui   xihuan t$_i$]]?
                buy what   DE person you   most like
         Lit: 'The person that bought what do you like most?'

Such a question may be interpreted as asking about the identity of the person who you like, in terms of the thing that the person bought. Since the *wh*-phrase *shenme* 'what' stays put within the relative clause containing it, the pied-piping movement does not violate Subjacency or the CED. Similarly, in deriving the LF representations for (121) and (122), LF movement may pied-pipe an entire sentential subject or an adjunct clause, in each case obeying Subjacency and the CED in full.

Given the pied-piping approach, then, (120)–(122) are grammatical not because they disobey Subjacency but because the relevant *wh*-phrase does not move out of an island. In other words, these sentences are only apparent counterexamples to the LF-Subjacency hypothesis. As long as pied-piping remains a possibility, Subjacency effects are entirely invisible for these sentences.

Fiengo *et al.* (1988) examined Nishigauchi (1986) and, while finding the pied-piping hypothesis attractive, they saw two major problems with it, one theoretical and one empirical. The theoretical issue has to do with the question of why large-chunk pied-piping of the type being entertained is possible in LF, but not in overt Syntax. As the following examples show, overt pied-piping is very limited:

(128) a. Whose mother did you see?
      b. Who did you see pictures of?
      c. ?Of whom did you see pictures?
      d. *Pictures of whom did you see?
      e. *Pictures that who gave you are most funny?
      f. *That who should pay for this would be most reasonable?
      g. *Because John talked to who did you get jealous?

Instead of saying that Subjacency applies only to S-Structure but not to LF, the pied-piping hypothesis amounts to the claim that restrictions against large-chunk pied-piping obtain in overt but not covert Syntax. In the absence of an explanation as to why this should be true, the problem posed by S-Structure Subjacency is not solved, but simply reassigned.

Empirically, there is also a problem in that the pied-piping hypothesis does not get the semantics right for certain sentences. The hypothesis claims that movement does not violate an island constraint because the *wh*-phrase contained in a given island never moves out of the island. This claim cannot be maintained in view of sentences of the following kind:

(129)   mei-ge ren   dou mai-le [san-ben [shei xie   de] shu]?
       every person all buy-LE three-CL who write DE book
       'Who is the author x such that everyone bought three books that x wrote?'

In the above sentence, the *wh*-phrase *shei* 'who' is contained in the complex NP *san-ben shei xie de shu* 'three books that who wrote,' which is itself an existentially quantified NP. As indicated in the translation, the sentence has a reading according to which the *wh*-phrase has the widest scope and the existential NP headed by *shu* 'book' has the narrowest scope, while the subject *mei-ge ren* 'everyone' has an intermediate scope. This indicates that the question can be answered by supplying the identity of a single author, with the resulting sentence understood in the distributive sense, i.e., each person bought three different books.

(130)   mei-ge ren   dou mai-le [san-ben [Lisi xie   de] shu].
       every person all buy-LE three-CL Lisi write DE book
       'Everyone bought three books written by Lisi.'

The availability of this reading means that *shei* 'who' in (129) must be allowed to move out of the complex NP and beyond the subject *mei-ge ren* 'everyone' to give the following LF representation, assuming that quantifiers undergo Quantifier Raising (QR; May 1977) by adjoining to IP:

(131)   [$_{CP}$ shei$_i$ [$_{IP}$ mei-ge ren$_j$ [$_{IP}$ [san-ben t$_i$ xie   de shu]$_k$ [$_{IP}$ t$_j$ dou mai-le t$_k$]]]]
          who   every person three-CL write DE book   all buy-LE

But this move violates Subjacency and destroys the original purpose of the pied-piping hypothesis.[24]

Fiengo *et al.* (1988) proposed a different version of the pied-piping hypothesis that is free from both the theoretical and empirical problems that Nishigauchi's faced. Their proposal rests on the assumption that a *wh*-phrase undergoes both QR (adjunction to IP) and *wh*-movement (to Spec of CP), and that it is QR, not *wh*-movement, that may perform large-chunk pied-piping. First, it is uncontroversial that a *wh*-phrase is both an interrogative phrase and an existential quantifier. Assuming that each quantificational NP (QNP) undergoes QR (by adjunction to IP) in LF, then it follows that every *wh*-phrase undergoes QR and, under the current approach, also *wh*-movement. Now, when a QNP (interrogative or otherwise) is contained in another NP, as in *pictures of everybody/somebody/who*, the containing NP may also be construed as a QNP, also subject to QR. This is so, because just as *someone* is a quantifier ranging over individuals, *pictures of someone* may be construed as a quantifier ranging over picture sets defined by their owners. That is, assuming a small domain, if *someone* is an existential quantifier ranging over {John, Bill, Mary}, then *pictures of someone* may be an existential quantifier ranging over the set {pictures of John, pictures of Bill, pictures of Mary}. Thus, a sentence like (132) may have (133) as its LF representation:

(132)   Pictures of everybody are on sale.

(133)   [$_{IP}$ Everybody$_i$ [$_{IP}$ [pictures of t$_i$]$_j$ [$_{IP}$ t$_j$ are on sale]]]

That is, QR may first target the containing NP *pictures of everybody* and perform a "pied-piping QR," before applying to the smaller NP *everybody*. And for a *wh*-question like (134), QR may apply first by pied-piping a complex NP, followed by *wh*-movement into CP, as indicated in (135):

(134)   ni   zui   xihuan [shei xie   de shu]?
          you most like   who write DE book
          'For which x, x a person, you like books that x wrote?'

(135)   [$_{CP}$ shei$_i$ [$_{IP}$ [t$_i$ xie   de shu]$_j$ [$_{IP}$ ni zui   xihuan t$_j$]]]?
          who   write DE book you most like

---

[24] Von Stechow (1996) pointed out another way the pied-piping hypothesis fails to represent the correct meaning, suggesting that LF reconstruction following pied-piping may be required.

Fiengo *et al.* (1988) follow Nishigauchi in taking Subjacency and the CED to be applicable in both overt and covert Syntax, though the island effects are sometimes invisible. This they attribute to two independent factors: (a) the possibility of pied-piping under QR (an adjunction operation), and (b) the ability of adjunction to "debarrierize" a barrier. The latter is a corollary of the idea – developed in the Barriers framework of Chomsky (1986b) and adopted in much other work (e.g., Kayne 1994) – that adjunction of a phrase α to a category node A does not create an *additional* node on A, but simply breaks up the node into two segments {A1, A2} and places the adjoined category between them. Thus, suppose α adjoins to A and then moves into a higher position:

(136) $\dots \alpha_i \dots [_{A1} t_i \ [_{A2} \dots, t_i \ \dots \ ]]$

Then neither of these steps crosses the category A in its entirety. Step one crosses segment A2, while step two crosses segment A1. The first step has not quite left the category A, and the second step has not quite originated from "within" A. If we suppose that A is a barrier of movement, such as the crucial "bounding node" (Chomsky 1973) that is part of the definition of Subjacency or the CED, then movement of α in "one fell swoop" directly from the position t_i would cross one full barrier. However, a stepwise movement as depicted in (136) would be allowed, since in neither movement is the relevant barrier node crossed in full. This is why adjunction to a barrier has the effect of debarrierizing that barrier, thereby sidestepping Subjacency. Thus, given the S-Structure in (134), movement of *shei* 'who' out of the relative clause directly into the matrix Spec of CP would be prevented by Subjacency. However, a stepwise derivation as indicated in (135) is allowed. First, the complex NP containing *shei* is pied-piped under QR and adjoins to IP, crossing one segment of the bounding node. In the next step, *shei* is moved into CP, again crossing only a segment of the IP. Subjacency is satisfied in full. The same applies to the other cases of apparent island violations.

We can now see that, although similar in spirit, Fiengo *et al.*'s (1988) account does not suffer from the theoretical and empirical problems associated with Nishigauchi's account. Empirically, Fiengo *et al.*'s account does allow a *wh*-phrase to move out of an island (after the island has undergone QR), so the problem associated with (129) does not arise. The correct semantics can be obtained, with the scope order 'who' > 'everybody' > 'three books that . . . bought,' as in the LF representation (131). The possibility of large-chunk pied-piping in LF is not considered a property of LF *wh*-movement but of QR, so the question does not arise as to why covert *wh*-movement is able to pied-pipe more freely than overt *wh*-movement. The ability of QR to pied-pipe large constituents follows without stipulation from the meaning of a QNP: in the event of any QNP contained in another (non-definite) NP, the containing NP may also be construed as a QNP.[25] Finally, as for why QR pied-piping takes place only in LF, the answer is simply that QR is an operation of LF.

Note that the QR pied-piping hypothesis not only explains those cases of LF movement that do not exhibit island effects, it also fares well with those cases that do, including adjunct *wh*-questions and internally headed relative clauses (IHRCs). We saw that adjuncts like *weishenme* 'why,' *zenme* 'how,' and the A-not-A constituent exhibit island effects that are attributed to the ECP, because their traces under covert movement fail to be antecedent governed. Note that while it takes crossing two bounding nodes to constitute a Subjacency violation, one barrier is enough to prevent antecedent government under the ECP. Thus, consider the following schema, where an adjunct *wh*-phrase has been moved out of an island that has been adjoined to IP under QR:

(137) $[_{CP}$ Wh-adjunct$_i$ $[_{IP}$ $[_{island}$ . . . t_i . . . $]_j$ $[_{IP}$ . . . t_j . . . $]]]$

This movement does not violate Subjacency, because the higher IP does not count as a second bounding node for a violation to occur. However, it does violate the ECP, because one barrier has been crossed (a relative clause, a sentential subject, or an adjunct phrase), making antecedent government impossible.[26]

As for IHRCs, the reason they cannot sidestep Subjacency is quite simple. In IHRCs, the internal head raises to the head NP position in LF. Unlike *wh*-phrases which are QNPs subject to QR, there is no reason to assume the internal head to be a quantifier subject to QR. The option of pied-piping a whole island under head-raising is also ruled out, because that would give the wrong semantics: the

---

[25] This is not possible if the containing NP is definite, as in *that picture of everybody*.

[26] A question arises as to what if the adjunct in (137) is adjoined to the island itself first, thereby debarrierizing the island, before moving into Spec of CP. Such a derivation can be ruled out in one of at least two ways. One is that while QR may adjoin to IP, it does not adjoin a QNP to a CP or PP (such as that of a relative clause, sentential subject, or adjunct clause). Another is to assume, in effect, that while adjunction may void a barrier of movement, it does not void a barrier of government. In other words, while only a full barrier counts as a bounding node for Subjacency, a weaker boundary, such as a segment of a barrier, is enough to block proper government (cf. Fukui 1991). This latter hypothesis is independently motivated by the existence of other weak islands, such as negative clauses and complements of factive or non-bridge verbs, which block antecedent government though not (argument) movement:

(i)   *Why$_i$ didn't he say that [John was late t_i]?
(ii)   *Why$_i$ did he whine that [John left t_i]?
(iii) *How$_i$ did you regret that [John fixed the car t_i]?

relative clause would be understood as modifying the whole island. A relative clause headed by the phrase *pictures of the boy* says something about the pictures, not about the boy. That seems to be true for all languages. IHRCs therefore display a full array of island restrictions.

7.4.4   *Non-movement and unselective binding*

If certain *wh*-phrases in situ do not exhibit island effects, one possible explanation is simply that they indeed remain in situ, in LF as well as in overt Syntax. This is the approach pursued in Aoun and Li (1993a, b) and Tsai (1994a), among others. One of the most important empirical arguments that has been adduced concerns the interaction of some focus words such as *only* and *wh*-phrases in various constructions (those with Antecedent Contained Deletion, scope interaction, etc.). We shall briefly discuss the basic paradigm regarding the distribution of *only* in *wh*-questions (see Aoun and Li 1993a for further details).

As pointed out in the literature, *only* is associated with an element in its c-command domain (see, among others, Anderson 1972, Kuroda 1969, Jackendoff 1972, Rooth 1985, Kratzer 1989, and Tancredi 1990). This is illustrated by the following sentences:

(138) a. He only **likes** Mary. (He doesn't love her.)

      b. ta zhi **xihuan** Mali.
        he only like   Mali
        'He only likes Mali.'

(139) a. He only likes **Mary**. (He doesn't like Sue.)

      b. ta zhi xihuan **Mali**.
        he only like   Mali
        'He only likes Mali.'

For the purpose of our discussion, it is relevant that the postverbal object associated with *only* cannot undergo overt movement: it cannot be topicalized as in (140), nor can it be (*wh-*) moved to form questions or relative structures as in (141).

(140) a. ***Mary**$_i$, he only likes t$_i$.

      b. ***Mali**$_i$, ta zhi xihuan t$_i$.
        Mali he only like
        'He only likes Mali.'

(141) a. ***Who**$_i$ does he only like t$_i$?

      b. *[ta zhi xihuan t$_i$ de] na-ge ren$_i$
         he only like   DE that-CL person
        'the person that he only likes x'

The following generalization, which Tancredi (1990) calls the Principle of Lexical Association (PLA), encodes the restriction at work with *only*:

(142)   Principle of Lexical Association
An operator like *only* must be associated with a lexical constituent in its c-command domain.

Aoun and Li (1993a: 206–210), based on a generalization regarding quantifier phrase (QP) interaction and Antecedent Contained Deletion (ACD), argue that the PLA must apply to covert movement as well. The PLA thus provides a test for the presence or absence of (overt and covert) movement. Interestingly, a *wh*-phrase can be associated with 'only' in Chinese:

(143) a. ta zhi   xihuan **shei**?
            he only like   who
            '**Who** does he only like?'

       b. ta zhi   xihuan zai **nar**   kan   shu?
            he only like   at   where read book
            '**Where** does he only like to read?'

Were *wh*-phrases in such instances to undergo movement, it would be unexpected that *only* could still be associated with them, as illustrated in (140)–(141).

The facts in (138)–(143) suggest that an in situ *wh*-phrase stays in situ even at LF. It does not undergo movement covertly. How, then, are the facts noted in the previous section that were captured by a movement analysis to be accommodated? The solution lies in a better understanding of the morpho-syntactic behavior of *wh*-words.

It has been noted in various works (see, among others, Cheng 1991, Huang 1982b, Kim 1989, 1991, Kuroda 1965, A. Li 1992b, and Nishigauchi 1986) that, in some languages such as Chinese, *wh*-words not undergoing overt movement to form questions are actually not interrogative expressions in the same way that *wh*-words in English are. Unlike English *wh*-words, which are generally analyzed as interrogative expressions, *wh*-words in Chinese do not have inherent interpretations as regards their "quantificational force": depending on the contexts in which they occur, they may be interpreted as universal or existential quantifiers or as interrogative expressions. They are lexically underspecified but syntactically disambiguated for their quantificational force. In the context of the adverbial expression *dou* 'all, uniformly' (as in (144a)), a *wh*-phrase acquires the interpretation of universal quantification. In (144b), the conditional clause (assumed to contain an existential quantifier) gives an existential quantification interpretation to the *wh*-expression. And in (144c), the *wh*-expression is interpreted as an interrogative in the context of the *wh*-question marker *ne*.[27]

(144) a. shei dou xihuan shu.
    who all like   book
    'Everyone likes books.'

   b. ruguo ni   xihuan shei, jiu   qing ta   lai.
    if   you like   who then ask him come
    'If you like someone, then invite him over.'

   c. shei xihuan ni   ne?
    who like   you Q
    'Who likes you?'

In other words, a *wh*-phrase is lexically an "indeterminate" category[28] that exhibits "quantificational variability effects" (QVE) of a kind similar to what has been observed with indefinites under "adverbs of quantification" (Lewis 1975). As the following sentences show, the indefinite NP *a farmer* may be paraphrased as a universal or one of several possible existential NPs:

(145) a. A farmer nowadays is always rich.
    = Every farmer nowadays is rich.

   b. A farmer nowadays is sometimes rich.
    = Some farmers nowadays are rich.

   c. A farmer nowadays is seldom rich.
    = Few farmers nowadays are rich.

   d. A farmer nowadays is never rich.
    = No farmers nowadays are rich.

Such QVEs suggest that the indefinite *a farmer* might not be an inherent existential quantifier, but is perhaps best treated as a variable unselectively bound by an appropriate adverb of quantification which gives rise to its quantificational force, i.e.:[29]

(146) a. (Always_x) (a farmer$_i$ nowadays is rich).
   b. (Sometimes_x) (a farmer$_i$ nowadays is rich).
   c. (Seldom_x) (a farmer$_i$ nowadays is rich).
   d. (Never_x) (a farmer$_i$ nowadays is rich).

---

[27] *Ne* is optional and only occurs in root clauses. In embedded questions we might take the selecting predicates to be the contexts that give the *wh*-phrases their interrogative force. An alternative is to say that the interrogative is the default value, in the absence of contexts that force (or license) non-interrogative universal and existential quantification.

[28] The term "indeterminate" is first used by Kuroda (1965) for a parallel property of Japanese *wh*-phrases.

[29] As in Heim (1982) and other related works. We return to the unselective binding approach to donkey anaphora in Chapter 9.

In the same spirit, Aoun and Li (1993a) suggest that a *wh*-phrase is not an inherent quantificational expression, but a variable licensed and bound by an appropriate operator that gives rise to its quantificational force. In the case of interrogation, Aoun and Li (1993a) suggest that the *wh*-phrase is a variable bound by an interrogative operator generated in a question projection (or a Σ projection along the lines of Laka 1990). Simplifying the presentation, we may use the following schema, with a question operator and a *wh*-phrase coindexed, to represent the relation between a *wh*-element and the question operator (abbreviated as Qu) that licenses and binds the *wh*-element.

(147) $[_{CP}$ Qu$_i$ $[_{IP}$ ... *wh*$_i$ ... $]]$

A similar approach is suggested in Tsai (1994a). One of Tsai's arguments turns on the important observation that English *wh*-forms, too, may exhibit QVE by being associated with different operators, except that this QVE occurs at the level of morphology. There are three series:

(148) a. Universal   b. Existential   c. Interrogative
          whoever   somewhat   who
          whatever   somewhere   what
          wherever   somehow   where
          whenever   anywhere   when
          however   nowhere   how
                                                  why

At the morphological level, we can see that each item here exemplifies a structure of operator binding. In the first series, a *wh*-word is bound by the operator *ever* which gives it the force of universal quantification, and in the second series the operator *some* binding a *wh*-word results in existential quantification. It is then natural to assume that, in the last series, each *wh*-word receives an interrogative reading because it is bound (word-internally) by an abstract interrogative Q operator (Aoun and Li (1993a) made a similar claim regarding *wh*-interrogatives in English).

Thus both English and Chinese exhibit QVE effects with respect to their *wh*-words, these effects being the results of their being bound by different operators. The difference is that while these effects are observed in the lexicon in English, they are observed in the syntax in Chinese. That is, in English, each word is "operator-variable complete" and enters the syntactic component each with a fixed, inherent quantificational force, whereas in Chinese, this binding occurs right in syntax and each *wh*-phrase enters from the lexicon underspecified for its quantificational force. To put it another way, while an English interrogative word takes the *synthetic* form containing both the [+Q] feature and the *wh*-word in it, the Chinese interrogative "word" takes the *analytic* (discontinuous) form of $[OP_i \ldots wh_{io} \ldots]$. Since the English *wh*-word enters the syntactic derivation with [+Q], overt movement is triggered to satisfy (or "check") a relevant feature in C. In Chinese, overt movement does not occur because the operator OP satisfies the C's requirement and the *wh*-word itself does not have the necessary [+Q].[30]

Tsai's explication of this English–Chinese difference is quite insightful as it explains why Chinese and English differ in the way they do with respect to *wh*-movement. In particular, it reduces the parametric difference between these two languages to a difference in the nature of their lexical items, in accordance with the widely-accepted Lexical Parameterization Hypothesis (Borer 1984), as a special case of the general analytic–synthetic difference between the two languages.[31] In addition, consideration of QVE at the syntactic level also leads to the suggestion that Chinese *wh*-questions generally involve unselective binding, but not covert movement.[32]

Assuming no movement, how do we then account for the facts that have been shown to fall under the LF-movement hypothesis? Consider the selection and scope properties noted in (98)–(103), for example. The generalization we saw earlier was that the selectional restrictions of various predicates differ with respect to whether they require, allow, or prohibit an interrogative operator in the Spec of their complement CP, and this distinction was made by the LF movement of a *wh*-phrase into an appropriate Spec of CP position. In unselective binding, this is

[30] Tsai argues that Japanese *wh*-phrases have a status between Chinese and English. Based on Watanabe (1992), Nishigauchi (1991), and others, it is shown that the operator (such as *-ka* and *-mo*, and by assumption *-Q*) responsible for giving a *wh*-phrase its quantificational force may be merged to a full NP/DP or PP. Thus, while the interrogative "word" may span over a whole sentence in Chinese, it may span over an NP/DP or PP in Japanese.

[31] In Huang's original typology, the two languages differ in where *wh*-movement applies, but it is not clear why the Chinese–English difference could not be the reverse. For the Lexical Parameterization Hypothesis, cf. also Manzini and Wexler (1987), Chomsky (1995), and Fukui (1995), among others.

[32] It should be noted that while the morphological difference in their *wh*-words explains why English and Chinese differ with respect to overt movement, this fact itself is independent, as a matter of logic, of the question whether in situ *wh*-phrases undergo LF movement. Cheng (1991, 1995), for example, argues for a distinction between *licensers* and *binders*. In particular, she treats the variability of *wh*-phrases as a matter of polarity licensing. Thus, while a *wh*-word is licensed as a universal quantifier in the presence of *dou*, as an existential quantifier in an affective context, and as an interrogative in the domain of a (possibly covert) question particle, she assumes that such QNPs (the interrogative one included) nevertheless still undergo LF movement. We agree that there is important reason for the distinction between licensing and binding. For example, the environments which license an existential reading of a *wh*-phrase range from negation to conditionals to *yes-no* and A-not-A questions and more, and it is difficult to see each of them as hosting an existential quantifier.

quite simply achieved without resort to movement. The relevant Spec of CP is base-generated with a question operator Qu, coindexed with a *wh*-phrase. The selectional requirements of each matrix predicate are met by the presence (or absence) of this operator. The sentences in (98)–(100) are represented as in (149)–(151).

(149) a. [Qu$_i$ [Zhangsan yiwei [[Lisi mai-le shenme$_i$]]]]?
       'For which x: x a thing, Zhangsan thinks Lisi bought x?'

   b. *[[Zhangsan yiwei [Qu$_i$ [Lisi mai-le shenme$_i$]]]].
       'Zhangsan thinks [for which x: x a thing, Lisi bought x].'

(150) a. *[Qu$_i$ [Zhangsan xiang-zhidao [[Lisi mai-le shenme$_i$]]]]?
       'For which x: x a thing, Zhangsan wonders Lisi bought x?'

   b. [[Zhangsan xiang-zhidao [Qu$_i$ [Lisi mai-le shenme$_i$]]]].
       'Zhangsan wonders [for which x: x a thing, Lisi bought x].'

(151) a. [Qu$_i$ [Zhangsan jide [[Lisi mai-le shenme$_i$]]]]?
       'For which x: x a thing, Zhangsan remembers Lisi bought x?'

   b. [[Zhangsan jide [Qu$_i$ [Lisi mai-le shenme$_i$]]]].
       'Zhangsan remembers [for which x: x a thing, Lisi bought x].'

The scope property of each *wh*-word is directly represented by these structures: it is equivalent to the scope of the Qu operator that binds it.[33]

What about generalizations concerning movement constraints? First, we saw that argument *wh*-phrases in situ do not exhibit island effects. This is of course what we expect under the non-movement approach. But what about adjunct *wh*-phrases? If there is no LF *wh*-movement, it's not immediately clear why adjuncts are restricted by movement constraints like the ECP.

In answer to this question, two options have been proposed in the literature. One claims that while *wh*-arguments do not move in LF, *wh*-adjuncts nevertheless do (Tsai 1994a). This approach assumes that an adjunct *wh*-phrase can be an operator but cannot function like a variable as argument *wh*-phrases do. In other words, adjuncts like *weishenme* 'why,' *zenme* 'how,' and the A-not-A constituent are inherently interrogative (with inherent [+Q] features) like English interrogative *wh*-phrases, and therefore they also move to Spec of CP (albeit covertly), with ensuing island effects. The plausibility of this idea is supported by several considerations, though some questions remain. First, in English, we see that the adjunct *why* does not pattern with other *wh*-words in having a lexical QVE. Compare the following with the words we saw in (148): *whyever, *somewhy, *anywhy. The adjunct *why* has only an interrogative interpretation. In Chinese, too, adjuncts

---

[33] Generalizations regarding Weak Crossover and the Specificity Condition (cf. note 22) can likewise be captured under this account. What is needed is a broader definition of a variable: in addition to an A$'$-bound empty category (under movement) or a pronominal (in the case of a resumptive pronoun), any DP/NP that is directly A$'$-bound is defined as a variable.

like *weishenme, zenme*, and A-not-A do not receive an existential quantificational reading in an affective context, in the way that *wh*-arguments do. The following sentences illustrate the versatility of *shenme* 'what' in various contexts.

(152) a. ta   mei zuo shenme.
      he   not do   what
      'He did not do anything in particular.'

   b. ni   zuo-le shenme ma?
      you   do-LE   what   Q
      'Did you do something?'

   c. ni   xiang-bu-xiang mai shenme?
      you   want-not-want   buy what
      'Would you like to buy something or not?'

   d. wo yiwei   ta zuo-le shenme.
      I   thought he do-LE   what
      'I thought he did something.'

   e. ni   kan! ta yiding faxian-le   shenme le, buran   zenme
      you look he definite discover-LE what   LE, otherwise why
      name gaoxing?
      so   happy
      'Look, he must have discovered something; otherwise why is he so happy?'

   f. ruguo ni   xihuan shenme, wo jiu   ba ta mai-xia-lai.
      if   you like   what   I   then BA it buy-down-come
      'If you like something, I will buy it.'

As pointed out by A. Li (1992b) (cf. also J. Lin 1998), a *wh*-phrase takes on an existential quantifier reading in a variety of contexts, including negation (a), *yes-no* questions (b), A-not-A questions (c), non-factive predicates (d), expressions of probability or inference (e), and conditional clauses (f).[34]

By contrast, *weishenme* 'why,' A-not-A, and (to a lesser degree) *zenme* 'how' do not receive an existential reading under these contexts. The following sentences are either ungrammatical, or grammatical only under an interrogative reading:

(153) a. *ta hui weishenme hen hao   yun   ma?
       he will why   very good fortune Q
       'Will he get lucky for some reason?'

   b. ??ta hui zenme xiu che ma?
       he will how   fix car Q
       'Will he fix cars in some way?'

---

[34] By and large these are the elements that do not assert or imply the truth of the propositions they modify. A superset of the traditional "affective contexts," these contexts have more recently come under the term *nonveridicality* (Giannakidou 1999, etc.). According to Giannakidou, a propositional operator F is nonveridical iff F_P does not entail P.

(154) a. *ruguo ta weishenme hao yun,   ni jiu hui yinwei
    if   he why   good fortune you then will because
    na-ge yuanyin hao yun.
    that-CL reason   good fortune

    b. *ruguo ta zenme xiu che, ni jiu yinggai yong na-ge
      if   he how   fix car, you then should use   that-CL
      fangfa xiu che.
      method fix car

(155)   ni   yiwei [ta weishenme/zenme/shi-bu-shi xiu-le nei-bu che le] ne?
    you think he why/how/be-not-be   fix-LE that-CL car LE Q
    Interrogative readings only:
    a. 'Why do you think that s/he fixed the car t?'
    b. 'How do you think that s/he fixed the car t?'
    c. 'Do you think that s/he has fixed the car (or do you think s/he has not)?'

If, indeed, adjunct *wh*-phrases can never function like variables, it is logical to assume that they are operators and undergo movement at LF. Furthermore, *wh*-adjuncts also differ from arguments in that they cannot occur under *zhi* 'only':

(156) a. ta zhi xiu-le nar-bu   che?
    he only fix-LE which-CL car
    'He fixed only which car?'

    b. *ta zhi   weishenme xiu-le che?
      he only why   fix-LE car

    c. *?ta zhi zenme xiu-le che?[35]
      he only how   fix-LE car

    d. *ta zhi yuan-bu-yuanyi   xiu che?
      he only willing-not-willing fix car

Recall our discussion of the PLA (142) above. The grammaticality of (156a) suggested to us that the *wh*-phrase *nar-bu che* 'which car' does not move in LF. Then, by the same reasoning, the ungrammaticality of (156c–d) might suggest that a *wh*-adjunct has moved, causing a violation of the PLA.[36]

However, although *wh*-adjuncts cannot be interpreted as existential inderminates, on other occasions they can behave like variables. Cheng and Huang (1996) have argued that in "bare conditional" sentences, as illustrated below, the *wh*-phrases in situ are best analyzed as variables unselectively bound by appropriate adverbs of quantification (see also Chapter 9 on donkey anaphora). In such

[35] *Zenme* 'how' seems to induce less severe island effects than *weishenme* 'why' in a variety of environments. This difference is observed in other languages as well.
[36] Adjunct *wh*-constituents are also excluded under Negation, and this again can be explained by the ECP as a violation of Ross' "Inner Island" constraint, as suggested in Rizzi (1990).

constructions, however, we see that both argument and adjunct *wh*-phrases are acceptable:[37]

(157)   ta xie   shenme, wo jiu   xie   shenme.
         he write what,   I   then write what
         'I will write whatever he writes.'

(158) a. ta weishenme mei lai,   wo jiu   weishenme mei lai.
         he why   not come I   then why   not come
         'I did not come for the same reason he did not come.'

      b. ta zenme xiu che, ni jiu   yinggai zenme xiu che.
         he how   fix car, you then should how   fix car
         'You should fix cars in the same way he fixes cars.'

So the movement hypothesis is somewhat of a double-edged sword as regards the behavior of adjunct *wh*-phrases in situ.

An alternative to a movement approach to adjuncts is to claim that a *wh*-adjunct also does not undergo movement. However, their relationship to the Qu operator is more restricted because *wh*-adjuncts are not referential. Details aside, Aoun and Li (1993a) suggested that a *wh*-adjunct is underlyingly bound by a Qu operator in its local CP. The local Qu operator, if not located in the Spec of an interrogative C^0, must move to a higher Spec of CP where such a C is available. This gives a long-distance adjunct question the following representation:

(159)   [$_{CP}$ Qu$_i$ [$_{IP}$ ta   renwei [$_{CP}$ t$_i$ [$_{IP}$ Lisi weishenme$_i$ mei lai   ]]] ne]?
                        he   think   Lisi why   not come   Q

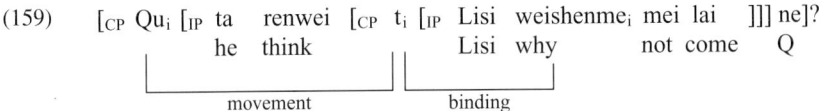

Here the relation between t$_i$ and *weishenme* 'why' is one of binding, and that between *Qu* and t$_i$ one of movement. The possibility of interpreting an adjunct long-distance but not across an island is then reduced to the existence of movement, not of the *wh*-adjunct itself, but of an abstract operator locally binding it.

Both varieties of the non-movement approach to *wh*-in-situ thus critically employ an abstract movement strategy to account for observed locality effects. The original covert movement hypothesis is not abandoned, but made more precise and hence strengthened.

---

[37] A-not-A forms are completely excluded from such conditionals though:

(i)   *ta gao-bu-gaoxing, wo jiu   gao-bu-gaoxing.
        he hap-not-happy, I   then hap-not-happy
        Intended: 'I will be either happy or not happy as he will be.'

7.5   Summary

In this chapter we have discussed all major types of questions in Chinese: *yes-no* questions, disjunctive questions, A-not-A questions, and *wh*-questions. We made some efforts to distinguish A-not-A questions from *yes-no* questions on the one hand and normal disjunctive questions on the other. We then argued for the need to distinguish between two types of true A-not-A questions, and we adopted a modular approach that derives their differences with respect to island sensitivity, lexical integrity, and the ban against P-Stranding. For *wh*-questions, we directed our attention to the in-situ strategy and addressed the question of how various similarities and differences between Chinese and English (and by extension, between *wh*-in-situ languages and *wh*-movement languages) can be insightfully captured. Although the apparent absence of syntactic movement had for some time put the *wh*-in-situ languages outside of a major part of general syntactic theory, a covert movement hypothesis has unearthed interesting insights into the syntax of *wh*-constructions and the nature of the syntax–semantics interface, with consequences for the theory of movement and of parametric syntax.

8

Nominal expressions

We have so far focused on clausal structures, touching briefly on nominal expressions in Chapter 6 when relative structures were discussed. Clausal structures are known to have parallels within nominal expressions (Chomsky 1970). This chapter focuses on the internal structure of nominal expressions.

For speakers of English, a striking fact about Chinese nominal expressions is their apparent "simplicity": as briefly noted in Chapter 6, Section 6.2.1, Chinese nouns are not inflected for number and do not need to occur with a definite or indefinite article (*the* or *a*). The absence of definite and indefinite articles does not prevent a bare noun from being interpreted as definite or indefinite. A generic interpretation is also possible. To illustrate, the bare noun *gou* 'dog' in the following examples can be interpreted as generic, definite, or indefinite. It can also be interpreted as singular or plural:

(1) a. *gou* hen congming.
        dog very intelligent
        'Dogs are intelligent.'

     b. wo kandao *gou*.
        I   saw   dog
        'I saw a dog/dogs.'

     c. *gou* pao-zou-le.
        dog run-away-LE
        'The dog(s) ran away.'

Clearly, bare nouns in Chinese can be the interpretive equivalents of the English [(definite/indefinite) article + (singular/plural) noun]. Is the semantic equivalency reflected syntactically?

The other side of the cursory English–Chinese comparison is that the Chinese nominal system might also appear to be more "complex" than that of English in some other respects. When nouns are counted, English simply combines a number and a noun, such as *three books*. When the number is greater than one, the noun must appear in the plural form. In contrast, Chinese needs a classifier to help with counting: the classifier for books, *ben*, must appear between 'three' and 'book' *san-ben shu*. The noun remains the same regardless of whether the number is greater than one. What is the role of a classifier in Chinese? What are its syntactic properties? Are a plural marker and a classifier mutually exclusive in particular languages? Do classifier languages use a plural marker at all? What are the structures of nominal expressions in Chinese in general? Do they have similar structures to those in English when they express similar meanings?

The syntactic representations of nominal expressions in Chinese and their relation to the general syntactic theory of nominal phrases have been investigated and debated since the advent of a more elaborate structure for nominal expressions – when the traditional label of NP was replaced by DP (determiner phrase, Abney 1987). This chapter serves to establish the internal structure of nominal expressions in Chinese. The investigation will help us address cross-linguistic issues such as the syntactic representation of bare nouns in determiner-less languages and the possibility of plural marking and classifiers being present in the same language. We will begin with the theoretical underpinnings of the debates on nominal structures and then turn to the various types of evidence toward establishing a nominal structure for Chinese similar to the one for English. We will conclude that nominal structures in different types of languages are basically identical. The evidence comes from (i) the distribution of different types of nominal expressions, (ii) the ordering of the constituents within nominal expressions, and (iii) the behavior of the Chinese plural/collective marker/morpheme, *-men*.

8.1   The issues

As shown in Chapter 3, Section 3.3.1, a clause generally has functional projections between the subject NP and the VP, including the Tense projection and/or the Aspect projection. Tense and Aspect are often inflectional morphemes. An "inflectional phrase" (IP) is often used to represent a clause. A typical clausal structure, thus, is [$_{IP}$ Subject [$_{I'}$ Infl [$_{VP}$ V Object]]]. The head of a clausal structure is a functional projection, Infl (which houses Tense, for instance). Infl takes a VP as its complement.

A clause often has a nominal counterpart: the following pair of examples has been widely used to illustrate the similarity between verbal and nominal categories (Chomsky 1970):

(2)   The enemy destroyed the city.

(3)   the enemy's destruction of the city

In both instances, the same arguments (the one that destroys and the one that is destroyed) appear with the verb and the deverbal noun.[1] The parallelism between the two structures suggests that their syntactic representations may be quite similar. We have seen that a clausal structure contains an Infl functional projection, in addition to the subject NP and the verb phrase. A nominal expression has traditionally been a projection headed by an N: [$_{NP}$...N...]. However, if the similarity between (2) and (3) is an indication of a parallelism in syntactic structures, a nominal expression may require a more complex form than [$_{NP}$ ... N ...]. This is what Abney (1987) proposed, highlighting the fact that nouns often occur with an article in English.

(4)   I saw *(the/a) cat.

Further, note that the constituents occurring within a nominal expression generally are restricted in their ordering, as shown in (5).

(5)   Demonstrative/Article + Number + Noun
       these/the   three   books
       *three these/the books
       *three books these/the
       *books three these/the

If the head of a nominal expression is the noun *books*, what is the relation of the demonstrative/article and number to the noun? How is the fixed ordering captured?

Semantically, there is also a parallelism between a verb and a noun. Both are essentially property-denoting expressions. That is, even though a nominal phrase in an argument position, such as the subject of (2), *the enemy*, is an individual-denoting expression, the noun *enemy* is the property predicated of a certain individual. *The* has the function of turning a property (predicate) to an entity (argument). In other words, the fact that a nominal phrase is an individual-denoting expression is largely due to the function of an article like *the*. This important function of the article seems to be lost in the syntactic representation of [$_{NP}$ ... N ...] for a nominal phrase.

In brief, the traditional representation of a nominal expression in argument positions as [$_{NP}$ ... N ...] does not accommodate the parallels between a nominal phrase and a clausal structure, the restrictions on constituency and ordering within nominal expressions, and the importance of articles. Because of these

---

[1] Even when a verb does not have a deverbal nominal form, it may appear in the gerundive form, forming a nominal expression with the same argument structure:

(i)   a. John built a space ship.
       b. John's building of a space ship

considerations, many linguists have come to recognize that an argument nominal phrase does not have the straightforward structure [$_{NP}$ ... N ...]. Rather, it has a functional head, a determiner (D), which takes a complement NP and projects to a maximal projection, a determiner phrase (DP). A DP and an NP are two distinct categories: a DP is an entity-denoting expression – an argument – and an NP is a property-denoting expression – a predicate. More specifically, an expression like *the book* should be projected as a DP containing an NP *book*: [$_{DP}$ *the* [$_{NP}$ *book*]].[2] The predicate–argument distinction can be illustrated by the following examples:

(6)   a. [*(The) captain of the team] will visit us tomorrow. (*the* obligatory in argument position)

    b. We elected him [captain of the team]. (*the* not required in predicate position)

An extensive investigation of the interpretation and distribution of different types of nominal expressions led Longobardi (1994) to propose that an empty D exists even in the cases of argument nominal expressions without an overt determiner. We will not repeat the details here. The main point is that there have been substantial arguments in the literature in support of a DP structure to represent a nominal expression as an argument.

This has consequences for our analysis of Chinese. As noted briefly at the beginning, bare nouns in Chinese can be definite or indefinite and may be singular or plural. They also occur in argument positions, functioning as a subject or an object. That is, a bare noun in Chinese functions like a full DP in English. Should a Chinese bare noun also then be represented as a DP? Two lines of research have been pursued: one aims to keep a one-to-one syntax–semantics mapping relation, and the other emphasizes correlations of cross-linguistic variation with respect to the use of classifiers, plural marking, and articles.

The first line of research takes the distinction between an NP and a DP seriously and assumes that structures and meanings strictly correspond to each other. An NP is always interpreted as a predicate (property-denoting), and a DP (entity-denoting) an argument. This move brings us closer to a one-to-one relationship between form and function, and it has also facilitated the "discovery" of more functional projections. For instance, in addition to a DP, a number phrase (NumP) has been proposed (see, for instance, Carstens 1991, Ritter 1991, 1995, and Valois 1991). A nominal phrase therefore has the structure [$_{DP}$ D [$_{Num}$ Num [$_{NP}$ N]]].[3] A strong claim stemming from this line of research is that all languages have

---

[2] We leave open the issue of whether *the* occupies the position of D or the Spec of D. For detailed discussions on the motivation for a DP and the constituents within a DP, see Abney (1987).

[3] Other functional projections have been proposed in the literature, such as Kase Phrase and Quantifier Phrase. We focus on D, Num, and Cl in this chapter.

identical nominal structures, regardless of whether they have all the appropriate lexical items to fill the positions.

The second line of research does not assume the existence of a universal structure. It highlights systematic empirical variations among different languages. For instance, some languages do not use plural marking. Such languages often use classifiers with their nouns instead. Moreover, many of these classifer languages also lack articles. As mentioned earlier, Chinese is such a language. Chierchia (1998) notes that there seems to be a correlation between the occurrence of articles, the use of plural marking, and the absence of classifiers. Nominal expressions have different properties in different types of languages. It is not necessary to assume that all languages project a DP or a NumP, especially when such projections are not realized morphologically. A language like Chinese may simply represent its arguments as NPs instead of DPs. An NP in Chinese can be an argument or a predicate. This line of research allows the same syntactic category to represent semantic functions. Some languages allow the category NP to represent an argument (Chinese); some others do not (English). A "semantic parameter" is required: NPs in some languages can function as arguments and predicates, and in some other languages only as predicates.

Which approach characterizes the properties of nominal expressions in Chinese more adequately? In what follows, we will show that adopting a DP structure (containing a NumP) in Chinese has important advantages in capturing (i) the structures and interpretations of different types of nominal expressions, (ii) order and constituency within nominal expressions, and (iii) the behavior of the plural/collective morpheme *-men*.

8.2   Projecting a DP – referential and quantity expressions

Once one looks past the fact that Chinese nouns are bare, it actually is not obvious that Chinese does not have overt morphological evidence for the projection of a DP. Interesting generalizations can be found in cases containing expressions of the form [number + classifier + noun], referred to as number expressions. The way these expressions are interpreted and how they interact with the general constraint in Chinese that disallows an indefinite nominal expression in subject or topic position provides support for a DP in Chinese. We first show that the interpretation of a number expression varies with the position where it occurs. Accordingly, an appropriate analysis to capture the correlation between distribution and interpretation should recognize two different structures for number expressions: NumP and DP. The success of such an analysis supports the existence of these projections in Chinese.

8.2.1   Number expressions as indefinite and quantity expressions

Number expressions [number + classifier + noun] in Chinese have gen-erally been regarded as non-definite expressions. They generally do not occur in subject or topic positions because these positions do not allow indefinite[4] expressions:[5]

(7) a. ??san-ge   xuesheng chi-le   dangao.
         three-CL student   eat-LE cake
         'Three students ate the cake.'

     b. ??san-ge   xuesheng hen   congming.
         three-CL student   very smart
         'Three students are smart.'

(8) a. *san-ge   xuesheng, wo yiwei chi-le   dangao.
         three-CL student   I   think eat-LE cake
         'Three students, I thought (they) ate the cake.'

     b. *san-ge   xuesheng, wo yiwei hen congming.
         three-CL student   I   think very smart
         'Three students, I thought (they) are smart.'

Bare nouns in subject and topic positions are definite expressions:[6]

(9)   xuesheng chi-le   dangao.
         student   eat-LE cake
         'The students ate the cake.'
         Not: '(Some) students ate the cake.'

(10)   xuesheng, wo yiwei chi-le   dangao.
         student   I   think eat-LE cake
         'The students, I thought (they) ate the cake.'
         Not: '(Some) students, I thought (they) ate the cake.'

---

[4] The terms "non-definite" and "indefinite" are used loosely. A subject can be definite or specific. Tsai (1996) suggests that number expressions in Chinese are not specific unless the number is 'one.' That is, 'one N' can be specific, but not 'two N' or any others. Looking ahead, we may claim that a specific nominal expression such as *yige xuesheng* 'a certain student' is derived by moving the number from the Num position to D (see Diesing 1992). This means that specific and definite expressions share the property that the D is lexically filled. We will not pursue the issue of "specific" and "definite." We will use the clearer "indefinite, non-specific" number expressions in our examples. Namely, our examples will consist mostly of number expressions with a number larger than 'one.'

[5] See Chao (1968), Li and Thompson (1981), Lee (1986), Shyu (1995), A. Li (1996), Tsai (1994a, 1996), and Xu (1995, 1996), among many others, on the distribution of indefinite nominal expressions and the prohibition against a subject or topic being indefinite.

[6] Bare nouns can also be interpreted as generic in the generic contexts. The issue of gener-icity will be addressed in Section 8.5.

However, number expressions are not always disallowed in subject or topic positions:[7]

(11) a. san-ge   xuesheng bu gou.
          three-CL student   not enough
          'Three students is not enough.'

      b. san-ge   xuesheng, wo xiang shi bu gou   de.
          three-CL student   I   think is not enough DE
          'Three students, I think is not enough.'

(12) a. san-ge   xuesheng dagai   chi-bu-wan   liang-ge dangao.
          three-CL student   probably eat-not-finish two-CL   cake
          'Three students probably cannot finish two cakes.'

      b. san-ge   xuesheng, wo xiang dagai   chi-bu-wan   liang-ge dangao.
          three-CL student   I   think probably eat-not-finish two-CL   cake
          'Three students, I think probably cannot finish two cakes.'

The possibilities of number expressions in subject or topic positions are systematic. They involve the notion of "quantity" (A. Li 1998). For instance, the verb 'enough/sufficient' in (11) expresses the sufficiency of a certain amount. The verb complex 'eat-not-finish' in (12) expresses the notion of the amount of students finishing the amount of cakes. That is, the subject and topic number expressions in (11)–(12) denote quantity. Examples (11)–(12) are contrasted with (7)–(8). The latter pair do not involve quantity-denoting expressions and are not acceptable with the number expressions in subject or topic positions. Let us conveniently label the number expressions in (11)–(12) "quantity number expressions" to capture the observation that they denote the notion of quantity. The number expressions in (7)–(8) will be called "non-quantity individual-denoting expressions" or "indefinite expressions" to highlight the fact that they refer to some entities/individuals (indefinite referents),[8] rather than denoting quantity. The question that arises from the contrast between (7)–(8) and (11)–(12) is why only the latter are acceptable.

8.2.2   Quantity vs. indefiniteness

A. Li (1998) argues that the two types of number expressions illustrated in (7)–(8) and (11)–(12) exhibit different syntactic behaviors, which leads us to

---

[7] There is a range of patterns that allow a number expression in the subject position, as discussed in Tsai (1994a, 1996) and A. Li (1996, 1998).

[8] "Indefinite referents" in the sense of denoting random objects in the discourse. Again, these terms are used very loosely. The main contrast to be made is between the one that mainly expresses quantity and the other that mainly denotes entities/individuals.

recognize their different structural representations. The main support comes from the facts concerning pronominal coreference/binding and scope interaction.

8.2.2.1 Pronominal coreference/binding

A quantity-denoting number expression does not corefer with a pronoun. Nor can it be an antecedent of a bound pronoun such as *ta* 'he' or *tamen* 'they.' These properties contrast with the coreferential and binding possibilities available to non-quantity individual-denoting expressions. The examples in (13) indicate that indefinite nominals (which are individual-denoting) can be coindexed with referential or bound pronouns.

(13) a. wo jiao liang-ge xuesheng$_i$ huiqu ba tamen$_i$ de chezi kai   lai.
         I   ask two-CL   student   return BA them   DE car   drive over
         'I asked two students to go back and drive their car over.'

      b. ni   ruguo neng zhaodao liang-ge bangshou$_i$, jiu   gankuai ba
         you if   can   find   two-CL   helper   then hurry   BA
         tamen$_i$ qing lai.
         them   invite come
         'If you can find two helpers, hurry and invite them over.'

      c. ta mingtian hui kandao san-ge   ren$_i$,   hai hui gen tamen$_i$
         he tomorrow will see   three-CL people and will with them
         zuo   pengyou.
         make friends
         'He will meet three people tomorrow and will make friends with them.'

In contrast, a quantity expression does not corefer with or bind a pronoun. Examples (14a–c) are not acceptable. If they can be accommodated (when disregarding the definiteness requirement on subject), their number expressions must be interpreted as denoting individuals, rather than quantities:

(14) a. *san-ge   ren$_i$ tai-bu-qi liang-jia ni   gei   tamen$_i$ de gangqin.
         three-CL man lift-not-up two-CL   you give them   DE piano
         'Three people cannot lift two (of the) pianos that you gave to them.'

      b. *liang-ge daren$_i$ bu ru   tamen$_i$ de san-ge   xiaohai you liliang.
         two-CL   adult not compare they   DE three-CL children have strength
         'Two adults are not as strong as their three children.'

      c. *ruguo liang-zhang chuang shui-de-xia   san-ge ren$_i$,   wo
         if   two-CL   bed   sleep-able-complete three-CL person I
         jiu   qing   tamen$_i$ lai.
         then invite them   come
         'If two beds can accommodate three people, I will invite them over.'

Similarly, the binding of a reflexive is not possible with quantity expressions. The contrast between (15a) and (15b) shows that the quantity number expression, though occupying the subject position c-commanding the reflexive, cannot be the antecedent of the reflexive (15a). This stands in contrast to the individual-denoting number expression in (15b), which can serve as a binder.

(15) a. Zhangsan$_i$ zhidao san-ge   ren$_j$ yiding   ban-bu-dong
          Zhangsan   know   three-CL people certainly move-not-move
          ziji$_{i/*j}$ de gangqin.
          self   DE piano
          'Zhangsan knows that three people certainly cannot move self's piano.'

      b. Zhangsan$_i$ jiao san-ge   ren$_j$ huiqu ba ziji$_{i/j}$ de gangqin
          Zhangsan   ask three-CL people return BA self   DE piano
          ban   lai.
          move over
          'Zhangsan asked three people to go and move self's piano over.'

8.2.2.2 Scope

Quantity number expressions behave differently from non-quantity ones with respect to scope interaction. A quantity number expression does not enter into scope relations with another one. For instance, (16) has only one reading: the amount of rice consumed by the amount of three people is five bowls:

(16)   san-ge   ren,   wo zhidao chi-de-wan   wu-wan fan.
         three-CL people I   know   eat-can-finish five-CL   rice
         'Three people, I know can finish five bowls of rice.'

This again contrasts with the non-quantity indefinite expressions, which can have scope interaction. The following sentence can have the fifteen-bowl interpretation; i.e, 'three people' has scope over 'five bowls of rice.'

(17)   wo rang san-ge   ren   chi wu-wan fan.
         I   let   three-CL people eat five-CL   rice
         'I let three people eat five bowls of rice.'

The facts in (13)–(17) show that, even though they share the same form [number + classifier + noun], the quantity and non-quantity number expressions differ in their possibilities of coreference with/binding of pronouns and scope interaction. These distinctions will follow naturally from their structural differences, as shown next.

8.2.3   Number phrase and determiner phrase

Taking the meaning to be an indication of the structure, we put forward the claim that the number of a quantity-denoting expression [number + classifier + noun] is a head, projecting a number phrase. When the phrase [number + classifier

+ noun] is individual-denoting, a logical possibility is that it is a DP: determiner is projected even though it is not filled by a lexical item. In other words, an expression like *san-ge ren* 'three-CL people' can be a number phrase with the Number head 'three,' indicating the quantity of 'three,' as in (18a). It can also be a DP with a null D head, as an individual-denoting expression (18b).

(18)   a. [NumP san   ge ren]
                three CL person
       b. [DP D [NumP san   ge ren]]
                       three CL person

Such a structural difference straightforwardly captures the contrasts discussed in the previous sections. The D of a DP is generally the locus of reference. If a quantity-denoting phrase does not have a D in its structure, it is expected that it does not enter into coreference or binding relations. Moreover, a number phrase does not quantify over individuals and does not interact with another expression scopally.

This way of distinguishing between a DP and a NumP has advantages over potential alternatives. Consider the alternative of not projecting a quantity expression as a NumP. It would then also be a DP – an indefinite nominal expression – always taking narrow scope with respect to other quantificational expressions. However, such an option fails to capture the differences between a true indefinite expression and a quantity-denoting expression. Recall that a contrast exists between (16) and (17): scope interaction is only manifested in (17) with non-quantity individual-denoting expressions. Such a contrast argues against reducing a quantity expression to an indefinite individual-denoting expression that always takes narrow scope. In (17), the first indefinite expression can take wide scope over the second indefinite expression. Were we to label a quantity expression as a narrow scope indefinite expression, we would still need to answer the question of why there are two types of indefinite expressions, one participating in scope interaction and the other, not. In addition, the coreference and binding possibilities also force us to distinguish two types of number expressions.

Moreover, equating a quantity-denoting expression with a narrow-scope indefinite expression wrongly groups together quantity expressions and other typical indefinite expressions such as non-interrogative *wh*-elements and those expressions preceded by the existential marker *you* 'have,' as shown in the next two sections.

8.2.4   Comparison with indefinite wh-*elements*

We have seen in Chapter 7 that a *wh*-phrase in Chinese is essentially a non-interrogative indefinite expression. Such indefinite expressions differ from quantity expressions by having the possibility of being coreferential with or bound by a pronoun: an indefinite *wh*-element can be coindexed with a coreferential or bound pronoun, but a quantity-denoting expression cannot. Compare (14) with (19a–b):

(19) a. ruguo ni   kandao shenme ren$_i$,   qing ba ta$_i$ dai   jinlai.
          if   you see   what   person, please BA him bring in
          'If you see anyone$_i$, please bring him$_i$ in.'

      b. ruguo ni   yao jiao shenme ren$_i$ huiqu ba ta$_i$-de
          if   you want ask what   person return BA his
          chezi kai lai, jiu qing   kuai jiao ba.
          car   drive come then please fast ask SFP
          'If you want to ask someone$_i$ to go and drive his$_i$ car over, please ask soon.'

Similarly, the binding of a reflexive is possible with a *wh*-indefinite, but not with a quantity-denoting expression. Compare (15a) with (20):

(20)   ruguo ni   yao jiao shenme ren$_i$ huiqu ba ziji$_i$-de
          if   you want ask what   person return BA self-DE
          chezi kai lai, jiu qing   kuai jiao ba.
          car   drive come then please fast ask SFP
          'If you want to ask someone$_i$ to go and drive self$_i$'s car over, please ask soon.'

8.2.5 *Comparison with* you *expressions*

An indefinite nominal in subject position in Chinese generally co-occurs with the existential quantifier *you* 'have.'

(21)   you   san-ge ren   lai-le.
          exist three-CL person come-LE
          'There were three people that came/Three people came.'

When another number expression occurs in a sentence similar to the one in (16), the first number expression takes wide scope. This contrasts with the lack of such a reading in (16):

(22) a. you   san-ge ren   chi-de-wan   wu-wan fan.
          exist three-CL person eat-can-finish five-CL rice
          'There exist three people that can finish five bowls of rice.'

      b. you   san-ge ren   tai-de-qi   liang-jia gangqin.
          have three-CL person lift-can-up two-CL   piano
          'There are three people who can lift two pianos.'

Example (22a) affirms the existence of three people, each of whom is able to finish five bowls of rice; (22b) affirms the existence of three people, each of whom can lift two pianos.

The contrast in interpretation between (16) and (22a–b) suggests that a number phrase in the former cannot be analyzed as an indefinite expression.

8.2.6   *Prohibition against an indefinite subject/topic*

The discussion so far has shown that a number expression of the form [number + classifier + noun] is structurally ambiguous: it may be a NumP, or it may be a DP with a null D (18a–b). The difference between these two structures is manifested in the possibilities regarding coreference/binding and scope interaction. More support for this conclusion came from a comparison of quantity-denoting number expressions with non-interrogative indefinite *wh*-expressions and indefinite individual-denoting expressions occurring with the existential marker *you*.

Distinguishing quantity-denoting NumPs and indefinite DPs structurally also enables us to capture the contrast in distribution between these two types, illustrated by (7)–(8) and (11)–(12). The former pair demonstrates the unacceptability of an indefinite DP in subject/topic positions; the latter pair shows the acceptability of a quantity-denoting NumP in these positions. DP and NumP are illustrated in (18a–b). The important distinction is that (18b), not (18a), contains a null category in the D position. This difference provides an account for the contrast in distribution between the two types of phrases: (18b) is not allowed in topic or subject position, as in (7)–(8); however, (18a) is possible, as in (11)–(12). The empty category in (18b) must meet well-formedness conditions (i.e., the Empty Category Principle; see Chapter 7). Longobardi (1994) argues that a null D, like other empty categories, must be properly governed. An object position is properly governed: it is governed by the lexical V.[9] An indefinite expression with a null D is possible in such a position. A topic position in Chinese does not allow an indefinite expression because no lexical item is available to govern a topic. For a subject, we may follow Aoun, Hornstein, Lightfoot, and Weinberg (1987) and take it to be in the Spec(ifier) of IP position, which is not lexically governed, either. An indefinite nominal in such a position is therefore not acceptable.

Alternatively, the contrast could be due to a condition on identifying a variable in D position. The variable in D needs to be licensed by an operator (quantificational element). The operator can be an existential closure adjoined to VP. A

---

[9]   A preposition behaves like a V in allowing an indefinite expression as its object. According to the lexical government approach of Longobardi, a P must be a lexical governor. This amounts to saying that the prohibition against preposition stranding cannot be reduced to the requirement of lexical government, if Longobardi's approach is to be adopted.

DP in the subject or topic position is too high to fall within the domain of the existential closure. The occurrence of an overt existential marker such as *you* saves the structure. We will return to the licensing of an indefinite phrase in Section 8.5.

The analysis proposed here can also accommodate many other distributional facts. For instance, an indefinite expression in the possessor position of an object contrasts with one in the possessor position of a subject or topic. The former is acceptable, like an object; the latter is unacceptable, like a subject:

(23) a. wo qu-guo yi-ge   pengyou-de jia.
          I   go-GUO one-CL friend-DE   home
          'I have been to a friend's home.'

      b. wo gei yi-ge   pengyou-de haizi zhao gongzuo.
          I   for one-CL friend-DE   child find work
          'I (will) find work for a friend's child.'

      c. *yi-ge   pengyou-de haizi bu hui zhaodao gongzuo.
          one-CL friend-DE   child not will find   work
          'A friend's child will not find work.'

      d. *yi-ge   pengyou-de haizi, wo tingshuo bu hui zhaodao gongzuo.
          one-CL friend-DE   child I   hear-say not will find   work
          'A friend's child, I heard that (he) will not find work.'

8.2.7   Summary

A number expression of the form [Num + Cl + N] in Chinese should be analyzed as a quantity-denoting expression represented by a NumP (18a) or an individual-denoting one represented by a DP containing an empty D (18b). The differences that we saw between (18a) and (18b) provide support for the existence in Chinese of a DP category, in addition to the existence of an independent NumP, not dominated by a DP.

The existence of a DP is further manifested in a wide range of facts concerning constituency and order within nominal expressions, as shown next.

8.3   Order and constituency within a DP

Recall that an individual-denoting number expression such as *san-ge ren* 'three-CL people' should have a full DP structure like the one below, where Num is filled by a number, Cl(assifier) by a classifier, and N(oun) by a common noun. D is null in this structure.

(24)

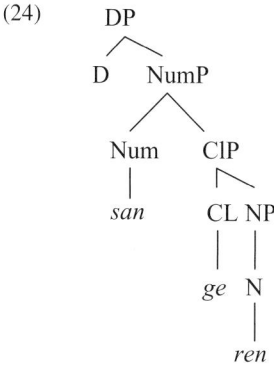

Since D is typically thought to be the locus of reference or definiteness, it should host all the expressions related to reference or definiteness, such as demonstratives, pronouns, proper names, and even definite bare nouns. This is indeed supported by the types of constituents allowed within a nominal expression and the possible orderings of those constituents.

8.3.1   Demonstratives

If demonstratives are in D, we should find [demonstrative + number + classifier + noun] according to the structure in (24). This is true:

(25)   zhe/na   san-ge   ren
        these/those three-CL person
        'these/those three people'

The interrogative demonstrative *na*[10] behaves in the same fashion:

(26)   na   san-ge   ren
        which three-CL person
        'which three people'

A demonstrative is sometimes followed by a classifier directly, without a number, although one may argue that the number 'one' is present underlyingly because the interpretation is singular:

(27)   zhe/na-ge   ren
        this/that-CL person
        'this/that person'

---

[10] The interrogative demonstrative *na* 'which' has a fall-rise tone, and the distant demonstrative *na* 'that' a falling tone.

8.3.2   Pronouns

In the recent generative literature, pronouns are often analyzed as the spell-out features of D (see, for instance, Longobardi 1994). This insight originally appeared in an earlier work by Postal (1969), who suggests that pronouns are like the definite article *the* in English. A definite article is in the D position; thus, a pronoun also occupies the D position. Our proposed DP structure indicates that a pronoun can be followed by number, classifier, and noun (which need not be overt):[11]

(28)   a. tamen liang-ge   (ren/xuesheng/langui/liulang han)
            they   two-CL   person/student/lazybones/vagrant
            'them two   people/students/lazybones/vagrants'

        b. ta/ni/wo yi-ge   (ren/xuesheng/langui/liulang han)
            he/you/I one-CL person/student/lazybones/vagrant
            'him/you/me a   person/lazybones/vagrants'

        c. women ji-ge   (ren/xuesheng/langui/liulang han)
            we   several-CL person/student/lazybones/vagrant
            'us   several   people/students/lazybones/vagrants'

The pattern [pronoun + noun] is also possible.[12]

(29)   a. tamen xuesheng
            they   student
            'them students'

        b. women laoshi
            we   teacher
            'us teachers'

        c. nimen haizi
            you   children
            'you children'

[11] As suggested by Dylan Tsai (personal communication), a pronoun taking a number phrase as its complement is interpreted very much like a verb with an adjunct as a complement (Larson 1988). Both have complements interpreted like modifiers.

[12] When the number and classifier expressions do not occur, the pronoun must be plural:

  (i)   ta zhe (yi)-ge xuesheng/langui
          he this one-CL student/lazybones
          'he, this student/lazybones'

  (ii)   *ta xuesheng/langui
           he student/lazybones
           'him student/lazybones'

This is quite similar to English: *he/him boy* is not acceptable but *them boys* is. See Noguchi (1997) for a possible answer to why such a constraint exists and relevant references.

These expressions can occur in all argument positions:

(30) a. wo xihuan tamen liang-ge (ren).
          I   like   them two-CL (person)
          'I like them two (people).'

      b. wo dui tamen liang-ge (xuesheng) hen you hao-gan.
          I to them two-CL   student   very have good-feeling
          'I have good feelings toward them two students.'

      c. tamen liang-ge (langui)   wo tingshuo hen xihuan zai yiqi.
          them two-CL   lazybones I hear   very like   at together
          'Them two (lazybones), I hear like to be together.'

(31) a. wo xian dai   tamen xuesheng hui qu.
          I first bring they student   back go
          'I will take them students back first.'

      b. tamen xuesheng bu hui xihuan gongke   de.
          they student   not will like   homework DE
          'They students will not like homework.'

      c. wo dui tamen xuesheng bu zai   yanfan-le.
          I to them student   not again tired-LE
          'I am no longer tired of them students.'

      d. tamen xuesheng, wo zhidao bu hui you shenme qian   de.
          they student   I know   not will have what   money DE
          'Them students, I know will not have much money.'

Thus, a DP structure [D + [Num + [Cl + [N]]]] captures the possible constituents
and their ordering: a pronoun is in D, number in Num, classifier in Cl, and noun
in N.

However, there are some complications. Unexpectedly, pronouns and demonstratives, which have both been claimed to occupy the D position, can occur
together:

(32) a. wo xihuan nimen zhexie guai haizi.
          I like   you   these good children
          'I like you these good kids.'

      b. wo dui tamen naxie liulanghan meiyou   yinxiang.
          I to they those vagrant   not-have impression
          'I do not have impressions of them those vagrants.'

      c. tamen naxie xuesheng, meigeren dou hen xihuan.
          they those student   everyone all very like
          'Them those students, everyone likes.'

Why can demonstratives and pronouns co-occur, if they both are in D? Several
options are available. The first is to maintain the claims so far but allow a more

complex structure: both pronouns and demonstratives are in the D position. They are in a double-headed D position or two separate D positions (D taking another DP as a complement). Another option is to generate a pronoun in Spec of D and a demonstrative in D. We will return to these options when we discuss the plurality issue in Section 8.4.

8.3.3   Proper names

Proper names are like pronouns in terms of their function: both denote designated entities. They also behave alike when occurring with number expressions or common nouns. The constituency and ordering facts show that proper names in Chinese occur in (the Spec of) D (see Section 8.4), followed by a pronoun or a demonstrative in the D position and a number expression: [proper name + pronoun/demonstrative + number + classifier + noun].

(33) a. wo xihuan Zhangsan, Lisi na   ji-ge   guai haizi.
         I   like   Zhangsan, Lisi those several-CL good children
         'I like Zhangsan, Lisi those several good kids.'

      b. wo dui Zhangsan zhe-ge xuesheng meiyou   shenme yinxiang.
         I   to Zhangsan this-CL student   not-have what   impression
         'I do not have much [of an] impression of Zhangsan this student.'

      c. Zhangsan zhe-ge ren,   wo yiwei   henduo ren   dou renshi.
         Zhangsan this-CL person I   thought many   person all know
         'Zhangsan this person, I thought many people know (him).'

      d. wo xihuan Zhangsan, Lisi tamen ji-ge   guai haizi.
         I   like   Zhangsan, Lisi they   several-CL good children
         'I like Zhangsan, Lisi them several good kids.'

A pronoun and a demonstrative may both appear in this order: [proper name + pronoun + demonstrative].

(34)   wo xihuan Zhangsan ta zhe-ge yonggong de xuesheng.
          I   like   Zhangsan he this-CL diligent   DE student
          'I like Zhangsan him this diligent student.'

When proper names and pronouns co-occur, the proper name can be singular and the pronoun can be plural (as shown by the suffix -men, as in tamen 'they'). That is, the pronoun need not agree with the proper name in number. However, the pronoun needs to be plural if the number following the pronoun is more than one.

(35) a. wo xihuan Zhangsan tamen (na)   san-ge.
         I   like   Zhangsan them   those three-CL
         'I like Zhangsan them (those) three.'

b. *wo xihuan Zhangsan ta   (na)   san-ge.[13]
   I   like   Zhangsan him those three-CL

Unlike pronouns, proper names cannot precede nouns directly.

(36) a. *wo xihuan Zhangsan/Zhangsan he   Lisi xuesheng.
         I   like   Zhangsan/Zhangsan and Lisi student

      b. *wo dui Zhangsan/Zhangsan he   Lisi xuesheng hen   guanxin.
         I   to Zhangsan/Zhangsan and Lisi student   very care

A number expression or a pronoun/demonstrative is required. It is most acceptable
to have both a number expression and a demonstrative/pronoun. In the following
examples, if the elements in the parentheses do not appear, the degree of acceptability decreases.

(37) a. wo xihuan Zhangsan he   Lisi ?(tamen/zhe) liang-ge guai haizi.
         I   like   Zhangsan and Lisi they/these   two-CL   good children
         'I like Zhangsan and Lisi (them/these) two good kids.'

      b. wo dui Zhangsan ??(zhe) yi-ge   xuesheng meiyou   shenme yinxiang.
         I   to Zhangsan this one-CL student   not-have what   impression
         'I do not have much impression of Zhangsan (this) one student.'

      c. Zhangsan ??(zhe) yi-ge   ren,   wo yiwei   henduo ren   dou renshi.
         Zhangsan this one-CL person I thought many   person all know
         'Zhangsan (this) one person, I thought many people know (him).'

      d. Zhangsan he   Lisi ?(tamen) liang-ge, wo tingshuo hen   xihuan zai yiqi.
         Zhangsan and Lisi they   two-CL   I hear   very like   at together
         'Zhangsan and Lisi (them) two, I heard (that they) like to be together.'

In brief, D is the locus of reference. It hosts demonstratives, pronouns, and proper
names. Therefore, these expressions can precede [(Num + Cl) + N]. There are
some more complex issues, such as what positions are occupied by a proper name,
a pronoun, and a demonstrative when they all occur before a number expression
simultaneously, and why a proper name behaves somewhat differently from a
pronoun (36)–(37). We will return to these questions in Section 8.4. The main
point in this section remains: the order and constituency of [D + Num + Cl+ N]
suggests the existence of a DP structure in Chinese.[14]

---

[13] This sentence is acceptable if it is interpreted as *Zhangsan tade na san-ge* 'those three
belonging to Zhangsan (him).'

[14] An important difference between the analysis proposed here and the analysis discussed
in Longobardi (1994) is that the former can base-generate a proper name (as well as a
pronoun) in (Spec of D) position, but the latter only base-generates a pronoun in the D
position and moves a proper name from N to D position.

8.3.4   *Common nouns*

Common nouns, in contrast to proper names and pronouns, are not base-generated in D or Spec of DP. Instead, they are base-generated in N. Accordingly, we expect that the order of [noun + number + classifier] cannot be base-generated. It cannot be derived by movement of N to D, either. This movement is ruled out by the Head Movement Constraint (Travis 1984), which disallows movement of one head across another.

(38)   a. *wo xihuan xuesheng liang-ge (ren).
          I   like   student   two-CL   (person)
          'I like students two.'

       b. *wo dui xuesheng liang-ge (ren)   hen   you   hao-gan.
          I   to   student   two-CL   person very have good-feeling
          'I have good feelings toward students two.'

       c. *xuesheng liangge (ren)   wo tingshuo hen xihuan zai yiqi.
          student   two-CL person I   hear   like   very   at   together
          'Students two, I hear like to be together.'

Moreover, it is expected that nouns, unlike proper names or pronouns, cannot be followed by demonstratives (and/or pronouns).

(38)   d. *wo xihuan xuesheng tamen/na   liang-ge (ren).
          I   like   student   (they/those) two-CL   (person)
          'I like students them/those two.'

       e. *wo dui xuesheng tamen/na liang-ge (ren)   hen   you   hao-gan.
          I   to   student   they/those two-CL   person very have good-feeling
          'I have good feelings toward students them/those two.'

       f. *xuesheng tamen/na liang-ge (ren)   wo tingshuo hen   xihuan zai yiqi.
          student   they/those two-CL   person I   hear   very like   at   together
          'Students them/those two, I hear like to be together.'

The distinction between proper names and pronouns on the one hand and common nouns on the other may be blurred because pronouns and proper names can sometimes function like common nouns, and common nouns can sometimes function like proper names. What is important, however, is that when common nouns function like proper names, they occupy the (Spec of) D position. When pronouns/proper names function like common nouns, they are in the N position. The expressions in (39) illustrate the cases of common nouns used as proper names and those in (40), the common noun usage of pronouns/proper names:[15]

(39) a. Didi   you   (common noun used as proper name)
         younger-brother again
         wang-le   dongxi le.
         forget-LE   thing   LE
         'Younger Brother forgot (his) stuff again.'

      b. [Didi   na yi-ge   hutu   (behaving like proper name)
          younger-brother that one-CL muddled
          dan] you   wang-le   dongxi le.
          egg   again forget-LE thing   LE
          'Younger Brother that muddled head forgot (his) stuff again.'

      c. [Didi   (ta) yi-ge   (behaving like proper name)
          younger-brother   he one-CL
          danshenhan] hen   wuliao.
          bachelor   very bored
          'Younger Brother him a bachelor is very bored.'

(40) a. wo kandao-guo yi-ge   Xiaoming.   (proper name used as common noun)
         I   see-GUO   one-CL Xiaoming
         'I have seen one Xiaoming.'

      b. *wo kandao-guo [yige   Xiaoming   (behaving like common noun)
          I   see-GUO   one-CL Xiaoming
          na-ge hutu   dan].
          that-CL muddled egg.
          'I have seen one Xiaoming that muddled head.'

In sum, a common noun can follow [(pronoun/demonstrative) + number + classifier] when it is base-generated and stays in the N position. It can precede [(pronoun/demonstrative) + number + classifier] when it is base-generated in the (Spec of) D position (used as a proper name). If a noun is base-generated in

---

[15] It is much harder for a pronoun to function like a common noun than it is for a proper name to do so (see Longobardi 1994).

    (i)   wo kandao-guo yi-ge   Li Denghui.
          I   see-GUO   one-CL Li Denghui
          'I have seen one Li Denghui.'

    (ii) *wo kandao-guo yi-ge   ta.
           I   see-GUO   one-CL him

    However, it is not entirely impossible for a pronoun to become a common noun. It is found in limited cases:

    (iii) jingzi-li   you san-ge   ta.
          mirror-inside have three-CL him
          'Inside the mirror are three hims.'

N and moves to D, it does not occur with [(pronoun/demonstrative) + number + classifier]. An expression [$_{DP}$ number + classifier + noun] has a null D and is interpreted as indefinite, occurring only in the positions allowing indefinite expressions (e.g., object positions). The form [noun + number + classifier] is acceptable only when the noun is interpreted as a proper name, as in (39). They are not acceptable when the noun is a common noun, even when the noun is interpreted as definite.

(41) a. wo ba xuesheng song hui jia le. ('student' interpreted as definite)
            I BA student send back home LE
            'I took the students home.'

      b. Definite N cannot be followed by [number + classifier]:
          *wo ba xuesheng liang-ge song hui jia le.
          I BA student two-CL send back home LE
          'I took the two students home.'

The contrast between (41) and (39b–c) is especially interesting. It shows that it is not definiteness that allows a proper name to be followed by [number + classifier]. Both proper names and definite common nouns are definite. It is structures and derivations that govern the possible constituents and their ordering. A proper name (and a common noun used as a proper name) is base-generated in (Spec of) D position. A definite bare noun, in contrast, must be generated in N and moved to D. Example (41b) is unacceptable because the sequence *xuesheng* + *liang-ge* cannot be base-generated or derived by movement.[16]

8.3.5   *Not appositives or adverbials*

It is important to point out that the expression discussed in the previous sections – [proper name/pronoun (+ demonstrative) + number + classifier + noun] – is not two separate units, such as a DP with an appositive (*John, the man I saw yesterday*, or *that man, the one in a black hat*) or a DP with an adverbial (such as [*John*] [*himself*]). First, let us compare our data with an apposition structure. In the former, the pronoun or proper name is not followed by a pause, in contrast to the obligatory presence of a pause between two elements in apposition structures. Moreover, pronouns and proper names contrast with definite nouns (with or without demonstratives) in our data. An apposition structure does not show such a contrast.

---

[16] The following sentence is acceptable because *xuesheng* 'student' and *liang-ge* 'two-CL' are two separate constituents.

  (i)   xuesheng, liang-ge yijing hui qu le.
          student two-CL already back go LE
          'Among the students, two have returned home.'

(42) a. *xuesheng zhege/xie ren
          student   this-CL   person

      b. xuesheng, ni   renshi de naxie, mingtian hui lai.
          student   you know DE those tomorrow will come
          'Students, those you know, will come tomorrow.'

      c. *zhe-ge xuesheng zhe-ge ren
          this-CL student   this-CL person

      d. zhe-ge xuesheng, chuan hong yifu   de, shi tade xuesheng.
          the-CL student   wear red clothes DE be his student
          'This student, wearing red clothes, is his student.'

      e. *naxie xuesheng (tamen) san-ge   ren
          those student   they   three-CL people

      f. naxie xuesheng, chuan hong yifu   de na san-ge, shi ta-de xuesheng.
          those student   wear red clothes DE that three-CL be his   student
          'Those students, the three students wearing red clothes, are his students.'

More than one appositive can occur with a nominal and the ordering of the two appositives is free, as in (43a–b). However, the DP structure in question allows only one form, as dictated by the structure of DP [D + Num + Cl + N] illustrated in (43c).

(43) a. naxie xuesheng, nimen qunian   jiao-guo, ta hen xihuan
          those students you   last.year teach-GUO he very like
          de, xianzai zai zher.
          DE now   at here
          'Those students, you taught last year and he likes very much, are now here.'

      b. naxie xuesheng, ta hen xihuan de, nimen qunian
          those students he very like   DE you   last.year
          jiao-guo, xianzai zai zher.
          teach-GUO now   at here
          'Those students, he likes very much and you taught last year, are now here.'

      c. *Zhangsan tamen liangge xuesheng tamen naxie langui
          Zhangsan them two-CL student   them those lazybones

An appositive follows an entire DP and does not occur between the constituents within a DP:

(44) a. Zhangsan tamen ji-ge   xuesheng, ni   jiaoguo   de
          Zhangsan they several-CL student   you teach-GUO DE
          naxie, xianzai zai zher.
          those now   at here
          'Zhangsan them several students, those you have taught, are now here.'

      b. *Zhangsan, ni   jao-guo   de naxie, tamen ji-ge   xuesheng . . .
          Zhangsan, you teach-GUO DE those, them several-CL student

    c. *Zhangsan tamen, ni   jiao-guo   de naxie, ji-ge   xuesheng . . .
       Zhangsan them,   you teach-GUO DE those several-CL student

Finally, the two elements in an apposition structure generally are both definite. For instance, a constituent in apposition to a pronoun cannot be an indefinite expression [number + classifier (+ noun)], as in (45a). However, the DP structure we are proposing does allow the form of [pronoun + [number + classifier (+ noun)]], as in (45b).

(45)   a. Appositive
        *wo dui tamen, liang-ge xuesheng, hen   hao.
         I   to   them   two-CL   student   very nice
        'I am very nice to them, two students.'

      b. DP Structure
        wo dui tamen liang-ge xuesheng hen   hao.
        I   to   them   two-CL   student   very nice
        'I am very nice to them two students.'

In brief, the DP expressions discussed in these sections are not appositives.

    Nor can such DPs be analyzed as nominal expressions plus adverbials. As observed in Lee (1986), important generalizations exhibited by the expressions containing an adverbial phrase such as *yi-ge ren* 'by oneself' in Chinese are:

(46)   a. The adverbial phrase is not part of the nominal expression. The adverbial and the nominal expression can be separated by other constituents; see (47).

      b. *Yi-ge ren* 'a person' seems to be the only expression that is used as an emphatic adverbial. Substituting the noun with *xuesheng* 'student,' for instance, is disallowed (48).

      c. The number of an adverbial expression is restricted to 'one'; see (49).

A modal can intervene between a nominal and an emphatic adverbial (47a), but not appear inside a DP (47c).

(47)   a. ta hui ziji/yi-ge   ren   lai   zher.
        he will self/one-CL person come here
        'He will come here by himself.'

        Compare:
      b. [tamen (na) liang-ge (langui)]   hui lai.
        they   that two-CL   lazybones will come
        'They two (both of them) (lazybones) will come.'

      c. *[tamen hui (na) liang-ge (langui)]   lai.
        they   will that two-CL   lazybones come

A DP allows nouns other than *ren* 'person,' such as *xuesheng* 'student,' in the N position, but not as an adverbial phrase:

(48) a. tamen (na)   liang-ge xuesheng hui lai.
          they   that two-CL   student   will come
          'They two (both of them) students will come.'

      b. ta yiding   yi-ge ren   lai   zher.
          he definitely one-CL person come here
          'He will definitely come by himself.'

      c. *ta yiding   yi-ge   xuesheng lai   zher.
          he   definitely one-CL   student   come here

A number other than 'one' loses the adverbial function.

(49)   *tamen yiding   liang-ge ren   lai   zher.
          they   definitely two-CL   people come here
          Not: 'They will definitely come here by themselves.'
          Not: 'They two (both of them) will definitely come here.'

8.3.6   Summary

The contrast between quantity-denoting and individual-denoting number expressions argues for the presence of a DP in Chinese. A DP structure is further supported by the constituents allowed within a nominal expression and their ordering. However, there is an important issue left unsolved: the position of proper names, pronouns, and demonstratives when they all occur within a nominal expression. Our discussion in the next section regarding the collective/plural morpheme *-men* in Chinese will help clarify this issue, as well as help refine the structure of nominal expressions and provide further support for a DP structure in Chinese.

8.4   Extension and revision: plurality

There is further advantage to projecting nominals as DPs in Chinese. According to A. Li (1999), a DP structure in Chinese provides an account for some quite puzzling facts regarding the so-called collective morpheme *-men* in this language. The differences in the behavior of *-men* and a "normal" plural morpheme (such as *-s* in English) arise from the structural difference between the type of language that allows a "collective" morpheme and one that allows a plural morpheme. The DP account also helps identify more correctly the types of languages that allow a plural or collective morpheme and the types that do not.

In the following subsections, we will introduce Li's DP account and incorporate the expanded data. We will first lay out the morpho-syntactic properties of the morpheme -*men* and then show that the contrast between -*men* in Chinese and -*s* in English can be more accurately captured by an analysis that takes into account the structural similarities and differences between the two languages: both languages project DPs, but Chinese additionally has a classifier projection that English lacks.

8.4.1 *Some puzzles about* -men

As is well known, Chinese does not have much inflectional morphology. In the nominal system, this means its nouns are not inflected for number, Case, or gender. Therefore, it is unexpected that the nominal expression in Chinese can have plural morphology. Indeed, in most relevant works, -*men* is labeled as a "collective" marker since it does not behave like a traditionally understood plural morpheme. Compare it to a regular plural morpheme such as the plural suffix -*s* in English. Unlike -*s*, which can be suffixed to nouns quite productively, the morpheme -*men* generally is only attached to a pronoun or a human noun,[17] as indicated in various dictionaries (e.g., *A Chinese–English Dictionary*, *Xiandai Hanyu Cidian* [Modern Chinese Dictionary]) and grammar works (such as Chao 1968, Li and Thompson 1981, Lü 1980, and Zhu 1982, among many others). More precisely, the following considerations pose challenges for analyzing -*men* as a plural marker.

First, unlike a regular plural morpheme, -*men* is not compatible with a [number + classifier] expression (i.e., a number phrase):[18]

(50)   *san-ge   xuesheng-men*
         three-CL   student-MEN
         'three student+*men*'

According to Iljic (1994), a number phrase expresses the number of individuals. A collective refers to a group as a whole. "Group" and "individual" expressions are not compatible.

---

[17] Norman (1988, p. 120) suggests that the restriction of -*men* to human-denoting expressions is the result of -*men*'s historical development: it evolved from the fusion of *mei* 'every, each' and *ren* 'person.'

[18] Iljic (1994) noted some counterexamples to the traditional observation that quantity expressions do not occur with N-*men*. He attributed these examples to appositive structures. However, while we do not deny the possibility of apposition in certain cases, we have shown in Section 8.3 and will show later in the text that there are acceptable non-apposition cases with -*men* and quantity expressions, which follow from our proposed structures.

Second, occurrence of *-men* makes a nominal expression definite. Quoting Rygaloff (1973) and Yorifuji (1976), Iljic (1994) wrote that "N-*men* always refers to the definite. As a rule, one can neither posit nor negate the existence of N-*men*."

(51) a. *you   ren-men   cf. you   ren
           have person+MEN   have person
                                 'there is/are some person(s)'

      b. *mei you   ren-men   cf. mei you   ren
           not have person+MEN   not have person
                                       'there is nobody'

This observation is further supported by the contrast in the following sentences, which differ minimally in the use of *-men*. The one with *-men* must refer to a definite group but the one without *-men* is vague in this respect (and also vague regarding number):

(52) a. wo qu zhao haizi-men
           I   go find   child-MEN
           'I will go find the children.'

      b. wo qu zhao haizi
           I   go find   child
           'I will go find the/some child/children.'

Third, a proper name can be suffixed with *-men* to express a group consisting of the person denoted by the proper name and others. An example given in Iljic (1994) is *Xiao Qiang-men*, which can mean the person Xiao Qiang and others in his group:[19]

(53)   Xiao Qiang-men shenme shihou lai?
          Xiao Qiang-MEN what   time   come
          'When are Xiao Qiang and company coming?'

---

[19] As noted by Iljic (1994: 111, note 5), even though many works in the literature mentioned the possibility of interpreting *Xiao Qiang+men* as Xiao Qiang and the others, the preference is to use *Xiao Qiang tamen* 'Xiao Qiang them.' In fact, a small survey of my own indicates that most speakers accept only the latter form to mean Xiao Qiang and the others. For the speakers I surveyed, *Xiao Qiang+men* is only used to denote a group of people with the same characteristics or the same name as Xiao Qiang. This is equivalent to the plural form of a proper name used as a common noun in English such as *I have met three Edisons in my life*. In this case, *-men* is used as a plural marker akin to *-s* in English. Anticipating the discussion later, *Xiao Qiang tamen san-ge* 'Xiao Qiang them three' is acceptable in the same way *tamen san-ge* is acceptable. *Xiao Qiang* occurs in the Spec of D with D being the pronoun. Also note that the "collective" reading is not possible with common nouns: *xuesheng-men* means a plurality of students rather than the student(s) and others. Again, anticipating the discussions later in the text, this will follow from the fact that common nouns are base-generated in N and receive a "regular" plural reading.

These three facts in (i–iii) certainly raise questions about -*men* being a plural marker. On the other hand, -*men* does exhibit some properties of a plural marker. Modulo the definiteness restriction, a common noun can be suffixed with -*men* to express plurality. A proper name denoting a person can be suffixed with -*men* to mean a group of people with the same name or characteristics of that person, and we call this the "plural reading." The plural reading is in contrast to the "collective" interpretation (a group anchored by an individual).

Not only is there a "plurality" interpretation of -*men*, there are also facts that do not immediately follow from the claim that -*men* is simply a collective marker. For instance, even though a "collective" -*men* can be suffixed to a definite expression taking the form of a proper name or a pronoun, this is not possible with the definite expressions consisting of a demonstrative.

(54) a. *zhe-ge/na-ge   ren-men
           this-CL/that-CL person-MEN
           'this/that person and the others'

      b. *ni-de na-ge   penyou-men
           your that-CL   friend-MEN
           'that friend of yours and the others'

These expressions, with -*men* attached to a definite expression containing a demonstrative-classifier [*zhe*/*na-ge*+ N] 'this/that + C1 + N,' intended to mean 'this/that person and the others,' are not acceptable. Under an analysis that intends to capture the distribution of -*men* in terms of the "collective" interpretation, it is difficult to define the difference between a proper name and a demonstrative expression 'this/that N' responsible for their different possibilities with -*men*.

Another puzzling fact about the collective analysis of -*men* is the seemingly complicated set of restrictions on the co-occurrence of a [number + classifier] expression. Recall that one of the arguments for the collective analysis of -*men* is the incompatibility of -*men* with a [number + classifier] expression. However, not all of the facts are in line with this argument. For instance, even though 'three-CL he-*men*' in (55a) is unacceptable, we find that 'he-*men* three-CL' is acceptable in (55b). Moreover, in a sentence like (55c), which is comparable to (55b) except for the replacement of the pronoun with a common noun, the use of -*men* becomes unacceptable again.

(55) a. *wo qing   san-ge   ta-men chi-fan.
           I   invite three-CL he-MEN eat-rice
           'I invited three them for a meal.'

      b. wo qing   ta-men   san-ge   (haizi) chi-fan.
           I   invite he-MEN   three-CL child   eat-rice
           'I invited them three-CL (children) for a meal.'

    c. *wo qing   pengyou-men san-ge   (ren)   chi-fan.
       I   invite friend-MEN   three-CL person eat-rice
       'I invited three friends for a meal.'

To complete the paradigm, (55d) has the same word order as (55a) and is not acceptable either.

(55)   d. *wo qing   san-ge   pengyou-men chifan.
         I   invite three-CL friend-MEN   eat
         'I invited three friends for a meal.'

What adds to the puzzle is that, when a proper name followed by a [number + classifier] expression is suffixed with *-men*, it only yields the collective reading – a group of people consisting of the person denoted by the proper name and other people related to him. It does not have the plural reading, denoting people with the same characteristics or the same name:

(55)   e. wo qing   Xiao-Qiang-men/xiaozhang-men san-ge   (ren)   chifan.[20]
         I   invite Xiao-Qiang-MEN/Principal-MEN   three-CL person eat
         'I invited Xiao-Qiang/the Principal and two others (in the group) for a meal.'
         Not: 'I invited three Principals/three people all named/all with the
         characteristics of Xiao Qiang.'

By contrast, (55f) is not acceptable at all, under either reading:

(55)   f. *wo qing   san-ge   Xiao Qiang-men/xiaozhang-men chifan.
         I   invite three-CL Xiao Qiang-MEN/Principal-MEN   eat
         'I invited Xiao Qiang/the Principal and two others (in the group) for a meal.'
         'I invited three principals/three people all named/all with the characteristics
         of Xiao Qiang.'

The behavior of *-men* can be summarized as follows:

(56)   P1: *-men* is suffixed to pronouns, proper names, and some common nouns.

        P2: Common nouns with *-men* must be interpreted as definite.

        P3: Attachment of *-men* to proper names yields two different interpretations, "plural" or "collective."

        P4: A pronoun/proper name with *-men* can be followed, but not preceded, by a number phrase. In the cases with proper names, only the "collective" reading

[20] If a speaker prefers to use *Xiao Qiang-tamen* in place of *Xiao Qiang-men*, this sentence is not acceptable. Address terms such as *xiaozhang* 'Principal' are also regarded as proper names: they are common nouns used as proper names. Not surprisingly, when used as a proper name, *xiaozhang-men san-ge* is possible as a collective (cf. the fourth property in (56)).

is possible when followed by a number phrase. Common nouns with *-men* do not occur with a number phrase.[21]

These facts do not follow from an account that analyzes *-men* as a collective morpheme. The unacceptability of *-men* suffixed to a definite expression with a demonstrative is not expected. The seemingly chaotic co-occurrence restrictions on a number phrase with *-men* are not captured. Moreover, the fact that an N-*men* expression can co-occur with the distributive marker *dou* (as in *xuesheng-men dou likai le* 'Each of the students has left.') raises questions about what exactly "collective" means. Recall that an argument for the "collective" status of *-men* is that a number phrase cannot occur with N-*men*. A collective group is not concerned with or compatible with individuals. The use of the distributive marker *dou* must involve individuals. For instance, an example like *tamen liangge dou jiehun le* 'Them two have been married' must be about two marriages, rather than the two of them being married to each other. The distributive use of *dou* with N-*men* directly contradicts the semantic account of a "collective" marker. On the other hand, there are facts suggesting that *-men* may be a plural morpheme. It can be attached to a proper name in the same way a true plural morpheme makes a plural proper name interpreted like a common noun (the plural reading). When it is attached to a common noun, it creates a plural entity.

8.4.2   Plural feature as head of NumP

Rather than relying on the "meaning" difference between "plural" and "collective," Li (1999) argues that the behavior of *-men*, in contrast to the English *-s*, can be more adequately captured in terms of structures.[22] Both *-men* and *-s* are generated in the Number head position.[23] An English nominal expression with *-s*

---

[21] Iljic (1994: 93) notes that there do exist cases where a number phrase precedes N-*men*, such as *ni-men si-wei taitai xiaojie-men* 'you four mesdames and mesdemoiselles' (McCawley, personal communication). Iljic also notes that this is a case of double apposition: *si-wei* is apposed to *nimen*, both being in turn (after a prosodic pause) referred to by *taitai xiaojie-men*. This contrasts with the expressions discussed in the text, which are quite acceptable without a pause. Further note that the said pattern is quite limited. It is mostly used when addressing the hearers directly. The following sentence, for instance, is not possible:

(i)   *wo kan-guo ta-men si-wei   taitai xiaojie-men.
       I   see-GUO them   four-CL Mrs.   lady-MEN
       'I saw them four mesdames/mesdemoiselles.'

[22] Feng and Tsai (2006) argue that prosody also plays an important role in the distribution of *-men*.

[23] Alternatively, it is possible that *-s* is generated with a noun and is raised to the Number projection to check the plural features or simply Agrees with the plural feature (cf. the

has the structure in (57) and a Chinese nominal expression with *-men* has the structure in (58). The only difference between the two lies in the absence of a Classifier projection in English and the presence of one in Chinese:

(57)

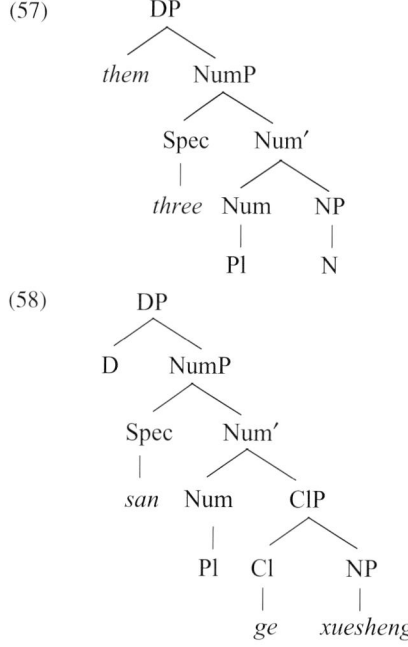

(58)

In both structures, a Plural feature appears as the Number head.[24] The Plural feature needs to be realized (or checked). In English, it is no problem for the Plural feature to be realized in N[25] (either N moves up to Num or the Plural feature lowers to N, if lowering is possible). In Chinese, however, the Plural feature cannot be realized in N because of the Head Movement Constraint: the Classifier head intervenes between N and Num. The plural feature is instead realized in D. In other words, while *-s* is realized on common nouns generated under the N node in English, *-men*

---

notion of Agree in Chomsky 2000, 2001). Also see Borer (2005) for *-s* being related to the Classifier projection.

[24] This contrasts with the quantity denoting expression [number + classifier + noun], where a number such as 'three' occupies the head Num position.

[25] Nothing prevents the Plural feature from being realized in D, or in both N and D. Further, note that English count nouns must have the plural suffix when denoting plurality, in contrast to the optionality of *-men* in Chinese. Therefore, the fact that a plural feature is not realized by an element base-generated in D in English may be due to the morphological requirement of the suffix *-s* needing an N as its host. Also see Borer (2005) claiming that *-s* has a classifier-like function.

in Chinese occurs with the elements in D. The claim that *-men* is realized on the elements in D captures all the facts in (56), as shown below.

Recall that pronouns and proper names are elements in (Spec of) D, where the plural feature can be realized. Accordingly, the structure in (62a–b) yields the ordering of number and classifier (and noun) expressions following a pronoun/proper name with *-men*.

(59) a. wo dui ta-men san-ge   (ren)   tebie   hao.
         I   to   them   three-CL person especially good
         'I am especially nice to them three.'

      b. wo dui Xiao Qiang-men san-ge   (ren)   tebie   hao.
         I   to   Xiao Qiang-MEN three-CL person especially good
         'I am especially nice to Xiao Qiang (them) three persons.'

      c. *wo dui san-ge   ta-men tebie   hao.
         I   to   three-CL them   especially good

      d. *wo dui san-ge   Xiao Qiang-men tebie   hao.
         I   to   three-CL Xiao Qiang-MEN especially good

A common noun is base-generated in N, with Number and Classifier preceding it. Such a noun cannot be affixed by *-men* because neither of them can move to the other, due to the intervening Classifier.

(60) a. *wo dui san-ge   xuesheng-men tebie   hao.
         I   to   three-CL student-MEN   especially good
         'I am especially nice to three students.'

      b. *wo dui xuesheng-men san-ge   (ren)   tebie   hao.
         I   to   student-MEN   three-CL person especially good

Example (60b) cannot be derived by moving a common noun from N to D because of the intervening Classifier. Examples (60a–b), with the presence of a classifier, are unacceptable regardless of whether the common noun is interpreted as indefinite or definite.

Nonetheless, a classifier need not be present. When it is not present, a common noun can be moved to D, suffixed with *-men*, and interpreted as definite, as we have shown in Section 8.3. Such a definite N-*men* expression cannot be preceded or followed by a [number + classifier] expression.

This analysis captures all the properties listed in (P4) of (56) except the exclusive collective reading for proper names followed by a number phrase. That reading will become clear after the discussion on the third property (P3), which concerns the ambiguity of proper names. A proper name can be base-generated in D to refer to a designated entity. In addition, it can function like a common noun, base-generated in N, denoting an entity/entities with the same name (*I met two Bills at the party.*

I like the Bill you like) or denoting some one(s) with the same characteristics. For instance, the proper name *A-Q* (a famous character in works by the Modern Chinese writer Lu Xun) can mean the kind of persons with the characteristics of A-Q, as in *He will be an A-Q* (cf. *He will be an Einstein* in English). When a proper name is generated in D (referring to a designated entity), it can be suffixed with *-men*, because no other heads intervene between the two. The collective reading (the particular individual and others in the group) is derived. When a proper name is generated in N (denoting the relevant characteristics) and moved to D, it yields the plurality reading of a group of people with the same characteristics. A proper name with *-men* is therefore ambiguous. However, the ambiguity is lost when a number phrase occurs (cf. (59b)). The lack of ambiguity is explained by our earlier account of why common nouns with *-men* must be interpreted as definite. Recall that, for an N to be suffixed with *-men*, a classifier cannot intervene. This suggests that, if a proper name is suffixed with *-men* and followed by a number phrase, the proper name should be generated in D rather than N. That is, *Xiao-Qiang-men san-ge* should not have the common noun-plural reading, referring to three people with the same characteristics of Xiao-Qiang. Replacing *Xiao-Qiang* with *Xiaozhang* 'Principal,' a common noun used as a proper name, also fails to bring out the common noun-plural interpretation. It only has the interpretation of 'Principal and the others in his group.' Moreover, this also captures the oddity of (61a–b), which use the name of famous people not present now. These cases strongly favor the interpretation of likeness in characteristics – common noun-plural reading, which is not available when a number phrase appears.

(61)   a. ??wo dui A-Q-men san/mei-ge   (dou) you   pianhao
          I   to   A-Q-MEN three/every-CL   all   have preference
          'I especially like A-Q them three/all.'

       b. ??wo dui Aiyinsitan-men san/mei-ge   (dou) hen   jingzhong.
          I   to   Einstein-MEN   three/every-CL all   very respect
          'I am very respectful of Einstein them three/all.'

In brief, if *-men* is realized on a nominal element in D, the properties in (56) are captured. This contrasts with a commonly recognized plural morpheme such as *-s* in English, which is suffixed to N. In the latter case, the plural nominal does not have to be definite because the N does not have to be raised to D to realize the plural feature. The difference between realizing the Plural feature in N in English and realizing it in D in Chinese is derived from the difference in nominal structures between the two languages: Chinese, not English, has a classifier morpheme occupying the head of a Classifier phrase. This structural difference also accommodates the fact that the order *three students* is possible in English, but in Chinese is unacceptable (60a). Furthermore, it follows that *(the) students three* is not possible in English,

either. As for pronouns, normally base-generated in D, -*s* cannot be suffixed to the
D pronoun in English (the affix -*s* requires its host to be an N). A number phrase
can follow a pronoun, because a NumP follows a D.

Thus, the so-called collective -*men* is not a peculiar morpheme whose distribution is random. A very straightforward account based on structural differences
captures the differences between -*men* in Chinese and a "regular" plural morpheme
such as -*s* in English. Both -*men* and -*s* are realizations of the plural feature under
Num. The latter is realized by an element in N, and the former in D. An intervening Classifier prevents an N from realizing the plural feature. This analysis
not only captures many interesting facts regarding nominal expressions in English
and Chinese but also enables us to define the minimal differences between the
two kinds of plural morphemes. Languages with a "collective" morpheme and
those with a "regular" plural morpheme vary only by one structural difference: the
presence/absence of a head Classifier.

8.4.3   *Proper name + pronoun + demonstrative*

Finally, the analysis of -*men* in Chinese can also help us decide on the
proper structure for more complicated nominal expressions. Recall that a nominal
expression in Chinese may have more than one element occurring above the NumP:
a proper name, a pronoun, and/or a demonstrative. With the behavior of -*men*
clarified, we are now in a better position to identify the structure for this form.

Let us begin with the longest case: those with proper names, pronouns, and
demonstratives. First of all, they must occur in the order [proper name + pronoun + demonstrative]. Second, nothing can intervene between any two of these
expressions. Individually, demonstratives can have their own plural form -*xie* (*zhexie*/*na-xie*) or be followed by a number + classifier (*zhe*/*na san-ge* 'these/those
three-CL'). They do not prevent a preceding pronoun from occurring with -*men*:

(62)   a. ta-men na-xie haizi
          they   those   children
          'them those children'

       b. ni-men zhe   san-ge   langutou
          you   these three-CL lazybones
          'you these three lazybones'

A proper name, however, does not occur with -*men* when a pronoun or a demonstrative appears:

(63)   a. *Xiao Qiang-men zhe/na   san-ge   langutou
          Xiao Qiang-MEN these/those three-CL lazybones

b. *Xiao Qiang-men tamen san-ge
   Xiao Qiang-MEN they   three-CL

Moreover, when followed by a plural *zhe-xie* 'these,' *na-xie* 'those,' *zhe/na san-ge*
'these/those three,' a pronoun must be in the plural form, regardless of whether or
not a proper name also occurs:

(64)   a. (Zhangsan) ta-men na-xie xuesheng
          Zhangsan they   those student
          '(Zhangsan) them those students'
       b. *(Zhangsan) ta na-xie xuesheng[26]
          Zhangsan he those   student
          'Zhangsan him those students'

In general, there seems to be agreement in number among all the elements, except
for the cases when a proper name and a pronoun co-occur: it is possible to have a
singular proper name with a pronoun attached with *-men*.

(65)   Zhangsan ta-men xuesheng
         Zhangsan they   student
         'Zhangsan them students'

In short, in the form [proper name + pronoun + demonstrative], the pronoun
and the demonstrative must agree in number but the proper name need not. The
pronoun, but not the proper name, can be attached to *-men* when a demonstrative
occurs. Recall that nothing can intervene between any two of the three elements.
Thus, we suggest that the form [proper name + pronoun + demonstrative] has the
structure below, where the demonstrative occupies the D position, the pronoun is
adjoined to D, and the proper name is in Spec of D:

(66)

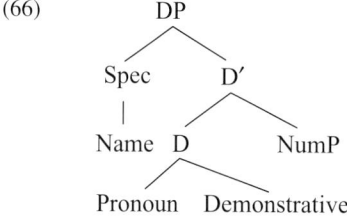

This structure allows *-men* to be adjoined to the pronoun when the plural feature
(*-men*) and a demonstrative both occur. The plural feature can move to D. A
demonstrative, morphologically, does not take the *-men* suffix. However, the plural

---

[26] This is possible when the pronoun is interpreted as a possessor: *Zhangsan ta (de) naxie*
xuesheng 'those students of (Zhangsan) his.'

feature can be realized on the pronoun that is also in D. The proper name is in the Spec of D and does not occur with *-men* when either a pronoun or a demonstrative occurs.

This analysis may also enable us to understand some variations on the facts presented so far. We observed one such variation in note 19: there are speakers who do not like a proper name followed by a number phrase directly. A pronoun and/or a demonstrative needs to intervene in such cases. Consequently, these speakers do not allow a proper name suffixed with *-men* to be followed by a number phrase, even though they do allow a proper name to be suffixed with *-men* when it is used as a common noun (see the discussions regarding (59)–(61)). It is possible that there is a change toward more consistency in progress: when a proper name is used as a common noun, it is base-generated in N. However, a true proper name is base-generated in Spec of D. When it is in Spec of D, it is not suffixed with the plural suffix (assuming that *-men* is only attached to the elements in D, as we have shown so far). This may also be related to the fact that the sequence [proper name + pronoun], occupying the Spec of D and the D positions, is very commonly used in colloquial speech. Examples like (67) are frequently found in colloquial speech.

(67) a. Zhangsan ta   shenme shihou lai?
          Zhangsan he what   time   come
          'When is Zhangsan him coming?'

      b. wo gen   Zhangsan ta chao-le   yi-jia.
         I   with Zhangsan he quarrel-LE one-fight
         'I had a quarrel with Zhangsan.'

8.5   Summary and some empirical complications

Nouns in Chinese are generally "bare" because they lack inflection for number or any other grammatical feature, nor do they require determiners. On the other hand, nouns in this language often occur with classifiers. Many interesting discussions have appeared in the literature on whether Chinese, being a classifier language, can have plural marking, and whether D and Num are syntactically represented. We showed that analyzing Chinese noun phrases as DPs, like those in non-classifier languages such as English, allows us to capture the facts regarding distribution, interpretation, constituency, and order. The presence of D is manifested in the distribution of different types of noun phrases. The projection of Classifier and number phrases helps us account for the complex behavior of the collective/plural morpheme *-men* in Chinese, as

compared to the plural morpheme *-s* in English. Therefore, classifiers and plural marking are not always in complementary distribution. The distribution of
these elements follows from the structure of DPs and the Head Movement Constraint. A classifier language like Chinese is therefore not much different from
a non-classifier language like English. It is possible to maintain a one-to-one
mapping between syntax and semantics cross-linguistically: the same structures
yield the same meanings and the same meanings are derived from the same
structures.

The proposal that Chinese noun phrases should be represented as DPs is promis-
ing. It may also help us sort out the complications in interpreting expressions of
the form [number + classifier + noun]. We conclude this chapter with a discussion
of this issue.

In Section 8.2, we distinguished expressions of the form [number + classifier + noun] ("number expressions") into two types: quantity-denoting expressions and indefinite individual-denoting expressions. The former, not the latter,
can occur in subject or topic positions – there is a prohibition against indefinite
subjects/topics. It seems uncontroversial that a topic should be definite unless
used contrastively. However, it is less clear how to formulate the indefinite subject constraint. An accompanying issue is the range of possible distributions and
interpretations of number expressions. Below, we review the issues and show
how the analysis in this chapter can accommodate the relevant wide-ranging sets
of data.

8.5.1   Non-quantity indefinite nominals in subject position

Lee (1986) observes that a number expression may occur in the subject
position in a variety of contexts: (a) when it is used referentially by modifying the
NP with a vivid description:

(68)   yige [gaogao shoushou] de jinfa   guniang ganggang lai   zhao ni.
         one   tall   thin   DE blonde girl   just.now come find you
         'A tall, thin blonde girl came to look for you just now.'

(b) when it occurs in a sentential subject:

(69)   a. [san-ge   pengyou chi(*-le) fan] duo hao.
          three-CL friend   eat-LE   rice very good
          'It would be very nice for three friends to have a meal.'

       b. [liang-ge xiaohai zou (*-le) gang-suo] hen   weixian.
          two-CL   children walk-LE   steel-rope very dangerous
          'It is dangerous for two children to walk on the tightrope.'

(c) when it occurs as part of a hypothetical clause:

(70) a. [ruguo yi-ge   ren   bu gou],   jiu   zhao wu-ge ren   qu.
          if   one-CL person not enough then find five-CL person go
          'If one person is not enough, then find five persons.'

      b. [yi-ge   nuren   jie-le-hun], keneng hui xiang sheng xiaohai.
          one-CL woman marry-LE   perhaps will want bear child
          '(If) a woman gets married, (she) will perhaps want to bear children.'

Or (d) when it appears to be "licensed" by modals and adverbs:[27]

(71) a. wu-ge ren   *(zhunneng)   wancheng renwu.
          five-CL person definitely.can complete task
          'Five persons can definitely complete the task.'

      b. liang-ge ren   *(keyi) chi shi-wan fan.
          two-CL   person   can   eat ten-CL rice
          'Two persons can eat ten bowls of rice.'

      c. yi-ge   nanren *(yinggai) yonggan.
          one-CL man   should   brave
          'A man should be brave.'

Fan (1985) also discusses several instances that seem to challenge the claim that
a subject cannot be indefinite. He gave the following generalizations concerning
when a non-definite (*wuding*) subject is possible:

(72) a. The predicates are mainly verbs, not adjectives.

      b. An intransitive verb needs to take a complex form. Example (73b) below is better
          than (73a).

      c. Acceptability varies with different styles of language.

(73) a. *yi-zhi   qingwa tiao-le.[28]
          one-CL frog   jump-LE
          'A frog jumped.'

---

[27] In addition, *dou* licenses a number expression in the subject position as in (i):

(i)   san-ge ren   *(dou) qu-le.
        three person   all   go-LE
        'The three persons all left.'

The number phrase associated with *dou* is interpreted as definite. See Liu (1990) for the
compatibility between *dou* and G-specific quantifiers.

[28] Example (73a) is actually acceptable when uttered in appropriate circumstances: a
person is looking at a group of frogs lying silently and without a movement. Sud-
denly, a frog makes a jump. This person can report this situation by using (73a).
This is expected under an account based on judgment types, as will be discussed
in the text shortly. Therefore, the issue is not a matter of simple vs. complex form
but is related to the readiness of imagining a situation when an event is noted and
reported.

b. yi-zhi qingwa tiao jin   shui-li le.
   one-CL frog   jump enter water-in LE
   'A frog jumped into the water.'

Zhu (1988) re-examines Fan's examples and notes that almost all the examples cited in Fan are from journalistic newspaper writings. The only examples representing speech are those in (74):

(74)   a. hei! yi xiaohai pa   shang qu-le.
          hey one child   climb up   go-LE
          'Hey, a child climbed up.'

       b. tui   men jin qu, yi laotou   tang zai chuang shang.
          push door in go one old.man lie at bed   on
          'Push the door and enter, (you see) an old man lying on the bed.'

Zhu adds some more examples (p. 61):

(75)   kuai lai   kan, liang mao dajia-le.
          quick come look two   cat fight-LE
          'Come look quick! Two cats are fighting.'

The characteristics of these examples, according to Zhu (p. 61), are (i) they are very short, (ii) they express unexpected new discoveries, and (iii) they depend on the current scene or a known knowledge background. Zhu further notes that such usage is often found in children's story books with pictures.

Within recent generative studies, Shyu (1995), following Kuroda's (1992) studies, notes that there is a distinction between stage-level and individual-level predicates (Carlson 1977, Diesing 1992, Kratzer 1989): stage-level predicates allow indefinite subjects but individual-level predicates do not.[29]

(76)   a. yi-ge   ren   lai-le/zheng   zai nian shu.
          one-CL person come-LE/right at   read book
          'A man came/is reading.'

       b. *yi-ge   ren   hen congming/gao.
          one-CL person very clever/tall
          'A/One man is very smart/tall.'

Extending Kuroda's studies further, Shyu discusses the difference between a root clause and a non-root clause. A root clause distinguishes between stage-level and individual-level predicates in the acceptability of an indefinite subject

---

[29] Sentences like (76a) are marked as acceptable by Shyu (1995), even though they are marked as unacceptable in some other literature (for instance, Lee 1986, Tsai 1994a). See the discussion later in the text for such variations in judgment.

(see (76a–b), (77a)); whereas a non-root clause, represented by a conditional clause in (77b) and Lee's examples in (70a–b), allows an indefinite subject.

(77) a. *yi-zhi   da   xiang   bizi   hen   chang.
           one-CL   big   elephant nose   very   long
           'A big elephant, nose is long.'

      b. ruguo   yizhi   da   xiang   bizi   hen   chang,   na   yiding   hen   keai.
          if   one   big   elephant nose   very   long   then   definitely   very   lovely
          'If an elephant's trunk is very long, then (it) must be lovely.'

What are the commonalities among the generalizations presented so far and how should we account for them? We show below that different types of number expressions need to be distinguished – a main point advocated in this chapter – and that all of them are accommodated by our analysis.

Empirically, it is clear that there is a contrast between a stage-level predicate and an individual-level predicate. To capture the difference, one option is to pursue the notion, along the lines of Tsai (1996), that an indefinite nominal is a variable which needs to be bound by an operator (Heim 1982). A sentence with a stage-level predicate, which expresses an event, contains an event operator; a sentence with an individual-level predicate does not. An indefinite subject nominal with a stage-level predicate can then be bound by an event operator, in the way that an existential closure licenses an indefinite nominal within a VP (Diesing 1992). This may also account for the fact that a conditional clause allows an indefinite subject NP, because a conditional clause is generally assumed to contain a necessity operator. Similarly, a modal may also provide a modality operator and allow an indefinite subject.

Such an analysis would predict that all sentences with stage-level predicates should allow indefinite nominals in subject position, as should conditional clauses and sentences with modals. However, as will be demonstrated, counterexamples to each of these predictions exist.

Let us begin with the examples containing stage-level predicates. Speakers generally agree that the addition of the existential *you* 'have' makes a clear difference in acceptability. That is, a number expression in the subject position is "saved" by *you* – the typical indefinite subject constraint.[30]

(78) a. ??(you)   yi-ge   ren   kan-guo   ta-de   dianying.
           have   one-CL   person   see-GUO   his   movie
           'A person has seen his movie.'

---

[30] Along the lines of distinguishing quantity vs. indefinite expressions, the sentences without *you* are acceptable if they are answers to a question of quantity, such as *ji-ge ren kanguo ta-de dianying?* 'How many people have seen his movie?' and *ji-ge ren bu kan ta-de dianying?* 'How many people did/will not see his movie?'

b. ??(you) yi-ge   ren   meiyou/bu   kan ta-de dianying.
    have one-CL person not-have/not see his movie
    'A person did not/does(will) not see his movie.'

c. ??(you) yi-ge   xuesheng na   shihou zai xuexiao.
    have one-CL student   that time   at school
    'A student is at school at that time.'

Modals do not seem to help in the following cases, in contrast to the instances we saw earlier (such as (71b–c)).

(79) a. ??yi-ge   ren   hui/keneng kan ta-de dianying.
       one-CL man will/may   see his   movie
       'A person will/may see his move.'

    b. ??(you) yi-ge   ren   keneng meiyou/bu   kan na   zhong dianying.
        have one-CL person may   not-have/not see that kind movie
        'A person might not have seen/may not see that kind of movie.'

    c. ??(you) yi-ge   xuesheng na   shihou hui/keneng zai xuexiao.
        have one-CL student   that time   will/may   at school
        'A student will/may be at school at that time.'

The question is why some sentences with stage-level predicates are acceptable with indefinite subjects but some others are not. A solution can be found in Kuroda's (1992) and Shyu's (1995) works, which incorporate the notion of thetic and categorical judgment.[31] A thetic judgment is expressed by a sentence that describes what is perceived by the speaker. According to Kuroda, it is a single cognitive act that recognizes the existence of an entity or event. A sentence of thetic judgment expresses "a simple recognition of the existence of an actual situation" (p. 23), "a direct response to the perceptual cognition of an actual situation, a perceptual intake of information about an actual situation" (p. 22). A sentence expressing a thetic judgment can have an indefinite (but referential) NP as its subject. The referent of the NP is only relevant to the unique current perceptual cognition. It is temporary.

A sentence can be ambiguous between describing a perceived situation (thetic judgment) and expressing a categorical judgment, which consists of two cognitive acts: the recognition of the Subject (Subject in the logical sense) and the acknowledgement of the Predicate of a Subject (p. 20). Such a logical Subject cannot be indefinite.

The sentences in (78)–(79) are not quite acceptable without *you* because none of them describe situations that are directly perceived. A speaker generally does

---

[31] Xu (1996) discusses "assertive" and "descriptive" sentences: the former might correspond to the sentences expressing categorical judgment, and the latter those of thetic judgment.

not directly observe someone else's earlier experiences, inaction,[32] future plans, etc. These sentences are quite odd when embedded under a perception verb such as 'look':

(80) a. *ni kan(-kan), yi-ge ren   kan-guo ta-de dianying.
    you look-look one-CL person see-GUO his movie
    '(Take a) look, a person has seen his movie.'

  b. *ni kan(-kan), yi-ge ren   meiyou/bu kan na-zhong dianying.
    you look-look one-CL person not-have/not see that-CL movie
    '(Take a) look, a person did not/does(will) not see that kind of movie.'

  c. *ni kan(-kan), yi-ge xuesheng na shihou zai xuexiao.
    you look-look one-CL student that time at school
    '(Take a) look, a student is at school at that time.'

  d. *ni kan(-kan), yi-ge ren hui/keneng kan ta-de dianying.
    you look-look one-CL man will/may see his movie
    '(Take a) look, a person will/may see his movie.'

In contrast, a speaker can directly observe someone's coming or reading (76a). A sentence expressing a thetic judgment is a direct response to the perceptual cognition of an actual situation. A sentence with an individual-level predicate, which denotes permanent properties of an individual, does not express a thetic judgment. This captures the intuition that individual-level predicates do not allow indefinite subjects.

A sentence containing a stage-level predicate does not always describe a situation that has been perceived. For instance, the following examples are not direct observations of situations that are reported. Rather, they express Predication relations. (*Zhangsan* is the Topic (Subject in Kuroda's term) and the stage-level predicate is Predicate of the Topic/Subject.)

(81) a. Zhangsan zuijin zenmeyang, hui-bu-hui lai   zher?
    Zhangsan lately how   will-not-will come here
    'How is Zhangsan lately? Will he come?'

  b. Zhangsan zao jiu lai-le.
    Zhangsan early then come-LE
    'Zhangsan came quite early.'

---

[32] Under certain circumstances, it is possible to observe someone's not doing something. For instance, one can perceive a situation of someone's not seeing a movie in this situation: everyone in a room is paying attention to the movie being shown, except for one person who lowers his head and reads his own book. Under such circumstances, it is possible to say *(ni kan(-kan), yi-ge ren meiyou zai kan dianying* '(You look), one person is not watching the movie.'

The substitution of *Zhangsan* with an indefinite is impossible in (81a–b). The ambiguity of sentences containing stage-level predicates – describing a perceived situation or not – may account for the variations in acceptability judgments: if the sentences are interpreted as expressing thetic judgment (describing a perceived situation), an indefinite subject is acceptable; if they express a categorical judgment (a Subject–Predicate relation), the subject cannot be indefinite.

This account also captures Zhu's generalization, since journalistic newspaper writings tend to report perceived situations/events. They are writings describing the reporter's or the witness's observation of events or occurrences. Thus, an indefinite subject is commonly used. The same is true with children's story books with pictures, which generally describe the pictures on the pages. The only examples from speech discussed by Zhu are those in (74)–(75), which are typical sentences describing perceived situations/events. Examples (74a–b) describe the scenes perceived. Example (75), with the verb *kan* 'look,' asks the hearer to observe the scene. Indeed, the canonical cases allowing an indefinite subject are those beginning with the expression *(ni) kan* 'look' or embedded under perception verbs such as 'see/dream':

(82)   kan, yi-pian feng   ye   diao xialai le.
         look one-CL maple leave fall   down LE
         'Look, a maple leave fell down.'

(83)   wo kandao/mengdao (de shi) yi-zhi   mao zai pa   shu.
         I   see/dream   DE be   one-CL cat   at   climb tree
         'I saw/dreamed that a cat was climbing a tree; What I saw/dreamed
         was that a cat was climbing a tree.'

As expected, topicalization is not possible in these cases when the subject is indefinite:

(84)   *wo kandao/mengdao (de shi), (na-ke) shu, yi-zhi   mao zai pa.
         I   see/dream   DE be   that-CL tree one-CL cat   at   climb
         'What I saw was/I saw that tree, a cat was climbing.'

In contrast, the following sentences are worse than (82)–(83) because they do not describe direct perceptions of situations. All the sentences are more acceptable if *you* 'have' occurs.

(85)   a. ??wo renwei/xiangxin yi-zhi   mao na   shihou zai pa   shu.
            I   think/believe   one-CL cat   that time   at   climb tree
            'I thought/believe that a cat was climbing a tree at that time.'
       b. ??wo xiang zhidao yi-zhi   mao na   shihou shi-bu-shi zai pa   shu.
            I   want know   one-CL cat   that time   be-not-be   at   climb tree
            'I want to know if a cat was climbing a tree at that time.'

  c. ??yinwei yi-zhi mao pa-guo shu, suoyi ta hen jinzhang.
    because one-CL cat climb-GUO tree so he very nervous
    'Because a cat has climbed a tree, he is very nervous.'

Similarly, this analysis captures Lee's observation that modifying an NP with a vivid description makes an indefinite expression acceptable in a subject position: vivid descriptions make the relevant sentence easier to interpret as a report on a perceived situation. As expected, such a vividly modified NP does not occur in a sentence containing an individual-level predicate.

(86) *yi-ge gaogao shoushou de jinfa guniang hen congming/ershi sui.
     one tall thin DE blonde girl very clever/twenty.years old
     'A tall, thin blonde girl is very clever/twenty years old.'

A further application of an analysis based on the notion of "thetic judgment" concerns the possibility of an indefinite subject in non-root clauses. First note that, contra the claim by Lee and Shyu that non-root clauses allow an indefinite subject (see (69)–(70) and (77a–b)), there are quite a few examples disallowing an indefinite subject in non-root clauses, as will be illustrated shortly. Moreover, if we go through all the examples discussed so far, we note that even though the notions of quantity interpretation and thetic judgment carried us a long way, they do not accommodate all the cases. We turn to these cases next.

8.5.2 *Non-root clauses, generic NPs*

   We have shown that a number expression can be a subject when it is a quantity-denoting expression or when the sentence expresses a thetic judgment. However, there are cases that do not fall under these two categories, such as the ones below:

(87) [yi-ge nuren jie-le-hun], keneng hui xiang sheng xiaohai.
    one-CL woman marry-LE perhaps will want bear child
    '(If) a woman gets married, (she) will perhaps want to bear children.'

(88) ruguo yi-zhi daxiang bizi hen chang, na yiding hen keai.
    if one-CL elephant nose very long then definitely very lovely
    'If an elephant's trunk is very long, then (it) must be lovely.'

Note that a conditional clause does not always license an indefinite subject NP:

(89) *ruguo yi-ge ren hen congming, wo (jiu) mashang
    if one-CL person very clever I then immediately
    qu zhao ta bangmang.
    go find him help
    'If a person is clever, I will go to find him to help (me) immediately.'

The question is what distinguishes (87)–(88) from (89). We would like to suggest that the number phrase in the former set, not the latter, is a generic expression. Note that the conditional clause in an example like (87) can be a relative clause without changing meaning:

(90)   yi-ge [[jie-le-hun] de nuren] keneng hui xiang sheng xiaohai.
         one   marry-LE DE woman perhaps will want   bear   child
         'A married woman perhaps will want to bear children.'

That the number phrase in (87) is a generic expression can be further illustrated by the fact that numbers other than 'one' change the acceptability of sentences:

(91)   *[san-ge   nuren   jie-le-hun], keneng hui xiang sheng xiaohai.
          three-CL woman marry-LE   perhaps will want   bear   child
          '(If) three women get married, (they) will perhaps want to bear children.'

Other examples fall into the same category. Example (88) and the following sentences are also examples of the generic use of the number phrase:

(92)   a. ruguo yi-ge   ren   zhong-le caipiao, ta hui biande hen fuyou.
           if   one-CL person hit-LE   lottery, he will become very rich
           'If a man wins the lottery, he will become very rich.'

       b. ruguo yi-ge   ren   hen congming dan bu yonggong, haishi
           if   one-CL person very smart   but not diligent   still
           meiyou   yong.
           not-have use
           'If a person is smart but not diligent, it still is no use.'

If we replace the number 'one' with 'two' or any other number, these sentences are not acceptable unless the existential *you* occurs before the number NP.

   In contrast, (89) does not have a generic interpretation. The indefinite subject needs to be supported by the existential *you*. Similarly, the following examples, including other conditionals headed by *jishi* 'even if' and *yaoshi* 'if,' require the use of *you* when the number phrase is not interpreted as generic or quantity:

(93)   a. ruguo *(you) yi-ge   ren   zai deng ta, ta jiu   dei
           if   have one-CL person at wait him he then should
           mashang   hui qu.
           immediately back go
           'If a person is waiting for him, he should go back immediately.'

       b. jishi   *(you) liang-ge ren   tai lan, women haishi neng
           even.though   have two-CL people too lazy we   still   can
           zuo wan   zhe-jian shi.
           do   finish this-CL   thing
           'Even though two people are too lazy, we still can finish doing this job.'

c. yaoshi *(you) yi-ge   ren   hen you qian,   women jiu
   if   have one-CL person very have money we   then
   qu zhao ta   zizhu.
   go find him sponsor
   'If a person is rich, we should go find him for sponsorship.'

Other adverbial clauses, such as time adverbials ('when,' 'before,' and 'after' clauses), also behave like conditionals. We will not elaborate further on this point.

With the possibilities of a generic interpretation clarified, we may conclude that number phrases in conditional clauses do not behave differently. They must be interpreted as quantity-denoting or generic; otherwise, they must be supported by existential *you*. Thus, the generalization is that a number phrase can be an individual-denoting indefinite only when it occurs in a sentence expressing thetic judgment. The clauses embedded under perception verbs accept indefinite subjects most easily because they are the typical cases of thetic judgment. Other types of subordinate clauses, such as the adjunct 'because,' 'although' clauses, and so forth are much harder to coerce into expressing thetic judgment; this explains their reluctance to accepting indefinite subjects.

The fact that an indefinite subject is possible inside a sentential subject can be captured in the same way: the subject in question must be either a quantity-denoting or a generic expression. Examples are (69a–b), repeated here.

(69) a. [san-ge   pengyou chi(*-le) fan] duo hao.
         three-CL friend   eat-LE   rice very good
         'It would be very nice for three friends to have a meal.'

      b. [liang-ge xiaohai zou(*-le) gang-suo] hen weixian.
         two-CL   child   walk-LE steel-rope very dangerous
         'It is dangerous for two children to walk on the tightrope.'

These number phrases are expressions of quantity: (69a) is acceptable under the interpretation that it is three friends eating together (rather than one person eating alone) that is nice and (69b) is acceptable under the interpretation that it is two children walking together on the tightrope (rather than one child alone) that is dangerous. Example (69b), for instance, does not have an interpretation like (94) where the number phrase denotes individuals that exist:

(94)   [you liang-ge xiaohai zou-zhe   gangsuo] hen weixian.
        have two-CL   child   walk-ZHE steel-rope very dangerous
        'It is dangerous that there are two children walking on the tightrope.'

A non-quantity, non-generic number phrase is not possible in the subject position
of a sentential subject:

(95) a. [yi-ge   ren   xia   qi]   hen wuliao.   – quantity
         one-CL person play chess very boring
         'It is boring for one person to play chess.'

      b. [yi-ge   gao-shou xia-cuo   qi]   hen bu keneng.   – generic
         one-CL high-hand play-wrong chess very not likely
         'It is unlikely for an expert to play chess wrong.'

In brief, it is not the distinction between root and non-root clauses that determines
the distribution of an indefinite subject. Examples of non-root 'because,' 'though'
clauses, and verb complement clauses all indicate that they do not behave differently from the root clauses. The apparent indefinite subject is actually interpreted
as a quantity or generic NP, just as in root clauses. The existential *you* is necessary
to make a non-quantity, non-generic reading available. The only contexts where
an indefinite subject is possible are in those sentences expressing thetic judgment.

The distinction between stage-level and individual-level predicates is only partially relevant. The more appropriate distinction is thetic judgment vs. categorical
judgment. A sentence with an individual-level predicate generally expresses categorical judgment. However, a sentence with a stage-level predicate may express
thetic or categorical judgment.

Relating this judgment distinction to our account of the distribution and interpretation of number phrases, we may adopt the structural difference suggested by
Kuroda (1992) for these two types of sentences. Kuroda suggests that thetic and
categorical judgment have different syntactic structures, reflected in the use of
different Case markers in Japanese. The subject of a sentence expressing categorical judgment is higher than the one expressing thetic judgment. It is possible that
the latter is in a lexically governed position or is bound by an operator situated
between the two types of subject positions. Either choice can be reduced to the
licensing of an empty D in a DP – the structure proposed for number expressions
in this chapter.

9

Anaphora

Much research in grammatical theory has shown that syntax plays an important role (together with semantics and pragmatics) in governing the possible referential meanings of nominal expressions. Three factors enter into the proper characterization of the syntax of anaphora: (a) the nature of the nominal expression in question (whether it needs a linguistic antecedent or not); (b) the structural relation between the expression and its antecedent if it has one; and (c) the nature of the antecedent itself.

In the generative literature, a distinction is made between three NP-types on the basis of their ability or inability to directly refer: anaphors, pronouns, and R-expressions. In Chinese, reflexive expressions like *ziji* 'self' and combinations of pronouns + *ziji* like *taziji* 'himself,' *nimenziji* 'yourselves,' etc. are anaphors since they are incapable of directly denoting entities in the outside world, but must each rely on a linguistic antecedent for their reference to be established. Personal pronouns like *ta* 'he/she' or *tamen* 'they' may be deictic (used without antecedents) or anaphoric (requiring antecedents). Other noun phrases (*Zhangsan, zhe-ge xiaohai* 'this child,' etc.) are R(eferential)-expressions, which do not require an antecedent for their reference to be established.

The possibility and location of an antecedent for a given expression is governed by structural principles, most prominently represented by the principles of *Binding Theory* in Chomsky (1981) and its subsequent developments. The "classical" version of Binding Theory includes the following three principles, known as Principles (or Conditions) A, B, and C:

(1) a. An anaphor is bound in its local domain. (Principle A)
    b. A pronominal is free in its local domain. (Principle B)
    c. An R-expression is free. (Principle C)

An antecedent for a given noun phrase (whether an anaphor or a pronominal) may be *referential*, denoting a definite entity (e.g., *John, zhe-ben shu* 'this book'), or it may be *quantificational*, ranging over sets (e.g., *mei-ge xiaohai* 'every child,' *na-ge xuesheng* 'which student'). Generally, when a pronoun takes a referential antecedent (as in (2)), it is said to be coreferential with that antecedent; when it takes a quantificational antecedent (as in (3)), it is said to be a variable bound by the quantificational antecedent:

(2)   John$_i$ thinks he$_i$ is smart.

(3)   Everybody$_i$ thinks he$_i$ is smart.

In (3), *he* is not coreferential with the group of persons in a given context that *everybody* ranges over, but its reference co-varies with the value of x, x a member of the group.

In 9.1 we will examine the basic facts of Chinese nominal expressions with particular emphasis on the conditions in (1). We will find that while Chinese is basically "well behaved" to some extent with respect to these principles, it also raises important issues that call for a closer look at the theory of anaphora. In Section 9.2 we discuss the problem raised by the long-distance binding of the reflexive *ziji* 'self.' The distinction between coreference and variable binding, together with the phenomenon of donkey anaphora, will be taken up in Section 9.3.

9.1   Binding Theory in Chinese

9.1.1   Reflexives and Principle A

In Chinese, a reflexive pronoun may take a "bare" (monomorphemic) form, *ziji* 'self,' or a "compound" form which combines *ziji* with a pronoun: *woziji* 'myself,' *niziji* 'yourself,' *taziji* 'himself,' *tamenziji* 'themselves,' and so forth. The behavior of the compound reflexive in Chinese is quite similar to its equivalent in English:

(4)   Zhangsan$_i$ zhidao Lisi$_j$ lao   piping   taziji$_{*i/j/*k}$.
         Zhangsan   know   Lisi incessantly criticize himself
         'Zhangsan knows that Lisi criticizes himself all the time.'

Like its counterpart in English, *taziji* 'himself' must take the local NP *Lisi* as its antecedent (represented by the fact that *Lisi* and *taziji* are coindexed with the subscript *j*). It cannot take the remote NP *Zhangsan* as its antecedent (hence *i), nor can it exist without an antecedent (hence *k). This pattern of behavior is predicted by Binding Principle A (BPA), as in (1a): an anaphor is bound in its local domain. The *k construal is unavailable, because BPA requires *taziji* to be bound (coindexed with an NP which c-commands it). The construal with *Lisi$_j$* is available, but not the construal with *Zhangsan$_i$*, because although binding obtains in both of these cases, in only the former does the NP bind the reflexive in its "local domain." Here, we shall take the "local domain" to be the "governing category (GC)" of Chomsky (1981) as revised in Huang (1983):[1]

(5) α is the governing category for β iff α is the minimal category containing β, a governor of β and a SUBJECT which, if β is an anaphor, is accessible to β.

The requirement of an "accessible subject" in the definition of a GC allows for an embedded subject anaphor to be bound by an NP in the immediately higher clause, but not beyond, as illustrated in (6):

(6)   [Zhangsan$_i$ zhidao [Lisi$_j$ renwei [taziji$_{*i/j/*k}$ zui congming]]].
       Zhangsan know   Lisi think   himself   most clever
       'Zhangsan knows that Lisi$_j$ thinks he$_j$ is the smartest.'

The compound reflexive *taziji* appears to be well behaved. When we turn to the bare reflexive *ziji*, however, the situation is rather different. First, in contrast to (4) and (6), the following sentences are ambiguous, permitting both a local and a long-distance construal of *ziji*:

(7)   Zhangsan$_i$ zhidao [Lisi$_j$ chang zai bieren mianqian piping   ziji$_{i/j}$].
       Zhangsan know   Lisi often at   others face   criticize self
       'Zhangsan$_i$ knows that Lisi$_j$ often criticizes him$_i$/himself$_j$ in the presence of others.'

(8)   Zhangsan$_i$ xiangxin [Lisi$_j$ renwei [ziji$_{i/j}$-de erzi zui   congming]].
       Zhangsan believe   Lisi think   self-DE son most clever
       'Zhangsan$_i$ believes Lisi$_j$ thinks that his$_{i/j}$ son is the smartest.'

This presents an important problem for BPA. The fact that *ziji* can be locally bound by *Lisi* suggests that it is an anaphor and not a pronoun, but then the possibility of a long-distance antecedent should be ruled out. It has been noted, however, that although local binding is *always* possible (provided that a local binder is available), long-distance binding is rather limited. For example, in contrast to (7)–(8) above, the following do not permit long-distance binding:

(9)   Zhangsan$_i$ zhidao [wo/ni$_j$ chang zai bieren mianqian piping   ziji$_{*i/j}$].
       Zhangsan knows I/you often at   others face   criticize self
       'Zhangsan$_i$ knows that I/you often criticize myself/yourself/*him$_i$ in the presence of others.'

---

[1] Chomsky (1986a) reformulated (5) with the notion of a closest CFC (complete functional complex) relative to 'BT-compatibility.' This amounts in effect to the following for (1a–b):

(a)   An anaphor is bound in the smallest CFC in which it can be bound.
(b)   A pronominal is free in the smallest CFC in which it can be free.

(10)   Zhangsan$_i$ xiangxin [wo/ni$_j$ renwei [ziji$_{*i/j}$-de erzi zui   congming]].
        Zhangsan believe   I/you think   self-DE   son most clever
        'Zhangsan$_i$ believes I/you think that my/your/*his$_i$ son is the smartest.'

Examples (9)–(10) differ from (7)–(8) only minimally in form, with the embedded subject *Lisi* having been replaced by *wo/ni* 'I/you.' This contrast, first observed by Y.-H. Huang (1984), illustrates what has come to be known as the 'Blocking Effect': in (9)–(10), a first/second-person local NP blocks long-distance binding by a third-person NP in the matrix clause (cf. also Huang, Huang, Teng, and Tiedeman 1984, Wang and Stillings 1984, Tang 1989). More generally, the generalization emerged that long-distance binding is possible only if the long-distance antecedent agrees with all local and intermediate potential antecedents in "phi-features" (person, number, and gender features), but is blocked otherwise. Thus, the following is also an example of blocking, where the matrix and embedded subjects do not agree in person:

(11)   ni$_i$ zhidao [wo$_j$ chang zai bieren mianqiang piping   ziji$_{*i/j}$].
        you know   I   often at others face   criticize self
        'You know that I often criticize myself/*you in the presence of others.'

(12)   ni$_i$ xiangxin [wo$_j$ renwei [ziji$_{*i/j}$-de erzi zui   congming]].
        you believe   I   think   self-DE   son most clever
        'You believe I think that my/*your son is the smartest.'

Another problem presented by the bare reflexive is that it can be *free*, without any linguistic binder at all.

(13)   zhe nanran yiding dui ziji you yisi,   buran   weishenme
        this man   must   to self have interest otherwise why
        lao   wang zher kan?
        always to   here look
        'This man must be interested in me; otherwise why would he keep looking this way?'

As pointed out by Yu (1992), however, a "free" *ziji* is not freely interpreted, but must be specifically interpreted as referring to the speaker, as the translation above shows.

Thus, the bare *ziji* may be unbound or long-distance bound, in violation of Principle A, but only under specific conditions. This problem has been the topic of much recent research, and will be the subject of our discussion in Section 9.2.

9.1.2   Pronouns and Principle B

Pronouns contrast sharply with reflexives: they have to be free in their governing categories, in accordance with Principle B. Thus, in contrast with (4), replacement of *taziji* with the pronoun *ta* gives an opposite pattern of possibilities:

(14)   Zhangsan$_i$ zhidao Lisi$_j$ lao   piping   ta$_{i/*j/k}$.
        Zhangsan know Lisi incessantly criticize him
        'Zhangsan knows that Lisi criticizes him all the time.'

In (4), *taziji* has reference *j* but not *i* or *k*, whereas in (14) *ta* may have *i* or *k* but not *j* as its possible references. Thus, in the environment illustrated here, pronouns and anaphors are complementary in their interpretations. In some environments, pronouns and reflexives may freely alternate. In the following examples, even though they occur in the same structural position, the pronoun *ta* is free and the anaphor *taziji* is bound in its GC:[2]

(15)   Zhangsan ji-le   [*ta*/*taziji*   *de* zhaopian] gei wo.
        Zhangsan send-LE he/himself DE photo   to   me
        'Zhangsan sent his/himself's photos to me.'

(16)   Zhangsan zong   yiwei [*taziji*/*ta*   zui   liaobuqi].
        Zhangsan always think himself/he most great
        'Zhangsan always thinks himself/he is the greatest.'

Principle B expresses the insight (after Lasnik 1976) that a proper syntactic theory of binding need only specify what a pronoun *cannot* refer to, not what its reference must be. Thus a pronoun need not be bound (having reference represented by *k* in (14)), or it can be bound outside its GC (*i*). Furthermore, an antecedent may occur in the pronoun's GC, as long as it does not c-command or bind it:

(17)   Zhangsan$_i$ de muqin hen guanxin ta$_i$.
        Zhangsan DE mother very caring   him
        'Zhangsan's mother is very concerned about him.'

9.1.3   Principles C and D

Another case of pronominal non-coreference that must be stipulated by grammar is illustrated below:

(18)   *ta$_i$ yiwei [wo bu xihuan Zhangsan$_i$].
        he think I   not like   Zhangsan
        *'He$_i$ thinks that I don't like Zhangsan$_i$.'

---

[2] This situation arises from the definition of a GC as given in (5): the GC for an anaphor must include an accessible subject but the GC for a pronoun need not. Thus an anaphor's GC may be larger than a pronoun's. In examples (15)–(16), when an anaphor occurs as the subject of an NP or an embedded clause, its GC is the main clause, but when a pronoun occurs in these positions, its GC is the NP or embedded clause itself. Thus, in (15)–(16), the anaphor is bound and the pronoun is free in their respective GCs. See Huang (1983) and Chomsky (1986a) for details.

Here, although *ta* is free (conforming to Principle B), the R-expression *Zhangsan* is bound, in violation of Principle C. Following Lasnik (1976), it has generally been assumed that (18) and (19) are ruled out in the same way, by Principle C:

(19)   ?*Zhangsan$_i$ yiwei [wo bu xihuan Zhangsan$_i$].
        Zhangsan think I   not like   Zhangsan
        '?*Zhangsan$_i$ thinks that I don't like Zhangsan$_i$.'

However, contrary to this earlier position, Lasnik (1991) presents evidence for a separate condition, which we shall dub Principle D, that applies to (18) but not to (19):

(20)   Principle D:
        A less referential expression may not bind a more referential one.

According to (20), (18) is in violation of Principle D because the binder *ta* is less referential than the bindee *Zhangsan*, but (19) is not, because the binder and the bindee are equal in their degree of referentiality.[3] Lasnik bases his argument on the fact that in Thai and Vietnamese, sentences corresponding to (19) are fully acceptable while those corresponding to (18) are ruled out completely. This fact poses a problem for the conception that (18) and (19) are ruled out by the same Principle C. But with the postulation of Principle D, the requisite distinction follows if one assumes that while Principle C does not apply in Thai and Vietnamese, Principle D does, perhaps universally. This argument has some validity for the Chinese examples here as well: for many speakers, (18) sounds worse than (19). This can be attributed to the fact that while both (18) and (19) violate Principle C, (18) additionally violates Principle D: (18) is doubly ill-formed. The following sentences also seem ill-formed at the same level as (18) and considerably worse than (19):

(21)   *na-ge   xuesheng$_i$ yiwei [wo bu xihuan Zhangsan$_i$].
        that-CL student   think I   not like   Zhangsan
        *'That student$_i$ thinks that I don't like Zhangsan$_i$.'

(22)   *ta$_i$ yiwei [wo bu xihuan na-ge   xuesheng$_i$].
        he think I   not like   that-CL student
        *'He$_i$ thinks that I don't like that student$_i$.'

An additional argument for Principle D comes from the fact that, for Chinese, such a constraint must be formulated differently from Principle C. Whereas Principle C simply prohibits the binding of an R-expression by a c-commanding NP, a proper formulation of Principle D for Chinese is needed to exclude more illegal cases.

---

[3] "Less referential" means "more anaphoric." We assume a referentiality hierarchy like this: Proper name > NP with demonstrative > pronoun > anaphor.

Thus, (23) and (24) are fully well-formed where neither R-expression of each coindexed pair c-commands the other. This is as predicted by Principle C:

(23)   Zhangsan$_i$-de mama   conglai dou bu zebei Zhangsan$_i$.
        Zhangsan-DE mother ever   all   not scold Zhangsan
        'Zhangsan's mother never scolded Zhangsan.'

(24)   zhe-ge xiaohai$_i$-de mama yixiang dou tanhu zhe-ge xiaohai$_i$.
        this-CL child-DE   mother ever   all protect this-CL child
        'This child's mother always protected this child.' [e.g., against any blame]

However, the following continue to be quite bad even in the absence of c-command:

(25)   *ta$_i$-de mama yixiang dou tanhu   Zhangsan$_i$.
        he-DE mother ever   all   protect Zhangsan
        Lit: 'His mother always protected Zhangsan.'

(26)   *zhe-ge xiaohai$_i$-de mama yixiang dou tanhu   Zhangsan$_i$.
        this-CL child-DE   mother ever   all protect Zhangsan
        Lit: 'This child's mother always protected Zhangsan.'

(27)   *ta$_i$-de mama yixiang dou tanhu   zhe-ge xiaohai$_i$.
        he-DE mother ever   all   protect this-CL child
        Lit: 'His mother always protected this child.'

The relevant difference responsible for the contrast between (23)–(24) and (25)–(27) is that in the ungrammatical cases, the first member of each coindexed pair is less referential than the second member, whereas in the grammatical cases, the first member is higher than or equal to the second member in its degree of referentiality. The contrast shows that while Principle C as currently formulated is more or less adequate for Chinese, Principle D must be strengthened so as to rule out certain cases where the strict notion of c-command does not obtain. Specifically, the bad cases are those where the less referential NP stands in a somewhat "weaker" relation than strict c-command to the more referential NP. An appropriate version of Principle D for Chinese might be as follows:

(28)   Principle D′:
        A less referential expression may not bind, or weakly bind, a more referential one.

In (25)–(27), NP_1 weakly binds NP_2 in the sense that, although it does not itself directly bind NP_2, the NP that immediately contains it does bind NP_2.[4] That

---

[4] This definition of "weak c-command" is simplified for the basic cases. The contrast between (23)–(24) and (25)–(27) persists even when the first member of each pair is

Chinese requires the notion of "weak binding" in the formulation of Principle D but not Principle C shows that these two principles cannot be collapsed.

In sum, we have seen in this section that the basic facts of anaphora in Chinese fall generally under the principles of Binding Theory supplemented with an appropriate version of Principle D. There is a major problem, however, presented by the bare reflexive *ziji*, which can be bound by a distant antecedent outside of its GC or simply unbound, under certain circumstances. In the next section we examine the bare reflexive in more detail.

9.2   The bare reflexive *ziji*

The problem presented by the bare reflexive would not be particularly interesting if it were to behave in complete disregard for BPA. If such were the case, the problem would be easily solved by simply categorizing it as an item that falls outside the purview of this principle. The problem is interesting because on the one hand, *ziji* can *always* be interpreted as being locally bound (hence an anaphor in the sense of BPA) and, on the other hand, non-local binding (or no binding) is possible *only* under specific circumstances: a long-distance bound *ziji* is subject to blocking, and a free *ziji* must refer to the speaker.[5] These situations occur only with the bare, monomorphemic *ziji* but not the compound reflexive. That is, the long-distance reflexive is characterized jointly by the following three properties:[6]

---

further embedded under the subject:

(i)   Zhangsan$_i$-de jiejie-de pengyou changchang bang Zhangsan$_i$ zuo gongke.
      Zhangsan-DE sister-DE friend   often   help Zhangsan do homework
      'Zhangsan's sister's friend often helped Zhangsan with his homework.'

(ii) *ta$_i$-de jiejie-de pengyou changchang bang Zhangsan$_i$ zuo gongke.
      he-DE sister-DE friend   often   help Zhangsan do   homework
      'His sister's friend often helped Zhangsan with his homework.'

This suggests a recursive definition of "weak c-command": α weakly c-commands β iff α is immediately contained in an NP that c-commands β or weakly c-commands β. See Huang (1982b) and T.-H. Teng (1985) for related discussion. The latter proposed a modification of the definition of "weak c-command" which obtains iff α is contained in any maximal phrase that c-commands β.

[5] A "generic" use of an unbound *ziji* has sometimes been noted (e.g., Li and Thompson 1981) for sentences like *ziji de guoshi, ziji fuze* 'self's fault, self take-charge' (i.e., 'One should personally be responsible for one's own fault'). In line with Tang (1989), we take these instances of *ziji* to be the adverbial *ziji* 'by oneself, alone, etc.' or adjectival 'own' modifying a null generic pronoun like 'one' or 'you.'

[6] Henceforth, we shall use the term "long-distance reflexive" to include both cases where it has an antecedent outside of its GC and where it has no antecedent but refers to the speaker.

(29)   Properties of the long-distance (LD) *ziji*
      a. Monomorphemicity
      b. Blocking Effect
      c. Speaker-orientation

This raises the interesting question why this cluster of conditions makes a long-distance reflexive (LDR) possible. Let us consider some previous attempts to answer this question.[7,8]

9.2.1   Two approaches to the long-distance ziji

Among the various attempts to cope with the problematic behavior of *ziji*, two different strategies can be distinguished: (a) a syntactic approach that reanalyzes the facts so that they cease to be problems for Binding Theory; (b) a functional/pragmatic approach that appeals to non-syntactic factors. We will see that an adequate account should include a combination of these two strategies.

---

[7] The discussion that follows in this section is based heavily on Huang and Liu (2001). See also Cole, Hermon, and Lee (2001), Pan (2001), Y. Li (1993b), and references cited there for related but somewhat different views.

[8] Other interesting properties of Chinese reflexives have been noted. One of them is "subject-orientation," i.e., the antecedent of a given reflexive must be a subject but not an object or indirect object, etc. The other property is that a reflexive may be bound by an antecedent that does not quite c-command, but only "sub-command," the reflexive (in the terminology of Tang 1989). Subject orientation is illustrated in (i):

(i)   Zhangsan$_i$ yijing   tongzhi Lisi$_j$ ziji$_{i/*j}$-de fenshu le.
    Zhangsan already inform Lisi self-DE   grade   LE
    'Zhangsan$_i$ already told Lisi$_j$ his$_{i/*j}$ grade.'

In (i), *ziji* may only be bound by *Zhangsan* but not by *Lisi* (unlike the situation in English *John told Bill about himself*, which allows both construals).
    Tang's (1989) notion of sub-command is based on sentences like (ii):

(ii)   Zhangsan$_i$-de jiao'ao   hai-le   ziji.
    Zhangsan-DE arrogance hurt-LE self
    'Zhangsan's arrogance ended up hurting him.'

The antecedent *Zhangsan* does not quite c-command the reflexive *ziji*, but is the subject (Specifier) of a larger NP (i.e., *Zhangsan de jiao'ao* 'Zhangsan's arrogance') that does, and binding is possible when the larger NP itself is not a potential binder (*ziji* in Chinese is inherently animate). (See Tang 1989 and Huang and Tang 1991 for fuller details and Kayne 1994, which allows for a simplification of the notion.)
    Note also that neither subject-orientation nor sub-command is a specific property of long-distance *ziji* ((i) and (ii) are themselves examples of local binding). Also, neither of them is a specific property of the bare *ziji*; they apply to the compound *taziji* as well. Therefore, we will not consider these properties in the following discussion.

9.2.1.1   The formal syntactic approach: *ziji* as an anaphor

One important attempt employing the syntactic strategy sought to re-analyze apparent LD binding as involving a number of successive steps of local binding, each in full satisfaction of Priniciple A. This has the result of making both LD *ziji* and the local *ziji* anaphors. Tang (1989) developed an early account using this strategy, with the proposal of an LF-reindexing rule. Following an idea of Lebeaux (1983), Chomsky (1986a), Pica (1987), and Battistella (1989) proposed that the LDR was made possible by *ziji* undergoing LF head-movement across clause boundaries. This line of approach was developed most fully in a number of papers by Cole, Hermon, and Sung (see Cole, Hermon, and Sung 1990, Cole and Sung 1994, Cole and Wang 1996, inter alia). According to this hypothesis, the monomorphemic *ziji* obligatorily moves in LF to I^0 of the minimal IP containing it, and optionally moves to head a higher IP. Thus the sentence in (30) has the LF structure (31) representing the LD construal of *ziji*:

(30)   [$_{IP}$ Zhangsan I^0 yiwei [$_{IP}$ Lisi I^0 piping-le   ziji]].
         Zhangsan   think   Lisi   criticize-LE self
         'Zhangsan thinks that Lisi criticized himself/him.'

(31)   [$_{IP}$ Zhangsan [$_I$ ziji]$_i$ [$_{VP}$ yiwei [$_{IP}$ Lisi [$_I$ t'$_i$] [$_{VP}$ piping-le   t$_i$]]]]

According to this hypothesis, binding of *ziji* by *Zhangsan* is possible because the reflexive has moved to the matrix I^0 position, where it is locally bound by the matrix subject. The successive I-to-I movement is itself a strictly local process. Thus what we have is an *apparent* case of LD binding that actually consists of successive steps, each obeying strict locality principles. In addition to putting away an important apparent counterexample to Principle A, this approach also provides an attractive explanation of some of the properties associated with the LDR. In particular, the requirement of monomorphemicity follows, because only the monomorphemic *ziji* (and not its polymorphemic cousins) is an X^0 category which can undergo head-movement. Hence only the bare *ziji* exhibits apparent LD binding. The Blocking Effect also follows, under the assumption that I^0 agrees with its Specifier in phi-features. Because the Head Movement Constraint (HMC, of Travis 1984) requires *ziji* to move to the lower I^0 before it moves to the higher I^0, *ziji* (and its trace t') must agree with the Specs of their IPs, which means the two Specs themselves must also agree in phi-features.

Using a similar strategy, Huang and Tang (1991) developed an LF adjunction account, whereby *ziji* may be adjoined to a local IP and be bound by the next local binder outside of IP. Successive IP adjunction then creates other binding possibilities, each a local matter. This account also derives the monomorphemicity and the Blocking Effect, in a somewhat different fashion. In particular, although both the bare and the compound reflexives are anaphoric in lacking reference, the former is doubly so because it also lacks "phi-features" (person, number, and gender features). It is suggested that on the application of BPA in overt Syntax the bare reflexive must first have its phi-features fixed on the basis of its local antecedent. This allows for its reference to be fixed at a later point, following (optional) LF movement. Monomorphemicity thus follows, because the latter possibility is excluded for the compound reflexive, which already has its reference fixed when BPA applies in overt Syntax. The Blocking Effect also follows in that the bare reflexive, having acquired its phi-features from the local antecedent prior to its LF movement, can take a higher antecedent only if that antecedent agrees in phi-features with the local antecedent.

Both the head-movement and the IP-adjunction account, then, treat the LD *ziji* as a special case of local *ziji*. Despite their apparent attractiveness, both the head-movement account and the IP-adjunction account suffer from important empirical problems. One clear problem is that, although these accounts provide an explanation for the first two properties – monomorphemicity and the Blocking Effect (29a, b) – neither had anything to say about the third property of the LDR (29c), the fact that it can occur free referring to the speaker, as observed by Yu (1992). Furthermore, several facts have since come to light surrounding the putative Blocking Effects.

First, as pointed out by Xue, Pollard, and Sag (1994), Blocking Effects may be induced by non-subjects. Since non-subjects do not enter into agreement with I^0, blocking is unexpected under the head-movement account.

(32)   Zhangsan$_i$ gaosu wo$_j$ Lisi$_k$ hen ziji$_{*i/*j/k}$.
        Zhangsan tell   me Lisi hate self
        'Zhangsan$_i$ told me$_j$ that Lisi$_k$ hated self$_{*i/*j/k}$.'

Second, a number asymmetry exists in the observed Blocking Effects: a plural local NP does not block a singular LD antecedent, though a singular local NP does block a plural LD antecedent (Tang 1989):

(33)   a. Zhangsan$_i$ juede tamen$_j$ lao   piping   ziji$_{i/j}$.
           Zhangsan feel they   incessantly criticize self
           'Zhangsan felt that they criticized themselves/him all the time.'

        b. tamen$_i$ juede Zhangsan$_j$ lao   piping   ziji$_{*i/j}$.
           they   feel Zhangsan incessantly criticize self
           'They felt that Zhangsan criticized himself/*them all the time.'

This raises a problem for any account that derives the Blocking Effect from the requirement of phi-feature agreement. Why should person agreement matter, but not number agreement?

Third, a *person* asymmetry also exists between first-/second- and third-person NPs with respect to their ability to induce Blocking Effects. As noted in Xu (1993; cf. also Pan 1997), it appears that although a local first/second-person NP may block a remote third-person NP from being an LD antecedent, a local third-person NP does not fully block a remote first/second-person NP from being an LD antecedent.

(34) a. Zhangsan$_i$ danxin wo/ni$_j$ hui piping   ziji$_{*i/j}$.
          Zhangsan worry I/you will criticize self
          'Zhangsan is worried that I/you might criticize myself/yourself/*him.'

      b. wo$_i$ danxin Zhangsan$_j$ hui piping   ziji$_{i/j}$.
          I   worry Zhangsan will criticize self
          'I am worried that Zhangsan will criticize himself/me.'

      c. ni$_i$ danxin Zhangsan$_j$ hui piping   ziji$_{i/j}$ ma?
          you worry Zhangsan will criticize self Q
          'Are you worried that Zhangsan will criticize himself/you?'

Finally, under some circumstances, even a third-person NP may induce blocking. One such circumstance, reported in Huang and Liu (2001), is when the local third-person subject is presented deictically, as in (35), where the pointing finger indicates that the speaker points to someone in the audience as he utters the sentence.

(35)   Zhangsan shuo ☞ **ta**   qipian-le ziji.
        Zhangsan say   he/she cheat-LE self
        'Zhangsan said that he/she cheated himself/herself.'

Another situation where a third-person NP may induce blocking is when multiple occurrences of *ziji* are involved. The relevance of the following example was first pointed out by Pan (1997), who attributed it to C. L. Baker. The available readings are summarized in (36a–i):

(36)   [Zhangsan renwei [Lisi zhidao [Wangwu ba ziji$_1$-de shu   song-gei-le
          Zhangsan think   Lisi know   Wangwu BA self-DE book give-to-LE
        ziji$_2$-de pengyou]]].
        self-DE friend
        'Zhangsan thinks that Lisi knows that Wangwu gave self's books to self's friends.'

      a.   ziji$_1$ = ziji$_2$ = Wangwu
      b.   ziji$_1$ = ziji$_2$ = Lisi
      c.   ziji$_1$ = ziji$_2$ = Zhangsan
      d.   ziji$_1$ = Wangwu, ziji$_2$ = Lisi
      e.   ziji$_1$ = Wangwu, ziji$_2$ = Zhangsan
      f.   ziji$_1$ = Zhangsan, ziji$_2$ = Wangwu
      g.   ziji$_1$ = Lisi, ziji$_2$ = Wangwu
      h.   *ziji$_1$ = Zhangsan, ziji$_2$ = Lisi
      i.   *ziji$_1$ = Lisi, ziji$_2$ = Zhangsan

In this sentence, there are two occurrences of *ziji* and three c-commanding subjects. As indicated above, the two occurrences of *ziji* may refer to the same antecedent, in which case any of the c-commanding subjects can be the antecedent (a, b, c). The two occurrences of *ziji* may also refer separately, so long as one of them is locally bound by *Wangwu* (d, e, f, g). Crucially, if both occurrences of *ziji* are to be LD bound, then they must be bound by the same LD antecedent (as in (b, c)), but not separately bound (as in (h, i)). This range of possibilities indicates that a third-person NP does not induce blocking when it is itself a non-binder or local binder of *ziji*, but does so when it is itself an LD binder of *ziji*. In the illicit cases (h, i), the intermediate subject *Lisi* is the LD binder of one occurrence of *ziji*, and it prevents the other *ziji* from being bound by the matrix subject *Zhangsan*.

All of these complications are unexpected under the formal accounts discussed here. In fact, they call into serious question the very existence of a generalization concerning Blocking Effects in terms of feature agreement, and also to all accounts designed to derive this putative generalization.

9.2.1.2   The discourse-functional approach: *ziji* as a logophor

Although the formal approach came into vogue after the relevant facts were introduced by Y.-H. Huang (1984), the first account proposed in Huang *et al.* (1984) was, in effect, a functional one. Essentially, the proposal was that the Chinese LD reflexives are not true anaphors in the sense of Binding Theory, but a special kind of anaphoric expression referring to the matrix subject as the "speaker" of the embedded clause, following Kuno's (1972) "direct discourse complementation" analysis of certain pronouns in English. According to Kuno, under one coreferential reading the sentence (37a) is a direct report of the matrix subject's inner feelings, and under this reading it should be analyzed as having been directly derived from (37b) as its underlying structure:[9]

(37)   a. John said that he saw Bill.
         b. John said, "I saw Bill."

In the terms of earlier generative studies, the claim is that the transformational process that forms an indirect complement structure from its direct discourse underlying source converts the first-person pronoun *I* in (37b) directly into the third-person pronoun *he* in (37a), without going through the intermediate step (38):

(38)   John said that John saw Bill.

---

[9] There is another reading according to which John need not have *consciously* ascribed the experience of having seen Bill to himself using the first-person pronoun. This was not the reading under discussion by Kuno.

In other words, the pronoun *he* is not a result of pronominalizing *John* but one of direct conversion from *I* in the speech of its antecedent, i.e., the matrix subject and "speaker" of the complement clause. The matrix subject may be the actual speaker of the direct discourse complement as in (37b), or a "virtual speaker" (e.g., thinker, feeler, fearer, knower, experiencer, etc.) in situations like (39):

(39)   a. John was afraid that he might lose her.
       b. John feared in his mind: "I might lose her."

The use of a pronoun that originates from the first-person *I* in Kuno's system has now come to be known as the *logophoric* use, after Clements (1975) and Hagège (1974). Huang *et al.* (1984) suggested, following Kuno (1972), that the reflexive *ziji* in its LD construal was permitted when it corresponds to *wo* 'I' in the direct discourse representation of a sentence in which it occurs. Thus, in its LD construal in (40a), the bare reflexive *ziji* is a logophor.

(40)   a. Zhangsan$_i$ manyuan Lisi chang piping   ziji$_i$.
          Zhangsan   complain Lisi often   criticize self
          'Zhangsan$_i$ complained that Lisi often criticized him$_i$.'

       b. Zhangsan manyuan, "Lisi chang piping   wo."
          Zhangsan complain, Lisi often   criticized me
          'Zhangsan complained, "Lisi often criticized me." '

The logophoric reflexive is not the result of reflexivizing *Zhangsan* on identity with its own matrix subject, but the result of converting from the speaker-referring *wo* 'me' in the underlying direct discourse.

Huang *et al.* (1984) argued that this analysis offers a natural explanation for the Blocking Effect. Recall that in a sentence like (40a), an embedded subject *wo/ni* 'I/you' in place of the third-person *Lisi* would block LD construal of *ziji* (see also (7)–(12) above). The direct-discourse underlying source would be either (41a) or (41b):

(41)   a. Zhangsan manyuan, "wo chang piping   wo."
          Zhangsan complain   I   often   criticize me
          'Zhangsan complained, "I often criticize me." '

       b. Zhangsan manyuan, "ni   chang piping   wo."
          Zhangsan complain   you often   criticize me
          'Zhangsan complained, "you often criticize me." '

In (41a), there are two instances of *wo*, the first one referring to the speaker of the entire discourse, and the second one referring to the matrix subject, the speaker of the complement clause. This perspective conflict makes communication very difficult if not impossible. The same explanation applies to (41b), where the embedded subject *ni* 'you' is an addressee from the perspective of the (external) speaker but the object *wo* is the "speaker" from the perspective of the matrix subject. In other words, the Blocking Effect occurs as a perceptual strategy to avoid conflicting references to speech act participants at different levels.

Although the discourse/functional *logophoric* account provided a rather natural explanation of the Blocking Effect, for various reasons the idea was put aside as researchers turned their attention to a syntactic *anaphoric* account postulating LF operations. As the various problems for the anaphoric analysis have come to light, it now appears that the LD *ziji* lends itself more comfortably to a logophoric analysis. A reconsideration of those problems will make this clear.

First, we noted earlier that the LF-movement theories failed to explain the property of speaker orientation when *ziji* is without any binder (see (13)). This is, without any further explanation, exactly what is expected from the logophoric account.

Second, the functional account explains the phenomenon of blocking much more precisely than the formal, LF-movement account. We noted the following five problems for the LF-movement accounts:

(42)   a. Non-subjects may induce blocking (see (32)).

   b. A number asymmetry exists with respect to blocking: a plural does not block a singular LD antecedent, but a singular blocks a plural antecedent (see (33)).

   c. A person asymmetry also exists: a first/second-person NP blocks a third-person LD antecedent, but not vice versa (see (34)).

   d. Deictic third-person NPs also induce blocking (see (35)).

   e. Multiple occurrences of LD *ziji* may cause blocking (see (36)).

Consider (42c) first. The explanation provided by Huang *et al.* (1984) for the Blocking Effect is that the occurrence of *wo* 'I' or *ni* 'you' in a sentence necessarily "anchors" the sentence to the perspective of the speaker, and this prevents a distinct NP from being an LD antecedent of *ziji* because it would require a distinct perspective from which to refer to *ziji* in the first person. Blocking thus arises from a strategy to avoid conflicts in perspectives. However, in the event that the LD antecedent in question is itself *wo* 'I' or *ni* 'you,' the perspective of the speaker and that of the LD antecedent are one and the same. There is no conflict, hence no blocking. Furthermore, a third-person NP elsewhere in the sentence is normally neutral, as it remains in the third person whether viewed from the external speaker's or from the LD antecedent's perspective. Therefore, although a first- or second-person NP blocks a third-person LD antecedent, a third-person NP does not block *wo* or *ni* – or indeed any other NP – from being an LD antecedent.

An exception to the above occurs, however, if a third-person NP is presented in a fixed, non-neutral perspective. This is what happens when it is deictically presented as in (42d). The speaker's pointing finger necessarily anchors a given utterance to the current time-space in the speaker's presence, and blocking ensues as in (35).

Condition (42e) describes another situation where a third-person NP induces blocking: when multiple occurrences of *ziji* are involved with distinct LD antecedents. The generalization from (36) is that a long-distance antecedent-*ziji* relation precludes the possibility of other such LD relations, because each distinct LD relation implies a speech act with one distinct perspective. In Huang *et al.*'s (1984) terms, the unavailable readings of (36) are those for which the underlying representation would be something like the following: *Zhangsan thinks, "Lisi knows, 'Wangwu gave my book to my friend,'"* where one occurrence of *my* refers to Zhangsan, and the other occurrence refers to Lisi, a very hard situation indeed to sort out.

Furthermore, note that nothing in the logophoric account requires a first- or second-person NP to be a subject in order for an utterance to be anchored to the external speaker's perspective. Thus, while (42a) presents a serious problem for the agreement-based LF-movement theory, it presents no problem for the logophoric theory at all.

Finally, since the logophoric account concerns the (actual or virtual) speaker's perspective, it is natural that only person features seem to matter in producing Blocking Effects, but number features do not. Condition (42b) does not pose a problem for the logophoric account as it does for the agreement-based LF-movement account.[10]

In this section we have seen that a syntactic anaphoric account that treats both LD and local *ziji* as instances of an anaphor faces important problems. Under the logophoric account of the LD *ziji*, these problems do not arise, and the relevant facts receive a natural explanation. This seems to be a strong argument in favor of treating the LD *ziji* as a logophor. Note that this conclusion entails an extra cost, since we must now recognize two different morphemes having the same form *ziji* – the LD reflexive *ziji* as a logophor and the local *ziji* as an anaphor. We shall see below that this extra cost is indeed justified.[11]

9.2.2   *Logophoricity and anaphoricity*

9.2.2.1   **The dual status of *ziji***

As indicated above, Kuno (1972) demonstrated the importance of what has now come to be known as logophoricity for analyzing one salient reading

---

[10] As for the source of the number asymmetry itself, see Huang (2002) for the proposal that attributes it to the inherent distributivity of logophoric antecedents.

[11] The logophoric account explains both the Blocking Effect and the property of speaker-orientation, but does not by itself explain the property of monomorphemicity. We shall suggest below that the logophor is an operator in the semantics of logophoricity, and that while the bare reflexive is an operator, the compound reflexive is not. See also note 13 below.

of (37a), repeated below, as a direct report of the matrix subject's inner feelings:

(43)   John said that he saw Bill.

Under this reading, the sentence may be seen as the speaker's report on an event in which John literally said, "I saw Bill." But that is not the only scenario that makes (43) true with intended coreference between *John* and *he*. Suppose that while watching an old video, John remarked, "The little boy saw Bill" without realizing that the little boy in the video was actually John himself. On the other hand, the speaker (who filmed the video twenty years earlier) does know that the little boy is indeed John, and therefore may report that John did *in effect* say that he saw Bill. Such a report is not a report on the matrix subject's direct feeling, but the speaker's own knowledge of the relevant event or state of affairs.

Although in English the same pronoun is used in reports of both "the speaker's own knowledge" and "the subject's direct feeling," Hagège (1974) and Clements (1975) report on some West African languages where the distinction is grammaticalized. In these languages, a distinct set of logophoric pronouns exist for the sole purpose of referring to an antecedent "whose speech, thoughts, feelings, or general state of consciousness are reported." Another case where this distinction is grammaticalized is provided by the Italian possessive reflexive *proprio*, in contrast to the pronoun *suoi*, as illustrated by the pair below (from Chierchia 1989: 24):

(44)   a. Pavarotti crede che i **proprio** pantaloni siano in fiamme.
         'Pavarotti believes that **self's** pants are on fire.'

         b. Pavarotti crede che i **suoi** pantaloni siano in fiamme.
         'Pavarotti believes that **his** pants are on fire.'

Chierchia (1989) explains the difference between (44a) and (44b) by employing Lewis' (1979) distinction between *de se* and *de re* beliefs, which roughly corresponds to Kuno's distinction between "the matrix subject's direct feeling" and "the speaker's knowledge" (more on the distinction in Section 9.2.3 below). Both (44a) and (44b) assert the coreference of Pavarotti with the man whose pants are on fire, but while (44a) with *proprio* expresses a *de se* belief by Pavarotti (being disposed to say, "My pants are on fire!" and run for the extinguisher, for example), (44b) with *suoi* expresses a *de re* belief where the coreference relation, known to the speaker, may or may not be part of Pavarotti's own belief. In other words, while *suoi* is a normal anaphoric pronoun, *proprio* is a logophor.

The existence of logophoric pronouns in addition to normal coreferential pronouns in such languages raises the question of why logophors don't seem to exist in others (e.g., Chinese). This question is answered if we say that Chinese does have a logophor in the form of LD *ziji*, but it is homophonous with the local anaphor *ziji*. In other words, the "extra cost" of recognizing two uses of *ziji* is not *a priori* unjustified.[12]

9.2.2.2 Logophoric *ziji*: Source, Self, and Pivot

Sells (1987) provided a useful taxonomy of logophoric phenomena in terms of three primitive roles of the antecedent of a logophor.

(45)   a. Source: the one who is the intentional agent of the communication
       b. Self: the one whose mental state or attitude the proposition describes
       c. Pivot: the one with respect to whose (time–space) location the content of the proposition is evaluated

In other words, a logophor refers to a person whose (a) speech or thought, (b) attitude or state of consciousness, and/or (c) point of view (perspective) is being reported. This person may be the speaker (the external Source, Self, or Pivot) or an internal protagonist denoted by an argument of the sentence. For some Chinese speakers, all three types of logophoricity are available, as illustrated in (46), though for others the case of a (pure) Pivot antecedent is considerably more difficult to obtain:

(46)   a.   Zhangsan shuo [pashou   tou-le   ziji-de pibao].
            Zhangsan shuo pickpocket steal-LE self-DE purse
            'Zhangsan said that the pickpocket stole his purse.'

       b.   [Ziji$_i$-de xiaohai mei de jiang] de xiaoxi shi   Lisi$_i$ hen shiwang.
            self-DE child   not get prize DE news   make Lisi very disappointed
            'The news that his$_i$ child didn't win the prize made Lisi$_i$ very disappointed.'

       c.   ??[Zhangsan lai   kan ziji$_i$] de shihou, Lisi$_i$ zheng zai kan shu.
            Zhangsan come see self   DE moment Lisi now   at read book
            'Lisi$_i$ was reading when Zhangsan came to visit him$_i$.'

In (46a), *Zhangsan* may be understood as the Source antecedent of *ziji*. In (46b), *Lisi* is the internal Self whose mental state is being reported. Example (46c) may be understood as reporting an event from the perspective of *Lisi*, the Pivot. Sells (1987) notes that there is an implicational relation among these three types of logophoric antecedent: if a sentence is interpreted as reporting on the speech or thought of an internal Source antecedent, the same antecedent must also be a Self whose mental state is described and a Pivot from whose perspective the report is

---

[12] Languages that have a distinct set of logophors in addition to pronouns may also possess a distinct set of (local) anaphors. In Italian, local anaphors come in two forms: the clitic form *si* and the full form *se stesso*, which is inflected with appropriate phi-features.

made or perceived. Similarly, if a sentence simply reports on the mental state or consciousness of its antecedent (Self), it must also be the case that the sentence is evaluated from the viewpoint of the antecedent (Pivot). The reverse does not hold, however. Thus, in (46c) the speaker simply empathizes with *Lisi* but does not purport to be reporting on his mental state (as in (46b)) or his speech or belief (as in (46a)). Sells suggests that these roles characterize certain cross-linguistic variations, and shows that languages differ as to whether they permit one, two, or all three kinds of logophoric antecedents. Following Huang and Liu (2001), we assume that these three labels express a progressive degree of liberation in the linguistic expression of logophoricity, Source being the "core," Self being the "extended core" (i.e., the "virtual Source"), and Pivot yet further extended (i.e., the "virtual Self"). Thus some languages may permit logophoric reference to the Source only, others allow either Source or Self, and still others allow all three roles; but we do not expect to find languages allowing Pivot as a logophoric antecedent but specifically excluding antecedents that denote the Source. As indicated above, while some Chinese speakers find (46c) difficult to accept, no one – so far as we know – finds (46c) acceptable *and* (46a) or (46b) unacceptable.

There is evidence that LD binding of *ziji* by a Source or Self is binding in the context of "attitudes *de se*." Suppose that Zhangsan saw a pickpocket running away with his purse without realizing that it was his own purse. He might kindly report it to the police but would not be disposed to say, "A pickpocket stole *my* purse." In this case, (46a) would not be an appropriate description of Zhangsan's deed. An appropriate description would need to replace the reflexive with a pronoun, as in (47):

(47)   Zhangsan shuo [pashou   tou-le   ta-de pibao].
        Zhangsan shuo pickpocket steal-LE his   purse
        'Zhangsan said that the pickpocket stole his purse.'

The LD *ziji*, then, is like Italian *proprio* in being limited to logophoric uses, here a case of logophoric *ziji* referring to the internal Source.

Example (46b) is a case of binding by an internal Self. That this is the case can be appreciated by comparing it with the unacceptable (48):

(48)   *[Lisi$_i$-de xiaohai mei de jiang] de xiaoxi shi   ziji$_i$ hen shiwang.
        Lisi-DE child   not get prize DE news   make self very disappointed
        'The news that Lisi's$_i$ child didn't win the prize made him$_i$ very disappointed.'

The contrast between (46b) and (48) shows that backward reflexivization is acceptable but forward reflexivization is not, which is somewhat surprising from what we know in general about anaphora. For example, pronominalization in the same context can be in either direction:

(49) a. [Lisi$_i$-de xiaohai mei de jiang] de xiaoxi shi   ta$_i$ hen shiwang.
          Lisi-DE child   not get prize DE news   make him very disappointed
          'The news that Lisi's$_i$ child didn't win the prize made him$_i$ very disappointed.'

      b. [ta$_i$-de xiaohai mei de jiang] de xiaoxi shi   Lisi$_i$ hen shiwang.
          his   child   not get prize DE news   make self very disappointed
          'The news that his$_i$ child didn't win the prize made Lisi$_i$ very disappointed.'

The reason is that LD *ziji* requires its antecedent to be disposed to describe the relevant event or proposition referring to himself by *wo* 'I/me.' Example (46b) is well-formed, because the antecedent *Lisi* is an Experiencer disposed to say or think, "My child did not win the prize . . ." But in (48) the antecedent *Lisi* is not an Experiencer, and the sentence does not purport him to be so disposed to describe the event in these terms.

Because a *de se* reading presupposes consciousness on the part of the protagonist denoted by the antecedent, the following contrast is expected:

(50) a. Zhangsan$_i$ kuajiang-le [[changchang piping   ziji$_i$ de] naxie ren$_j$].
          Zhangsan praise-LE   often   criticize self DE those person
          'Zhangsan$_i$ praised those people who criticize him$_i$ a lot.'

      b. ??Zhangsan$_i$ kuajiang-le [[houlai sha si   ziji$_i$ de] naxie ren$_j$].
          Zhangsan praised-LE   later   kill die self DE those person
          'Zhangsan$_i$ praised those persons who later killed him$_i$.'

In (50a) the relative clause describes an event that *Zhangsan* could be aware of at the time he praised his critics. His praise might even have been based on the fact that he had knowingly benefited from the criticism. In (50b) the relative clause is assumed to describe an event known only to the speaker, not to *Zhangsan*.

As indicated above in connection with (46c), some speakers allow for an LD *ziji* to be bound by a Pivot antecedent denoting a protagonist from whose point of view a given sentence is presented. For these speakers, binding is possible as long as the speaker takes the antecedent's point of view, even though the Pivot may not have a *de se* attitude about the reported proposition or event. We submit that Pivot binding is an extension of Self binding, in the sense that it acquires "virtual consciousness" in virtue of the speaker's empathy with the Pivot. The fact that it is not the core, but the extended, case of logophoricity explains why (46c) is not as readily acceptable as (46a–b).

9.2.2.3 Anaphoric *ziji*: locally bound

Our logophoric analysis of the LD *ziji* implies that the locally bound *ziji* is mostly not a logophor. This must be the case because the local reflexive does not meet the *de se* requirement of a logophor. Consider the following examples of local *ziji*: in (51) *ziji* is bound by a co-argument, and in (52) *ziji* is contained in an NP and bound by a co-argument of that NP. In both cases, *ziji* is bound in its GC as defined in (5).

(51) a. Zhangsan piping-le   ziji.
          Zhangsan criticize-LE self
          'Zhangsan criticized himself.'

      b. Zhangsan gen ziji guo-bu-qu.
          Zhangsan with self pass-not-go
          'Zhangsan gave himself a hard time.'

      c. Zhangsan ji-le   yi-ben shu gei ziji.
          Zhangsan send-LE one-CL book to   self
          'Zhangsan sent a book to himself.'

(52) a. Zhangsan piping-le   ziji-de pengyou.
          Zhangsan criticize-LE self-DE friend
          'Zhangsan criticized his own friend.'

      b. Zhangsan gen ziji-de didi   guo-bu-qu.
          Zhangsan with self-DE brother pass-not-go
          'Zhangsan gave his own brother a hard time.'

      c. Zhangsan ji-le   yi-ben shu gei ziji   de   erzi.
          Zhangsan send-LE one-CL book to   self-DE son
          'Zhangsan sent a book to his own son.'

In these sentences, binding is possible even when no logophoric conditions hold. In each case, the local binder is not, or need not be, a Source, Self, or Pivot. For example, since these sentences are reports on an action performed by Zhangsan, but not of his speech or thought, the notion Source is irrelevant. Second, these sentences do not require the speaker or hearer to take the empathy focus of Zhangsan, but can be uttered entirely from the speaker's own viewpoint. Third, consciousness, which we saw as a common property of logophoricity, clearly also does not obtain. Thus (51a) and (52a) are entirely licit even though Zhangsan may not be aware that the person he was criticizing was actually himself or his own friend. It is also easy to imagine a scenario in which the following holds true with Zhangsan, even at the time of his death, still not knowing who he was victimized by:

(53)   Zhangsan$_i$ bei ziji$_i$ (de pengyou) hai-si-le.
       Zhangsan by self DE friend   wrong-death-LE
       'Zhangsan was wronged to death by himself/his own friend.'

In other words, *ziji* may be locally bound in non-logophoric contexts and therefore cannot be treated as a logophor. From here, we can expect that local *ziji* also should not exhibit any Blocking Effects. This expectation is borne out in full.

In the following examples, the intervening first- and second-person pronouns do not induce blocking:

(54)   Zhangsan$_i$ gaosu wo ziji$_i$-de fenshu.
        Zhangsan tell   me self-DE grade
        'Zhangsan told me about his own grade.'

(55)   ta$_i$ xiang ni   tidao   ziji$_i$-de quedian   le ma?
        he to   you mention self-DE shortcoming LE Q
        'Did he mention his own shortcoming to you?'

(56)   ta zheng-tian dui-zhe wo chuipeng ziji.
        he whole-day to-ZHE me boast   self
        'He boasted about himself in front of me all day long.'

(57)   Zhangsan ba wo dai-hui   ziji-de jiali.
        Zhangsan BA me bring-back self-DE home
        'Zhangsan brought me back to his own home.'

We therefore conclude that it is important to distinguish between the anaphoric and the logophoric uses of *ziji*, each with its distinct properties. The LD *ziji* whose antecedent falls outside of its governing category is a logophor, and as a logophor it exhibits logophoric effects: *de se* attitudes, consciousness, perspectivity, and blocking. The local *ziji* does not exhibit any logophoric effects, but is subject to local binding in accordance with Principle A.[13]

9.2.3   Logophoricity: syntax and semantics

Although Kuno's (1972, 1987) early observations and discussion of the discourse/pragmatic effects of anaphora provide valuable insights into the nature of logophoricity in an intuitively satisfactory way, his account in terms of direct-discourse representations did not mesh with a sophisticated theory of semantics and of the syntax–semantics interface. Sells (1987) treats logophoricity in terms of the three primitive roles (Source, Self, and Pivot) within Discourse Representation

---

[13] When occurring as the subject (or contained in the subject) of an embedded clause, *ziji* may be treated either as a logophor or an anaphor:

(i)   Zhangsan yiwei [ziji zui   congming].
       Zhangsan think self most clever
       'Zhangsan thinks that he is the smartest.'

This sentence may describe a situation where Zhangsan says mentally, "I am the smartest," so *ziji* can be analyzed as a logophor. On the other hand, since *Zhangsan* occurs within the GC of *ziji*, (i) may be a case of anaphor binding as well. See Huang and Liu (2001) for further discussion showing that local binding of *ziji* should be defined in terms of the GC, rather than as a matter of predicate reflexivity (as proposed in Reinhart and Reuland 1993), or as a relation between co-arguments (as in Pollard and Xue 1998).

Theory, while Chierchia (1989) argues that logophoricity can be integrated into an interpretive theory by independently needed notions without recourse to such newly postulated primitives.

Chierchia adopts Lewis' (1979) distinction between *de re* and *de se* beliefs and capitalizes on his insight that, while the *de re* readings of attitudinal sentences express a relation between a believer and a proposition, the *de se* readings express a relation between a believer and a property. In the former, a believer holds a certain proposition to be true; in the latter, a believer (knowingly) ascribes a property to himself/herself. Chierchia proposes that this distinction can be captured in semantic representation by treating the complement clause either as a propositional argument (the *de re* reading), or as a secondary predicate (the *de se* reading). Thus the *de re* and *de se* readings of (58) are respectively as in (59):

(58)   Pavarotti believes that his pants are on fire.

(59)   a. (λx (believe (x, x's pants are on fire))) (P)
        b. believe (P, λx (x's pants are on fire))

The structure of secondary predication in (59b) is appropriate for the *de se* reading, given that certain other known structures of secondary predication also permit only *de se* interpretations. These include structures of obligatory control. Note that a *de se* reading is obligatory in (60a) but not in (60b):

(60)   a. John claims [PRO to be innocent].
        b. John claims that he is innocent.

Taking obligatory control to be (secondary) predication (as in Williams 1980, Chierchia 1984, etc.), (60a) has the following representation:

(61)   claims (John, λx (innocent (x)))

How would a semantic representation like (59b) or (61) be related to, or derived from, the syntactic structure of a logophoric sentence? It seems to us that a possible answer is readily available from Huang and Tang's (1991) original LF-adjunction analysis of the LD *ziji*.[14] According to Huang and Tang, an LD *ziji* is adjoined to an IP immediately below its antecedent. This gives rise to an LF representation like (62):

(62)   [$_{IP}$ Zhangsan yiwei [$_{IP}$ ziji$_i$ [$_{IP}$ Lisi changchang piping   t$_i$]]]
        Zhangsan think   self   Lisi often   criticize

---

[14] A head-movement analysis is also possible, if additional assumptions are made about the nature of an operator and general movement constraints on head-movement.

In other words, *ziji* is treated as an operator binding its own trace as a variable. This process is thus on a par with the (overt) null operator movement we postulated for the long passive (see Chapter 4, Section 4.1.2.). The structure (62) is parallel to the semantic representation that would be appropriate under Chierchia's system, either (63a) or the somewhat more fancy (63b):

(63)   a. (Zhangsan thinks λx (Lisi often criticizes x))
        b. thinks (Zhangsan, λx (often criticizes (Lisi, x)))

The IP-adjoined *ziji* in (62) corresponds to the lambda operator in the semantic representations in (63). The status of the LF-adjoined *ziji* is thus on a par with a null operator, an anaphoric operator in this case. As is commonly assumed in the literature, a null operator is the syntactic correlate of a lambda operator. Thus we can see the LF-adjunction of *ziji* as a process of creating an operator–variable construction out of a complement clause – in semantic terms, of creating a predicate out of an argument, for direct translation into its semantic representation. In LF, just as a null operator, the IP-adjoined *ziji* needs to be locally bound by *Zhangsan* in (62). This is the process of "strong binding" or predication in the sense of Chomsky (1982, 1986a). In semantics, each (secondary) λ-predicate must be predicated on its subject, a result easily obtained from strong binding. Thus, LF IP-adjunction of *ziji* provides a convenient syntax–semantics interface for the interpretation of logophoric sentences.

In fact, we can also think of the IP-adjunction process as creating a structure to directly represent Sells' concept of a Source, Self, or Pivot at the interface between discourse and syntax. In light of important recent works on the "cartography of the left periphery" (Cinque 1999, 2002, Rizzi 1997, 2002, etc.), it is plausible to assume that a functional category exists which provides a "gate" from which discourse factors are processed. In particular, we may assume that the *ziji*-adjoined structure is in fact a Source Phrase (or Self or Pivot Phrase, as the case may be). Assuming this to be the structure for (62), with *ziji* in Spec of SourceP, we have:

(64)   [$_{IP}$ Zhangsan yiwei [$_{SourceP}$ ziji$_i$ [$_{IP}$ Lisi chang piping   t$_i$]]]
        Zhangsan think   self   Lisi often criticize

Coindexing *ziji* with *Zhangsan* fulfills the requirement of strong binding or predication, and the resulting representation can be read as "Zhangsan thinks of himself as the Source (the 'me') such that Lisi often criticizes that Source."[15]

If this hypothesis proves to be on the right track, we now have a new conclusion about the LF-movement hypothesis. Although we have seen that LF movement

---

[15] A similar proposal making use of a POV (Point-of-View) Phrase has been made by Nishigauchi (1999).

cannot be the right mechanism for capturing the Blocking Effect, it provides a natural representation at the syntax–semantics interface and the interface between grammar and discourse. Furthermore, despite the appearance of long-distance binding, a local relation still holds between the operator *ziji* and its logophoric antecedent.[16]

9.3   Bound anaphora and donkey anaphora

At the beginning of this chapter, we noted that the proper characterization of nominal anaphora depends on three ingredients: (a) the nature of the nominal expression in question; (b) the structural relation between the expression and its antecedent if it has one; and (c) the nature of the antecedent itself. We saw that (a) matters, as evidenced by the need to distinguish among anaphors, pronominals, and R-expressions. The second ingredient (b) also matters, as we saw, in that the various nominal expressions need to obey the appropriate principles of Binding Theory. As for the third ingredient, binding possibilities vary with respect to the nature of an antecedent involved, specifically whether it is referential or quantificational.

9.3.1   *Pronouns in coreference or as bound variables*

The distinction between referential and quantificational NPs plays an important role in both the syntax and the semantics of natural languages. The former include proper names and definite or specific descriptions (e.g., *John, the boy, a certain guy*), and the latter are made up of quantified NPs – universal (e.g., *everyone, both men*) or existential (e.g., *somebody, two girls, a few of the apples*, and *wh*-phrases like *who, which dog*, etc.). Unlike a referential NP, which directly denotes an individual or individuals, a quantificational NP *ranges over* a set or sets of individuals but does not denote any specific member of the set. With respect to anaphora, this distinction amounts to a difference between coreference and variable

---

[16] As indicated above in footnote 9, although the logophoric account explains (a) the Blocking Effects of LD binding and (b) speaker-orientation of the free *ziji*, it does not, by itself, explain the property of monomorphemicity. One possible answer we suggest here is that the bare *ziji* is an operator, and as an operator it is subject to LF movement (like quantificational NPs and null operators). On the other hand, the compound reflexive with a pronominal prefix is a variable on a par with normal bound pronouns that do not undergo movement. It is important to remember that bare *ziji* is an XP category exhaustively dominating an X^0 category. As an operator it undergoes XP movement. There is also evidence that it may move as an X^0 category. Huang (2002) argues that this happens with the local *ziji*: the X^0 *ziji* adjoins to the local governing verb and forms a reflexive predicate with it (cf. *self-criticizing, self-inflicting*, etc.), thus giving rise to the property of distributivity that is not observed with sentences with the compound reflexive.

binding. In both (65a) and (65b) the pronoun *his* refers to what its antecedent refers to, i.e., the individual whose name is *John* or the boy whose reference has been established in context:

(65) a. John$_i$ loves his$_i$ mother.
      b. The boy$_i$ loves his$_i$ mother.

In both cases, we have a pronoun in coreference. In each sentence in (66), however, the antecedent does not refer to any particular individual, but specifies a set {x}, such that x is a person:

(66) a. Everyone$_i$ loves his$_i$ mother.
      b. Someone$_i$ loves his$_i$ mother.
      c. Who$_i$ loves his$_i$ mother?

In the Principles and Parameters framework, while referential NPs are treated as arguments of sentences, quantificational NPs (QNPs) are treated as operators, each binding a variable in argument position. Such an operator–variable configuration is created when the QNP is A′-moved to Spec of CP (under *wh*-movement as in (66c) for English *wh*-questions) or adjoined to IP (under Quantifier Raising (QR) of May 1977) at the level of Logical Form. The sentences in (66) have the following LF representations:

(67) a. [Everyone$_i$ [t$_i$ loves his$_i$ mother]]
      b. [Someone$_i$ [t$_i$ loves his$_i$ mother]]
      c. [Who$_i$ [t$_i$ loves his$_i$ mother]]

These representations are then each interpreted through a restrictive quantification formula, having the following informal forms:

(68) a. For all x: x a person, x loves x's mother.
      b. For some x: x a person, x loves x's mother.
      c. For which x: x a person, x loves x's mother.

Notice that in each of (67), the pronoun *his* has the trace t_i as its antecedent. Since the antecedent is itself a variable, the referential value of the pronoun *co-varies* with the value assigned to its antecedent, as shown in (68). In each case, the pronoun is used as a bound variable.

9.3.2   *Variable binding: scope, accessibility, and disjointness*

The distinction between coreference and variable binding is an area that has not been addressed by Binding Theory. Although all pronouns are governed by Principles B and D, there are additional restrictions on the use of bound variable pronouns that do not hold of coreferential ones. We can see this by comparing (69) with a referential antecedent *Zhangsan*, with (70) with a quantificational antecedent *mei-ge ren* 'everyone.' As shown in (69), a pronoun may take a c-commanding antecedent outside its local domain (see (a–b)), or a non-c-commanding antecedent occurring either locally (i.e., (c)), or at a distance (as in (d–e)):[17]

(69) a. Zhangsan$_i$ xiwang women hui xihuan ta$_i$.
          Zhangsan hope   we   will like   him
          'Zhangsan hopes that we will like him.'

      b. Zhangsan$_i$ hen danxin ta$_i$-de muqin.
          Zhangsan very worried his   mother
          'Zhangsan is very worried about his mother.'

      c. Zhangsan$_i$-de muqin hen danxin ta$_i$.
          Zhangsan-DE mother very worried him
          'Zhangsan$_i$'s mother is very worried about him$_i$.'

      d. wo kandao Zhangsan$_i$ de shihou, ta$_i$ zheng zai chi fan.
          I   see   Zhangsan DE time   he right at eat rice
          'When I saw Zhangsan, he was having dinner.'

      e. wo kandao ta$_i$ de shihou, Zhangsan$_i$ zheng zai chi fan.
          I   see   him DE time   Zhangsan right at eat rice
          'When I saw him, Zhangsan was having dinner.'

In (70), whereas quantificational binding is possible where the antecedent *mei-ge ren* 'everyone' c-commands the pronoun (as in (a–b)), the indexings shown in (70c–d) are out:

(70) a. mei-ge ren$_i$ dou xiwang women hui xihuan ta$_i$.
          everyone   all hope   we   will like   him/her.
          'Everyone hopes that we will like him/her.'

      b. mei-ge ren$_i$ dou hen danxin ta$_i$-de muqin.
          everyone   all very worried his/her mother
          'Everyone$_i$ is worried about his/her$_i$ mother.'

      c. ??mei-ge ren$_i$-de muqin dou hen danxin ta$_i$.
          everyone-DE mother all very worried him/her
          'Everyone$_i$'s mother is worried about him/her$_i$.'

---

[17] In fact, nothing in Binding Theory requires a pronoun to have an antecedent at all. The following may be said of a pickpocket caught in action by a closed-circuit camera:

(i) ni kan-kan, ta na-le   shoubiao, jiu zheme zou-le   chuqu!
     you look-look, s/he take-LE watch,   then thus walk-LE out
     'Look! S/he took the watch and walked out just like that!'

And such a *deictic* use of a pronoun is also grammatical in each of the examples in (69), though in the absence of a larger context, each sentence in isolation tends to favor the coreferential reading.

    d. *wo kandao mei-ge ren$_i$ de shihou, ta$_i$ zheng zai chi fan.
       I   see   everyone   DE time   s/he right   at   eat rice
       *'When I saw everyone, s/he was having dinner.'

    e. *wo kandao ta$_i$ de shihou, mei-ge   ren$_i$ dou zheng zai chi fan.
       I   see   him/her DE time   everyone all   right at   eat rice
       *'When I saw him/her$_i$, everyone$_i$ was having dinner.'

The question we want to address is what makes quantificational binding impossible in (70c–e). What we have seen in (69) and (70) suggests the generalization that a pronoun may take a quantificational antecedent only under c-command by the antecedent, though the c-command requirement does not hold of a non-quantificational antecedent.[18] There is evidence, however, that this requirement is too strong. The following examples clearly permit a bound variable reading for the pronoun *ta*, showing that c-command per se is not a necessary condition for quantificational binding:

(71) a. mei-ge ren$_i$ shou-dao de xin   shangmian dou xie-zhe   ta$_i$ jia
       everyone   receive   DE letter on   all   write-ZHE his/her home
       de dizhi.
       DE address
       'For all x, the letter that x received has x's home address written on it.'

      b. mei-ge ren$_i$ xihuan de xiaoshuo dou rang ta$_i$ xiang-qi-le
       everyone   like   DE novel   all   cause him think-up-LE
       tongnian   wangshi.
       childhood old-event
       'For all x, the novel that x likes causes x to remember x's childhood.'

In both (71a) and (71b), the antecedent *mei-ge ren* 'everyone' occurs within a relative clause modifying the subject, hence failing to c-command the pronoun in the main clause, but the pronoun can have a bound variable reading.[19]

---

[18] Cf. Reinhart (1976) for the c-command requirement on quantificational binding in English; also Reinhart (1983), who maintains a distinction between variable binding and coreference for definite NP antecedents as well. Thus (69a–b) are treated as cases of variable binding on a par with (70a–b), but (69c–e) are treated as cases of coreference. In the latter cases, the pronouns are not seen as depending for their reference on the antecedents.

[19] In English, there is also evidence that quantificational binding does not require strict c-command. In the following examples, the pronouns are clearly used as bound variables:

    (i)   The election of no president$_i$ will please any of his$_i$ opponents.

    (ii)   Applications from every student$_i$ must each be accompanied by his$_i$ or her$_i$ parents' signatures.

If c-command is not a necessary condition, then what explains the ill-formedness of (70c–e)? We would like to suggest that these examples illustrate the need for three requirements that make the binding of a pronoun by a QNP possible, drawing on works by Chomsky (1976), Higginbotham (1980a, b), and Aoun and Li (1990):

(72)   Conditions on Bound Variable Pronouns:
        A pronoun may have a QNP as its antecedent only if

        a. the QNP is interpreted as having scope over the pronoun,
        b. the QNP is accessible to the pronoun, and
        c. the pronoun is locally A′-free (as well as A-free).

Consider first the scope requirement, (72a). The relevance of this requirement can be seen by comparing (71) with (73):

(73) a. *mei-ge ren$_i$ dou shou-dao de xin   shangmian xie-zhe
         everyone   all receive   DE letter on   write-ZHE
         ta$_i$ jia   de dizhi.
         his/her home DE address
         *'The letter that everyone received has his/her home address written on it.'

      b. *mei-ge ren$_i$ dou xihuan de xiaoshuo rang ta$_i$ xiang-qi-le
         everyone   all like   DE novel   cause him/her think-up-LE
         tongnian   wangshi.
         childhood old-event
         *'The novel that everyone likes causes him/her to remember his/her childhood.'

The examples in (71) and (73) are identical with respect to the structural relations between *mei-ge ren* 'everyone' and the pronoun *ta*: the quantifier is a constituent of a relative clause modifying the subject, whereas the pronoun occurs in the main clause. The crucial difference lies in the position of the adverbial *dou*, which serves as a licenser and scope marker for a universal quantifier to its left. In each of (71) *dou* occurs in the matrix clause and *mei-ge ren* has scope over the entire sentence. The universal QNP is interpreted *distributively* in each case, as indicated in the translation, so that each person may be understood as having received a separate letter or having his/her own favorite novel. The bound variable reading is available. In each of (73) on the other hand, *dou* occurs within the subject relative clause and the QNP *mei-ge ren* has scope internal to the relative clause. The QNP is interpreted *collectively* in these cases, so that everybody is understood to have received the same letter, or have the same favorite novel. The bound variable reading is unavailable in these examples.

Assuming that QNPs are adjoined to their scope position in LF under QR, note that the scope requirement (72a) amounts to the claim that a QNP must A′-bind the pronoun at LF. For illustration, the LF representations of (71a) and (73a) are as in (74) and (75) respectively, after *mei-ge ren* has been raised to its appropriate scope positions:

(74)   [$_{\text{IP}}$ mei-ge ren$_i$ [$_{\text{IP}}$ [$_{\text{NP}}$ t$_i$ shou-dao de xin] . . . dou xie-zhe ta$_i$ jia   de dizhi]].
        everyone   receive DE letter   all written his home DE address
        'Everyone is such that each letter s/he received has his/her home address on it.'

(75)   *[$_{\text{IP}}$ [$_{\text{DP}}$ [$_{\text{IP}}$ mei-ge ren$_i$ [$_{\text{IP}}$ t$_i$ dou shou-dao]] de xin] . . . xie-zhe ta$_i$ jia
                  everyone   all receive   DE letter   written his home
        de dizhi].
        DE address
        *'The letter that everyone received has his/her home address on it.'

That is, although the c-command requirement is too strong as a requirement of overt Syntax, c-command at LF is indeed a necessary condition that quantificational binding must meet. In addition to the contrasts between (71) and (73), this requirement also correctly rules out the indexing in (70d). As indicated in the English translation, *mei-ge ren* in (70d) has scope internal to the clause within the time adjunct. The relevant LF representation is as in (76):

(76)   *[[$_{\text{IP}}$ mei-ge ren$_i$ [$_{\text{IP}}$ wo kandao t$_i$]] de shihou], ta$_i$ zheng zai chi fan.
          everyone   I see   DE time   s/he right at eat rice
        *'When I saw everyone, s/he was having dinner.'

The bound variable reading of the pronoun is ruled out. Example (76) differs from (71)–(73) in that the universal QNP *mei-ge ren* occurs in an object position, and this somehow prevents it from taking scope over the matrix clause. In subject position, matrix scope is possible, as seen in (77) with its LF representation in (78):

(77)   mei-ge ren$_i$ jingguo zheli de shihou, wo dou gen ta$_i$ da zhaohu.
        everyone   pass   here DE time, I   all with him do greeting
        'Everyone is such that when s/he passes by here, I always say hello to him/her.'

(78)   [$_{\text{CP}}$ mei-ge ren$_i$ [$_{\text{CP}}$ [t$_i$ jingguo zheli de shihou], [$_{\text{IP}}$ wo dou gen ta$_i$
            everyone   pass   here DE time,   I   all with him
        da zhaohu]]].
        do greeting

In other words, in Chinese, relative clauses seem to be scope islands for a universal QNP in object position, though not for a subject universal QNP. In contrast, conditional clauses seem to be absolute islands for a universal QNP even in subject position:

(79)   *ruguo mei-ge ren$_i$ jingguo zheli, wo dou hui gen ta$_i$ da zhaohu.
          if   everyone   pass   here I   all will with him/her do greeting
        *'If everyone passes by here, I will always greet him/her.'

(80)   *bixu mei-ge ren$_i$ jingguo zheli, wo cai dou hui gen ta$_i$ da zhaohu.
        must everyone pass   here I   then all will with him/her do greeting
        *'Only if everyone passes by here, I will always greet him/her.'

This account of the impossible indexing in (70d) also provides us with an account of a difference between the universal and interrogative QNPs. For example, replacement of *mei-ge ren* in (70d) with *shei* 'who' yields an acceptable bound reading:

(81)   ni   kandao shei de shihou, ta   zheng zai chi fan ne?
        you see   who DE time   s/he right at eat rice Q
        'Who is the person x such that when you saw x, x was having dinner?'

In the same manner, substituting a *wh*-phrase for *mei-ge ren* in the conditionals in (79) and (80) yields acceptable indexings.

(82)   ruguo shei$_i$ jingguo zheli, ni jiu hui gen ta$_i$ da zhaohu ne?
        if   who   pass   here you then will with him/her do greeting Q
        'Who is the person x such that if x passes by here, you will greet x?'

(83)   bixu shenme-ren$_i$ jingguo zheli, ni cai hui gen ta$_i$ da zhaohu ne?
        must what-person   pass   here you then will with him/her do greeting Q
        'Who is the person x such that only if x passes here will you greet x?'

In short, a bound variable reading for a pronoun is possible only if the quantificational antecedent has scope over the pronoun. Examples (80)–(83) permit a bound variable reading because the *wh*-phrase has matrix scope (these sentences are direct questions), but (70d) and (79)–(80) do not permit such a reading because *mei-ge ren* is incapable of having matrix scope.

We have seen that the ill-formedness of (70d) follows from the scope requirement (72a). Let us now consider (70e), repeated below:

(70e)   *wo kandao ta$_i$ de shihou, mei-ge ren$_i$ dou zheng zai chi fan.
        I   see   him/her DE time   everyone   all right at eat rice
        *'When I saw him/her$_i$, everyone$_i$ was having dinner.'

Example (70e) differs from (70d) in that the pronoun and the intended antecedent have swapped their positions. The pronoun occurs now within the temporal adjunct and the QNP occurs as the main clause subject. As the main clause subject, the QNP can have scope over the entire sentence. The indexing indicated in (70e) therefore satisfies the scope requirement (72a). However, binding is not possible in (70e) any more than it is in (70d). Similar problems arise from sentences with existential and interrogative QNPs:

(84)   *wo kandao ta$_i$ de shihou, (you) yi-ge ren$_i$ zheng zai chi fan.
        I   see   him DE time   (have) someone right at eat rice
        *'When I saw him$_i$, someone$_i$ was having dinner.'

(85)   *ni   kandao ta$_i$ de shihou, shei$_i$ zheng zai chi fan ne?
        you see   him DE time   who right at eat rice Q
        *'When you saw him$_i$, who$_i$ was having dinner?'

These examples illustrate the relevance of the accessibility requirement, (72b). The term *accessibility* is first due to Higginbotham (1980b), but the classical version of this requirement is the so-called "Leftness Condition" of Chomsky (1976):

(86)   The Leftness Condition
        A variable cannot be the antecedent of a pronoun to its left.

The Leftness Condition is a condition applied to LF representations, and it rules out configurations that result from raising a QNP (under QR) across a non-c-commanding pronoun (i.e., Weak Crossover configurations). The indexings indicated in (70e) and (84)–(85) are ruled out, because their LF representations (such as (87) for (70e)) are in violation of the Leftness Condition:

(87)   *[mei-ge ren$_i$ [wo kandao ta$_i$ de shihou, t$_i$ dou zheng zai chi fan]]
        everyone   I   see   him DE time   all right at eat rice

Higginbotham argues that the Leftness Condition should be abandoned in favor of a non-linear notion of accessibility that refers crucially to the notion c-command. To simplify our discussion, a QNP is accessible to a pronoun iff the QNP (a) c-commands the pronoun or (b) is contained in an NP that is itself accessible to the pronoun.[20] A pronoun can be bound by a QNP only if the QNP is accessible to the pronoun. We shall adopt Higginbotham's version for its descriptive superiority, and note that, as far as our examples are concerned, the condition of accessibility obtains the correct results. Take the contrasting pair (81) and (85), for example. In (81), the *wh*-phrase *shei* does not c-command the pronoun, but it is contained in an NP (headed by *shihou* 'time') that does, so it is accessible to the pronoun. In (85), the *wh*-phrase neither c-commands the pronoun nor is contained in an NP that does, so it is not accessible to bind the pronoun as a variable. This applies to the universal *mei-ge ren* and the existential *yi-ge ren* in (70e) and (84), respectively, as well.

   We have now accounted for the ungrammatical status of (70d) and (70e) by attributing them to the scope requirement and the accessibility requirement, respectively. This leaves us with (70c), repeated below:

(70c)   ??mei-ge ren$_i$-de muqin dou hen danxin ta$_i$.
        everyone-DE   mother all   very worried him/her
        'Everyone$_i$'s mother is worried about him/her$_i$.'

---

[20] Some important details are left out here. For a review of the various accounts to remedy the Leftness Condition, see Huang (1994a).

Similar sentences with existential or interrogative QNPs have the same status:

(88)   ??shei$_i$-de muqin zui   danxin   ta$_i$.
        who-DE mother most worried him/her
        'Whose$_i$ mother is most worried about him/her$_i$?'

(89)   ??you-ge ren$_i$-de muqin hen danxin   ta$_i$.
        someone-DE   mother very worried him/her
        'Someone$_i$'s mother is worried about him/her$_i$.'

These sentences are problematic because they all meet the scope and accessibility requirements, but binding is rather hard to obtain for some speakers (though others have no problem with such a reading). In this connection we find that the sentences improve somewhat when the pronoun is further embedded.

(90)   mei-ge ren$_i$-de muqin dou hen guanxin   ta$_i$ de gongke.
        everyone-DE   mother all very concerned s/he DE schoolwork
        'Everyone$_i$'s mother is concerned about his$_i$/her$_i$ schoolwork.'

(91)   shei$_i$-de muqin shuo-guo ta   de-le   jiang le?
        who-DE mother say-Exp s/he get-LE prize LE
        'Whose mother said that s/he had won a prize?'

Earlier we showed that examples like (71a) permit quantificational binding:

(71a)   mei-ge ren$_i$ shou-dao de xin   shangmian dou xie-zhe
        everyone   receive   DE letter on   all write-ZHE
        ta$_i$ jia   de dizhi.
        his/her home DE address
        'For all x, the letter that x received has x's home address written on it.'

Here the pronoun is fairly deeply embedded. If the pronoun occurs as the object of the main clause, the bound reading becomes somewhat degraded too:

(92)   ??mei-ge ren$_i$ shou-dao de xin   dou piping   ta$_i$.
        everyone   receive   DE letter all criticize him/her
        'For all x, the letter that x received criticizes x.'

These contrasts, if they are real, suggest that the problem with (70c) and (88)–(89) lies not with the QNP, but with the pronoun occurring "too close" to the quantificational antecedent. This reminds us of similar observations made in Aoun and Li (1989) concerning some speakers, and the generalization they drew: a quantificationally bound pronoun, besides being A-free in its governing category (Principle B), also must be locally A′-free – free from any A′-binder within the minimal potential domain of A′-binding (i.e., an A′ disjointness requirement). Suppose that DP and IP each constitute a potential A′-binding domain. The unacceptability of (70c) and (88)–(89) then follows because in each case the QNP is required to have the matrix IP as its scope, but the object pronoun must be A′-free from any QNP in the same domain, which poses a contradiction. On the other hand, in the acceptable (90) and (91), the pronoun *ta* is A′-free in its local A′-binding domain (the DP *ta de gongke* 'his/her schoolwork' in (90), and the embedded IP in (91)). This makes it possible for the pronoun to be quantificationally bound in the matrix IP.

To summarize, we have seen in this section that for a pronoun to be used as a bound variable, its quantificational antecedent must have scope over the pronoun and be accessible to it and, possibly, the pronoun itself must be locally A′-free (in addition to being A-free in accordance with Binding Theory). Most of these conditions (especially with respect to scope and accessibility) have been shown to obtain in English and other languages that are typologically quite different from Chinese, so their relevance in Chinese lends support to the idea that these principles reflect properties of Universal Grammar. Indeed, given the highly subtle and abstract nature of the interpretive matters that concern us, which are mostly unavailable in the primary data that trigger early language growth, it would be surprising if the conditions governing the bound variable use of the pronoun in Chinese were fundamentally different from those employed for other languages.

9.3.3   Indefinites and donkey anaphora

The conditions on quantificational binding – scope, accessibility, and possibly minimal disjointness – are expected to apply to all QNP types, including universal, existential, and interrogative QNPs. While they do work generally for the examples we have encountered, a problem remains with certain sentences containing existential QNPs, as illustrated below:

(93)   wo kandao yi-ge ren$_i$ de shihou, ta$_i$ zheng zai chi fan.
        I   see   someone DE time   s/he right   at   eat rice
        'When I saw someone, he was having dinner.'

This is to be compared with (70d), repeated below as (94):

(94)   *wo kandao mei-ge ren$_i$ de shihou, ta$_i$ zheng zai chi fan.
         I   see   everyone DE time   s/he right   at   eat rice
        *'When I saw everyone, s/he was having dinner.'

Recall that the indexing in (94) was ruled out because it fails the scope requirement, as *mei-ge ren* 'everyone' has scope internal to the *when*-clause. A problem arises, however, under the same internal-scope interpretation of *yi-ge ren* 'someone.' The sentence can be read (as can its English translation) as saying that when there was some person x such that I saw x, x was just having dinner. Under such a reading (93) clearly also fails the scope requirement, but in this case coindexing *ta* with *yi-ge ren* is allowed.[21]

The available indexing in (93) indicates that Chinese also has its own version of a "donkey pronoun" and the problems associated with it. "Donkey sentences" are illustrated by examples like (95), attributed originally to Peter Geach:

(95) a. If a farmer owns a donkey, he beats it.
       b. Every farmer who owns a donkey beats it.

The problem these sentences raise is that, under the traditional treatment (following Bertrand Russell) of an indefinite NP as an existential quantifier, the scope of *a donkey* is limited within the first subordinate or relative clause that contains it (as in (95)). Yet apparent binding of the pronoun outside its scope is possible. This is exactly the problem we saw with (93). More examples are given below. These include not only normal indefinites as in (96)–(97), but also *wh*-indefinites as in (98) (see Chapter 7 and A. Li 1992b), and *wh*-interrogatives as in (99). The crucial fact to observe is that in each case, the indefinite antecedent of a pronoun does not have scope over the pronoun, but the pronoun is apparently bound by it.

(96)   ruguo ni   zhaodao yi-ge   xin pengyou, qing ba ta   jieshao   gei wo.
       if   you find   one-CL new friend,   please BA him/her introduce to me
       'If you find a new friend, please introduce him/her to me.'

(97)   shi nian qian wo jiao-guo   yi-ge   hao xuesheng. zuijin ta   lai
       ten year ago I   teach-GUO one-CL good student   recently s/he come
       zhao-le wo.
       seek-LE me
       'Ten years ago I taught a very good student. Recently s/he came to see me.'

(98)   yaoshi shei   xihuan zhe ben shu, wo jiu   mai yi ben song gei ta.
       if   someone like   this-CL book I   then buy one-CL give-to him/her
       'If anyone likes this book, I will buy a copy for him/her.'

(99)   buguan   shei lai   zhao wo, dou bie   rang ta   jinlai.
       regardless who come seek me, all don't let   him/her enter
       'No matter who comes to look for me, don't let him/her come in.'

---

[21] Example (93) also allows a reading according to which *yi-ge ren* has wide scope, extending over the entire matrix sentence, i.e., 'Someone x was such that when I saw x, x was having dinner.' This parallels the direct question reading of (81). Under this reading, the scope principle is fully satisfied.

9.3.3.1 Two approaches to donkey anaphora

The paradox raised by donkey sentences has been a topic of great interest and controversy in the recent past. Two prominent approaches to the paradox have been influential: the "E-type strategy" of Evans (1980), and the Discourse Representation Theory (DRT) of Heim (1982) and Kamp (1981).

Evans (1980) adopted the traditional Russellian view of the indefinite as an existential quantifier and denied the bound-variable status of the pronoun. According to Evans (1980), the pronoun belongs to a new type (called the "E-type") which refers "to the object(s), if any, which verify the antecedent quantifier-containing clause" (p. 340). According to this analysis, the antecedent of *it* in (95) is not the indefinite *a donkey*, but something akin to a definite description, like *the donkey that he (the farmer) owns*. Thus (95) can be paraphrased as: *If a farmer owns a donkey, he beats the donkey that he owns*. The E-type pronoun constitutes a fourth type of pronoun, distinct from (a) the deictic, (b) the coreferential, and (c) the bound-variable pronouns.[22] Because such a pronoun is not a bound variable, it does not have to occur in the scope of the indefinite quantifier to which it is related.[23]

In the DRT analysis of Kamp (1981) and Heim (1982), on the other hand, an indefinite NP like *a donkey* or *a farmer* is treated not as a quantifier, but as a variable, akin to the pronoun associated with it. A central observation that has been taken to motivate such a view is the fact that an indefinite NP does not seem to have inherent quantificational force, but exhibits quantificational variability under various adverbs of quantification (Lewis 1975). Thus the indefinites in (95a) may have the quantificational force of *all*, *most*, or *some* depending on the type of adverbs they occur with:

(100) a. Always, if a farmer owns a donkey, he beats it.
    = **All** farmers (x) and donkeys (y) are such that if x owns y, then x beats y.
  b. Usually, if a farmer owns a donkey, he beats it.
    = **Most** farmers (x) and donkeys (y) are such that if x owns y, then x beats y.
  c. Sometimes, if a farmer owns a donkey, he beats it.
    = **Some** farmers (x) and donkeys (y) are such that if x owns y, then x beats y.

These variations are captured by treating each indefinite NP and any pronoun associated with it as a variable bound by the adverb of quantification. In the

---

[22] In a sense, one might regard the E-type pronoun as a "virtual" deictic pronoun. A normal deictic pronoun directly refers to an individual that may be identified with a pointing finger, while a donkey pronoun refers to an individual identified by a definite description inferred from, but not expressed in, the text.

[23] In fact, a donkey pronoun cannot be c-commanded by its indefinite antecedent. A sentence like *Someone believes he's innocent* does not have an E-type interpretation of the pronoun. This may follow from Binding Principle C and the assumption that the E-type pronoun is a definite description, hence an R-expression in the sense of Principle C.

following representation, the operator "unselectively" binds the variables *a farmer*, *a donkey*, *he*, and *it*.

(101)   Always$_{i,j}$, if a farmer$_i$ owns a donkey$_j$, he$_i$ beats it$_j$.

Given the universal force of *always*, (101) represents the interpretation indicated in (102):

(102) $\forall x\ \forall y$ ((x is a farmer & y is a donkey & x owns y) $\rightarrow$ (x beats y))

In the absence of an overt adverb of quantification, an implicit necessity operator (i.e., *necessarily*) is assumed in a conditional like (95), again giving rise to a universal interpretation of the sentence.

The unselective binding analysis of the DRT treats not only the donkey pronouns, but also the indefinites, as variables occurring in the scope of (adverbial) binders. For the E-type analysis, an indefinite is a normal quantifier and a new category is recognized for the donkey pronoun. For the DRT, a donkey pronoun is a normal bound variable but, in addition to a normal bound variable, a new kind of bound variable is posited in the form of an indefinite NP.

The facts about donkey sentences in English largely carry over to Chinese, and so the controversy over the two approaches applies as well. In the rest of this chapter, we will make two points. First, on grounds of generality, the E-type strategy should be preferred for the donkey sentences we have discussed so far. Second, the unselective binding strategy is nevertheless independently needed, for an account of certain donkey sentences in Chinese.

9.3.3.2   Two types of donkey sentences

Our first point is that although unselective binding nicely captures the phenomenon of quantificational variability, the strategy lacks generality as a solution to the problem posed by pronouns that are related to quantificational antecedents but lie outside their scopes. Compare (98) and (99) above for example. In (98) we have the *wh*-indefinite *shei* 'someone' and a related donkey pronoun *ta*. The sentence may be analyzed in terms of binding under an implicit necessity operator (NEC), as in (103), representing the meaning of (104):

(103)   NEC$_i$ [[yaoshi ... shei$_i$ ...], [wo jiu ... ta$_i$ ...]]
            if   someone   I   then   him/her

(104) $\forall x$ ((x likes this book) $\rightarrow$ (I will buy a copy for x))

However, in (99) the donkey pronoun *ta* is related to an interrogative *shei*. The strategy of treating the interrogative and the pronoun as variables unselectively bound by a wide-scope adverb of quantification is not available. The reason is that the interrogative interpretation requires *shei* (qua variable in the spirit of DRT) to be bound by a question operator having embedded scope under *buguan* 'regardless of,' which selects an embedded question as its complement.

(105)   buguan [[Q_i [shei$_i$ lai   zhao wo]], dou bie   rang ta$_i$ jinlai].
         regardless   who come seek me,   all don't let   him/her enter
         'No matter who comes to look for me, don't let him/her come in.'

The binder Q of the variable *shei* still does not have the pronoun *ta* in its scope, and so the scope requirement is still not satisfied. The problem also remains when universal QNPs and plural indefinites are involved:

(106)   ruguo mei-ge ren dou dao-qi-le, jiu   jiao tamen yiqi   jinlai.
         if   everyone all arrive-LE then tell them together enter
         'If everyone has arrived, tell them to come in together.'

(107)   yaoshi tai shao ren   lai,   jiu   qing tamen xian hui jia
         if   too few person come then ask them first go home
         denghou tongzhi.
         wait   notice
         'If too few people arrive, then ask them to go home to wait for further notice.'

In (106) the position of *dou* 'all' shows that *mei-ge ren* has scope within the *if*-clause. Similarly, *tai shao ren* 'too few people' in (107) is naturally interpreted as a narrow scope existential. Unlike singular indefinites which exhibit quantificational variability under frequency adverbs, plural indefinites such as *few people*, *many students*, etc., and universals do not, and binding under a wide-scope adverb of quantification does not yield the right semantics. To account for the pronouns in (105)–(107) an E-type strategy would presumably be needed. In each case, the pronoun may be paraphrased as a definite description on the basis of the clause that contains its antecedent: 'the one who comes to see me,' 'all those who have arrived,' and 'the few who have come.' In other words, the strategy of unselective binding lacks general applicability and, on grounds of theoretical parsimony, should be dispensed with, all else being equal.[24]

However, all else is not equal, and thus our second point is that the unselective binding strategy is necessary after all. We show that the strategy is independently motivated, not for the sentence types we have examined, but for a type of conditional sentence illustrated below.

---

[24] The argument from quantificational variability is also not fully compelling for the unselective binding analysis of singular indefinites. While unselective binding obtains variability by directly manipulating the quantificational force of the indefinite noun phrase, in the E-type analysis the variability can be derived, indirectly, by having the adverb quantify over (minimal) situations described by the clauses containing the indefinites.

(108)   shei xian lai,   shei xian chi.
         who first come,   who first eat
         'If x comes first, x will eat first.'
         (Whoever comes in first eats first.)

(109)   shei xian jinlai, wo xian da shei.
         who first enter, I first hit who
         'If x enters first, I shall hit x first.'
         (I will beat up whoever comes in first.)

The existence of sentences of this type has been noted for several decades. Cheng and Huang (1996) first noted their theoretical relevance to the current debate. These sentences have the syntax and semantics of conditionals, as evidenced in part by the fact that the element *jiu* 'then' may optionally occur in the consequent clause:

(110)   shei xian lai,   shei jiu xian chi.
         who first come   who then first eat
         Intended reading: same as (108).

(111)   shei xian jinlai, wo jiu xian da shei.
         who first enter, I   then first hit who
         Intended reading: same as (109).

These conditionals differ in form from normal *if. . . then* conditionals like (106)–(107) in that they do not have an overt leading element such as *ruguo* or *yaoshi* 'if' in the antecedent clause. These "bare conditionals" have several important properties that distinguish them from normal *if*-conditionals. First, each sentence contains two identical occurrences of a *wh*-word, one in the antecedent clause and one in the consequent clause. These two occurrences are identical both in form and in reference. Second, the *wh*-word in the consequent clause cannot be replaced by a pronoun or a definite description (see (112a–b)), or be completely missing from the consequent clause (see (112c)):

(112) a. *shei xian jinlai, **ta**   xian chi.
           who first enter s/he first teach

      b. *shei xian jinlai, **zhe-ge ren**   xian chi.
           who first enter this-CL person first eat

      c. *shei xian jinlai, wo hui hen gaoxing.
           who first enter, I   will very happy

A bare conditional may contain more than one *wh*-word in the antecedent clause, but for each such word in the antecedent clause, an identical *wh*-word is found in the consequent. As a result, each bare conditional may contain two, or four, or six *wh*-words, etc.

(113) a. shei yan shei, shei xiang   shei.
           who act   who   who   resemble who
           'If [actor] x plays [character] y, x resembles y.'

    b. shei xihuan shenme, shei jiu   mai shenme.
           who   like   what   who   then buy what
           'If x likes y, then x buys y.'

These properties distinguish the bare conditionals from normal *if*-conditionals. A normal *if*-conditional does not require the existence of an anaphoric element in the consequent clause (114c), and if one does exist in the consequent clause, it may take the form of a pronoun or a definite description (114a–b):

(114) a. ruguo shei xian jinlai, **ta**   jiu   xian chi.
           if   who   first enter   s/he then first eat
           'If someone comes in first, then s/he will eat first.'

    b. yaoshi shei xian jinlai, **nei-ge ren**   jiu   xian chi.
           if   who   first enter   that-CL person then first eat
           'If someone comes first, then that person will eat first.'

    c. yaoshi shei xian jinlai, wo hui   hen   gaoxing.
           if   who   first enter   I   will very happy
           'If someone comes in first, I will be very happy.'

In this respect, the normal *if*-conditionals behave on a par with the following sentences with *dou* (the "*dou*-conditionals"):

(115) a. (buguan)   shei xian jinlai, **ta**   dou keyi xian chi.
           regardless who   first enter   s/he all   can   first eat
           'No matter who comes in first, s/he will get to eat first.'

    b. (buguan)   shei xian jinlai, **nei-ge ren**   dou keyi xian chi.
           regardless who   first enter, that-CL person all   can   first eat
           'No matter who comes in first, that person will get to eat first.'

    c. (buguan)   shei xian jinlai, wo dou hui   hen   gaoxing.
           regardless who   first enter   I   all   will very happy
           'No matter who comes in first, I will be very happy.'

Neither the normal *if*-conditionals nor the *dou*-conditionals go well with a *wh*-word in the consequent clause:

(116)   ??ruguo shei xian jinlai, jiu   rang shei xian chi.[25]
             if   who   first enter   then let   who   first eat

[25] The strength of the grammaticality judgment with the *if*-conditionals varies somewhat among speakers. If the antecedent clause does not contain *ruguo* 'if' but the consequent clause does contain *jiu* 'then,' many speakers allow a free alternation between a pronoun

(117)   *(buguan)   shei xian jinlai, wo dou rang shei xian chi.
         regardless who first enter I all let who first eat

Following Cheng and Huang (1996), we take the systematic contrasts between bare conditionals and *if-* and *dou-*conditionals to indicate that while the *if-* and *dou-*conditionals are best treated via the E-type strategy, the bare conditionals exemplify unselective binding *par excellence.* According to Heim's (1982) schema, unselective binding involves a tripartite structure consisting of an operator, a restriction, and a nucleus. In a conditional sentence, an adverb of quantification serves as the operator, the antecedent clause maps into the restrictive clause, and the consequent maps into the nuclear clause. The operator binds a variable in both the restriction and the nucleus. Under the tripartite schema, (109) would be appropriately represented as in (118):

(118) NEC_i $shei_i$ xian jinlai, wo xian da $shei_i$
         who first enter I fist hit who
         OP_i (Restriction)   (Nucleus)

Example (113a) would be represented by multiple unselective binding as in (119):

(119) $NEC_{i,j}$ $shei_i$ yan $shei_j$, $shei_i$ xiang $shei_j$
         who act who who resemble who
         $OP_{i,j}$ (Restriction)   (Nucleus)

Note that in both (118) and (119), the operator *directly* and *locally* binds both the *wh-*variable(s) in the antecedent clause and those in the consequent clause – since neither of the *wh-*variables c-commands the other. The two occurrences of *shei* 'who' in (118), in other words, are of equal status, with neither construed as being anaphoric to the other. This explains why both occurrences of the same variable take the form of identical *wh-*phrases. The *wh-*phrase in the consequent clause cannot be replaced by an anaphoric pronoun or a definite description (implying 'familiarity'), because its status is equal to that in the antecedent clause, not

---

and a *wh-*phrase:

(i)   shei xian jinlai, wo jiu xian da shei/ta.
       who first enter I then first hit who/him/her

We shall consider such "half-bare" conditionals to have the status of either *if-*conditionals (when they take a pronoun in the consequent clause) or bare conditionals (when they take a *wh-*word). The conditions under which the alternation is possible are somewhat complicated, depending in part on where the anaphoric pronoun or *wh-*word is. See Cheng and Huang (1996) and Lin (1996) for additional discussion. Details aside, what is important here is that if a particular sentence type allows an anaphoric pronoun, then it also allows a definite description in the consequent clause; and if an anaphoric pronoun is prohibited, so is a definite description.

anaphoric to it. The tripartite representation also explains why a *wh*-variable must occur in both the antecedent and the consequent clause. Assuming that natural language quantification is both restrictive and non-vacuous, the following bare conditionals are ungrammatical because neither of these requirements has been satisfied. These sentences are as "strange" as their English translations sound:

(120) a. *shei xian jinlai, wo xian da Lisi.
           who first enter I first hit Lisi
           (*'For all x such that x comes in first, I shall hit Lisi first.')

     b. *Lisi xian jinlai, wo xian da shei.
         Lisi first enter I first hit who
         (*'For all x such that Lisi comes in first, I hit x first.')

Our explanation of the properties of bare conditionals in terms of unselective binding also means that the *if*- and *dou*-conditionals are *not* examples of unselective binding, but are more appropriately treated using the E-type strategy. Because the E-type strategy treats the indefinite *wh*-phrase as an existential or interrogative quantifier having scope internal to the antecedent clause, no variable is needed (or tolerated) in the main or consequent clause. This explains the grammaticality of (114c) and (115c). If a reference is to be made from the main clause to the bound variable within the antecedent clause, such a reference will necessarily be anaphoric in nature, referring to whatever value the antecedent variable is assigned. It depends on the variable as its antecedent, and hence takes the form of an anaphoric pronoun or definite description, as in (114a–b) and (115a–b). Note that pronouns and definite descriptions are distributed in the same way: they are both allowed in *if*- and *dou*-conditionals, but both disallowed in bare conditionals. This provides an additional argument for Evans' treatment of the donkey pronoun as being on a par with a definite description.

In summary, there are two types of donkey sentences in Chinese: bare conditionals and *if*- and *dou*-conditionals. The bare conditionals provide strong evidence for the unselective binding mechanism as proposed in the DRT. Although the DRT account was first developed on the basis of "normal" conditional sentences involving donkey pronouns, our argument from bare conditionals serves, ironically, to reaffirm the appropriateness of an E-type strategy for the treatment of such donkey pronouns.

9.4   Summary and conclusion

This chapter has examined an important area of Chinese syntax as it relates to semantic interpretation, concerning the reference of nominal expressions. We have seen that, while the general patterns of NP reference in Chinese conform to general principles of binding, a number of phenomena specific to Chinese contribute to our understanding of the formal nature of the syntax–semantics interface and the interface between grammar and discourse, as part of human linguistic competence. Among these, the pattern of pronominal non-coreference helps to establish the need for an independent Principle D. The dual status of the bare reflexive *ziji* argues for the need to distinguish an anaphor governed by syntactic principles and a logophor governed by a combination of syntactic and functional principles operating at the grammar–discourse interface. The differential behaviors of definite and quantificational NP anaphora demonstrate the relevance of scope, accessibility, and locality for a theory of variable binding. The patterns of various conditional sentences show that both the E-type strategy and the unselective binding strategy are necessary for a proper theory of donkey anaphora in natural language.

The fact that the matters concerning us seem in large part to conform to general principles should not be surprising. Given the abstract nature of these matters from the point of view of the language learner, it is natural that they reflect the inner workings of the mind and part of the device that the child brings to the task of language acquisition. On the other hand, it is also clear that our understanding of these inner workings will not be complete without the in-depth examination and analysis of individual languages.

References

Abbreviations used in the references:

CLS: Papers from the annual regional meeting of the Chicago Linguistic Society
NELS: Proceedings of the annual conference of the North East Linguistic Society
WCCFL: Proceedings of the West Coast Conference on Formal Linguistics

Abney, Steven. 1987. The English noun phrase in its sentential aspect. Doctoral dissertation, MIT, Cambridge, Mass.
Åfarli, Tor A. 1994. A promotion analysis of restrictive relative clauses. *The Linguistic Review* 11: 81–100.
Alexiadou, Artemis. 1997. *Adverb placement: a case study in antisymmetric syntax.* Amsterdam: John Benjamins.
Alexiadou, Artemis, Paul Law, Andre Meinunger, and Chris Wilder. 2000. Introduction. In *The syntax of relative clauses*, ed. Artemis Alexiadou, Paul Law, Andre Meinunger, and Chris Wilder, 1–52. Amsterdam: John Benjamins.
Anderson, Stephen. 1972. How to get even. *Language* 48: 893–906.
    1992. *A-morphous morphology*. Cambridge: Cambridge University Press.
Aoun, Joseph, Norbert Hornstein, David Lightfoot, and Amy Weinberg. 1987. Two types of locality. *Linguistic Inquiry* 18: 537–577.
Aoun, Joseph and Y.-H. Audrey Li. 1989. Constituency and scope. *Linguistic Inquiry* 20: 141–172.
    1990. Minimal disjointness. *Linguistics* 28: 189–204.
    1993a. *Syntax of scope.* Cambridge, Mass.: MIT Press.
    1993b. *Wh*-elements in-situ: syntax or LF? *Linguistic Inquiry* 24: 199–238.
    1993c. On some differences between Chinese and Japanese. *Linguistic Inquiry* 24: 365–372.
    2003. *Essays on the representational and derivational nature of grammar: the diversity of wh-constructions*. Cambridge, Mass.: MIT Press.
Authier, J.-Marc and Lisa Reed. 1992. On the syntactic status of French affected datives. *The Linguistic Review* 9: 295–311.
Baker, Mark. 1988. *Incorporation: a theory of grammatical function changing*. Chicago: University of Chicago Press.
    1996. *The polysynthesis parameter*. New York: Oxford University Press.
    2002. Building and merging, not checking. *Linguistic Inquiry* 33: 321–328.
Baker, Mark, Kyle Johnson and Ian Roberts. 1989. Passive arguments raised. *Linguistic Inquiry* 20: 219–251.

Barss, Andrew. 1986. Chains and anaphoric dependencies. Doctoral dissertation, MIT, Cambridge, Mass.

Barss, Andrew, Ken Hale, Ellavina Tsosie Perkins, and Margaret Speas. 1991. Logical form and barriers in Navajo. In *Logical structure and linguistic structure*, ed. by C.-T. James Huang and Robert May, 25–48. Dordrecht: Kluwer.

Battistella, Edwin. 1989. Chinese reflexivization: a movement to INFL approach. *Linguistics* 27: 987–1012.

Bender, Emily. 2000. The syntax of Mandarin *ba*: reconsidering the verbal analysis. *Journal of East Asian Linguistics* 9: 105–145.

Bennett, Paul A. 1981. The evolution of passive and disposal sentences. *Journal of Chinese Linguistics* 9: 61–89.

Bianchi, Valentina. 1999. *Consequences of antisymmetry: headed relative clauses.* New York: Mouton de Gruyter.

Borer, Hagit. 1984. Restrictive relatives in Modern Hebrew. *Natural Language and Linguistic Theory* 2: 219–260.

    2005. *Structuring sense.* (Vol. 1: *In name only*; Vol. 2: *The normal course of events.*) New York: Oxford University Press.

Bowers, John. 1993. The syntax of predication. *Linguistic Inquiry* 24: 591–656.

Bresnan, Joan. 1982. The passive in lexical theory. In *The mental representation of grammatical relations*, ed. Joan Bresnan, 3–86. Cambridge, Mass.: MIT Press.

Browning, Marguerite A. 1987. Null operator constructions. Doctoral dissertation, MIT, Cambridge, Mass.

Carlson, Greg N. 1977. Amount relatives. *Language* 53: 520–542.

Carstens, Vicky. 1991. The morphology and syntax of determiner phrases in Kiswahili. Doctoral dissertation, University of California, Los Angeles.

Chao, Yuen-Ren. 1968. *A grammar of spoken Chinese*. Berkeley: University of California Press.

Chen, Ping. 1988. Lun xiandai hanyu shijian xitong de sanyuan jiegou [On the triplex structure of the temporal system in Modern Chinese], *Zhongguo Yuwen* 5: 401–422.

Cheng, Lisa L.-S. 1986. Clause structures in Mandarin Chinese. Master's thesis, University of Toronto.

    1991 [1997]. *On the typology of wh-questions*. Doctoral dissertation, MIT, published by Garland, New York, 1997.

    1995. On *dou*-quantification. *Journal of East Asian Linguistics* 4: 197–234.

Cheng, Lisa L.-S. and C.-T. James Huang. 1994. On the argument structure of resultative compounds. In *In honor of William Wang*, ed. Matthew Chen and Ovid T.-L. Tzeng, 187–221. Taipei: Pyramid Press.

    1996. Two types of donkey sentences. *Natural Language Semantics* 4: 121–163.

Cheng, Lisa L.-S., C.-T. James Huang, and C.-C. Jane Tang. 1996. Negative particle questions: a dialectal comparison. In *Microparametric syntax and dialect variation*, ed. James R. Black and Virginia Motapanyane, 41–78. Amsterdam: John Benjamins.

Cheng, Lisa L.-S., C.-T. James Huang, Y.-H. Audrey Li, and C.-C. Jane Tang. 1993. Three ways to get passive. Ms., University of California, Irvine; USC; and Academia Sinica.

    1996. *Hoo, hoo, hoo*: the causative, passive, and dative in Taiwanese. In *Contemporary studies on the Min dialects, Journal of Chinese Linguistics Monograph* 14, ed. Pang-Hsin, 146–203.

Cheng, Lisa L.-S. and Yafei Li. 1991. Multiple projections and double negation in Mandarin Chinese. Paper presented at North American Conference on Chinese Linguistics, Cornell University.

Cheng, Lisa L.-S. and Rint Sybesma. 1999. Bare and not-so-bare nouns and the structure of NP. *Linguistic Inquiry* 30: 509–542.

Cheung, Hung-Nin Samuel. 1973. A comparative study in Chinese grammars: the *ba*-construction. *Journal of Chinese Linguistics* 1(3): 343–382.

Chierchia, Gennaro. 1984. Topics in the syntax and semantics of infinitives and gerunds. Doctoral dissertation, University of Massachusetts, Amherst.

   1989. Anaphora and attitudes *de se*. In *Semantics and contextual expression*, ed. R. Bartsch, J. van Benthem, and P. van Emde Boas, 1–31. Dordrecht: Foris.

   1998. Reference to kinds across languages. *Natural Language Semantics* 6: 339–405.

Chiu, Bonnie. 1995. An object clitic projection in Mandarin Chinese. *Journal of East Asian Linguistics* 4: 77–117.

Chomsky, Noam. 1970. Remarks on nominalization. In *Readings in English transformational grammar*, ed. Roderick Jacobs and Peter S. Rosenbaum, 184–221. Waltham, Mass.: Ginn & Company.

   1973. Conditions on transformations. In *A festschrift for Morris Halle*, ed. Steven Anderson and Paul Kiparsky, 232–286. New York: Holt, Rinehart and Winston.

   1976. Conditions on rules of grammar. *Linguistic Analysis* 2: 303–351.

   1977. On *wh*-movement. In *Formal syntax*, ed. Peter Culicover, Thomas Wasow, and Adrian Akmajian, 71–132. New York: Academic Press.

   1981. *Lectures on government and binding*. Dordrecht: Foris.

   1982. *Some concepts and consequences of the theory of government and binding*. Cambridge, Mass.: MIT Press.

   1986a. *Knowledge of language*. New York: Praeger.

   1986b. *Barriers*. Cambridge, Mass.: MIT Press.

   1995. *The Minimalist Program*. Cambridge, Mass.: MIT Press.

   2000. Minimalist inquiries: The framework. In *Step by step*, ed. Roger Martin, David Michaels, and Juan Uriagereka, 89–156. Cambridge, Mass.: MIT Press.

   2001. Derivation by phrase. In *Ken Hale: a life in language*, ed. Michael Kenstowicz, 1–52. Cambridge, Mass.: MIT Press.

Cinque, Guglielmo. 1990. *Types of A′-dependencies*. Cambridge, Mass.: MIT Press.

   1999. *Adverbs and functional heads: a cross-linguistic perspective*. New York: Oxford University Press.

   2002. *Functional structure in DP and IP: the cartography of syntactic structures*, vol. 1, Oxford Studies in Comparative Syntax. New York: Oxford University Press.

Clements, George N. 1975. The logophoric pronoun in Ewe: its role in discourse. *Journal of West African Languages* 2: 141–177.

Cole, Peter and Gabriella Hermon. 1994. Is there LF *wh*-movement? *Linguistic Inquiry* 25: 239–262.

Cole, Peter, Gabriella Hermon, and Cher Leng Lee. 2001. Grammatical and discourse conditions on long-distance reflexives in two Chinese dialects. In *Long distance reflexives*, Syntax and semantics 33, ed. Peter Cole et al., 141–195. New York: Academic Press.

Cole, Peter, Gabriella Hermon, and Li-May Sung. 1990. Principles and parameters of long distance reflexives. *Linguistic Inquiry* 21: 1–22.

Cole, Peter and Cher Leng Lee. 1997. Locality constraints on yes-no questions in Singapore Teochew. *Journal of East Asian Linguistics* 6: 189–211.

Cole, Peter and Li-May Sung. 1994. Head movement and long-distance reflexives. *Linguistic Inquiry* 25: 355–406.

Cole, Peter and Chengchi Wang. 1996. Antecedents and blockers of long-distance reflexives: the case of Chinese *ziji*. *Linguistic Inquiry* 27: 357–390.

Contreras, Heles. 1987. Small clauses in Spanish and English. *Natural Language and Linguistic Theory* 5: 225–244.

Dahl, Östen. 1981. On the definition of the telic-atelic (bounded-nonbounded) distinction. In *Tense and aspect*, Syntax and semantics 14, ed. Philip Tedeschi and Annie Zaenen, 79–90. New York: Academic Press.

Del Gobbo, Francesca. 2003. Appositives at the interface. Doctoral dissertation, University of California, Irvine.

Demirdache, Hamida. 1991. Resumptive chains in restrictive relatives, appositives and dislocation structures. Doctoral dissertation, MIT.

Di Sciullo, Anna Maria and Edwin Williams. 1987. *On the definition of word*. Cambridge, Mass.: MIT Press.

Diesing, Molly. 1992. *Indefinites*. Cambridge, Mass.: MIT Press.

Dowty, David. 1979. *Word meaning and Montague grammar*. Dordrecht: Reidel.

 1991. Thematic proto-roles and argument selection. *Language* 67: 547–619.

Emonds, Joseph. 1978. The verbal complex V′-V″ in French. *Linguistic Inquiry* 9: 151–175.

Ernst, Thomas. 1988. Chinese postpositions? – again. *Journal of Chinese Linguistics* 16: 219–245.

 1994. Conditions on Chinese A-not-A questions. *Journal of East Asian Linguistics* 3: 241–264.

 2002. *The syntax of adjuncts*. Cambridge: Cambridge University Press.

Ernst, Thomas and Chengchi Wang. 1995. Object preposing in Mandarin Chinese. *Journal of East Asian Linguistics* 4: 235–260.

Evans, Gareth. 1980. Pronouns. *Linguistic Inquiry* 11: 337–362.

Fan, Jiyan. 1985. Wuding NP zhuyuju [Sentences with indefinite NP subjects]. *Zhongguo Yuwen* 5: 321–328.

Feng, Shengli. 1994. Prosodic structure and compound words in Classical Chinese. In *New Approaches to Chinese Word Formation*, ed. Jerome Packard, 197–260. Berlin: Mouton de Gruyter.

 1995. Guanyue lilun yu Hanyu de beidong ju [GB theory and passive sentences in Chinese]. *Zhongguo Yuyanxue Luncong [Studies in Chinese Linguistics]* 1: 1–28.

 1998. Short passive in Modern and Classical Chinese. Ms., University of Kansas.

 2000. *Prosodic syntax in Chinese*. Shanghai: Shanghai Jiaoyu Chubanshe.

Feng, Shengli and W.-T. Tsai. 2006. Shuo *men* de weizhi: cong jufa-yunlu de jiemian tanqi [On syntactic positions of *men* – An interface between prosody and syntax]. *Yuyanxue Luncong* 32: 46–63. Shanghai: Shangwu Yinshuguan.

Fiengo, Robert. 1977. On trace theory. *Linguistic Inquiry* 8: 35–62.

Fiengo, Robert, C.-T. James Huang, Howard Lasnik, and Tanya Reinhart. 1988. The syntax of wh-in-situ. *WCCFL* 7: 81–98.

Fiengo, Robert and Robert May. 1994. *Indices and identity*. Cambridge, Mass.: MIT Press.

Frei, Henri. 1956. The ergative construction in Chinese: theory of Pekinese *pa*. *Gengo Kenkyu* 31: 22–50.

Freidin, Robert. 1991. *Foundations of generative syntax*. Cambridge, Mass.: MIT Press.

Fu, Jingqi. 1994. On deriving Chinese derived nominals: evidence for V-to-N raising. Doctoral dissertation, University of Massachusetts, Amherst.

Fukui, Naoki. 1991. Strong and weak barriers. In *Current English linguistics in Japan*, ed. H. Nakajima, 77–93. Berlin: Mouton de Gruyter.

    1995. The principles-and-parameters approach: a comparative syntax of English and Japanese. In *Approaches to language typology*, ed. Masayoshi Shibatani and Theodora Bynon, 327–371. Oxford: Oxford University Press.

Fukui, Naoki and Margaret Speas. 1986. Specifiers and projections. *MIT Working Papers in Linguistics* 18: 128–172.

Gasde, Horst-Dieter. 2004. *Yes/no* questions and A-not-A questions in Chinese revisited. *Linguistics* 42: 293–326.

Giannakidou, Anastasia. 1999. Affective dependencies. *Linguistics and Philosophy* 22: 367–421.

Givón, Tom. 1984. *Syntax: a functional-typological introduction*. Amsterdam: John Benjamins.

Goldberg, Lotus. 2005. Verb-stranding VP ellipsis: a cross-linguistic study. Doctoral dissertation, McGill University, Montreal, Quebec.

Goodall, Grant. 1987. On argument structure and L-marking with Mandarin Chinese *ba*. *NELS* 17(1): 232–242.

    1990. X'-internal word order in Mandarin Chinese and Universal Grammar. *Linguistics* 28: 241–261.

Greenberg, Joseph. 1963. Universals of language. Cambridge, Mass.: MIT Press.

Grimshaw, Jane. 1990. *Argument structure*. Cambridge, Mass.: MIT Press.

    1991. Extended projection. Ms., Rutgers University.

    2000. Extended projection and locality. In *Lexical specification and insertion*, ed. Peter Coopmans, Martin Everaert, and Jane Grimshaw, 115–133. Amsterdam: John Benjamins.

Gruber, Jeffrey. 1965. Studies in lexical relations. Doctoral dissertation, MIT.

Gu, Yang. 1992. The syntax of resultative and causative compounds in Chinese. Doctoral dissertation, Cornell University.

Hagège, C. 1974. Les pronoms logophoriques. *Belletin de la Societe de Linguistique de Paris* 69: 287–310.

Hagstrom, Paul. 2006. A-not-A questions. In *The Blackwell companion to syntax*, ed. Martin Everaet and Henk van Riemsdijk. Vol. 1, 173–214. Malden, Mass.: Blackwell.

Hale, Kenneth and Samuel Jay Keyser. 1987. A view from the middle. *Lexicon Project Working Papers* 10, Center for Cognitive Science, MIT.

    1993. On argument structure and the lexical expression of syntactic relations. In *The view from Building 20*, ed. Kenneth Hale and Samuel Jay Keyser, 53–109. Cambridge, Mass.: MIT Press.

    2002. *Prolegomenon to a theory of argument structure*. Cambridge, Mass.: MIT Press.

Hashimoto, Anne Yue. 1971. Mandarin syntactic structures. *Unicorn* 8: 1–149.

Hashimoto, Mantaro. 1969. Observations on the passive construction. *Chi-Lin* 5: 59–71. [Project on Chinese Linguistics, Princeton University.]

    1987. Hanyu beidongshi de lishi quyu fazhan [The historical and geographical development of Chinese passive constructions]. *Zhongguo Yuwen* 196: 36–49.

Haspelmath, Martin. 1997. *From space to time: temporal adverbials in the world's languages*. Munchen: Lincom Europa.

Hawkins, John. 1983. *Word order universals*. New York: Academic Press.

Heim, Irene. 1982. The semantics of definite and indefinite noun phrases. Doctoral dissertation, University of Massachusetts, Amherst.

Her, One-Soon. 2007. Argument-function mismatches in Mandarin Chinese: a lexical mapping account. *Lingua* 117: 221–246.

Higginbotham, James. 1980a. Pronouns and bound variables. *Linguistics Inquiry* 11: 679–708.

1980b. Anaphora and GB: some preliminary remarks. *NELS* 10: 223–236.

1985. On semantics. *Linguistic Inquiry* 16: 547–593.

1996. Semantic computation. Ms., Oxford University.

Hoekstra, Teun. 1988. Small clause results. *Lingua* 74: 101–139.

Hoekstra, Teun and Ian Roberts. 1993. Middle constructions in Dutch and English. In *Knowledge and language*, vol. 2, ed. Eric Reuland and Werner Abraham, 183–220. Dordrecht: Kluwer.

Hoji, Hajime. 1985. Logical form constraints and configurational structures in Japanese. Doctoral dissertation, University of Washington, Seattle.

Homma, Shinsuke. 1995. Syntax of possessive passive in Japanese. *Tsukuba English Studies* 14: 1–40.

Hornstein, Norbert and Amy Weinberg. 1981. Case theory and preposition stranding. *Linguistic Inquiry* 12: 55–91.

Hoshi, Hiroto. 1991. The generalized projection principle and the subject position of passive constructions. *Journal of Japanese Linguistics* 13: 53–89.

1994a. Passive, causative, and light verbs: a study on theta role assignment. Doctoral dissertation, University of Connecticut.

1994b. Theta-role assignment, passivization, and excorporation. *Journal of East Asian Linguistics* 3: 147–173.

Hsieh, Miao-Ling. 2001. Form and meaning: negation and question in Chinese. Doctoral dissertation, University of Southern California.

2004. Wh-phrase and word order in nominal phrases. Paper presented at the 16th NACCL, University of Iowa, May 2004.

Huang, C.-T. James. 1974. Constraints on transformations. Master's thesis, National Taiwan Normal University.

1982a. Move *wh* in a language without *wh*-movement. *The Linguistic Review* 1: 369–416.

1982b [1998]. Logical relations in Chinese and the theory of grammar. Doctoral dissertation, MIT; edited version published by Garland, New York, 1998.

1983. A note on the binding theory. *Linguistic Inquiry* 14: 554–561.

1984a. On the distribution and reference of empty pronouns. *Linguistic Inquiry* 15: 531–574.

1984b. Phrase structure, lexical integrity, and Chinese compounds. *Journal of Chinese Language Teachers Association* 19: 53–78.

1988a. On 'be' and 'have' in Chinese. *Bulletin of the Institute of History and Philology* 59(1): 43–64.

1988b. Hanyu zhengfan wenju de mozu yufa [A modular grammar of Chinese A-not-A questions]. *Zhongguo Yuwen* 1988: 247–264.

1988c. *Wo pao de kuai* and Chinese phrase structure. *Language* 64: 274–311.

1989. Pro drop in Chinese: a generalized control approach. In *The null subject parameter*, ed. Osvaldo Jaeggli and Ken Safir, 185–214. Dordrecht: D. Reidel.

1991. Modularity and Chinese A-not-A questions. In *Interdisciplinary approaches to language*, ed. Carol Georgopolous and Robert Ishihara, 305–322. Dordrecht: Kluwer.

1992. Complex predicates in control. In *Control and grammar*, ed. Richard K. Larson, Sabine Iatridou, Utpal Lahiri, and James Higginbotham, 109–147. Dordrecht: Kluwer.

1993. Reconstruction and the structure of VP: some theoretical consequences. *Linguistic Inquiry* 24: 103–138.

1994a. Logical Form. In *Government and binding theory and the minimalist program*, ed. Gert Webelhuth, 127–173. Oxford: Blackwell.

1994b. Verb movement and some syntax-semantics mismatches in Chinese. *Chinese Languages and Linguistics* 2: 587–613.

1994c. More on Chinese word order and parametric theory. In *Syntactic theory and language acquisition: crosslinguistic perspectives*, vol. 1, ed. Barbara Lust et al., 15–35. Mahwah, New Jersey: Lawrence Erlbaum.

1997. On lexical structure and syntactic projection. *Chinese Languages and Linguistics* 3: 45–89.

1999. Chinese passives in comparative perspective. *Tsing Hua Journal of Chinese Studies* 29(4): 423–509.

2002. Distributivity and reflexivity. In *On the formal way to Chinese languages*, ed. Sze-Wing Tang and Luther Liu, 21–44. Stanford: Center for the Study of Language and Information; distributed by Cambridge University Press; also in *Proceedings of the Center of Excellence International Symposium*, ed. Nobuko Hasegawa, Kanda University, Japan, 2001.

2005. On syntactic analyticity and the other end of the parameter. Lecture notes from LSA 2005 Linguistic Institute course. Ms., Harvard University.

2006. Resultatives and unaccusatives: a parametric view. *Bulletin of the Chinese Linguistic Society of Japan* 253: 1–43.

To appear. Ta-de laoshi dang-de hao [On the analysis of '*ta de laoshi dang-de hao*']. To appear in *Papers commemorating the centennial of Professor Lü Shuxiang*. Beijing: Shangwu Yinshuguan.

Huang, C.-T. James, Yun-Hua Huang, Te-Hsiang Teng, and Robyne Tiedeman. 1984. Reflexives in Chinese and the teaching of Chinese. *Proceedings of the first World Conference on Chinese Languages*, 205–215. Taipei: World Chinese Language Association.

Huang, C.-T. James and C.-S. Luther Liu. 2001. Logophoricity, attitudes and *ziji* at the interface. In *Long distance reflexives*, Syntax and Semantics 33, ed. Peter Cole et al., 141–195. New York: Academic Press.

Huang, C.-T. James and Masao Ochi. 2004. Syntax of *the hell*: two types of dependencies. *NELS* 34: 279–293.

Huang, C.-T. James and C.-C. Jane Tang. 1991. The local nature of the long-distance reflexives in Chinese. In *Long-distance anaphora*, ed. Jan Koster and Eric Reuland, 263–282. Cambridge University Press. Also in *NELS* 19, 1989.

Huang, Shizhe. 1996. Quantification and predication in Mandarin Chinese: A case study of *dou*. Doctoral dissertation, University of Pennsylvania, Philadelphia.

Huang, Yun-Hua. 1984. Chinese reflexives. *Studies in English Literature and Linguistics* 10: 163–188.

Iljic, Robert. 1994. Quantification in Mandarin Chinese: two markers of plurality. *Linguistics* 32: 91–116.

Ishii, Yasuo. 1991. Operators and empty categories in Japanese. Doctoral dissertation, University of Connecticut, Storrs.

Ito, Junko. 1986. Head-movement at PF and LF: the syntax of head internal relatives. *University of Massachusetts Occasional Papers in Linguistics* 11: 109–138.

Jackendoff, Ray. 1972. *Semantic interpretation in generative grammar*. Cambridge, Mass.: MIT Press.

——— 2002. *Foundations of language*. New York: Oxford University Press.

Jaeggli, Osvaldo. 1981. *Topics in Romance syntax*. Dordrecht: Foris.

Jiang, Zixin. 1990. Some aspects of the syntax of topic and subject in Chinese. Doctoral dissertation, University of Chicago.

Kamp, Hans. 1981. A theory of truth and semantic representation. In *Formal methods in the study of language*, ed. J. A. G. Groenendijk, T. M. V. Janssen, and M. B. J. Stokhof, 277–321. Amsterdam: Mathematical Centre.

Kayne, Richard S. 1975. *French syntax and the transformational cycle*. Cambridge, Mass.: MIT Press.

——— 1994. *The antisymmetry of syntax*. Cambridge, Mass.: MIT Press.

Kim, Soowon. 1989. *Wh*-phrases in Korean and Japanese are QPs. In *MIT Working Papers in Linguistics* 11: 119–138.

——— 1991. Chain scope and quantification structure. Doctoral dissertation, Brandeis University.

Kitagawa, Yoshihisa. 1986. Subjects in Japanese and English. Doctoral dissertation, University of Massachusetts, Amherst.

Kitagawa, Yoshihisa and S.-Y. Kuroda. 1992. Passive in Japanese. Ms., University of Rochester and University of California, San Diego.

Klavans, Judith. 1980. *Some problems in a theory of clitics*. Bloomington, Indiana: Indiana University Linguistics Club.

Koopman, Hilda. 1984. *The syntax of verbs*. Dordrecht: Foris.

Koster, Jan. 1978. *Locality principles in syntax*. Dordrecht: Foris.

Kratzer, Angelika. 1989. Stage-level and individual-level predicates. In *Papers on quantification*, 42–45. GLSA, University of Massachusetts, Amherst.

——— 1996. Severing the external argument from the verb. In *Phrase structure and the lexicon*, ed. Johan Rooryck and Laurie Zaring, 109–137. Dordrecht: Kluwer.

Krifka, Manfred. 1995. Common nouns: a contrastive analysis of English and Chinese. In *The generic book*, ed. Gregory Carlson and Francis Jeffry Pelletier, 398–411. Chicago: University of Chicago Press.

Kung, Hui-I. 1993. The mapping hypothesis and postverbal structures in Mandarin Chinese. Doctoral dissertation, University of Wisconsin, Madison.

Kuno, Susumu. 1972. Pronominalization, reflexivization, and direct discourse. *Linguistic Inquiry* 3: 161–195.

——— 1973. *The structure of the Japanese language*. Cambridge, Mass.: MIT Press.

——— 1976. Subject raising. In *Japanese generative grammar*, Syntax and semantics 5, ed. by Masayoshi Shibatani, 17–49. New York: Academic Press.

——— 1987. *Functional syntax*. Chicago: University of Chicago Press.

Kuo, Chin-Man. 1996. The interaction between *daodi* and *wh*-phrases in Mandarin Chinese. Ms., University of Southern California.

Kuroda, S.-Y. 1965. Generative grammatical studies in the Japanese language. Doctoral dissertation, MIT.

1969. English relativization and certain related problems. In *Modern studies in English*, ed. David A. Reibel and Sanford Schane, 264–287. Englewood Cliffs, N. J.: Prentice-Hall.

1988. Whether we agree or not. *Lingvisticae investigationes* 12: 1–47.

1992. *Japanese syntax and semantics: collected papers.* Dordrecht: Kluwer.

Laenzlinger, Christopher. 1998. *Comparative studies in word order variation: adverbs, pronouns, and clause structure in Romance and Germanic.* Amsterdam: John Benjamins.

Laka Mugarza, Miren Itziar. 1990. Negation in syntax: on the nature of functional categories and projections. Doctoral dissertation, MIT.

Larson, Richard. 1988. On the double object construction. *Linguistic Inquiry* 19: 335–392.

1991. The Projection of DP (and DegP). Ms., State University of New York, Stony Brook. [To appear in *Essays on shell structure*, ed. Richard Larson. London: Routledge.]

Lasnik, Howard. 1976. Remarks on coreference. *Linguistic Analysis* 2: 1–22. [Reprinted in Lasnik 1989.]

1989. *Essays on anaphora.* Dordrecht: Kluwer.

1991. On the necessity of binding conditions. In *Principles and parameters in comparative grammar*, ed. Robert Freidin, 7–28. Cambridge, Mass.: MIT Press.

1999. *Minimalist analysis.* Malden, Mass.: Blackwell.

2001. When can you save a structure by destroying it? *NELS* 31: 301–320.

Lasnik, Howard and Robert Fiengo. 1974. Complement object deletion. *Linguistic Inquiry* 5: 535–571.

Lasnik, Howard and Mamoru Saito. 1993. *Move ⟨: conditions on its application and output.* Cambridge, Mass.: MIT Press.

Law, Paul. 2006. Adverbs in A-not-A questions in Mandarin Chinese. *Journal of East Asian Linguistics* 15: 97–136.

Lebeaux, David. 1983. A distributional difference between reciprocals and reflexives. *Linguistic Inquiry* 14: 723–730.

Lee, H.-T. Thomas. 1986. Studies on quantification in Chinese. Doctoral dissertation, University of California, Los Angeles.

Lewis, David. 1975. Adverbs of quantification. In *Formal semantics of natural language*, ed. Edward L. Keenan, 3–15. Cambridge: Cambridge University Press.

1979. Attitudes *de dicto* and *de se*. *The Philosophical Review* 88: 513–543.

Li, Charles N. and Sandra A. Thompson. 1974. Co-verbs in Mandarin Chinese: Verbs or prepositions? *Journal of Chinese Linguistics* 23: 257–278.

1976. Subject and topic: a new typology of language. In *Subject and topic*, ed. Charles N. Li, 457–489. New York: Academic Press.

1979. The pragmatics of two types of yes-no questions in Mandarin and its universal implications. *CLS* 15: 197–206.

1981. *Mandarin Chinese: a functional reference grammar.* Berkeley: University of California Press.

Li, Fengxiang. 1997. Cross-linguistic lexicalization patterns: diachronic evidence from verb-complement compounds in Chinese. *Sprachtypologie und Universalien-forschung* 50(3): 229–252.

Li, Jen-I Jelina. 1997. The *ba* construction in Mandarin Chinese: a serial verb analysis. In *Current issues in linguistic theory*, 140: Clitics, pronouns and movement, ed. James R. Black and Virginia Motapanyane, 175–216. Amsterdam: John Benjamins.

Li, Linding. 1980. Dongbu de jushi [On the verb-complement construction]. *Zhongguo Yuwen* 2: 93–103.

Li, Xiaoguang. 1997. Deriving distributivity in Mandarin Chinese. Doctoral dissertation, University of California, Irvine.

Li, Y.-H. Audrey. 1985. Abstract case in Mandarin Chinese. Doctoral dissertation, University of Southern California, Los Angeles.

1987. Duration phrases: distributions and interpretation. *Journal of Chinese Language Teachers Association* 22.3: 27–65.

1990. *Order and constituency in Mandarin Chinese*. Dordrecht: Kluwer.

1992a. DOU: Syntax or LF. Paper presented at the fourth North American Conference on Linguistics, University of Michigan, Ann Arbor.

1992b. Indefinite *wh* in Mandarin Chinese. *Journal of East Asian Linguistics* 1: 125–155.

1996. Definite and indefinite existential constructions. *Studies in the Linguistic Sciences* 26: 175–191.

1998. Argument determiner and number phrases. *Linguistic Inquiry* 29: 693–702.

1999. Plurality in a classifier language. *Journal of East Asian Linguistics* 8: 75–99.

2005. Ellipsis and missing Objects. *Yuyan Kexue [Linguistic Sciences]* 4: 3–19.

2006. Chinese *ba*. In *The Blackwell companion to syntax,* ed. Martin Everaert and Henk van Riemsdijk, vol. 1, 374–468. Malden, Mass.: Blackwell.

2007. Theories of empty categories and Chinese null elements. *Yuyan Kexue [Linguistic Sciences]* 6: 37–47.

Li, Yafei. 1983. Existential sentences and the category of the locative words. Paper presented at the First Harbin Conference on Generative Grammar, Harbin.

1985. Empty categories and the ECP. Master's thesis, Shandong University, Jinan, China.

1990. On V-V compounds in Chinese. *Natural Language and Linguistic Theory* 8: 177–207.

1993a. Structural head and aspectuality. *Language* 69: 480–504.

1993b. What makes long distance reflexives possible? *Journal of East Asian Linguistics* 2: 135–166.

1995. The thematic hierarchy and causativity. *Natural Language and Linguistic Theory* 13: 255–282.

1997a. Remarks on Chinese word order. *Zhongguo Yuyanxue Luncong [Studies in Chinese Linguistics]* 1(1): 29–33.

1997b. Chinese resultative constructions and the UTAH. In *New approaches to word formation in Chinese*, ed. Jerome Packard, 285–310. Berlin: Mouton de Gruyter.

1997c. Head-government and X′-theory. *The Linguistic Review* 14: 139–180.

1997d. An optimized UG and biological redundancies. *Linguistic Inquiry* 28: 170–178.

1999. Cross-componential causativity. *Natural Language and Linguistic Theory* 17: 445–497.

2003. Localizers in Chinese and the cost of computation. Ms., University of Wisconsin, Madison.

2005. *X: a theory of the morphology-syntax interface.* Cambridge, Mass.: MIT Press.

In progress. Fathoming the depth of UG. Ms., University of Wisconsin, Madison.

Li, Yafei, Vivian Lin, and Rebecca Shields. 2005. Adverb types and the nature of minimality. Ms., University of Wisconsin, Madison.

Li, Ying-Che. 1974. What does "disposal" mean? Features of the verb and noun in Chinese. *Journal of Chinese Linguistics* 2: 200–218.

Liang, Donghan. 1958. Lun ba zi ju [On the *ba* construction]. In *Yuyanxue Luncong* 2: 100–119. Shanghai: Xinzhishi Chubanshe.

Lieber, Rochelle. 1983. Argument linking and compounds in English. *Linguistic Inquiry* 14: 251–285.

Lin, Jowang. 1992. The syntax of *zenmeyang* 'how' and *weishenme* 'why' in Mandarin Chinese. *Journal of East Asian Linguistics* 1: 293–332.

1994. Object expletives, definiteness effect and scope interpretation. *NELS* 24: 287–301.

1996. Polarity licensing and *wh*-phrase quantification in Chinese. Doctoral dissertation, University of Massachusetts, Amherst.

1997. Restrictive vs. nonrestrictive relative clauses in Chinese. Paper presented at the 7th International Conference on Chinese Linguistics. Leiden University, June 1997.

1998. On existential polarity *wh*-phrases in Chinese. *Journal of East Asian Linguistics* 7: 219–255.

2003. Temporal reference in Mandarin Chinese. *Journal of East Asian Linguistics* 12: 259–311.

2006. Time in a language without tense: the case of Chinese. *Journal of Semantics* 23: 1–53.

Lin, Jowang and Jane Tang. 1995. Modals as verbs in Chinese: a GB perspective. *Bulletin of the Institute of History and Philology, Academia Sinica* 66: 53–105.

Lin, Shuang-Fu. 1974. Locative construction and *ba* construction in Mandarin. *Journal of the Chinese Language Teachers Association* 9(2): 66–83.

Lin, T.-H. Jonah. 2001. Light verb syntax and the theory of phrase structure. Doctoral dissertation, University of California, Irvine.

Liu, Feng-Hsi. 1990. *Scope Dependency in English and Chinese.* Doctoral dissertation, University of California, Los Angeles.

1997. An aspectual analysis of *ba*. *Journal of East Asian Linguistics* 6: 51–99.

1998. A clitic analysis of locative particles. *Journal of Chinese Linguistics* 16: 48–70.

Longobardi, Giuseppe. 1994. Reference and proper names. *Linguistic Inquiry* 25: 609–666.

2001. The structure of DPs: some principles, parameters, and problems. In *The handbook of contemporary syntactic theory*, ed. Mark Baltin and Chris Collins, 562–603. Malden, Mass.: Blackwell.

Lu, Bingfu. 1998. Left-right asymmetries of word order variation: a functional explanation. Doctoral dissertation, University of Southern California.

Lu, Hui-Chuan. 1994. Second preverbal NP's in Chinese. Paper presented at NACCL-6, University of Southern California, May 1994.

Lü, Shuxiang. 1955. *Ba* zi yongfa de yanjiu [The study of *ba* sentences]. In *Hanyu yufa lunwenji* [*Collected papers on Chinese grammar*], ed. Shuxiang Lü, 176–199. Beijing: Kexue Chubanshe.

1980 [1984]. *Xiandai hanyu babai ci* [800 words of contemporary Chinese]. Beijing: Shangwu Yinshuguan.

Manzini, Rita and Kenneth Wexler. 1987. Parameters, binding and learnability. *Linguistic Inquiry* 18: 413–444.

Marantz, Alec. 1984. *On the nature of grammatical relations*. Cambridge, Mass.: MIT Press.

May, Robert. 1977. The grammar of quantification. Doctoral dissertation, MIT.

McCawley, James D. 1994. Remarks on the syntax of Mandarin *yes-no* questions. *Journal of East Asian Linguistics* 3: 179–194.

McConnell-Ginet, Sally. 1982. Adverbs and logical form: a linguistically realistic theory. *Language* 58: 144–184.

Mei, Kuang. 1978a. Is Chinese an SOV language? Ms., National Taiwan University.

1978b. The *ba* construction. *Bulletin of the College of Arts, National Taiwan University*, 145–180.

Mei, Tsu-Lin. 1978. *Xiandai hanyu xuanzewen jufa de laiyuan* [On the historical origin of Modern Chinese disjunctive questions]. *Bulletin of the Institute of History and Philology, Academia Sinica* 49.1: 15–36.

Munn, Alan B. 1993. Topics in the syntax and semantics of coordinate structures. Doctoral dissertation, University of Maryland, College Park.

1998. ATB movement without identity. In *Proceedings of the 14th Eastern States Conference on Linguistics (ESCOL-97)*, 150–160. Cornell Linguistics Club Publications, Cornell University, Ithaca, NY.

Murasugi, Keiko. 1991. Noun phrases in Japanese and English: A study in syntax, learnability, and acquisition. Doctoral dissertation, University of Connecticut, Storrs.

2000a. An antisymmetry analysis of Japanese relative clauses. In *The syntax of relative clauses*, ed. Artemis Alexiadou, Paul Law, Andre Meinunger, and Chris Wilder, 167–188. Amsterdam: John Benjamins.

2000b. Japanese complex noun phrases and the antisymmetry theory. In *Step by step: essays on minimalist syntax in honor of Howard Lasnik*, ed. Roger Martin, David Michaels, and Juan Uriagereka, 211–234. Cambridge, Mass.: MIT Press.

Ning, Chunyan. 1993. The overt syntax of topicalization and relativization in Chinese. Doctoral dissertation, University of California, Irvine.

Nishigauchi, Taisuke. 1986. Quantification in syntax. Doctoral dissertation, University of Massachusetts, Amherst.

1991. Construing *wh*. In *Logical structure and linguistic structure*, ed. C.-T. James Huang and Robert May, 197–232. Dordrecht: Kluwer.

1999. Point of view and phrase structure. *Theoretical and Applied Linguistics at Kobe Shoin* 2: 49–60.

Noguchi, Tohru. 1997. Two types of pronouns and variable binding. *Language* 73: 770–797.

Norman, Jerry. 1988. *Chinese*. Cambridge: Cambridge University Press.

Ogle, Richard. 1974. Natural order and dislocated syntax. Doctoral dissertation, University of California, Los Angeles.

Pan, Haihua. 1997. Constraints on reflexivization in Chinese. New York: Garland.

2001. Why the blocking effect. In *Long distance reflexives*, Syntax and Semantics 33, ed. Peter Cole et al., 279–316. New York: Academic Press.

Paris, Marie-Claude. 1979. *Nominalization in Mandarin Chinese*. Paris: University Paris VII.

Pesetsky, David. 1987. *Wh*-in-situ: movement and unselective binding. In *The representation of (in)definiteness*, ed. Eric Reuland and Alice ter Meulen, 98–129. Cambridge, Mass.: MIT Press.

1995. Zero syntax. Cambridge, Mass.: MIT Press.

Peyraube, Alain. 1980. *Les constructions locatives en chinois moderne*. Paris: Edition Langages Croises.

1996. Recent issues in Chinese historical syntax. In *New horizons in Chinese linguistics*, ed. C.-T. James Huang and Y.-H. Audrey Li, 161–213. Dordrecht: Kluwer.

Pica, Pierre. 1987. On the nature of the reflexivization cycle. *NELS* 17: 483–499.

Pollard, Carl J. and Ping Xue. 1998. Chinese reflexive *ziji*: syntactic reflexives vs. nonsyntactic reflexives. *Journal of East Asian Linguistics* 7: 287–318.

Pollock, Jean-Yve. 1989. Verb movement, Universal Grammar, and the structure of IP. *Linguistic Inquiry* 20: 365–425.

Postal, Paul. 1969. On so-called 'pronouns' in English. In *Modern studies in English*, ed. David Reibel and Sanford Schane, 201–244. Englewoods Cliffs, N. J.: Prentice Hall.

Qu, Yanfeng. 1994. Object noun phrase dislocation in Mandarin Chinese. Doctoral dissertation, University of British Columbia, Vancouver.

Reinhart, Tanya. 1976. The syntactic domain of anaphora. Doctoral dissertation, MIT.

1983. *Anaphora and semantic interpretation*. Chicago: University of Chicago Press.

Reinhart, Tanya and Eric Reuland. 1993. Reflexivity. *Linguistic Inquiry* 24: 657–720.

Ritter, Elizabeth. 1991. Two functional categories in noun phrases: evidence from modern Hebrew. In *Perspectives on phrase structure: heads and licensing*, Syntax and semantics 25, ed. Susan Rothstein, 37–62. New York: Academic Press.

1995. On the syntactic category of pronouns and agreement. *Natural Language and Linguistic Theory* 13: 405–443.

Rizzi, Luigi. 1990. *Relativized minimality*. Cambridge, Mass.: MIT Press.

1997. The fine structure of the left periphery. In *Elements of grammar*, ed. Liliane Haegeman, 281–338. Dordrecht: Kluwer.

2001. Relativized minimality effects. In *The handbook of contemporary syntactic theory*, ed. Mark Baltin and Christopher Collins, 89–110. Oxford: Blackwell.

2002. *Functional structure in DP and IP: the cartography of syntactic structures*, vol. 2, Oxford Studies in Comparative Syntax. Oxford: Oxford University Press.

Rooth, Mats. 1985. Association with focus. Doctoral dissertation, University of Massachusetts, Amherst.

Rosenbaum, Peter S. 1970. A principle governing complement subject deletion. In *Readings in English transformational grammar*, ed. Roderick A. Jacobs and Peter S. Rosenbaum. Waltham, Mass.: Ginn & Company.

Ross, John R. 1967. Constraints on variables in syntax. Doctoral dissertation, MIT.

1983. Inner islands. Ms., MIT.

Rygaloff, Alexis. 1973. *Grammaire élémentaire du Chinois*. Paris: PUF.

Safir, Ken. 1986. Relative clauses in a theory of binding and levels. *Linguistic Inquiry* 17: 663–689.

Sag, Ivan and Carl Pollard. 1991. An integrated theory of complement control. *Language* 67: 63–113.

Saito, Mamoru. 1985. Some asymmetries in Japanese and their theoretical implications. Doctoral dissertation, MIT.

Saito, Mamoru and Keiko Murasugi. 1989. N′ deletion in Japanese and the DP hypothesis. Paper presented at the 1989 Annual Meeting, Linguistic Society of America, Washington DC.

Sanders, Gerald and James H.-Y. Tai. 1972. Immediate dominance and identity deletion. *Foundations of Language* 8: 161–198.

Sauerland, Uli. 2000. Two structures for English restrictive relative clauses. In *Proceedings of the Nanzan GLOW*, ed. Mamoru Saito, 351–366. Nanzan University, Nagoya, Japan.

2003. Unpronounced heads in relative clauses. In *The interfaces: deriving and interpreting omitted structures*, ed. Kerstin Schwabe and Susanne Winkler, 205–226. Amsterdam: John Benjamins.

Schachter, Paul. 1973. Focus and relativization. *Language* 49: 19–46.

Schlyter, Suzanne. 1974. Une hiérarchie d'adverbes et leur distribution – par quelle transformation? In *Actes du colloque Franco-Allemand de grammaire transformationnelle*, vol. 2, ed. Christian Rohrer and Nicolas Ruwet, 76–84. Tübingen: Niemeyer.

Sells, Peter. 1985. Restrictive and non-restrictive modification. CSLI Report No. CSLI-85-28, Stanford University.

1987. Aspects of logophoricity. *Linguistic Inquiry* 18: 445–479.

Shao, Jingmin and Chunli Zhao. 2005. Zhishi ba ziju han shengyin bei ziju ji qi yuyong jieshi [Cognitive interpretation of *ba*-construction and *bei*-construction]. *Chinese Language Learning* 4: 11–18.

Shen, Jiaxuan. 2004. Dongjiesi *zhui-lei* de yufa he yuyi [On the syntax and semantics of *zhui*-lei 'chase-tired']. *Yuyan Kexue* 3(6): 3–15.

Shen, Li. 1992. On the passive *bei* in Mandarin Chinese. Ms., Kyoto University.

Shi, Dingxu. 1992. The nature of topic comment constructions and topic chains. Doctoral dissertation, University of Southern California, Los Angeles, California.

2000. Topic and topic-comment constructions in Mandarin Chinese. *Language* 76: 383–408.

Shyu, Shu-Ing. 1995. The syntax of focus and topic in Mandarin Chinese. Doctoral dissertation, University of Southern California.

Simpson, Andrew and Zoe Wu. 2002. From D to T – Determiner incorporation and the creation of tense. *Journal of East Asian Linguistics* 11: 169–209.

Smith, Carlota. 1964. Determiners and relative clauses in generative grammar. *Language* 40: 37–52.

1991. *The parameters of aspect*. Dordrecht: Kluwer.

Soh, Hooi Ling. 1998. Object scrambling in Chinese: a close look at post-duration/frequency phrase positions. *NELS* 28.2: 197–211.

Sportiche, Dominique. 1988. A theory of floating quantifiers and its corollaries for constituent structure. *Linguistic Inquiry* 19: 425–451.

von Stechow, Arnim. 1996. Against LF Pied-Piping. *Natural Language Semantics* 4: 57–110.

Stowell, Tim. 1981. Origins of phrase structure. Doctoral dissertation, MIT.

Sun, Chaofen. 1996. *Word order change and grammaticalization in the history of Chinese*. Stanford, Calif.: Stanford University Press.

Svorou, Soteria. 1994. *The grammar of space*. Amsterdam: John Benjamins.

Sybesma, Rint. 1992. Causatives and accomplishments: the case of the Chinese *ba*. Doctoral dissertation, Leiden University.

1999. *The Mandarin VP*. Dordrecht: Kluwer.

Tai, James. 1973. Chinese as an SOV language. *CLS* 9: 659–671.

1984. Verbs and time in Chinese: Vendler's four categories. *CLS* 20: *Parasession on lexical semantics*, 289–296.

Tancredi, Chris. 1990. Syntactic association with focus. In *Proceedings from the First Meeting of the Formal Linguistic Society of Mid-America*, 289–303. University of Wisconsin–Madison.

Tang, C.-C. Jane. 1989. Chinese reflexives. *Natural Language and Linguistic Theory* 7: 93–122.

1990. Chinese phrase structure and the extended X′-theory. Doctoral dissertation, Cornell University.

Tang, Sze-Wing. 1998. Parametrization of features in syntax. Doctoral dissertation, University of California, Irvine.

1999. The passive constructions in Cantonese and their agent argument. Ms., Hong Kong Polytechnic University.

Tang, Ting-Chi. 1977. *Studies in transformational grammar of Chinese*, vol. 1: *Movement transformations*. Taipei: Student Books.

1979. *Studies in Chinese syntax*. Taipei: Student Books.

Teng, Shou-Hsin. 1975. *A semantic study of transitivity relations in Chinese*. Berkeley: University of California Press.

1985. Hanyu dongci de shijian jiegou [The temporal system of verbs in Mandarin]. *Yuyan Jiaoxue yu Yanjiu* [Language Teaching and Research] 4: 7–17. [Reprinted in *Studies on modern Chinese syntax*, ed. Shou-hsin Teng, 2003, 261–269.]

Teng, Te-Hsiang. 1985. On pronominal reference in Chinese. Master's thesis, National Taiwan Normal University, Taipei.

Tenny, Carol. 1994. *Aspectual roles and the syntax-semantics interface*. Dordrecht: Kluwer.

Thompson, Sandra. 1973. Transitivity and the *ba* construction in Mandarin Chinese. *Journal of Chinese Linguistics* 1: 208–221.

Tiee, Henry Hung-Yeh. 1986. *A reference grammar of Chinese sentences with exercises*. Arizona: The University of Arizona Press.

Ting, Jen. 1995. A non-uniform analysis of the passive construction in Mandarin Chinese. Doctoral dissertation, University of Rochester.

1996. A non-uniform analysis of the passive construction in Mandarin Chinese. Paper presented at the 8th North American Conference on Chinese Linguistics, University of Illinois, May 1996.

1998. Deriving the *bei*-construction in Mandarin Chinese. *Journal of East Asian Linguistics* 7, 319–354.

2003. The nature of the particle *suo* in Mandarin Chinese. *Journal of East Asian Linguistics* 12: 121–139.

Ting, Jen and Yafei Li. 1997. Manner *-de* and resultative *-de*. Paper presented at the 6th Conference of the International Association of Chinese Linguistics, University of Leiden, June 1997.

Travis, Lisa. 1984. Parameters and effects of word order variation. Doctoral dissertation, MIT.

1988. The syntax of adverbs. *McGill Working Papers in Linguistics/Cahiers linguistiques de McGill*, Special Issue (May): 280–310.

Tsai, W.-T. Dylan. 1994a. On economizing A-bar dependencies. Doctoral dissertation, MIT.

1994b. On nominal islands and LF extraction in Chinese. *Natural Language and Linguistic Theory* 12: 121–175.

1996. Subject specificity, raising modals and extended mapping hypothesis. Paper presented at the Symposium on the Referential Properties of Noun Phrases, City University of Hong Kong, June 1996.

Tsao, Feng-Fu. 1977. A functional study of topic in Chinese. Doctoral dissertation, University of Southern California.

Ura, Hiroyuki. 1996. Multiple feature-checking: a theory of grammatical function splitting. Doctoral dissertation, MIT.

Valois, Daniel. 1991. The internal syntax of DP. Doctoral dissertation, University of California, Los Angeles.

van Voorst, Jan. 1988. *Event structure*. Amsterdam: John Benjamins.

Vendler, Zeno. 1967. *Linguistics in philosophy.* Ithaca, New York: Cornell University Press.

Vergnaud, Jean-Roger. 1974. French relative clauses. Doctoral dissertation, MIT.

Wang, Huan. 1957 [1984]. *Ba* zi ju he *bei* zi ju [On the *ba* sentences and *bei* sentences]. Shanghai: Shanghai Jiaoyu Chubanshe.

Wang, Jia-Ling and Justine T. Stillings. 1984. Chinese reflexives. In *Proceedings of the First Harbin Conference on Generative Grammar*, ed. Chunyan Ning et al., 100–109. Harbin: Hcilongjiang University Press.

Wang, Li. 1954. *Zhongguo yufa lilun* [Theory of Chinese grammar]. Beijing: Zhonghua. Shuju.

Wang, Mingquan. 1987. Transitivity and the *ba*-construction in Mandarin. Doctoral dissertation, Boston University.

Wang, Peter C. T. 1970. A transformational approach to Chinese *ba* and *bei*. Doctoral dissertation, University of Texas, Austin.

Wang, William S.-Y. 1967. Conjoining and deletion in Mandarin syntax. *Monumenta Serica* 26: 224–236.

Washio, Ryuichi. 1993. When causatives mean passive. *Journal of East Asian Linguistics* 2: 45–90.

Watanabe, Akira. 1992. Subjacency and S-Structure movement of wh-in-situ. *Journal of East Asian Linguistics* 1: 255–292.

Wei, Pei-Chuan. 1994. Guhanyu beidongshi de fazhan yu yanbian jizhi [On the development and mechanism of change of the passive construction in Classical Chinese]. *Chinese Languages and Linguistics* 2: 293–319.

Williams, Edwin. 1980. Predication. *Linguistic Inquiry* 11: 203–238.

Winkler, Susanne and Kerstin Schwabe. 2003. Exploring the interfaces from the perspective of omitted structures. In *The Interfaces: deriving and interpreting omitted structures*, ed. Kerstin Schwabe and Susanne Winkler, 1–26. Amsterdam: John Benjamins.

Wu, Jianxin. 1997. More on A-not-A questions: a model-theoretic approach. *WCCFL* 16: 463–477.

1999. Syntax and semantics of quantification in Chinese. Doctoral dissertation, University of Maryland, College Park.

Wu, Meng. 1982. *Ba* zi yongfa er li [Two examples for the usage of *ba*]. *Zhongguo Yuwen* 1982(6): 434.

Xiao, Z. Richard, Anthony McEnery, and Yufang Qian. 2006. Passive constructions in English and Chinese: a corpus-based contrastive study. *Languages in Contrast* 6: 109–149.

Xing, Gongwan and Ma Qingzhu, ed. 1992. *Xiandai hanyu jiaocheng.* Tianjin: Nankai University Press.

Xu, Liejiong. 1986. Free empty category. *Linguistic Inquiry* 17: 75–94.

1993. The long-distance binding of *ziji. Journal of Chinese Linguistics* 21: 123–141.

1995. Definiteness effects on Chinese word order. *Cahiers de Linguistique Asie Orientale* 24: 29–48.

1996. Limitations on subjecthood of numerically quantified noun phrases: a pragmatic approach. Paper presented at Symposium on Referential Properties of Chinese Noun Phrases, City University of Hong Kong, June 1996.

Xu, Liejiong and Terence Langendoen. 1985. Topic structures in Chinese. *Language* 61: 1–27.

Xue, Ping, Carl J. Pollard, and Ivan A. Sag. 1994. A new perspective on Chinese reflexive *ziji. WCCFL* 13: 432–447.

Yang, Liu. 2006. *Ba* zi ju yu *bei* zi ju [On *ba* sentences and *bei* sentences]. *Xiandai Yuwen (Yuyan Yanjiu)* 5: 64–65.

Yang, Suying. 1995. *Ba* and *bei* constructions in Chinese. *Journal of the Chinese Language Teachers Association* 30: 1–36.

Yong, Shin. 1993. The aspectual phenomena of the *ba* construction. Doctoral dissertation, University of Wisconsin, Madison.

Yorifuji, Atsushi. 1976. *Men* ni tsuite [A study on the suffix *-men*]. *Areal and Cultural Studies* 26: 73–88.

Yu, X.-F. William. 1992. Challenging Chinese reflexive data. *The Linguistic Review* 9: 285–294.

Zhang, Jie. 2004. Contour tone licensing and contour tone representation. *Language and Linguistics* 5: 925–968.

Zhang, Min. 1990. A typological study of *yes-no* questions in Chinese dialects: a diachronic perspective. Doctoral dissertation, Peking University.

Zhang, Ning. 1997. Syntactic dependencies in Mandarin Chinese. Doctoral dissertation, University of Toronto.

Zhang, Wangxi. 2001. The displacement of the *ba*-sentences. *Yuyan jiaoxue yu yanjiu* 3: 1–10.

Zhu, Dexi. 1982. *Yufa jiangyi* [Lecture notes on grammar]. Beijing: Shangwu Yinshuguan.

1991. V-neg-VO yu VO-neg-V liang-zhong fanfu wenju zai hanyu fangyan-li de fenbu [The distribution of V-neg-VO and VO-neg-V questions in Chinese dialects]. *Zhongguo Yuwen* 1991: 321–332.

Zhu, Xiaonong. 1988. Hypothesis-induction in grammatical studies. *Journal of East China Normal University (Philosophy and Social Sciences)* 4: 59–66.

Zoerner, Cyril Edward. 1995. Coordination: the syntax of & P. Doctoral dissertation, University of California, Irvine.

Zou, Ke. 1995. The syntax of the Chinese *ba*-construction and verb compounds: a morpho-syntactic analysis. Doctoral dissertation, University of Southern California.

Zwicky, Arnold. 1985. Clitics and particles. *Language* 61: 283–305.

Index